Israeli-Palestinian Conflict in the Francophone World

Routledge Studies in Cultural History

1. **The Politics of Information in Early Modern Europe**
Edited by Brendan Dooley and Sabrina Baron

2. **The Insanity of Place/The Place of Insanity**
Essays on the History of Psychiatry
Andrew Scull

3. **Film, History, and Cultural Citizenship**
Sites of Production
Edited by Tina Mai Chen and David S. Churchill

4. **Genre and Cinema**
Ireland and Transnationalism
Edited by Brian McIlroy

5. **Histories of Postmodernism**
Edited by Mark Bevir, Jill Hargis, and Sara Rushing

6. **Africa after Modernism**
Transitions in Literature, Media, and Philosophy
Michael Janis

7. **Rethinking Race, Politics, and Poetics**
C.L.R. James' Critique of Modernity
Brett St Louis

8. **Making British Culture**
English Readers and the Scottish Enlightenment, 1740–1830
David Allan

9. **Empires and Boundaries**
Rethinking Race, Class, and Gender in Colonial Settings
Edited by Harald Fischer-Tiné and Susanne Gehrmann

10. **Tobacco in Russian History and Culture**
From the Seventeenth Century to the Present
Edited by Matthew P. Romaniello and Tricia Starks

11. **History of Islam in German Thought**
From Leibniz to Nietzsche
Ian Almond

12. **Israeli-Palestinian Conflict in the Francophone World**
Edited by Nathalie Debrauwere-Miller

Israeli-Palestinian Conflict in the Francophone World

Edited by Nathalie Debrauwere-Miller

Routledge
Taylor & Francis Group
New York   London

First published 2010
by Routledge
711 Third Avenue, New York, NY 10017

Simultaneously published in the UK
by Routledge
2 Park Square, Milton Park, Abingdon, Oxfordshire OX14 4RN

First issued in paperback 2014

Routledge is an imprint of the Taylor and Francis Group, an informa business

© 2010 Taylor & Francis

Typeset in Sabon by IBT Global.

All rights reserved. No part of this book may be reprinted or reproduced or utilised in any form or by any electronic, mechanical, or other means, now known or hereafter invented, including photocopying and recording, or in any information storage or retrieval system, without permission in writing from the publishers.

Trademark Notice: Product or corporate names may be trademarks or registered trademarks, and are used only for identification and explanation without intent to infringe.

Library of Congress Cataloging in Publication Data

Israeli-Palestinian conflict in the Francophone world / edited by Nathalie Debrauwere-Miller.
    p. cm.—(Routledge studies in cultural history ; 12)
    Includes bibliographical references and index.
    1. Arab-Israeli conflict—1993—Foreign public opinion, French. 2. Public opinion—France. 3. Zionism—France. 4. Arab-Israeli conflict—Mass media and the conflict. 5. Arab-Israeli conflict—Literature and the conflict. 6. Intellectuals—France—Attitudes. 7. Jews—France. 8. Muslims—France. 9. France—Ethnic relations. I. Debrauwere-Miller, Nathalie.
    DS119.76.I8258 2010
    956.04—dc22
    2009027617

ISBN 978-0-415-99587-0 (hbk)
ISBN 978-1-138-87017-8 (pbk)
ISBN 978-0-203-88205-4 (ebk)

Contents

Acknowledgments ix

Introduction: France and the Israeli-Palestinian Conflict 1
NATHALIE DEBRAUWERE-MILLER

PART I:
Alternative History of Zionism and the Jewish Question, 1914–1950

1 Tracing the Shadow of Palestine: The Zionist-Arab Conflict and Jewish-Muslim Relations in France, 1914–1945 25
ETHAN KATZ

2 The Paradoxes of Zionism in the Work of Albert Cohen 41
PHILIPPE ZARD

3 "One Nation (In)divisible?": Sartre and the Jewish Question 55
LAWRENCE R. SCHEHR

PART II:
Francophone Literature and Cinema on the Conflict, 1957–2000

4 Slimane Benaïssa, or the Voice of Dissidence 67
CYRIL ASLANOV

5 The Israeli-Palestinian Conflict in France: A Conflict in Search of Novelistic Representations 81
ANNY DAYAN-ROSENMAN

6 When "*L'Essence Arrose de Haine*": The Reinvention of
   Identity in Francophone Tunisian Literature   93
   LAMIA BEN YOUSSEF ZAYZAFOON

7 Otherwise Occupied: The Israeli-Palestinian Conflict in the
   Francophone Cinema   105
   LINCOLN Z. SHLENSKY

PART III:
Violence, Martyrdom and Terrorism, 1970–2007

8 The Agony for Justice   123
   FETHI BENSLAMA

9 Out of Palestine: Jean Genet's Shooting Stars   141
   BRUNO CHAOUAT

PART IV:
Muslim-Jewish Relations in France, 1990–2008

10 The War Comes Home: Muslim-Jewish Relations in Marseille
   during the 1991 Gulf War   163
   MAUD S. MANDEL

11 Hung Up on Being Fair and Left Hanging between the Israeli-
   Palestinian Conflict and the "Banlieues"   180
   JOHANN SADOCK

12 Jews and Arabs in Postcolonial France, a Situated Account of a
   Long Painful Story of Intimacy   193
   NACIRA GUÉNIF-SOUILAMAS

PART V:
Judeocentrism, Anti-Semitism and French Intelligentsia, 2000–2008

13 A New Judeocentrism? On a Recent Trend in French Thought   209
   JEFFREY MEHLMAN

14 Dual Narratives on the Middle East Conflict: Analysis of a
   French Literary Genre, 1967–2006   222
   DENIS CHARBIT

15 How One Becomes a Traitor   232
   ESTHER BENBASSA

Contributors   251
Index   257

Acknowledgments

First of all, I am very grateful to Bruno Chaouat and Lawrence R. Schehr for their support of this daunting project since its conceptual stages, and for facilitating my contact with some remarkable scholars who, in spite of the sensitive nature of the topic, agreed to contribute to this volume.

I also owe a debt of gratitude to Alan Astro who graciously offered to translate Esther Benbassa's article. Many thanks are also due to Robert St. Clair, Robert Watson and Rachel Nisselson for translating the chapters by Fethi Benslama, Philippe Zard and Anny Dayan-Rosenman. We all know what is at stake in the difficult and often thankless "task of the translator."

Finally, I want to express my sincere gratitude to Esther Benbassa, Lynn Ramey and Martine Prieto for their attentive reading of my text, and to Paul B. Miller for his generous editorial assistance and for his constant support and encouragement.

Introduction
France and the Israeli-Palestinian Conflict
Nathalie Debrauwere-Miller

While there is no shortage of media coverage and scholarship on the Israeli-Palestinian conflict in the United States and elsewhere in the English-speaking world, this enduring and tragic conflict does not elicit the passionate response here as it does in France and the Francophone world (especially in North Africa).[1] With the historical proximity of both Jewish and Muslim Francophone populations in France and its ex-colonies, war in the Middle East reverberates much more intensely in these regions than in the United States. Since France has the largest Jewish and Muslim communities in Europe,[2] enmity in Israel and Palestine mobilizes the corresponding respective demographics in France, producing in some ways a mirror image of the conflict. Given this cultural, political and contextual specificity through which the Israeli-Palestinian conflict is perceived in France, this volume offers a multidisciplinary approach, the common aim of which is to gauge and elucidate the representation of the conflict and its reverberations among French and Francophone Jewish and Arab Muslim communities. One of the goals of the collection is to explore the various antagonistic ideological positions and to question how the multitudinous interpretations of the conflict influence the mobilization of adversarial ethnicities beyond the borders of Israel and Palestine.

After the Second Intifada,[3] "*al-Aqsa*," in 2000, the Israeli-Palestinian conflict begins to expand rhetorically into a generalized Jewish-Arab conflict, specifically in the French suburbs[4] of Paris, Marseille and Lyons, and generates semantic and ontological slippage or displacement among terms such as "Jew," "Israelite," "Israeli" and "Zionist" as well as "Palestinian," "Arab," "Muslim" and "terrorist." This volume attempts to clarify these aspects for Anglo-American readers by addressing the following questions: to what extent is the "importation" of the conflict into France a reality, a mediatic fiction or an ideological construction? Do Jews and Arabs really represent an irreconcilable ethical and historical opposition? Is the Jewish question really distinct from the Arabic question, as Gil Anidjar[5] articulates it? How does the conflict impact North African, Arab Muslim and Jewish communities in France? While some historical and religious conflicts fade into oblivion, the Israeli-Palestinian hostilities persist as a historically transcendent conflict, paradoxically (given the precise geo-historical demarcation outlined above) unrestrained by periodic or geographic boundaries.

HISTORICAL BACKGROUND

This book owes its origin to the acknowledgment of a necessity to examine the impact that the Arab-Israeli conflict has had in France among the Jewish and Francophone communities of the Maghreb,[6] and more generally of North Africa; and consequently to clarify certain aspects regarding the renewed outbreak of anti-Semitism that has affected the Jewish population of France, specifically since the Second Intifada of 2000 and the 2003 Iraq War.[7] It remains true that no conflict in the world has provoked as many repercussions as this one, and the goal of this book is to lay out its causes and its effects, as well as its various historical stages. The alliances formed, unformed and re-formed between France, Israel and Palestine over the course of the years have influenced the perceptions of the conflict held by French and North African writers, historians and intellectuals, whether Jewish or Arab.

The "passion" in France for Middle Eastern affairs belies the ambivalent politics toward the Israeli-Palestinian conflict. Three stages appear to have marked this particular relationship between France and the Israeli-Arab conflict: the first, starting with the end of the Second World War until the War of June 1967, the second from 1967 until the 1990s and the final stage from the 1990s to the present time. When the state of Israel was proclaimed in May 1948, France was practically Israel's sole ally among the international powers. The United States, hoping to succeed the British as the tutelary power in the region, showed signs of ambiguity and declined to sell arms to the Israelis. As for Great Britain, a former colonial power in the region, it remained the faithful ally of the Arabs.[8] This informal alliance was, of course, both circumstantial and strategic. The age-old Franco-British rivalry was exacerbated by the ousting of the French from Syria and Lebanon, which effectively pushed France into the arms of Zionism. In the wake of the Shoah and Nazi atrocities, Zionist ideology was perceived as especially legitimate in France, with its collective guilt for the deportation to the death camps of 75,721 Jews (of which only 2,500 survived).[9] Some of these complex issues are explored in this volume by Ethan Katz.

Several additional factors sealed the Franco-Israeli alliance. One was Nasser's nationalization of the Suez Canal in July 1956 that led to a tripartite war conducted jointly by Israel, France and Great Britain, and which concluded through the intervention of the Soviet Union, the United States and the United Nations. Another, to a lesser degree, was the progressive decolonization of the countries of the Maghreb under French protectorate or colonization since the nineteenth century or beginning of the twentieth century, ending in 1962 with the victory of Algerian forces for national independence (the Front de Libération Nationale). France at that time provided Israel with the technological means to build the atom bomb. During this period, according to Farouk Mardam-Bey and Elias Sanbar, the 1948 *Nakba*,[10] the situation of the Palestinians and the status of the refugees had little effect on public opinion, and Arabs were still generally perceived as being "nostalgic for Nazism."[11] It was not until the war with Lebanon (the fifth Arab-Israeli conflict, June 4, 1982) and the massacres of Sabra and Shatila[12] that French public opinion and the intelligentsia were mobilized. With the First Intifada of 1987, however, the French, and more generally the Europeans, "discovered" the Palestinian people, heightening their consciousness of Palestinians sufferings which had become so manifest.

Beginning with the decolonization of the African continent from 1955 to 1966, and specifically after the Algerian War for Independence against French occupation (1954–1962), the first wave of Maghrebian and North and West African immigration arrived in France, leading to the establishment of its three largest minority groups: Sephardic Jews,[13] Arab Muslims and black Africans (Muslim for the most part); Nacira Guénif-Souilamas develops these aspects in Part IV of this volume. The cohabitation between Jews and Muslims Arabs was not new. The long history of Judeo-Muslim relations goes back to the Middle Ages and becomes particularly pivotal in the colonial societies of the Maghreb. The status of Jews and Arabs differed, however, according to each country. In Morocco, although Sultan Mohammed Ben Youssef protected his Jewish subjects, Jews were kept in a state of daily degradation and humiliation. Moroccan Jews, even under colonization, remained for the most part Moroccan subjects, like their Tunisian coreligionists, and did not benefit from the condition of the Algerian Jews.[14]

In Algeria, the hostility between Jews and Arabs grew all the more in that the Jews, who had been considered as second-class individuals because of their status as *dhimmis*[15] before French colonization, obtained French citizenship with the Cremieux Decree of October 24, 1870. This "Francization" of their community contributed to the "de-Arabization" of the Jews as well as to the "de-Judaization" of the Muslim tradition, but separated Jews forever from Muslim Algerians (Benbassa 2006: 46). However, Algerian anti-Semitism, on the rise in the 1930s due to an increase in European immigration among other factors, was reinforced by the rise of the Vichy regime in 1940.[16] Marcel Peyrouton, the ex-governor general of Algeria and interior minister under Vichy, in 1940 was in charge of the abrogation of the Cremieux Decree and refused all new petitions for French citizenship on the part of Jews and Muslims. Algerian Jews had the same status at that time as the German Jews after the Nuremberg laws. While the Muslim and Jewish communities were opposed to each other largely as a result of colonialism, the repeal of the Cremieux Decree in 1940, the application of *numerus clausus* and the systematic inferiorization of the Jew paradoxically created a kind of rapprochement with the Muslim, who had been denied full citizenship since the beginning of colonization.[17] Nonetheless, Algerian Jews identified themselves increasingly with France, and despite the forcible return to their former status of natives during the Vichy period, they chose on a massive scale to be repatriated to France when Algeria became independent; this exile put an end to two thousand years of Jewish presence on Algerian soil. The example of Algeria, however, remains unique in the history of the Maghreb.

In any case, nineteenth-century Westernization generated diverse modes of Judeo-Arab relationships in all the Muslim countries, often resulting in new types of interethnic tensions. The analysis in 1974 by the writer and philosopher Albert Memmi, a native of Tunisia, is devoid of any nostalgia for that remote period because, for him, "the famous idyllic life of the Jews in Arab countries" is "a myth" and because "the truth" regarding the situation of Tunisian Jews was hardly to be envied, for they were "first of all a minority in a hostile environment; as such we suffered from every fear, every anxiety, the constant feeling of fragility of those who are too weak [. . .]. Cohabitation with the Arabs was not only uneasy, it was filled with threats, periodically acted upon."[18] In Part II of this volume, Lamia Ben Youssef Zayzafoon's chapter discusses Memmi's perspective. Nonetheless, the Jews of these Arab countries inevitably harbored a secret nostalgia for being Jewish Arabs, since this cultural mode of being was manifest in their mores, food, music and language, even as they trembled at the prospect of pogroms and the future of their children in this "atmosphere of sneaky and sometimes open segregation" (Memmi 1974: 54). For Memmi, the Jewish experience in an Arab land was that of someone who was doubly colonized, at the same time by the Arabs and then by the French. It is in this sense that he considers Zionism legitimate as the final liberation of an oppressed people who would find a certain degree of security only during French colonization: "Arab Jews distrusted Muslims even more than the Europeans and dreamed of Eretz Israel long before the Russians and the Poles. [. . .] Jews lived very badly in countries under Arab domination. The State of Israel is not the result of the misfortunes of the Jews of Europe alone" (Memmi 1974: 56, 58). Thus, in so noting, he deconstructs the myth created by the Parisian and European Left after 1967 which argued that Jews somehow had always lived in harmony with their Semitic brothers, and that Arabs, as oppressed people themselves, could not be anti-Semites (Memmi 1974: 56). By situating the Jews on the side of the colonized, Memmi justifies the creation of Israel as a phenomenon comparable to the independence of Algeria, Tunisia and Morocco, countries liberated from colonial oppression: "Zionism was likewise the national liberation movement of the Jews, just as it was for other national liberation movements, in the Maghreb, in Africa and in the world" (Memmi 1974: 149).[19]

The second historical stage of political and diplomatic relations between France and the Israeli-Arab conflict began when General de Gaulle adopted his controversial positions in 1967 which were later pursued practically to the letter by Georges Pompidou, Valéry Giscard d'Estaing and François Mitterrand until the First Intifada of 1987. Although opinions diverge as to the ambivalences in French politics, historians and commentators agree with near unanimity about the rupture that occurred in the wake of the Six-Day War launched by Israel on June 5, 1967. While the French government continued to affirm a certain sympathy for Israel, it nonetheless progressively adopted a sympathetic position toward Palestinians and Arab countries. On June 2, after repeated warnings, France suspended its arms shipments to Israel and eight other countries in the region, and this embargo would be rigorously applied against Israel in January 1969.[20] De Gaulle condemned the Israeli attack on June 10, 1967, but the true rupture was provoked in his press conference of November 27, 1967. Furious that Israel had, despite his previous objections, engaged in (and, moreover, won) a war of preemption—or, depending on one's perspective, a war of aggression—against the Arab states, de Gaulle laid out his government's position and articulated an unfortunate judgment on the Jews as "an elite people, self-assured and domineering." I quote what I consider to be the most revealing portions of de Gaulle's speech:

> One might have asked oneself, and many Jews did indeed ask themselves, whether the planning of this community in lands acquired under more or less justifiable conditions and in the midst of Arab populations fundamentally hostile to it, would not lead to ceaseless and interminable friction and conflict. Some even feared that the Jews, scattered hitherto but who had remained what they had always been, that is an élite people, self-assured and domineering, might, once they were reunited, turn the very moving hopes they had formed over nineteen centuries: 'Next year in Jerusalem,' into a burning ambition of conquest. (...).
>
> Once the Algerian affair had been brought to an end, we resumed the same policy of friendship and cooperation with the Arab peoples of the East which had been France's policy in that part of the World for centuries past. (...). Of course, we did not fail to tell the Arabs that for us the State of Israel was a fait accompli and that we would not permit its destruction.
>
> But, alas, the drama did arise. (...)
>
> We know that France's voice was not heeded. Israel attacked and in six days of fighting seized the objectives she wanted. Now, in the territories she has captured, she is organizing an occupation which can but be accompanied by oppression, repression and expulsion; and the resistance which is being displayed there she, in her turn, calls terrorism.[21]

Although de Gaulle's position was not strictly speaking pro-Arab, his tone was anti-Israeli, for not only did he accentuate Israel's expansionism and its occupation as provoking "oppression, repression, expulsions," and the Israeli tendency to equate the subsequent resistance to terrorism, but he also disputed the "more or less justifiable" conditions for acquiring Palestinian lands. Above all, he qualified the Jews as "an elite people. . . domineering," arousing the concern of French Jews because these terms were disturbingly reminiscent of the *Protocols of the Elders of Zion*. They were more affected by de Gaulle's words than Begin or Ben Gurion, for whom the conference on the whole "rather expressed admiration and deference."[22] De Gaulle did however attempt on several occasions to explain himself by reaffirming his sympathy for Israel. But Raymond Aron's response denounced the general's "Machiavellianism" which forced French Jews to take a position vis-à-vis Israel, and violated the taboo that had served as an impediment to anti-Semitism: "General de Gaulle knowingly, voluntarily, opened up a new period in Jewish and perhaps anti-Semitic history. Anything became possible once more. Everything started over again. It was not, of course, a question of persecution; only of 'ill-will.' It was not a time for hatred; it was a time for suspicion."[23]

From then on, the so called "Arab politics" and the distrust of Israel became a Gaullist dogma, and subsequently a more or less obligatory feature of the foreign policy of the Fifth Republic, regardless of the political allegiance of the head of state. Under President Valéry Giscard d'Estaing, France recognized the Palestinian Liberation Organization (PLO) and established formal relations in 1974 when Giscard d'Estaing's Minister of Foreign Affairs, Jean Sauvagnargues, met with Yasser Arafat in the French Embassy in Beirut. During its tenure in power from the 1960s to the 1990s, the Left was itself split between the pro-Israeli commitment of Gaston Deferre and that of Robert Pontillon; the gradual assumption of leadership positions in the Socialist Party by a new generation that had been marked by anticolonialist and anti-imperialist struggles in the 1960s had the effect of attenuating the philo-Zionism of the old school (Barnavi 2002: 33–36).

The Middle Eastern politics of François Mitterrand (president from 1981 to 1995) displayed these tensions at the heart of his political family. He declared himself "Zionist" and resumed the dialogue interrupted by de Gaulle fourteen years earlier by becoming the first French president to make an official visit to Jerusalem. Yet Mitterrand had discovered the misery of the Palestinian refugees in Gaza and met with Yasser Arafat in January 1974. His historic 1982 speech before the Knesset mentioned explicitly the PLO as a key organization for the future peace process (contradicting indirectly Israel's claim that the PLO was a terrorist group) and advocated the creation of a Palestinian state. But his statement was swept aside by the Prime Minister Begin and the Minister of Defense Ariel Sharon, and repudiated by the Arab world. A few months later, Mitterrand ordered the intervention of the French troops as part of the international force in Lebanon to protect and rescue Yasser Arafat and the *fedayin* at a moment in which they were under siege in Beirut by the Israeli army. Moreover, the French navy rescued Arafat and 4,000 Palestinian fighters in December 1983, reinforcing his opposition both to the radical "alliance" (Syria, Libya, Iran) as well as to the Israeli army. Mitterrand invited Arafat to the Champs Elysée in May 1989 after Arafat had recognized the legitimacy of the state of Israel in November 1988, and he rescued him once again from the "alliance" that was contesting the Palestinian authority. During this historical visit in Paris, Arafat pronounced the "expiration" of the PLO charter from 1964 that called for the destruction of Israel. As for Lionel Jospin, Mitterand's prime minister, up until the uproar at the University of Bir-Zeit in 1999 where he was booed by the Palestinian students for labeling the Lebanese Hezbollah as "terrorist," he might be ideologically situated at the point of intersection of these two trajectories within the Socialist Party, since he displayed both pro-Palestinian and pro-Israeli tendencies.

The positions held by Jacques Chirac (in office from 1995 to 2007) regarding the Arab world and the numerous Arab relations and friendships he maintained during his presidency were evident to the public. Close relations between Arafat and France continued under Chirac, who recognized Arafat as the legitimate president upon his election in 1996. Moreover, his ties to Israel remained very ambiguous. He was depicted, on the political landscape, as being the "pro-Arab philo-Semite."[24] But his speech in July 1995 acknowledging unambiguously the Vichy government's share of responsibility for the fate of Jews in France during the Nazi occupation reassured French Jews who would remain grateful to him for this unprecedented gesture. Chirac was the first to break with the unspoken dogma of the Fourth and Fifth Republics (from de Gaulle to Mitterrand) that depicted Vichy (French fascist state from 1940 to 1944) as simply a monstrous parenthesis within the history of the French Republic, and Marshall Pétain as a poor Nazi puppet.

It remains to be seen what the politics of the new president of the Republic will be; Nicolas Sarkozy, after he was elected in 2007, went to Jerusalem where he pronounced his first speech to the Knesset and renewed the "Franco-Israeli friendship" while supporting the partition of Jerusalem and a solution for Palestinian refugees in the peace process. Nonetheless, as Finkielkraut has stated, "it is not the State that is in hot pursuit of the Jews, it is public opinion. And public opinion does not so much mean the opinion of reporters or editorialists, however severe they may be, but outraged listeners and readers."[25]

REPERCUSSIONS OF THE CONFLICT IN FRANCE

It is in the course of the third historical stage of the relationship between France, Israel and Palestine, from 1990 until today, that the so-called "French passion" for the Israel-Arab conflict begins, because it is centered on questions of identity and community that directly affect the country as a whole. We therefore need to examine the diverse reactions of the French public and intelligentsia to the effects of the conflict that have spilled over into French society. Can one truly speak of a conflict "imported" into France? In other words, does the undeniable rise in internal tensions between the Jewish and Arab Muslim communities stem from the importation of the Israeli-Palestinian conflict? Are Arab Muslim youths or those of Arab origin (third-generation immigrants) the responsible parties in the new expressions of Judeophobia[26] which are seen in France, especially since the Second Intifada in the fall of 2000 and the 2003 Iraq War? Further, has there not been an aggravation of Islamophobia[27] since September 11, conflating Islam with terrorism, as well as a certain defamation of Arabs deemed responsible for the destruction of the republican idea of public education and French secularism, for unemployment, for the rise in violence and crime, and especially for the drift toward "communitarism"?[28] At least three factors, analyzed in the course of this volume, must be taken into consideration to understand what is at stake in these questions: socioeconomic considerations, the question of religion, and finally the political-ideological component.

When the decolonization of the African continent took place (1955–c. 1966), the Jacobin Republic, born of the French Revolution of 1789 and based on a universalist idealistic tradition, was destabilized by the arrival en masse of immigrants from the Maghreb who changed the geographical map of French society. Since the French Revolution, the French republican model based on a "universalist" ideal has been considered the guarantor of identity. Micro-identitarian racial, ethnic, religious or gender categories fall beyond the umbrella of "citizen" and have been regarded with suspicion. After the 1960s, this republican system had to henceforth confront the communitarian withdrawal of these minorities that had only recently settled in France and were challenging the universalist republican discourse. This discourse is by definition opposed to communitarism in the sense that the French Republic does not recognize within its politic body anything other than the French citizen, which conceives of the individual as universal and guarantees equality and liberty to that individual without regard to sex, race or ethnicity. Nevertheless, this republicanism, in which citizens are the only viable political agents, has fallen into crisis since the Fifth Republic (1958 to the present) and even more so since the 1990s (with its social and economic upheavals).

The rift between ideologues is reproduced in intellectual debates within the respective discourses on identity, multiculturalism and minority. Although such a notion of minority identity may seem fundamental in a North American intellectual context, identitarian vindications constitute a very complex and conflictive phenomenon in France. The controversy of the "veil" in France, which culminated in March 2004 with a law prohibiting the wearing of the garment in public schools, is one of the most symptomatic examples of the fear generated by communitarism. Though the law ostensibly affects all religions in its proscription of external religious signs and symbols, its real target was Islam, perceived as a threat to the law of *laïcité* or secularism established in 1905 (which relegated all the manifestations of religious particularism to the private sphere). It was also intended as a protective measure against the risks of proselytism in republican schools. In this sense, communitarism is perceived as synonymous with tribalism in distinction to legitimate particularism. The dual concern of this volume is to gauge this complexity, these micro-identities and their integration in French culture, while at the same time exploring the repercussions of the Jewish-Arab conflict and the conditions of this rift in French society between the republican universalism model and the politics of micro-identities. These particular issues are discussed in the chapters by Lawrence R. Schehr and Nacira Guénif-Souilamas.

For some politicians, sociologists, or idealogues—like Houria Bouteldja— French republican universalism has proven to be an inadequate and incommensurable model to address cultural differences and the conflict of cultures and ethnic and minority identities since the decolonization of Africa. They vindicate an identity-based and separatist system that recognizes communitarism or multiculturalism in order to confront the question of integrating the second and third generations of Beurs[29] and North and West African immigrants in France. For this current of thought, the dysfunction of French-style republican integration requires one to refashion society according to a multicultural model, to forge an American-style model of a multi-communitarian society in place of a model of assimilation, and to move toward pluralist citizenship. Republican France has not solved the problem of how to integrate these Arab Muslim minorities as full-fledged citizens, and has engendered this communitarian space where they become the prey of Islamic fundamentalism.[30] Others, on the other hand—like Fadela Amara—are still advocating republican universalism with French citizenship as the most efficient category for addressing the problems of assimilation faced by Arab Muslim women and men concentrated in these low-income suburban zones. But some intellectuals—like Finkielkraut or Taguieff—argue that it is the Muslim (Arab and black) youth from these "suburbs" (*banlieues*) who for the most part prove to be resistant to the norms required for republican integration and openly display a growing contempt for France and the "impious" West (Taguieff 2002: 173).[31] It is of course impossible to find a consensus on how best to settle the question of the efficacy of the assimilation model versus a multi-communitarian society, and which would also take into account, justly and correctly, the social reality of those suburban developments.

In any case, the communitarian "retrenchment," supposedly characterizing the working-class Maghrebians, Muslims from North and West Africa, and to a lesser extent Sephardic Jews, who share the same space of the low-income *banlieues*, becomes more evident from the 1990s on, with the social and economic decline that has affected the suburban developments in particular. Each community acts out its resentments against the other, and the rancor is magnified in this era of the Israeli-Palestinian conflict, with the relative success and ease of integration into French society by the North African Jews which has exacerbated the hostility of some Arab Muslims. The Jews likewise feel a resentment; marked by the traumatic experience of their precipitous departure from North Africa, perceived as an expulsion, they fear for their coreligionists in Israel whom they believe to be threatened by the same fate (Benbassa 2006: 69).

The second factor concerns religion. The young Maghrebians and Muslims ensconced in low-income suburban high-rise developments are on the front line of social injustice. Of modest backgrounds, they often face social and ethnic discrimination, and then as a compensation for the social injustice they turn toward what has been called, since the early 1990s, "*l'islam des caves*" or "cellar Islam." This Islam of "obscurantism," to use Fadela Amara's expression, is a fundamentalist Islamic current developed in the wake of the Muslim Brotherhood, spreading erroneous interpretations of the Koran among Muslim youth. The new preachers, these "cellar imams," preach a forceful Islam with its intolerant religious propaganda inciting racist and Judeophobic agitation, all the while increasing acts of discrimination instead of reducing them. The universalist and secular discourse upheld by the first and second generations of immigrants in the name of individual and secular freedom is spurned by these alienated youths in favor of a religious communitarism which bestows considerable powers upon these fundamentalist imams, who are now effectively in charge of settling problems that arise in the low-income suburban developments.[32] Meanwhile, the Sephardic Jews of the Maghreb might not lack in this religious communitarian spirit either,[33] since that is how they lived in Arab countries as a means of security and self-protection. According to Mardam-Bey and Sanbar, they also prove to be more religious and observant than the Ashkenazi Jews with deeper roots in France who—ever since the period of Franco-Judaism at the end of the nineteenth century and referring to themselves as "Israélites"[34]—relegated their religious beliefs to the private sphere out of concern for their emancipation and in order to assimilate into the French republican value system. Arguably, Maghrebian Sephardic Jews, however, have in general a conception of religion that does not distinguish between public and private spheres (Mardam-Bey 2005: 287).

Finally, the third factor concerns nationalist ideology. This supposedly "tribal" communitarism particular to the Arab Muslims and the Sephardic Jews living in these suburban developments was further strengthened after the Second Intifada of 2000, and it has spread in the form of a "Diasporic nationalism" without any territorial claims (Sanbar 2005: 292–295; see also Benbassa 2006: 69–70). Further, terrorism, the rise in Islamic fundamentalism, the question of immigration and the failure of integration, withdrawal into one's community to the detriment of French republican values—all these factors obscure the reality of the conflict and contribute to creating guidelines for identity for numerous Jews, Maghrebians and Muslims in France. Arab Muslims in the Diaspora then reconstruct an identitarian unity in defense of the Palestinian cause by aligning themselves with the Palestinians as well as with all those who would challenge the West, deemed to be responsible for the lost honor of the Arab world. The question of Palestine thus symbolizes the ideal of Arab Muslim and Beur youth who enter into solidarity through a communitarism that is in opposition to the Jews (Sanbar 2005: 295). In addition, even though they are French, they often have to deal with the difficulties of being accepted, so that in their internal rebellion they identify themselves with the youth of the Intifada, the mirror image of themselves as outcasts and rebels. This support for the Palestinians often drifts toward a new Judeophobia that, whether voluntary or not, confuses "Jews," "Israelis" and "Zionists." Zionism is their *bête noire*, representing a demonized figure of colonialism now assimilated to racism and racial discrimination. Since the creation of Israel, a Westernized "anti-Semitism" has filtered virulently into the Arab world in the form of anti-Semitic films, books and documentaries borrowing from European anti-Semitic stereotypes dating from the 1920s, the 1930s and the Second World War. These Judeophobic discourses are carried by satellite along Arab networks into the homes of Arab Muslims in Europe and in France, and add fuel to the fire of sermons preached by the "cellar imams" (Benbassa 2006: 72).[35] Hatred of the Jews has become a kind of release mechanism for a segment of young Muslims, and indeed a dangerous and pernicious obsession.

As for the Jews, nationalism throughout the Diaspora unites them all over the world and has become consolidated in the course of the evolution of the Israeli-Palestinian conflict, as discussed in this volume by Maud S. Mandel, who shows how Marseille's Jewish population responded angrily and publicly to the attacks against Israel during the 1991 Gulf War. But this solidarity was particularly evident after the 1967 War in that the triumphal victory has given them a sense of dignity that had been lost since the Shoah. Arguably, the 1967 War might have even contributed to the historical "revenge" of the Jews against the Arabs since their forced exile following the decolonization of Algeria: "Already disappointed by Gaullism, Algerian Jews in particular would become even more so by French politics in the Middle-East, and their allegiance to the State of Israel has become the principal pole of identity for the Jew, allowing that State to speak on behalf of the Jews of the world" (Mardam-Bey 2005: 288; Benbassa 2006: 70–73). Now, in insisting on the "communitarism" of Algerian Jews and their unconditional support for Israel, might Mardam-Bey not be reviving the old accusation of the divided allegiance of the Jew that characterized the anti-Semitic discourses of the nineteenth and twentieth centuries in Europe—a divided allegiance spared the Maghrebian Muslims? According to Finkielkraut, by wondering about or questioning the bond that unites the Jews of France to Israel, Jews have been made to feel an embarrassed defensiveness regarding the state of Israel since the Second Intifada, a sentiment that has cornered them into a protective communitarism. For Brauman, on the other hand, "at the cost of considering themselves as traitors, the Jews of France must vibrate in harmony with a State—Israel—that contradicts the republican form in which they recognize themselves" (Brauman 2006: 211–214) and, shaken by all these contradictions, the Jews prefer to defend themselves against hostility in a communitarian withdrawal. The two intellectuals, nevertheless, deplore the transformation of the French nation into a multi-communitarian ("multicultural") society, forcing the French, however, to renew their thinking about the Republic by refusing to stigmatize a communitarian ideal in the name of an abstract republican model.

DEBATES AMONG INTELLECTUALS

The Middle East conflict not only reveals but amplifies a serious malaise in France, becoming over the course of the years a prime subject of debate among French intellectuals,[36] now brought to the forefront by the media, as demonstrated by Jeffrey Mehlman's chapter in Part V of this volume. As the journalist Elisabeth Lévy said: "Since the beginning of the second Intifada in October 2000, the Middle East and anti-Semitism are subjects that get people angry and even drive them crazy. Every flare-up of violence over there, every manifestation of tension here, fan the flames of the civil war among intellectuals. [. . .] Some are Zionists, others not. The former are accused of a lack of sensitivity for the suffering of the Palestinians and of unconditional support for Israel, the latter of indifference to the torment of the Jews in France and of complacency towards terrorism. Each has its victims" (Lévy 2006: 14–15).

As for the fallout of the Jewish-Arab Muslim conflict in its Judeophobic form, here too opinions diverge, opening up onto a multiplicity of points of view and opposed narratives. Taking a position regarding anti-Semitism in France is a complex matter when some discourses exaggerate the gravity of anti-Semitic aggression of Arab-Muslim origin, while others diminish the seriousness of these acts so as not to stigmatize the young blacks and Arab Muslims living in the *banlieues*. There has been an undeniable increase in anti-Jewish attacks and an undisputed and open aversion for Jews expressed by certain Arab Muslim milieus in France.[37] For Taguieff, anti-Zionism has become a "euphemism" for a modern "anti-racist anti-Semitism," as spoken about by Finkielkraut, that consists of hurling the accusation of racism against Jews in order to justify Judeophobia (Taguieff 2002: 42–43). On the other hand, Brauman, following Mardam-Bey, denounces what he considers to be an intolerable "coercion using the charge of anti-Semitism" that is widespread in France and which would preclude any criticism of Israel on the pretext that such attacks stem from a desire to annihilate Israel (Brauman 2006: 178).[38] Similarly, Benbassa, conceiving of anti-Semitism as the "metaphor for the ills of French society," wonders about the fear that has seized Jews of France since 2000 by offering a hypothesis on the displacement of meaning of the term "anti-Semitism": "Should we not see here, too, the expression of this new diasporic nationalism, centered on the defense of Israel and quick to classify any criticism of it in the anti-Semitic category" (Benbassa 2006: 71)? Can we speak of a continuity between a certain form of criticism addressed against Israel, the principle of anti-Zionism and modern Judeophobia?

From one verbal slippage to another, we at times wind up with discursive excesses regarding the expansion of Judeophobia of Arab Muslim origin in France, and the "importation" of the conflict.[39] These excesses incite some to interpret the effects as an "Intifada of the *banlieues*" or, for others, to accuse the diasporic Jewish institutions in France of "Zionization" or "Israelization" (Mardam-Bey 2005: 288). Thus, Finkielkraut argues that "we are undergoing in France the fallout of anti-Semitism breaking out today in Africa and in the Arab Muslim world. Let us not be mistaken about which period we are dealing with. The spirit blowing over our country is not the spirit of Drumont—except in a residual, quasi folkloric way—it is the spirit of Durban" (Finkielkraut 2006: 176). Whereas for Brauman, even though the Israeli-Palestinian affair is also "a French and universal affair" because it resonates with colonial history and with the history of the Jews and Arabs in France, "anti-Semitism cannot be summarized by the cliché of an imported conflict" (Brauman 2006: 213). He thereby aligns himself with the arguments of Sanbar and of Mardam-Bey, who reject the idea of an imported conflict and for whom Islamophobia, just as much as Judeophobia, "carr[ies] the label: 'Made in France'" (Sanbar 2005: 291)![40]

Whether or not it is directly imported, it would be irresponsible and absurd not to admit the fallout of the Middle East conflict in France among the communities under discussion here. And, moreover, there is clearly a political recuperation from the Israeli-Palestinian conflict and from its direct repercussions in terms of Judeophobia, anti-Semitism and racism against the Arab Muslim community. For these terms are the object of an ideological and political usage that French intellectuals[41] denounce in unison because they concur in finding in such usage the many analogies that lurk there, through metonymic displacement, which can be exploited symbolically for the ideal "victim" or the ultimate "wretched of the earth." Nevertheless, these intellectuals discern these victimizing constructions only in the opposing ideological camp. Such constructions thus might legitimize the outbreaks of violence in the suburban developments on the pretext that they are motivated by the social rebellion of young people who have not been integrated. The diverse interpretations of the French riots of 2005 in the low-income suburbs, which exploded after the accidental death of two young boys pursued by the police, are an illustration of this internal schism in France regarding social issues, cultural diversity and racism, as discussed in this volume by Johann Sadock. Does the fact that there is originally a real problem in France regarding the acceptance and assimilation of Arab Muslim minorities justify making absolute victims of them?

Might it not be the same with the construction of a victimized "Palestinian terrorist," justified and encouraged by public opinion for incarnating, more strongly than anyone else, the revolt against an unjust destiny? (See Bruno Chaouat's chapter in Part III of the volume.) Taguieff deplores the mediatic "setting up of the Palestinians in the convenient position of the oppressed and victims, transfigured just as easily into the Marxist utopia of the Proletariat—as the class bearing the future of the world—as into the Islamist mythology of *djihad* led [...] by the true believers against the world of the impious and the infidels" (Taguieff 2002: 105).

Finally, and this is one of the most disturbing aspects of all, in the 1980s but especially since the beginning of the twenty-first century,[42] the enmity between Jews, blacks and Arab Muslims has initiated a new phase with renewed focus on the atrocities of slavery and colonization, and the demands that they be inscribed in the collective French memory on the same level as the "duty of memory" for the Shoah. We are then only a step away from scandalous extremes in the rivalry of memory and victimhood where blacks, Arab Muslims and Jews seek recognition for their status as victims, and uphold themselves as the standard bearers of victimization.[43] This provokes against Jews—specifically since the Barbie trial in 1987—odious judgments that accuse Jewish grief—based perhaps on the effects of the uniqueness of the Shoah—of obstructing the memory of the world's suffering.[44] Could those militating for memory, who may have instituted the exceptionality of the Shoah into a cult, be responsible for this catastrophic competition of memorialization and its excesses that are profoundly symptomatic? Since 1980, might there be a "religion of memory"? Finkielkraut objects to it in these terms:

> It is not a particular community but the religion of humanity that set up the memory of the Shoah as a supreme commandment; it is democracy that wanted Auschwitz to remain inscribed in the collective consciousness as a perpetual call to order, as a prohibition against going to sleep. [...] The obsession with the Shoah is not a Jewish affair. It is because our societies have placed equality at the foundation of living together that a sacred terror surrounds the names of Auschwitz, of Treblinka, of Maidanek or of Sobibor. And that the Jews should not be the exclusive heirs of the obligations born of the duty of memory (Finkielkraut 2006: 235).

Nevertheless, we are obliged to note that the horror of the Shoah is sometimes used in France, whether naively or perversely, by certain Jewish and non-Jewish milieus, on the one hand to legitimize the impunity of Israel where its politics cannot be defended, or to support Israel when it presents itself to the world as the response to the Shoah. But does challenging impunity necessarily imply a questioning of the right to exist? These issues are discussed in the last part of this volume, especially in Benbassa's chapter.

As Brauman argues, "overexposure by the media and the singular symbolic implications of the Israeli-Palestinian conflict confer upon commemorations of the Shoah an overflow of meanings that are easy to exploit" (Brauman 2006: 238). That said, however, Judeophobia prospers with or without any complicity with Israel, and the memory of the Shoah often turns against Jews who must henceforth see themselves taking on the role of executioner or persecutor.

CONCEPTUAL APPROACHES

In this book, the diverse methodologies incorporate historical, sociological, theoretical, literary and psychoanalytical interpretations of the conflict and its direct consequences in France among its Jewish and Arab Muslim populations. Each section of the book is organized historically, and the principal historical markers are the beginning of modern Zionism until the First and Second Intifadas (1987 and 2000) up to our time.

In Part I, "Alternative History of Zionism and the Jewish Question, 1914–1950," the question of Zionism, and the tragedy of the Shoah and its memory are at the heart of the Israeli-Palestinian conflict and its direct fallout in France, for they constitute the stakes of the conflict and nurture its tumultuous discourse since the creation of Israel. The first part begins with the premises of the Jewish-Arab relationship in France at the moment when Zionism preceded the creation of Israel, then during the horror of the Shoah and after the liberation of the camps. This first section begins with three chapters that explore the years between the early Zionist movement and the establishment of Israel in 1948. In "Tracing the Shadow of Palestine: The Zionist-Arab Conflict and Jewish-Muslim Relations in France, 1914–1945," Ethan Katz undertakes a significant historical analysis of events from 1914 to 1945 in France. He demonstrates that in interwar France, largely through the lens of two more central issues—colonial Algeria and the rise of fascism—the question of Palestine had already became a concern for Jews and Muslims. Subsequently, World War II heightened tensions between Jews and Muslims in France over the Arab-Zionist conflict. Philippe Zard, in "The Paradoxes of Zionism in the Work of Albert Cohen," shows the role that Zionism plays in Albert Cohen's writing. In his early years, Cohen, as a high-ranking official in the United Nations, adopted the cause of Zionism in *Revue Juive* as an ideology of national rebirth. After World War II, however, he elaborated in his fiction a metaphysics of Judaism which was no longer compatible with the historical and political development of Zionism. Lawrence R. Schehr's chapter, "'One Nation (In)divisible?': Sartre and the Jewish Question," emphasizes the importance of the historical context in his analysis of Jean-Paul Sartre's *Réflexions sur la question juive*. Though this key text was written in the fall of 1944, the extent of the destruction of European Jewry at the hands of the Third Reich was not yet common knowledge. Therefore, Schehr demonstrates how Sartre's reflections treat anti-Semitism as a domestic problem revealing the internal contradictions of republican ideals, as an ongoing divisive force within France that expresses a nostalgic return to a past that never was and a desire for a future that cannot be.

Part II, "Francophone Literature and Cinema on the Conflict, 1957–2000," comprises four chapters that address the specific role of literature and cinema. In "Slimane Benaïssa, or the Voice of Dissidence," Cyril Aslanov explores, from a sociolinguistic perspective, the work of the Francophone writer Slimane Benaïssa and the space of literary discourse in his plays. Aslanov theorizes that the choice of the French language helped Benaïssa to escape the pressure of the dominant discourse in Algeria and provides the writer an alternative to the politics of "re-Arabization" that characterize the Algerian sociolinguistic horizon since independence. Benaïssa adopts a subversive viewpoint in his attempt to bridge the gap between Jews and Arabs, and draws on his experience with his Algerian Sephardic friend, André Chouraqui. Anny Dayan-Rosenman's "The Israeli-Palestinian Conflict in France: A Conflict in Search of Novelistic Representations," shows, through a selection of Jewish French writers, how their texts dramatize the departure from their native North Africa, their connection to Israel before their emigration and their stages of disillusionment—often described from a derisive angle. In "When 'L'Essence Arrose de Haine': The Reinvention of Identity in Francophone Tunisian Literature," Lamia Ben Youssef Zayzafoon focuses on the discursive production of the conflict in the works of four Tunisian-born Francophone intellectuals and writers. This chapter examines how each author reproduces, reinvents or resists the Eurocentric categories of "the Jew," "the Mohammedan," "the Arab," "the Semite" and "the anti-Semite," as well as the "Islamophobe" neologism of the 1980s, in their formulations of the conflict, and how they maintain to various degrees critical positions vis à vis the twin nationalist discourses of Arabism and Zionism. In the final chapter of Part II, "Otherwise Occupied: The Israeli-Palestinian Conflict in the Francophone Cinema," Lincoln Z. Shlensky argues that Francophone cinema treats the conflict as an arena for addressing the unresolved traumatic history of Europe's treatment of cultural and religious others in the twentieth century. He discusses two major cinematic modes (drama and essay film genres) in which the Israeli-Palestinian conflict has been treated since the 1960s and in doing so discerns a reconceptualization of the cultural codes and historical dilemmas or traumas that pertain to the history of Francophone culture within and outside of Europe.

Part III, "Violence, Martyrdom and Terrorism, 1970–2007," includes two chapters related to the question of the seduction of violence. In "The Agony for Justice," Fethi Benslama analyzes the condition of "suicide bombers" in the Islamic world and specifically in what he calls "the Hezbollah laboratory" in Lebanon (under French mandate from 1920–1943). He examines the recent change in the humanity's understanding of death and how the construction of a discourse on witnessing and death has a direct impact on the unconscious as well as its reverberations on the Islamic masses. Bruno Chaouat's "Out of Palestine: Jean Genet's Shooting Stars" focuses on Genet's memoir of the Palestinian revolution in *Un captif amoureux*. Chaouat argues that, for Genet, Palestinians are mere tropes for nomadism and subversion of the law and that his oeuvre presents the ambiguous confusion between anti-Zionism and the metaphysics of European anti-Semitism. He also shows how Genet, with his glorification of the suicide bomber, supported the subaltern Palestinians because they were the most apt to be the rebels and the most likely to resist the Western world.

Part IV, "Muslim-Jewish Relations in France, 1990–2008," addresses the question of the "imported" conflict in the heart of the Jewish and Arab Muslim communities in the French "cités" (low-income suburban developments). Maud S. Mandel's "The War Comes Home: Muslim-Jewish Relations in Marseille during the 1991 Gulf War" investigates the relations between Muslims (of North African origin and representing at least one quarter of Marseille's population) and the Jewish community in Marseille (the third largest in Western Europe) during the Gulf War. Despite the ethnic violence of recent years, Mandel claims that Marseille has been the most successful of all of France's cities at maintaining peaceful interethnic relations and explains this "harmonious" rapport by examining the reaction of Muslims and Jews to the U.S.-led attack on Iraq in 1991 and Iraq's subsequent decision to bomb Israeli cities. Yet Mandel shows how the various responses reflected diverse links to the French state rather than investments in Middle East politics. In "Hung Up on Being Fair and Left Hanging between the Israeli-Palestinian Conflict and the 'Banlieues,'" Johann Sadock gives his personal account on the "importation" of the conflict in the French *banlieues* (low-income suburban developments). He provides insights on how matters are represented and how conflicts are scripted in and among communities. Also, in shedding light on current incarnations of the debate, Sadock integrates it into larger concepts that relate to the cultural clash between cities and suburbs during the Second Intifada of 2000 and in the riots of 2005. In the last chapter of Part IV, "Jews and Arabs in Postcolonial France, a Situated Account of a Long Painful Story of Intimacy," Nacira Guénif-Souilamas argues that recent interactions between Jews and Arabs seem to always be mediated by the cultural, political or historical French frame of reference. However, the enduring relation between Jews and Arabs in North Africa exceeds the boundaries of French history. In order to explain tensions and ties among communities, Guénif-Souilamas focuses on the story of "Marie and the RER D" (a false anti-Semitic attack) and the story of a personal dialogue between a Jew and an Arab in contemporary France.

Part V, the final section of the volume, "Judeocentrism, Anti-Semitism and French Intelligentsia, 2000–2008," includes three chapters with cogent analyses of current aspects and debates on the new Judeophobia, the pro-Palestinian anti-Semitism, the instrumentalization of the Shoah and the duty

18 *Nathalie Debrauwere-Miller*

of remembrance. In "A New Judeocentrism? (On A Recent Trend in French Thought)," using the word "Judeocentrism" as a synonym of anti-Semitism and, on the other hand, as another name for Judaism, Jeffrey Mehlman assesses the fallout from a trauma the French intellectual class is still trying to absorb, and situates this trauma somewhere between the hysteria over Renaud Camus' comments regarding what he perceived as the overrepresentation of Jews on French radio and the relative indifference to the first violent stages of the Parisian variant of the Second Intifada in 2000. Mehlman also examines the seductiveness of antiracist anti-Semitism and the symptom of a new Judeocentrism in French thought. Denis Charbit's "Dual Narratives on the Middle East Conflict: Analysis of a French Literary Genre" presents a corpus of books on the Arab-Israeli conflict that were published in France from the Six-Day War until the aftermath of the Second Lebanon War. These books have in common a dialogue between two authors, each one representing a side of the conflict, and Charbit analyzes the initial confrontation of two opposed narratives revealing the increasing interest within French society. Part V concludes with Esther Benbassa's testimonial "How One Becomes a Traitor" which divulges some of the personal ramifications that the discursive positions on the Israeli-Palestinian conflict have generated in France. Between 2000 and 2006, Benbassa finds herself at the center of controversy in the French Jewish community and discovers to her detriment that, as a Jew, she cannot criticize Israel. She also questions the conventional assessment that Jews are massively endangered in France, and refuses to view the Shoah as the defining event of modern Jewish history. Her personal account reveals a long history of dissentions within the Jewish world.

With the heterogeneity of approaches, I hope the chapters of this collection will help Anglophone readers achieve a broader view of the issues at stake in dealing with the repercussions of the Israeli-Palestinian conflict in the Francophone (Jewish and Arab Muslim) communities in France.

NOTES

This introduction was written and completed in the Fall 2008 before the Gaza War that began on December 27, 2008.
1. *"Francophonie"* is both a cultural and political concept (and in some ways a legacy of colonialism) that refers to lands where French is spoken. However, in the present collection of essays, "Francophone" will refer to diasporic communities or texts written by writers, historians or intellectuals from North Africa or of Maghrebian and North African origin. I regret the volume could not entertain a wider notion of Francophone population (the Caribbean, Quebec and West Africa) but the Francophone North Africans are those who are most directly impacted and concerned by the Middle East conflict and therefore merit the majority of attention here.
2. There are about 600,000 Jews and around 5 million Arab Muslims in France.
3. The popular uprising in the occupied Palestinian territories which designates a political or military contestation. The term in Arabic signifies "sudden

movement, uprising, war of stone-throwing." The First Palestinian Intifada against the Israeli army broke out on December 9, 1987, at the Jabbalyya refugee camp in Gaza. The Second Intifada, since designated as the "Al-Aqsa Intifada," started on September 28, 2000, in the Palestinian territories after Ariel Sharon, the head of the Likud Party, visited the esplanade of the Mosques in Jerusalem. Sharon's visit to the Dome of the Rock—the symbol of national identity—was interpreted by the Palestinians as an act of provocation.
4. In this context and along the volume, the word "suburbs," a translation of the French words "banlieue" or "cité," refers to the densely packed communities, inhabited for the most part by poor immigrants, in the outer suburbs of French cities. In this Introduction, "banlieue" and "cité" are usually translated as "low-income suburban developments." All translations of quotations are mine unless otherwise indicated.
5. Gil Anidjar, *The Jew, the Arab, A History of the Enemy* (Stanford, CA: Standford University Press, 2003).
6. Which in Arabic means the "setting sun," and encompasses all the countries of Northwest Africa (Morocco, Algeria, Tunisia), from the Mediterranean to the Sahara. Tunisia was under French protectorate from 1881 to 1956, Morocco under French protectorate from 1912 to 1956 (and Spanish protectorate in the Rif and Ifni regions until 1934), and Algeria was under French colonization from 1830 to 1962.
7. Though anti-Arab racism has likewise seen an upward curve in France since September 11, it is not directly linked to the Israeli-Palestinian conflict and not perpetrated by the Jewish community. On the contrary, the expansion of Judeophobia of arguably Arab Muslim origin in France is related to the Middle-East conflict.
8. Elie Barnavi and Luc Rosenzweig, *La France et Israël, Une affaire passionnelle* (Paris: Perrin, 2002), 30–37.
9. This was out of a total Jewish population of about 700,000 in France and North Africa in the 1940 census. 23% of the Jews from France were deported. See Esther Benbassa, *Histoire des Juifs de France* (Paris: Seuil, 1997), 251, and André Kaspi, *Les Juifs pendant l'occupation* (Paris: Seuil, 1991), 177.
10. This word in Arabic means "catastrophe." It was used by the Palestinians to indicate the day the state of Israel was created, May 14, 1948, leading to the exiling of many thousands of Palestinians.
11. Farouk Mardam-Bey and Elias Sanbar, *Etre Arabe* (Paris: Sindbad, 2005), 278. Subsequent references to this volume will be indicated parenthetically in the text.
12. Names of two refugee camps of Palestinians set up in Lebanon. Two days after the assassination of the Lebanese president Bashir Gemayel, the massacre was committed by Lebanese Christian militias under the passive observation of the Israeli army, September 16–18, 1982.
13. Before the decolonization of North Africa, the majority of the Jews in France were Ashkenazi. The term Ashkenazi, which appears in the Bible, refers to Noah's great-grandson and later to Germania and Lotharingia in Talmudic writings. By extension it then referred to European Jews (from Flanders and the Rhine valley), and then mainly to central and eastern Europe. The Zionist movement originated with the Ashkenazim and they constituted the first waves of immigration to Palestine. The term "Sephardic" designates Jews from the Mediterranean basin. It refers to the Jews living in Spain and Portugal in the Middle Ages, expelled from 1492 on. Many of them took refuge in North Africa. After Algerian independence, almost all the Jews left Algeria to settle in France, followed by tens of thousands of Jews from Morocco, Tunisia, Egypt and other countries, all natives of the Arab world and of

French culture. From 1956 to 1966, French Jewry was thus "Sephardized." According to Barnavi, 68 percent of the French Jews are Sephardic whereas 22 percent are Ashkenazi, in *Lettre ouverte aux Juifs de France* (Paris: Stock, 2002), 17.
14. In Tunisia, 7,000 Jews were granted French nationality between 1911 and 1940, and during the French protectorate about a quarter of the Jews became French. See Esther Benbassa and Jean-Christophe Attias, *Juifs et musulmans, Une histoire partagée, un dialogue à construire* (Paris: La découverte, 2006), 52. Subsequent references to this book will be indicated parenthetically in the text.
15. The particular status of the "people of the book" (Jews and Christians) requiring the payment of a special tax, the *giziya*, and the renunciation of political activity in exchange for Islamic protection in the countries where they reside.
16. French fascist state established from 1940 to 1944 with Marshall Pétain at its head.
17. "Even though anti-Jewish measures in North Africa were at times interpreted as a French concession to Muslim pressures, the Muslim elite, who had received a Western education and was disposed towards the resistance, seems to have supported the Jews." Michaël Marrus and Robert Paxton, *Vichy et Les Juifs* (Paris: Calmann-Lévy, 1981), 275. My translation.
18. Albert Memmi, *Juifs et Arabes* (Paris: Idées/Gallimard, 1974), 50. Subsequent references to this volume will be indicated parenthetically in the text.
19. See Anidjar, *Jew*, for an opposite opinion.
20. Henri Rousso, *Le Syndrome de Vichy de 1944 à nos jours* (Paris: Seuil, 1987), 158.
21. In Raymond Aron, *France, Israel and the Jews* (New York: Frederick A. Praeger, 1969), 9–11. See also Samir Kassir and Farouk Mardam-Bey, *Itinéraires de Paris à Jérusalem, La France et le conflit israélo-arabe* (Washington: Institut des études palestiniennes, 2007), 77–80.
22. Freddy Eytan, *David et Marianne: La France, les Juifs et Israël: La raison et la passion* (Paris: Alain Moreau, 1986), 139.
23. Rousso, *Syndrome*, 159–160. And Aron, *Israel*, 25.
24. Barnavi, *France*, 29.
25. Rony Brauman and Alain Finkielkraut, *La Discorde Israël-Palestine, les Juifs, la France, Conversations avec Elisabeth Lévy* (Paris: Mille et une nuits, 2006), 210. Subsequent references to this book will be indicated parenthetically in the text.
26. Although the new "anti-Semitism" of the 2000s still assumes certain forms of the earlier version that marked the Second World War, following Taguieff I will use the neologism "Judeophobia" instead of the term "anti-Semitism" which no longer accounts for the worldwide anti-Jewish manifestations of our time. The term "anti-Semitism" was introduced in Germany in 1879 by Wilhelm Marr to designate the rejection of the Jews as an inferior race. It therefore had to do with establishing a distinction among the "Semitic" and the "Aryan/Indo-European" races. The new, post-Nazi Judeophobia is no longer based on a racial opposition but on religious, cultural and political aspects quite different from the anti-Semitism of the Dreyfus Affair or the state-sponsored racism of fascism and Nazism. See Pierre-André Taguieff, *La Nouvelle judéophobie* (Paris: Mille et un Nuits, 2002), 25.
27. This controversial neologism poses a problem for essayists who fear being accused of racism for criticizing Islam or for studying it as a historical phenomenon. But Islam designates simultaneously the Muslim religion and the entirety of the peoples, countries or cultures dominated by that religion. See

Introduction 21

Mardam-Bey, *Etre arabe*, 303. According to Benbassa, there are no exact statistics regarding the amount of violence committed against Arabs and blacks in France. *Juifs*, 71.
28. This neologism attempts to communicate the sense of French "communautarisme"—that is, the isolation or particularity of diverse cultural communities into separate enclaves.
29. These second and third generations of North Africans have attracted a series of labels to distinguish them from the majority and that they claim or reject. "Beurs"/"Beurettes" is one of these labels (a backslang expression formed by deformation of the *verlan* word for Arab, *rebeu*). It can be defined as a young person of Maghrebian origin born in France of immigrant parents.
30. The ideological vision of the Muslim religion and its challenge to a power, a regime or a society. A politico-religious movement calling for the complete and radical Islamization of the law, institutions and government in Islamic countries.
31. See also Michèle Tribalat, *Dreux, voyage au coeur du Malaise français* (Paris: La découverte, 1999).
32. See Fadela Amara, *Ni Putes ni soumises* (Paris: La découverte, 2003), 74.
33. For objections to tribalism and communitarism of the Sephardic Jews, see Shmuel Trigano, *L'Avenir des Juifs de France* (Paris: Editions du Panama, 2006).
34. The oldest name used to define a member of the nation formed by the twelve sons of Jacob. At the time of emancipation, the Jews designated themselves by the terms "Israelites" and "Hebrews" in reference to the Jewish religion rather than "Jews," a term which at the time carried a pejorative and racial connotation.
35. Using the republication of the *Protocols of the Elders of Zion*—that famous forgery concocted by the Czarist police—and their massive distribution from 1967 on, the Arab world has reconstructed the image of the Jew as responsible for a worldwide conspiracy, a permanent plot for universal domination in that it is supposed to manipulate everything, from finance to the media, from politics to industry. See Pierre André-Taguieff, *La Judéophobie des modernes: Des lumières au Jihad Mondial* (Paris: Ed. Odile Jacob, 2008).
36. Whereas for Alain Finkielkraut, André Taguieff, Bernard Henry-Lévy, André Glucksman and Sylvain Attal the new Judeophobia is perpetrated by extreme-left anti-Zionist groups and by Arab Muslim or black Muslim youth, Raphaël Confiant, Michel Wieviorka, Guillaume Weil-Raynal and Ivan Segré are opposed to this view, diminishing or denying the significance of anti-Semitic attacks of black and Arab Muslim origin in France since the 2000s.
37. For statistics on anti-Jewish acts, see Taguieff, *Judéophobie* and Benbassa, *Juifs*, 71. Certain anti-Jewish acts of aggression are analyzed in this volume: see the chapters by Melhman and Benbassa, as well as Guénif-Souilamas, whose interpretation corroborates, by opposition, that of Finkielkraut in *Discorde*, 177–178.
38. See *Antisémitisme: L'intolérable chantage: Israël-Palestine, une affaire française*. (Paris: La découverte, 2003). And Michel Wieviorka, *La tentation antisémite: Haine des Juifs dans la France d'aujourd'hui* (Paris : Laffont, 2005).
39. For a critical response to the new Judeophobia in France, see Guillaume Weill-Raynal, *Une Haine imaginaire? Contre-enquête sur le "nouvel antisémitisme"* (Paris: Armand-Collin, 2005).
40. See also Leila Shahid, Michel Warschawski and Dominique Vidal, *Les Banlieues, le Proche-Orient et nous* (Paris: Editions de l'atelier, 2006).

41. Among other intellectuals, Alain Finkielkraut, Rony Brauman, André Taguieff, Esther Benbassa and Bernard Henry-Lévy.
42. The French law *Taubira* voted on May 21 of 2001 promulgates the official commemoration of the slave trade and slavery as a crime against humanity.
43. About the disturbing competition among victims, see Guillaume Erner, *La société des victimes* (Paris: La Découverte, 2006) and Jean Michel Chaumont, *La Concurrence des Victimes (Génocide, Identité, Reconnaissance)* (Paris: La Découverte, 2002).
44. The black comedian, Dieudonné, was sentenced in February 2005 for "public defamation of a racial nature," after qualifying the memory of the Shoah as "memorial pornography" on the pretext that not enough of the sort is done for blacks and slavery because people place too much importance on the Jews and the Shoah. About the Barbie trial, see Alain Finkielkraut, *La mémoire vaine* (Paris: Gallimard, 1989).

Part I
Alternative History of Zionism and the Jewish Question, 1914–1950

1 Tracing the Shadow of Palestine
The Zionist-Arab Conflict and Jewish-Muslim Relations in France, 1914–1945

Ethan Katz

Though the day's events are little remembered now, October 29, 1944, witnessed the first large-scale confrontation between Jews and Muslims in France over the Palestinian question. That afternoon in Paris, an estimated 1,400 to 2,000 people gathered for a meeting of the *Organisation Sioniste de France*. While most attendees were Jewish, two to three hundred of them were Muslim.[1] Before the gathering began, several Muslims gained permission to address the audience. As the meeting started, French Zionist leader Marc Jarblum spoke first, lamenting the horrors of deportation and highlighting the heroism of Jewish resisters. He saluted the presence of Muslims in the hall, and assured them of the Zionists' desire not to dominate, but to work with the Arabs of Palestine.

When a Muslim, Zadoca, took the podium, trouble began. After a few preliminary remarks, he referred to "Zionist atrocities in Palestine," provoking outcry from the audience. Resisting the crowd's protests and Jarblum's instructions first to tame his remarks and then to leave the stage, Zadoca completed his speech. A Zionist orator sought to respond but found himself drowned out by Muslims chanting "Palestine to the Arabs!" and "Palestine to the Muslims!" As the atmosphere briefly calmed, French Zionist leader Joseph Fisher confronted the Muslims: "For the first time since the Liberation, such a protest takes place. It is an outrage against the harmony that currently reigns in France." Linking the known Nazi collaboration of Hadj Amin Mohammad al-Husseini, Grand Mufti of Jerusalem, with the protesters' behavior, Fisher continued: "Certain leaders of ours are in Jerusalem, but yours, the Mufti, is in Berlin, which explains everything." Muslims continued to shout their slogans. Zionist speakers could not be heard, and Jews instead chanted the Zionist anthem *Hatikvah*. French police intervened to disband the meeting.

La Terre Retrouvée, France's Zionist organ, would soon feature two articles converning the incident. The first underscored the difficulties faced by Jewish attendees: many still wondered about the fate of family and friends deported in the Shoah. In stark contrast, the same article contended that certain Muslim protestors were connected to the rabidly anti-Semitic, pro-Nazi *Comité Musulman de l'Afrique du Nord*.[2] Implying further disparities between the two groups, wrtiers for the newspaper recounted the conciliatory efforts of the meeting's Zionist leaders, asserted that most Muslims present "did not even understand French" and classified the protestors as part of the treacherous fifth column that had collaborated with the Germans and continued to sabotage French interests.[3] In internal correspondence, the Zionists referred to the Muslim speaker as a "hooligan," and reported that certain Muslim attendees came from anti-Semitic fascist groups.[4]

* * *

This event appears to challenge key aspects of the prevailing historiographies of Jewish-Muslim relations in the Francophone world, of French Zionism and of Muslims in France. First, it points to the longevity of Jewish-Muslim relations in twentieth-century metropolitan France, a subject that has received almost no attention from historians. Secondly, scholarship on North African Jewry has typically treated 1947–1948 as the first time that Zionism became a major source of division between Jews and Muslims residing in the French orbit.[5] Histories of French Zionism up to Israeli statehood, meanwhile, have ignored the very presence of Muslims in France, let alone their interactions with Jews around the question of Palestine.[6] Similarly, according to studies of the history of France's Muslims, politically active Muslims in France at this time focused on the question of colonial North Africa, not Palestine.[7]

In fact, Jewish-Muslim relations in metropolitan France began in earnest with the First World War. For much of the ensuing thirty years, Zionism among French Jews and Arab nationalism among French Muslims each attracted relatively small, if increasing numbers of active adherents.[8] At the level of articulated politics, however, where this chapter focuses, the Zionist-Arab conflict appears to have already had a growing influence on Jewish-Muslim interactions. After surveying the war years and the 1920s, this chapter concentrates on two flashpoints—Adolf Hitler's arrival to power in 1933 and the Arab Revolt in Palestine of 1936–1939—and their impact on interactions between Jews and Muslims in France regarding the issue of Palestine. While World War I marked a critical turning point for Jewish and Arab nationalism that affected Jewish-Muslim relations everywhere, subsequent developments in France followed their own path, driven by particularly French concerns. Two issues, the future of colonial Algeria and the struggle between fascism and antifascism, largely defined Jewish-Muslim political relations in France between the wars. This chapter argues that Jewish and Muslim portrayals and impressions of one another around these two issues colored perceptibly their impressions and representations of the Zionist-Arab conflict. Through Nazi and Vichy racial policy and the battles in North Africa, World War II heightened the interconnectedness of Palestine with the questions of both colonialism and fascism. By situating the events of October 29, 1944, in the context of the preceding thirty years, this chapter traces the manner in which the Palestinian question became a potent source of Jewish-Muslim tension in France by the end of the occupation period.[9]

* * *

The First World War brought roughly 390,000 North African Muslims to the French *métropole* as soldiers or laborers.[10] With about 38,000 Jews from the métropole and Algeria serving in the French armed forces and 85,000 more Jewish civilians in the métropole, for the first time, sizable numbers of Jews and Muslims began to interact in hexagonal France.[11] Through the end of the Ottoman Empire, the Balfour Declaration and the eventual creation of the British Mandate, World War I helped to galvanize both Zionism and Arab nationalism. Yet the war years witnessed no documented animus between Jews and Muslims in France around the Palestinian question. The few recorded interactions concerning the subject are even quite positive. From early in the war, a Jewish doctor named Charles Zalta was one of several Jews on the "Syro-Lebanese Committee," which advocated for Syrian autonomy or independence.[12] In November 1916, a Muslim from Jerusalem addressed a large Zionist meeting in Paris. While strongly urging Jews not to associate their ethnicity with political ambitions, he promised a warm welcome for Jews returning to Palestine.[13] Following the Balfour Declaration, French Zionist activity grew dramatically. *L'Univers Israélite*, the organ of traditional French Jewry, both gave voice to the profound ambivalence of native French Jews regarding the prospect of a Jewish state in Palestine, and devoted significant attention to the historic nature of the moment. It painted a picture of positive Jewish-Muslim coexistence in Jerusalem, stated that Muslims' "monotheistic faith makes them true children of Abraham" and underscored the need to respect the Muslim inhabitants and holy sites of Palestine.[14] In January 1918, as one writer gently advocated for a Jewish home in Palestine, in the same breath he praised the sacrifice of Algeria's Muslims in the war effort and alluded to the journal's already stated support for French citizenship for all Algerian Muslim soldiers.[15]

The interwar period saw considerable evolution in the Muslim and Jewish populations of France, with significant political consequences. Shortly after hostilities ended, many North African Muslim soldiers and laborers were "repatriated" by French authorities to their homes on the other side of the Mediterranean. But significant numbers of Algerians in particular, as well as many Moroccans and a small number of Tunisians, returned to France as seasonal laborers. Almost all male, they sent most of their earnings back to their families.[16] By 1937, the peak of Muslim interwar immigration, nearly 140,000 Algerians lived in France, along with about 10,000 Moroccans, and a handful of Tunisians and Middle Eastern Muslims.[17] Meanwhile, approximately 150,000 Jews came to France between the wars, bringing France's total Jewish population by the late 1930s to over 300,000. Seventy-five percent of the newcomers hailed from Eastern Europe. Two thirds of the other immigrants came from the Balkans and the Levant, and one third from either Germany or North Africa.[18]

As Muslims became a permanent presence in the métropole, a few began to affiliate politically, first with the *Parti Communiste Français* (PCF), and then with early North African nationalists. Meanwhile, both the *Alliance Israélite Universelle* (AIU) and the French Consistory, bastions of the prevailing ethos of Franco-Jewish devotion to the Republic and acculturation, became openly hostile to Jewish nationalism. Yet the Eastern European Jewish immigrants challenged such an outlook, taking a more active role in left-wing and Zionist groups than their French-born counterparts. Still, in the early to mid-1920s, growing Zionist-Arab tension in Palestine produced only tiny ripples among Jews and Muslims in France. At a Zionist student association gathering in Paris in April 1925, several Muslim protesters and a Muslim speaker created a disturbance and were removed from the meeting hall.[19] In February 1926, at a well-attended debate in Paris, Muslim and Jewish speakers traded anti-Zionist and anti-Arab barbs, but also remarks about possibilities for peaceful coexistence.[20] Stories in the mainstream Jewish press, though not ignoring frictions, remained hopeful about coexistence in Palestine.[21] France's Muslim press, on the rarer occasions when it commented on Palestine, tended to treat Jewish claims there as illegitimate, at times recalling Britain and France's unfulfilled promises to the Arabs.[22]

The riots of Palestine of August 1929, which resulted in the deaths of 133 Jews and 116 Arabs, and left more than 500 others wounded, marked a turning point in creating wider sympathy among French Jews for Zionism.[23] Yet they had little discernible impact on Jewish-Muslim relations in France. Through press stories, meetings, religious services and fundraising, thousands of French Jews across a wide spectrum absorbed and responded to news of the riots. The Muslim reaction, however, appears to have been rather muted.[24] The notable exception, in terms of both Muslim response and Jewish-Muslim interactions in the wake of the riots, occurred under the aegis of the now firmly anti-Zionist PCF. The PCF treated the riots as the start of an Arab national revolution against the imperialism of Zionism and its British sponsors. In the coming months, the communist press and tracts drew Muslim and Jewish workers to multiple meetings where speakers, in Arabic and Yiddish, expressed anti-imperialist solidarity regarding Palestine.[25]

* * *

Adolf Hitler's assumption of power in Germany in January 1933 set off a series of limited but revealing Jewish-Muslim political interactions in France. The Jewish community responded with a series of efforts on behalf of its coreligionists across the Rhine. In the communal press and associational meetings, French Jews detailed the suffering of German Jewry, denounced the Nazis, called for anti-German boycotts and pled for France to open its doors to German-Jewish refugees.[26] For France's Zionists, finding broader acceptance amidst the growing xenophobia and anti-Semitism of the late 1920s and 1930s, the situation in Germany prompted a flood of activity to bring German Jews to safety in Palestine. In early discussions of Palestine as a haven for German Jews, French Zionists rarely gave the territory's Arab inhabitants more than a passing reference.[27] Such a silence implied that the Jewish needs of the hour took precedence, with little regard for Arab opposition or concerns.

In mid-April, Muslim resistance to such a posture began to emerge. On April 13, 1933, in Paris, Jacir, representing the Arab Executive in Palestine, spoke at a meeting on Jewish immigration to Palestine in the wake of German anti-Semitism.[28] In his opening remarks, after declaring that no Palestinian Arab was anti-Jewish, Jacir exclaimed:

> [T]he doors of Palestine must be opened widely to persecuted Jews from Germany . . . but we warn the Zionists that as long as there will be England between the Jews and us, there will be . . . inevitably, misunderstandings. We will never allow the Zionists, strengthened by the support of [England], to become masters of our land. If on the contrary the Jews wish to come to collaborate with us, we can . . . in this case promise them a sure haven in Palestine.

Later in the meeting, Jacir's rhetorical attempt to separate "Jews" from "Zionists" met with a sharp rebuke from a Zionist leader. He mocked Jacir's speech as "nearly a declaration of love," blamed the Arab Executive for fomenting anti-Jewish attacks in Palestine and declared, "It was our country before you were there and no one, you hear me, will prevent us from returning to it!" In reply, Jacir insisted that the Arab uprisings were not against the Jews but the Zionists, admitting that "when the revolution explodes it is difficult to make distinctions," but concluding, "We went to war on the Allied side in order to liberate ourselves from the yoke of the Turks, not to suffer under another." Another Jewish speaker, recently returned from Palestine, responded that, absent the Arab Executive's provocations, the Arabs "would live fraternally with the Jews."

The attempts of the meeting's Jewish speakers to paper over or delegitimize Arab opposition to Jewish immigration to Palestine continued to link the Zionist cause with the needs of European Jewry. Jacir, meanwhile, sharply distinguished Jews and their humanitarian needs from Zionism as an imperialist enterprise. Each of these attitudes reflected wider contemporary discourses, often strategic, of the international Zionist and Arab nationalist movements. The Muslim newspaper *L'Ikdam* offered its own treatment, more particular to the concerns of France's Muslims, of the implications of

German anti-Semitism for Jewish-Muslim relations in the Mediterranean. In a mid-April article by coeditor Sadek Denden that received accolades from Jewish and Muslim readers, the journal sympathized with Germany's Jews, condemned Nazism, cited Muslim suffering at the hands of fascism and emphasized the cordiality of Jewish-Muslim relations in Algeria. By May, Denden even contended that recent disturbances between Jews and Arabs in Palestine must have been provoked by Christian Arabs, as the attitude shown toward Jews was "one that the Muslim religion condemns."[29]

Yet, in a two-part, follow-up article published in *L'Ikdam* in June and July, which had originally appeared in *Essounna*, a journal of the *Association des Oulemas Musulmans Algériens* (AOMA), the connections drawn between events in Germany and Jewish-Muslim relations in both Algeria and Palestine took a different turn.[30] Here, Sheikh Mohamed Saïd Ezzahiri contrasted centuries of Jewish prosperity in Islamic lands to suffering in Europe at the hands of Christian anti-Semites. He argued that Algeria's Jews had been better off before the arrival of the French. On the subject of Palestine, like Jacir, he sought to separate Jews from Zionists, whom he defined as "a band of social climbers recruited from scum who, with the goal of plunder, wanted to grab the generous Arab land of Palestine." "Many Israélites," he contended, did not support Zionism, instead seeing it "as a comedy or something more ridiculous."

Following Adolf Hitler's rise to power, Jews utilized the threat of fascism and anti-Semitism to underpin the justice of the Zionist enterprise. Certain Muslim responses suggested that antifascism could indeed unify Jews and Muslims against common discrimination. Other Muslim voices, though, strictly separated Jewish suffering from Zionism, linking the latter to imperialism, and therefore, to Muslim suffering. Soon, two events brought fascism and colonialism to the forefront of Jewish-Muslim political interactions in France, setting the stage for greater tension at the next outbreak of violence in Palestine.

* * *

On February 6, 1934, antirepublican riots erupted in Paris, bringing the threat of fascism to the center of French political life and of Jewish-Muslim political relations in France. Six months later, from August 3–6, Jewish-Muslim rioting occurred in Constantine, Algeria, that left twenty-eight Jews and four Muslims dead, with dozens more injured. The riots triggered a sense of crisis regarding Algeria and a new emphasis on ethnic difference in Jewish-Muslim political interactions in France. The event galvanized the *Étoile Nord-Africaine* (ENA), France's nascent Algerian nationalist party, which spent the succeeding weeks swelling its membership and finances through large meetings in which speakers demonized Algerian Jews by tying them to the ENA's chief target: the French colonial project. The French Jewish press repeatedly recounted the riots' horror, highlighting the civilized Frenchness of the Jewish victims in contrast to the savagery of the Muslim attackers.[31] In the years following these touchstone events, France's growing quasi-fascist, anti-Semitic parties heavily recruited Muslims. Simultaneously, leading Jewish and Muslim groups mobilized behind a new antifascist, left-wing bloc, whose platform included democratic reform in Algeria. Headed by the Jewish socialist deputy Léon Blum, this bloc came to power in May 1936 as the Popular Front (PF).

These political circumstances, emblematic of both international developments and their specifically French implications, largely shaped the effect of the Arab Revolt of 1936–1939 upon Jewish-Muslim relations in France. In this regard, a comparison of the impact of the revolt's first and second stages is instructive. The first phase, lasting from April to October 1936, began as a general strike and soon featured urban terrorism and attacks by roving rural bands. These events coincided roughly with the most hopeful period of the PF in France. Soon after the electoral victory of early May, Léon Blum disbanded the anti-Semitic, xenophobic far-Right leagues. The massive strikes of the "June Days" and the subsequent Matignon Accords brought landmark reforms for all French workers such as significant pay increases, the forty-hour work week and paid vacations. Colonial reform in Algeria appeared imminent. Blum lent his name to a proposal (the Blum-Viollette Plan) of citizenship for over 20,000 Algerian Muslims and of other measures for their social and economic advancement.

As events in Palestine unfolded alongside these developments, in the communal press and associational meetings, Jewish depictions of the revolt placed most of the blame on the Arabs. Yet while certain accounts demonized Arabs in general, many others argued that most did not support the revolt and that entente remained possible. These contrasting views often shared a colonialist vocabulary that implicitly linked the current questions in Algeria and Palestine. One May dispatch from *L'Univers Israélite*'s special envoy in Palestine included several accounts of Muslim violence, and concluded with the bold declaration: "Bloodied by the Arabs, Palestine will be rebuilt by the Jews."[32] Two weeks later, buried in a series of reports of Arab attacks on Jews, *L'Univers* included a story about Arabs who had protected Jews. Another report mentioned the Arab mayor of Haifa, "whose sympathies for the Jews are known," but only as one of two targets of recent Arab bomb attacks.[33] Thus even in highlighting instances of amicable relations, the newspaper framed them as exceptions in a sea of indigenous unrest against the civilizing, European Jewish colonial presence.

Diverse voices expressed other, sometimes more clearly French versions of this discourse. In a meeting of Sephardic Jewish leaders in Paris, two Jews of Algerian origin drew upon their connections to the Islamic world. William Oualid argued that Jews of Arab countries could facilitate reconciliation with the Arabs, whom he described as "only cousins for us, brothers, 'since Ishmael was the son of Abraham.'" Yet, seemingly referring to the 1934 Constantine riots, Benjamin Zaoui described the "Muslim character" as strange: "he can be your friend for 60 years, then, all of a sudden, for no reason, he will kill you in cold blood, you and your family."[34] In early July, *L'Univers Israélite* ran an article from a Parisian daily that underscored connections between Algeria and Palestine.[35] Author Pierre Fontaine began by noting, "The grave events in Palestine should not make us forget that France is the second Islamic power of Europe." Focusing on Charles Lévy, an Algerian Jew of Alsatian origin, who worked with Sétif's mayor to build modern housing units for Muslims, Fontaine painted a classically colonialist, if newly hopeful, picture of European benevolence and Muslim backwardness. Portraying Lévy as working to overcome the natural primitivism of Muslims, Fontaine highlighted a grateful Muslim who exclaimed, "This house is thanks to Mr. Charles." Calling Jewish-Muslim conflict elsewhere the work of "professional agitators," the author concluded: "The French example of Sétif shows that an alliance is not impossible." In the political moment, the article carried a powerful subtext: like France's new prime minister, like the Zionist pioneers, here was a European Jew who could help reform and civilize the Muslim world, and therein repair Jewish-Muslim relations.

During the early months of the Arab Revolt, the Muslim nationalists of the ENA, active supporters of the PF, took their own measured stance toward events in Palestine.[36] While certain activists had established contact with advocates for an Arab Palestine, and the ENA occasionally saluted the resistance in Palestine in meetings, the party had hardly made the issue a leading concern.[37] This fact, and the ENA's participation alongside many Jewish leaders and organizations in the battle against fascism and for colonial reform, helps explain why in late April, despite pressure from some members, party leaders postponed the possibility of a meeting regarding events in Palestine, even as they encouraged two Muslim student associations to mobilize around the issue.

On June 19, when the ENA, the communist *Secours Rouge* and the French *Bund*, or Jewish Labor Organization, participated in a meeting that drew a largely Muslim crowd of 500, the evening revealed the moment's both unifying and volatile dimensions. Leaders from the Radical Party and the PCF, two key components of the PF coalition, spoke. The statement adopted at the meeting's conclusion declared solidarity with the Palestinian people, and hatred for fascism, imperialism and anti-Semitism. An ENA speaker expressed sadness at the Arab-Jewish conflict in Palestine, stating, "our duty is to reconcile them by making them understand that they are [both] victims of capitalism and British imperialism." One speaker from the anti-Zionist *Bund* said that Jews were not enemies of Arabs, blaming Zionism and British imperialism for the current situation.[38]

Differences of ethnic or transnational affiliation also, however, resulted in heated debate. Ferdinand Corcos, a Jewish leader of the League of the Rights of Man, while acknowledging that Arabs had rights to citizenship in Palestine, argued that Jews had an unassailable claim to the land. He recounted at length Jews' ancient presence in Palestine, and contended that recent Jewish immigration had only elevated the Arab standard of living. Messali Hadj, the founder and head of the ENA, tempered his often fiery rhetoric, but only to a point. His attacks on previous French governments, and on British imperialism as worse than that of France, implied he had hope for the PF. He called for Jewish-Arab unity. But Hadj also bitterly denounced the words of Corcos, and contended that Britain currently supported the Jewish people, whom he argued would be sacrificed eventually if it did not understand "the sick work of Zionism."

Corcos and Hadj's opposing positions previewed the tenser atmosphere of the Arab Revolt's second stage. Lasting from autumn 1937 through spring 1939, this phase saw a dramatic growth in the number of participants in the rebellion, the introduction of Jewish terrorism against Arabs, markedly increased attacks and casualties and, for a time, an almost total loss of control by the British in large parts of Palestine. Meanwhile, France was far removed from the heady days of summer 1936. The slow pace of colonial reform had opened a rift between the PF and the ENA. As tensions boiled over in January 1937, the Blum government disbanded the ENA.[39] In June 1937, with the PF's momentum stalled, Blum resigned as prime minister. Reflecting the Jewish communists' ongoing anti-Zionism and the PCF's newly anti-immigrant posture, the Jewish PF broke down around the same time.[40]

For many French Jews, increasing anti-Semitism in Germany and Eastern Europe significantly colored reactions to the revolt's second stage. On the one hand, coverage in both the Zionist and traditional Jewish press, while often demonizing the Arab rebels as "terrorists," also acknowledged Arab suffering, criticized the terrorist attacks of Zionist groups and maintained hopes of Jewish-Arab entente.[41] At the same time, at large gatherings and in the press, Zionists and other Jewish activists depicted the attacks on Jews in Palestine as part of a wider crisis of anti-Jewish persecution. Noting the spread of fascism and the need for a refuge for Jews expelled from Germany and Italy, they described work on behalf of the Jewish homeland as more critical than ever.[42] The speaker at a July 1938 *Bund* meeting contended that the Arabs, "supplied by Hitler and Mussolini, have more bombs . . . than the Jews."[43] A September meeting of the Left Poalei Tsiyon featured a report on Jewish antifascist volunteers in Spain, and a documentation of the growing influence of Nazi propaganda among Palestinian Arabs.[44]

Indeed, in place of earlier hopes for colonial reform, fears of fascist influence in the Muslim world now colored Jewish perception of events in Palestine. The Zionist press reported that in Algeria, Muslim-targeted propaganda from the Nazis and the French far Right was increasing Jewish-Muslim friction in the context of the revolt. This issue aroused anxiety for Jews' larger prospects in the Muslim world.[45] Altogether, French Jews framed events in Palestine as part of a wave of anti-Semitism in Europe and the Maghreb.

Likewise, shifts in the wider political landscape significantly affected the reaction of various Muslim political groups to the second stage of the Arab

Revolt. Reconstituted illegally as the *Parti du Peuple Algérien* (PPA), the former ENA's press coverage of Palestine sharpened its tone. In a December 1937 *El Ouma* article, the author spoke of "the Jewish question" to allude to increased anti-Semitism in Europe, but declared that Palestine was not the answer.[46] He argued that the British merely used the Jews as an imperial instrument, and repeatedly referred to the two groups together as the "anglo-zionists." Insisting conflict was neither religious nor racial, he contended that the Arabs in Palestine did not fight the Jews as Jews but merely the British and the Zionists. "From the banks of the Ganges to the coasts of the Atlantic," extolled the author, "no Arab or Muslim can remain indifferent or insensitive to the sacrifices and sufferings of his brothers in Jerusalem or in Jaffa." The framing of the Jews of Palestine as British imperial agents, the venom of the article's denunciations and the language of Islamic solidarity all mirrored the ENA's earlier treatment of Jews in Algeria after the Constantine riots. Together, these elements suggested a new level of interest in the Palestinian question, and relative disinterest in the fate of Europe's Jews.

Over the next several months, *El Ouma* focused much of its verbal fire on its erstwhile partners of the PF, but once more turned attention to Palestine from autumn 1938 through spring 1939.[47] The PPA no longer linked the struggles against anti-Semitism and colonial oppression, treating them now as opposing questions. Articles described the Zionists as invaders set on driving all Arabs from the land. Arabs could not welcome "the invasion of their country by a den of insects ready to devour them."[48] While continuing formally to insist that it fought the Zionists and not the Jews, the PPA blurred the distinction. One *El Ouma* writer declared that "[t]he legendary cowardice and betrayal of the Jews no longer knows any bounds," and another spoke of the imminent "nightmare" of the "Judaization of Palestine."[49] Coverage lionized the Grand Mufti of Jerusalem and the Arab rebels.[50]

Meanwhile, throughout the revolt's second stage, the reform-oriented *Congrès Musulman* (CM), which remained loyal to the PF until its dissolution in 1938, maintained a more measured attitude regarding events in Palestine. *L'Entente Franco-Musulmane*, the organ of one of the driving forces within the CM, Mohammed Salah Bendjelloul's *Fédération des élus musulmans*, a Constantine-based group of Muslim notables, devoted considerable energy both to supporting the Blum-Viollette Plan and to denouncing fascism.[51] The newspaper also backed the demands of Palestinian Arabs. In December 1937, one writer for *L'Entente* argued that France, as a Muslim empire, should intervene in Palestine in defense of the Arabs.[52] In an October 1938 article, Bendjelloul partly blamed the Zionists for the crisis, but attacked the British far more harshly. He cited historical and contemporary fraternal relations between Jews and Muslims as signs that if Britain would simply leave Palestine, Jews and Arabs could coexist peacefully.[53] In July 1938, the International Congress of the World Assembly Against Racism and Anti-Semitism in Paris included a discussion of Palestine among several French

Jewish and Muslim leaders. Zionist Marc Jarblum echoed Muslim delegate M. Chalidi's call for Jewish-Arab reconciliation. The congress issued a plea to end the violence in Palestine and decided to create a commission, with equal Jewish and Arab representation, to investigate the situation.[54]

Yet, autumn 1938 saw the end of the PF, and of any realistic hope for the Blum-Viollette Plan to become law. In an environment of growing disillusionment, certain Muslim activists in France radicalized, and reached out to the Germans in hopes of an alliance of interests and arms, if not ideology.[55] At the same time, more direct Muslim activism on behalf of Palestinian Arabs emerged. In February 1939, a small group of Muslims in Paris founded the *Comité Nord-Africain de solidarité et d'aide aux victimes arabes en Palestine*. The organization soon published declarations in both *El Ouma* and *L'Entente* that reprised many of the themes from the former's contemporary coverage of events in Palestine, and termed Zionism "a kind of Jewish fascism."[56] Such developments signaled the degree to which the impact of Palestine on Jewish-Muslim relations in France, no longer tempered by the shared opportunities of the PF, had now become exacerbated by the political crises and divisions of the late 1930s.

* * *

From 1940 to 1945, the German occupation, France's internal divisions and the Shoah reshaped Jewish-Muslim relations in France. The anti-Jewish measures of the Vichy regime shattered the egalitarian ideals of the French Revolution long cherished by native French Jewry. They also necessitated greater self-reliance on the part of the French Jewish community. In these circumstances, French Zionism achieved the organizational unity that had long eluded it, and partnered with communal organizations to meet French Jews' basic needs. Many Zionists also took a leading role in the Jewish resistance, and helped to found the *Conseil Représentatif des Israélites de France* (CRIF) in 1944. Created to serve as the representative political body of all French Jewish organizations, in its opening charter, CRIF included all major Zionist demands regarding Palestine.[57]

While the Zionists became more integrated into France's Jewish institutional life and gained vital credibility, France's Muslims faced new political choices. Particularly during the first two years after the fall of France, many Muslims opted to support Vichy and/or the Germans. Just as the occupation made the questions of fascism and anti-Semitism inescapable, everyday realities, it also offered new prospects for the future of France's colonial empire. Both the occupiers and various collaborationist political parties heavily courted Muslim support, creating special Muslim sections. They often promised equal rights, religious autonomy, increased social benefits and generous salaries for the most active collaborators. While the perceived opportunity to improve their political, cultural or economic status acted as the primary motivation for many Muslim collaborators, the anti-Semitism of the collaborationists played an important role. From March 1941 to December 1942, the Service of Algerian Affairs of Marseille produced at least forty separate reports that discussed explicit Muslim expressions of anti-Semitism. Attempts by North African nationalist and far-Right parties in the 1930s to link Jews to French and British imperialism, widely accepted wartime anti-Jewish attitudes among the general French population and longtime Nazi propaganda in North Africa all seemed to converge in much of the Muslim popular imagination.[58]

Following the Anglo-American landing in North Africa in November 1942, the tide of Muslim opinion did begin to turn. Muslims joined the Resistance in growing numbers, and many eventually served in the Liberation armies. With the Allies framing the war as a struggle for freedom from tyranny, and the North African front assuming central importance, certain Muslim resisters hoped their participation would further their own battle for equality. Some Muslims, drawn by a sense of shared suffering, moral imperative or common hatred of the fascist enemy, defended or helped to save Jews.[59]

The forces of collaboration, however, saw to it that more oppositional terms of Jewish-Muslim interaction remained widespread. For many Muslims, distinctions between Zionists and Jews, increasingly tenuous on the war's eve, became nonexistent. Beginning in January 1943, the most successful Muslim collaborationist group, the *Comité musulman de l'Afrique du Nord*, filled the pages of its widely disseminated newspaper, *Er Rachid*, with virulently anti-Jewish screeds. The newspaper treated the war in large part as a struggle between monstrous Jewish masters, controlling the Allied forces, and proud Muslims, defended by the valiant Germans, fighting for freedom.[60] *Er Rachid* attacked the "Jewish invasion of Palestine" and ridiculed the very idea of a Jewish nation.[61] In April 1944, several collaborationist North African nationalists held a meeting in Paris to oppose Jewish immigration to Palestine. Speakers denounced the Jews as the source of repressive measures taken previously against the ENA/PPA, and called for unity against "Jewish powers." In February 1945, these Muslim leaders coordinated with the recently formed *Association des Amis de la Palestine Arabe* to organize a gathering in Paris, where audience members repeatedly chanted "Down with the Jews!" and "Death to the Jews!"[62]

* * *

The history traced here enables us to return to the incidents of October 29, 1944, with greater clarity. The Jewish role in and subsequent interpretation of this event reflected growing support for French Zionism, and a link in the minds of certain French Jews between Nazism and Muslim anti-Semitism. Muslim behavior articulated widely disseminated, enduring discursive connections between the prospect of fascist rule and Muslim liberation, and between alleged Jewish power and Muslim colonial suffering, along with growing solidarity with Palestinian Arabs. This chapter has sought to demonstrate that these conditions and cultural understandings emerged in the years before the war. At the same time, we can see how the events of World War II heightened the connection for many Jews and Muslims between the questions of fascism and/or colonialism, on the one hand, and the future of Palestine on the other.

More than sixty years later, many analysts tend to draw a direct causal link between the Israeli-Palestinian conflict and current Jewish-Muslim tensions in France. In fact, however, the haunting specters of Nazi and Vichy anti-Semitism, and of colonialism in North Africa, remain at the heart of these tensions, and of the way that the Middle East conflict is read onto them. For French Jews who vigorously condemn certain Muslims' rhetorical attacks on Israel or physical attacks on Jews or Jewish property, the memory of the Shoah understandably informs their fears. Those French Muslims who express solidarity with their Palestinian coreligionists as part of a larger attack on Jews, the West or both commonly articulate their attitudes as a continuation of the anticolonial struggle of their parents' generation. This chapter helps us to appreciate how like these memories, for Jews and Muslims in France, the events at their origins became grafted onto the Zionist-Arab conflict far earlier than current scholars (or practitioners) have dared to imagine.

ACKNOWLEDGMENTS

Many thanks to Laird Boswell, Nathalie Debrauwere-Miller, Jonathan Gribetz, Maud Mandel and Arieh Saposnik for their extremely valuable suggestions on earlier drafts of this chapter.

NOTES

1. *Archives de la Préfecture de Police* (APP) (Paris), BA 1811, report of October 29, 1944; Central Zionist Archives (CZA) (Jerusalem) S25/1985, letter to Central Office of Karen Kayemet L'Yisrael (KKL), November 11, 1944 [Hebrew]. Figures and accounts of the meeting come from these sources, CZA KKL 5/13146, letter from Fisher to Central Office of KKL, October 30, 1944; Rachel, "Le Meeting du 29 octobre à la Mutualité," *La Terre Retrouvée* (*TR*), 1 December 1944. All translations from French and Hebrew are my own. In discussing this and other meetings, when I have only referred to an individual by his first name, this is because it is the only name provided in the sources.
2. The newspaper mistakenly referred to the group as the *Comité Musulman Africain*.
3. Rachel; T.G., "Toujours la même main,"*TR*, 1 December 1944. All quotations above from Rachel.
4. CZA S25/1985, letter to Central Office of KKL.
5. See André N. Chouraqui, *Histoire des Juifs en Afrique du Nord* (Poitiers, 1985); Michael Laskier, *North African Jewry in the Twentieth Century: The Jews of Morocco, Tunisia, and Algeria* (New York: New York University Press, 1994).

6. Michel Abitbol, *Les Deux Terres Promises: Les Juifs de France et le sionisme* (Paris: Olivier Orban, 1989); Catherine Nicault, *La France et le sionisme, 1897–1948: Une rencontre manquée?* (Paris: Calman-Lévy, 1992).
7. See Benjamin Stora, *Ils Venaient d'Algérie: L'immigration algérienne en France (1912–1992)* (Paris: Fayard, 1992); Neil MacMasters, *Colonial Migrants and Racism: Algerians in France, 1900–1962* (New York: St. Martin's Press, 1997).
8. Paula Hyman, *From Dreyfus to Vichy: The Remaking of French Jewry, 1906–1939* (New York: Columbia University Press, 1979), 172 places the peak number of Zionists in the interwar years at 10,135. The lack of organized Arab nationalist groups in France during this period suggests a smaller number of Muslims.
9. Due to contemporary terminologies and demographics, I use "Arab" generally to refer to events in Palestine or accounts thereof, and "Muslim" for Muslims in France.
10. This number comprises 260,000 soldiers and 132,000 laborers. The majority of both were Algerians. For a more precise breakdown of soldiers, see Pascal le Pautremat, *La politique musulmane de la France au XXe siècle: De l'Hexagone aux terres d'Islam. Espoirs, réussites, échecs* (Paris: Maisonneuve et Larose, 2003), 146, 173. For laborers, see Stora, 14. When referring to Muslims in France, I mean those of North African descent.
11. For more precise figures on Jewish soldiers and civilians, Philippe E. Landau, *Les Juifs de France et la Grande Guerre: Un patriotisme républicain, 1914–1941* (Paris: CNRS Editions, 2000), 26, 33; Esther Benbassa, *The Jews of France: A History from Antiquity to the Present*, trans. M.B. DeBevoise (Princeton: Princeton University Press, 1999), 137.
12. APP, BA 1811, service des Renseignements Généraux (R-G), "Au sujet de sous-lieutenant Husson, du docteur Zalta, et du mouvement qu'ils ont provoqué dans les milieux Syriens, Libanais et Sionistes, July 30, 1915."
13. APP, BA 1811, report of November 27, 1916.
14. See A.P., "La route de Jerusalem," November 30, 1917; A.P., "Les Réunions du dimanche 23: Conférence Victor Bérard," *UI*, January 4, 1918; A.P., "Le Temple et la Mosqueé," *UI*, February 15, 1918 (quotation in text taken from here); Charles Wagner, "Jérusalem: centre de ralliement religieux du monde," speech reprinted in *UI*, May 3, 1918.
15. A.P., "Les Réunions," *UI*. For the first statement, P.R., "Un acte de justice," *UI*, December 14, 1917.
16. Le Pautremat, *Politique*, 291, 307.
17. Numbers of Algerians from McMasters, 223; Moroccans from APP, BA 2171, minutes of meeting of *Haut Comité Méditerrenéen*, October 28, 1937.
18. For the first figure and the percentages, Hyman, 68; for the second figure, Michel Roblin, *Les Juifs de Paris: Démographie—Économie—Culture* (Paris: Picard, 1952), 79.
19. APP, BA 2273, report on meeting of April 1, 1925; "Nouvelles Diverses," *Archives Israélites (AI)*, April 2, 1925.
20. APP, BA 1811, report of February 21, 1926.
21. See, e.g., J. Bielinky, "Le Problème sioniste," *UI*, June 19, 1925; "Discours de Lord Balfour," *AI*, April 23, 1925.
22. See, e.g., "Autour du Sionisme," *EA*, March 24, 1922; Gabriel Milliex, "Les Arabes et la Paix," *L'Ikdam*; January 26, 1923.
23. See Abitbol, chapter III. Arabs attacked Jews throughout the riots; most Arab casualties came at the hands of the British. Benny Morris, *Righteous Victims: A History of the Arab-Zionist Conflict, 1881–1999* (New York: Vintage Books, 2001), 113–116.

24. APP, BA 1811, report of August 29, 1929. It seems that no French Muslim press of the period survives.
25. Reports in APP, BA 1811; 1815, and in *UI*, *TR*, and *L'Humanité*.
26. See, e.g., H. Prague, "Hitler Chancelier!!!" *AI*, February 2, 1933; "Dernière Heure," *AI*, April 6, 1933; APP, BA 1815, reports of April 14, 15, 21, and May 16 and 17, on various meetings.
27. See e.g., "Ce qui se passe chez nous," *TR*, February 25, 1933; Joseph Fisher, "Une seule certitude: le Sionisme," *TR*, March 25, 1933; APP, BA 1815, reports of April 14 and 21, and May 17 and 30.
28. APP, BA 1815, "Meeting organisé par le 'Club du Faubourg,'" April 14, 1933. All quotations from this meeting come from this document. The vast majority of the Arab Executive's members were Muslim, though there is no indication if Jacir himself was Muslim or Christian.
29. Sadek Denden, "L'Antisémitisme hitlérien," *L'Ikdam*, April 15, 1933; idem, "L'Antisémitisme Hitlérien et L'Islam," *L'Ikdam*, May 15, 1933.
30. Mohamed Saïd Ezzahiri, "A propos de l'antisémitisme Hitlérien: Entre les Arabes et les Juifs," *L'Ikdam*, June 10, 1933; idem, "Entre les Arabes et les Juifs," trans. M. Lamoudi, *L'Ikdam*, July 1, 1933. Quotations come from the second article. The AOMA, founded in 1931, advocated Islamic reformism in Algeria.
31. For the response to the Constantine riots, I have drawn on the Jewish and Muslim press, and accounts in APP, BA 2170–2172.
32. J.M., "Les événements de Palestine: Après les émeutes à Jaffa," *UI*, May 8, 1936.
33. J.M., "Lettre de Palestine," *UI* May 22, 1936; "Les événements de Palestine," *UI*, May 1, 1936.
34. "Union Sépharadite d'Action Palestinienne," *UI*, May 22, 1936.
35. Pierre Fontaine, "Israélites et Musulmans à Sétif," *UI*, July 3, 1936. Reprinted from *Le Petit Parisien*.
36. The ENA's organ, *El Ouma*, does not survive from this period, admittedly limiting our perspective.
37. APP, BA 2170, reports of February 12, and May 2, 1936; BA 2171, reports of March 4, 1935 and April 30, 1936.
38. APP, BA 2171, reports of June 18 and 23, 1936; HA 26, "Meeting organisé par la 'Ligue Anti-Impérialiste,'" June 20, 1936; R.D., "Un meeting antisioniste à Paris," *UI*, June 26, 1936. Quotations from HA 26.
39. Stora, *Ils Venaient*, 44–45.
40. See Hyman, *Dreyfus*, 107, 213–216.
41. See, e.g., "Une nouvelle vague de terreur a déferlé sur la Palestine," *UI*, June 24, 1938; J. Ben Gad, "9 Ab 5698," *UI*, August 5, 1938; Joseph Fisher, "La Riposte à la terreur," *TR*, December 1, 1937; idem, "Pour nous entendre avec les arabes," *TR*, January 1, 1939.
42. J.B., "Pour la Palestine Juive," *UI*, September 23, 1938; APP, BA 1811, "Meeting palestinien organisée par les sionistes de droit," September 14, 1938; "Tous dans la bataille pour la Palestine, tous pour la Palestine, seule terre de salut!" *TR*, September 1, 1938.
43. APP, BA 1812, "Réunion organisée par le 'Medem Fairbond,'" July 29, 1938.
44. APP, BA 1811, "Meeting organisée par le 'Poalei Zion,'" September 10, 1938.
45. Elie Gozlan, "Lettre d'Alger," *TR*, October 15, 1938; El Habib, "Les relations judéo-musulmanes en Algérie,"; Jacques Bielinky, "Pour la sauvegarde de l'empire français," both in *TR*, November 1, 1938.
46. A. Yahiaoui, "La Palestine martyre," *El Ouma (EO)*, December 1937.
47. See, for example, Ibonn-Jala, "Ce que fut pour nous l'expérience du Front Populaire," *EO*, July 24, 1938.

48. Abdel-Moumen, "En Palestine: Les méfaits du sionisme," *EO*, August 27, 1938.
49. First quotations from Abdel-Moumen, "En Palestine," 27; the second from "L'acharnement des juifs contre le Grand Mufti de Jerusalem," two parts in *EO* of March and April, 1939. Reprinted from *Nation Arabe*.
50. "Une bataille aux environs de Nablouse en Palestine," *EO*, January–February 1939; "L'acharnement."
51. See repeated notices, "Autour du Projet Blum-Viollette"; and, e.g., Saint-Just, "L'action coujuguée Italo-Allemande Dans le Monde Musulman," *L'Entente Franco-Musulmane (EFM)*, August 25, 1938.
52. "La politique musulmane de la France et la Palestine," *EFM*, December 9, 1937.
53. Bendjelloul, "La question de la Palestine: Les musulmans et les juifs dans le monde," *EFM*, October 13, 1938.
54. J.B., "Le 2e Congrès International du Rassemblement Mondial contre le racisme et l'antisémitisme," *UI*, July 29, 1938; M. El Azziz Kessous, "Lettre de Paris," *EFM*, July 28, 1938.
55. Stora, *Ils Venaient*, 84–85.
56. "Protestations envoyées aux membres du Gouvernement anglais," *EO*, March 1939; "Comité de solidarité et d'aide aux victimes arabes en Palestine," *EFM*, February 23, 1939.
57. CZA/KKL5/13146, letter to Central Zionist Office, October 19, 1944; Abitbol, "Conclusion."
58. My accounts of Muslim choices reflect extensive research in APP, BA 1945–1950; 1954–1955; and *Archives Départementales des Bouches-du-Rhône* (ADBdR) (Marseille), 76 W 206–209; *Centre des archives d'outre-mer* (Aix-en-Provence), 5 I 87. Figures compiled from the latter two sources.
59. Scattered examples found in ADBdR, 76 W 206–209.
60. See, e.g., Aït Atmann, "Au delà de la voûte," *Er Rachid (ER)*, June 14, 1944.
61. "L'invasion juive en Palestine," *ER*, November 5, 1943; Aït Atmann, "Le juif errant veut arriver," *ER*, April 26, 1944.
62. APP, HA 29, lengthy report, "Activité du Parti du Peuple Algérien," undated, pp. 82–84; 98–100; 103.

2 The Paradoxes of Zionism in the Work of Albert Cohen

Philippe Zard
(Translated by Robert Watson)

Today the facts of Albert Cohen's Zionist engagement are established, even if their meaning continues to be a matter for discussion. The origin as well as the chronology of Cohen's engagement are known, in particular the determining role of two encounters: the first with André Spire, who became his literary and political mentor, and the second with Chaim Weizmann, whom Cohen entered into contact with in 1921 to propose his services. Weizmann brought the ephemeral *Revue juive* his intellectual support, his moral and political backing and sizeable financial contributions. From then on, Cohen's engagement on behalf of Zionism was never ceasing. While continuing to pursue his literary career, Cohen put to good use his relationship with the International Labor Organization (ILO) to, as much as he could, advance the Zionist cause. From 1939, first in Paris and then in London, Cohen's activities were concentrated on three fronts: the creation of a Jewish army to fight the Axis forces (which was aborted), a project to aide the refugees escaping to Palestine (which was largely crowned a success) and finally, the creation of a Committee of Intellectuals in Favor of the Zionist Cause ("Pro Causa Judaïca") between 1939 and 1940. While in England from 1940 to 1944, Cohen never lost sight of his combat in favor of a Jewish state.

Nevertheless, in the postwar period, Cohen's Zionist militancy seems to break off. The writer ended his activities under the auspices of the Jewish Agency. His last great political project was the creation of an "international passport" for the thousands of stateless refugees created by the war—a passport that he liked to say was his "most beautiful book."

To explain this abrupt disengagement, political factors have been invoked (the Franco-Zionist partnership undertaken by de Gaulle had foundered) as well as factors that are more strictly biographical (Cohen was retiring from the public arena to consecrate himself to literary creation). One can add this simple fact: if Cohen's struggle came to an end, it is because he had triumphed. For Cohen, the birth of Israel in 1948 was the culmination of a project that he had totally dedicated himself to. His repeated and enthusiastic public displays of solidarity with the state of Israel suffice to show that Cohen's distance from his earlier militancy should not be interpreted as an expression of disagreement or political disillusionment. To imagine a perfect continuity between the militant Cohen of the prewar period and the retiring Cohen of the postwar period, there is only one step that we will nevertheless refrain from taking. Because, whatever we concede to historical and personal contingencies, to analyze the relations between Cohen and Zionism is to be confronted with a series of paradoxes. The paradox of someone who was a militant Zionist "from the beginning," and yet never set foot in Israel; the paradox of someone who, in his literary work, points out a problematic fate in store for the Zionist adventure, as if it would never find its place.

THE 1920S: THE IDEOLOGICAL MOMENT

Paroles juives was Cohen's veritable entry into a literary career. In this work, Zionism is not evoked as such, but the last word of the collection ostensibly affirms a position of extraterritoriality: for not having returned to Zion, the poet writes his collection "in a foreign land, June–August 1920." *Paroles juives* presents itself to the reader as a book written in exile. Of course, nothing in *Paroles juives* is explicitly linked to Zionism. Nonetheless, Cohen's poetry works profoundly to prepare the conditions for a national movement. The national imperative necessitates a break with the Christian vision of the world in general and of the Jews in particular, to banish the teaching of contempt and to work toward a spiritual and political rearmament, even though centuries of Diaspora are held responsible of having alienated the Hebrew spirit. The articles of the *Revue juive*, and in particular the inaugural "Declaration,"[1] would add to this theme of Jewish revival—which affected a portion of the Jewish intelligentsia during the interwar period[2]—the concrete prospect of a return to Zion.

The "Declaration" presents itself as an uninhibited affirmation of Jewish national identity:

> The *Revue juive* is founded by men who know themselves to belong to a living race whose spiritual work has not yet been achieved, who has a mission to fulfill and must work to recognize it.

The recurrence of allusions to "race" in the Declaration can admittedly surprise the modern reader. Without doubt, from the end of the nineteenth century onward, the word "race" had already taken on a sinister tone (it was used by Jules Soury, Edouard Drumont, and Maurice Barrès to justify antisemitism). It remains the case that neither the word nor the concept of "race" had been definitively discredited and it was still widely used. The word was still imbued with its classical meaning; it continued to define a lineage, a "group of people who share common characteristics tied to a history, a community, present or past, a language, a civilization without any necessary biological reference" (*Thesaurus of the French Language*). Thus, the word has not always been used in the strictly biological sense given to it by the partisans of "racialism" and "racism." In its indeterminacy, it served to identify what exceeded the all too political categories of "nation," "people" or "society." The word "race" falls within the province of the infrapolitical or the metapolitical and refers to that which, before any political or social contract, "makes community." In 1925, Cohen's Zionism situates itself between a postromantic and post-Barresien imaginary of national energy and the Peguyiste model of the national mystique. The phrase and the idea of "human races" had not yet acquired the murderous connotation that fascism and Nazism would imbue. Even the appeal to heredity and the "infallible laws of blood" are not enough to establish a clear line of demarcation between humanist thought and reactionary thought. If Cohen's political concepts can seem to be antimodern, the values that he fights for are humanistic. Israel must find its place among the democratic nations. Moreover, Cohen committed himself to a project of internal cultural reform in the Jewish world. A statement such as this—"The Jewish world is simultaneously in a state of decline and resurrection. We must discern what is fit to survive and what we must, with gentleness, encourage to pass away"—cannot be understood independently of the debates that were taking place throughout the Zionist intelligentsia over the necessity to break with a tradition judged to be "fossilized" (the Jewish ghetto) in order to bring about a truly national modernity.

The discourse of the "Declaration" attempts to distance itself from any anti-European resentment and from any reactionary temptation. On the contrary, Cohen's text is recognition of debt to "the admirable West," to "Europe, the intelligent countenance of the world," to the adopted countries of the Diaspora "that we have great reason to love." Cohen's Zionism, far from setting itself against Europe, proposes to be its messenger, faithful to what has historically been the cosmopolitan and universal vocation of the Jewish people. The necessary transplanting "in the burning land where Israel's political poets dreamed of saving mankind" does not erase the foundational experience of wandering and Diaspora: "The great Dispersed one [Israel] must bring together the regions where its members have lived in faithfulness, and not without sufferings. Israel is one of Europe's most reliable members [. . .] The Revue juive will take on the difficult and useful role of a foreign journal [. . .] Through its work the Diaspora will seem nearer."

Finally, Cohen refuses to fall into the totalitarian trap where the theme of national genius risked leading him: this "Israel [who] returns to Israel" is not obsessed with its unity. The very experience of Diaspora unmade the ancient unity of the Hebrews; the intellectual work incumbent upon the "missionaries" of the *Revue juive* is "to discover, not the Jewish spirit, but the many great Jewish spirits, the remains left by the sages in a wandering Israel's heart and thought." We know that this hypothesis had already been the orientation for Cohen's article "Le Juif et les romanciers français"

[French Novelists and the Jew], which appeared in the *Revue de Genève* in March of 1923. The goal is to preserve, at the time of the assembly of the exiled, the precious plurality of the Jewish soul.

It would surely be fruitless to look for an absolute ideological coherence in this program. Albert Cohen's position is not so much that of a philosopher as an engaged writer, who works on two projects: to cause Europe to recognize the vocation of Israel, and to contribute to the realization within the Jewish world of the necessity of radical reform. To tell of and bring about this renewal, Cohen finds only the words, the ideas, the images and the myths that correspond the best to his poetic temperament: those associated with a humanist hope—in which European Judaism naturally fits—and a romantic imaginary of national rebirth, which Judaism needs in order to regain a sense of its own grandeur. The first imperative inscribes Zionism in an ideal of political normalization; the second is still full of messianic resonances.

This Zionism, still speculative, will successively find two properly literary expressions: the first in a poem contemporary to the "Declaration"; the second in an episode in Cohen's first novel, *Solal*, published in 1930.

Published on March 15, 1925, in the third issue of the *Revue juive*, the "Song of Zion"[3] celebrates "these brothers who are more courageous than us": "Ils construisent les grandes routes de Djeddah / D'Afuleh à Nazareth / Ils défrichent à Kalendia / Ils plantent sur le Carmel / Ils amènent l'eau à Gan Samuel [. . .] / Sous leurs mains qui ne font pas le mal / Les marais disparaissent à Merhavia / Des habitations s'élèvent à Talpioth / Et des usines à Tibériade / Usines laides pauvres petites vous élargissez mon cœur / Plus imposantes à mes yeux que leurs temples / Plus délicieuses que leurs palais" [They build the great roads of Djeddah / From Afuleh to Nazareth / They clear the way to Kalendia / They sow on Mount Carmel / They bring water to Gan Samuel [. . .] / Under their hands which do no evil / The marshes disappear in Merhavia / Houses are built in Talpioth / And factories in Tiberias / Poor ugly small factories you make my heart grow / More magnificent in my eyes than their temples / More delightful than their palaces].[4] But literary creation, when it has to submit to collective needs, quickly runs up against the limits of all militant poetry: Cohen does not become Tchernikovksy. "Venez avec moi sur le mont / Avec la palme faisons le salut / Aux fiancés de notre terre / Et disons-leur ces mots / Force et bonté / Force et bonté" [Come to the mountain with me / With a palm branch let us salute / The bridegrooms of our land / And let us say these words to them / Strength and goodness / Strength and goodness] (Cohen 1925: 345). Moreover, Cohen admits, in the heart of his work, the renunciation on which his poetry is founded, subordinated to the prosaic injunctions of reality and political communication: "Je dis paroles nues que tous entendent / J'accepte la tâche triste / Je dis les noms / Je dis les chefs / Je dis les villes" [I speak naked words that everyone understands / I accept the sad task / I say the names / I name the leaders / I name the cities]

(Cohen 1925: 343). The poet's abnegation, his poetic abdication: if he is to be a spokesman, his words must be transparent. This is the "sad task" of a minor poet who effaces himself before the order that he celebrates, crushed by the seriousness of a collective mission where humor, fantasy and contradiction must be left aside. The "Song of Zion" suffers from, at the same time, the anachronistic excess of its prophetic ethos ("Because my word is truth") and the work of self-renunciation ("And my mouth is without pride") that the militant poet forces himself to undertake (Cohen 1925: 346).

SOLAL: THE FICTIONAL MOMENT

> "Hier encore sans patrie
> Bientôt je poserai un pied calme sur les mottes
> Et cette herbe bleue la nuit [. . .]"
> [Even yesterday without a country
> Soon I will set my calm feet on the mounds of earth
> And this blue grass the night . . .]
>
> (Cohen 1925: 344)

Despite what he wrote in this excerpt from "Song of Zion," Cohen would never set foot on the land. He entrusts this journey, some years later, to fictional characters that could not be further from the utopian imagery that had nourished his poetry. What becomes of Zionism when Cohen moves from his poetic and political celebration to the realm of fiction? No more songs here: the novel breaks the spell, *the novel disenchants*.

Nothing naturally constrained the author to include the Zionist question in the tale of *Solal*. But in a work haunted by the permanence of anti-Semitism and by the ordeals of exile, it is not surprising that the cantor of a return to Zion, having now become a novelist, would make a place for this hope.

Solal's Zionist episode inserts itself in a singular way in the story, on which it seems to be arbitrarily grafted at first glance. The episode interrupts the story of Solal at the very moment when Aude, overcome by the material poverty and moral decay of their relationship, has just left him. The Zionist tribulations of Saltiel and the Valeureux unexpectedly intervene and introduce a brusque change of register.

It is however easy to discover the "secret chain" that links the two episodes. Solal, in his shabby room on the rue de Carouge, is at the absolute low of his depression and, for a moment, considers committing suicide. The protagonist seems to have arrived at the end of his Western experience. Conversely, the Valeureux happily begin an entirely new life in Palestine, which might seem like a response to the hero's despair. Chapter 31 is marked by a series of humiliating displacements and expulsions suffered by Solal and his wife. In contrast, Chapter 32 presents itself as a reappropriation of space and land, and offers a possible end to exile. Saltiel "had discovered that he had a country."[5] The "remains of Europe" (the Chateau de Saint-Germain where Solal tried to reconcile the irreconcilable: his Western life and his Jewish roots) are clearly positioned as the antithesis of Palestine, the rediscovered homeland. "'In brief, my friend,' he said to himself, 'we're much better in the land of Israel than in that town of Saint-Germanique, or whatever it's called, I've forgotten.'"[6] It would be difficult to better express the tragic precariousness of Jewish life in the 1930s (particularly in "Germanic" territory).

And yet, something takes place in this fiction that puts the Zionist venture in a disconcerting light. First example: the Zionist project is written about in a way that equates it with *farce*. The uncle Saltiel discovers his new homeland after a case of mistaken identity: "he had been taken [. . .] for an important Zionist leader who was to receive a private audience from the Pope" (Cohen 1930: 287). The topic of Zionism reappears in *Mangeclous* through another hoax, Mangeclous having sent Saltiel a fake telegram, supposedly from Chaim Weizmann, which announces the appointment of his little uncle to the post of prime minister in an imaginary Jewish Republic (Chapter 26). What Cohen the poet had celebrated as a struggle, Cohen the novelist presents as a farce.

The Valeureux's adventure begins with a misunderstanding and finishes with drama: the death (purported, it is true) of Saltiel and Salomon, which precipitates the departure of the survivors. Even though it means taking cues from the Gospel, the chapter's last pages are a veritable profession of Mangeclous' diasporic faith, seconded by Maïmon:

—Am I a population that I should stay in this Palestine? The salt should be scattered, not heaped up in one place.
—I think the old man speaks truth, said Mangeclous. We are the salt, as I said. I am in a hurry to go and salt other countries (Cohen 1930: 300).

In light of this passage, Cohen's distance from his earlier advocacy of Zionism is unquestionable. Is this distancing political in origin? Was Cohen suddenly overtaken by skepticism toward the Zionist ideal that had for ten years inspired his combat? This conclusion would be hasty, inasmuch as the narrator intervenes directly in the chapter to praise the pioneers' work in terms similar to those of the "Song of Zion":

All these old wanderers knew they were clumsy. Did that matter? They were working in the heat of the sun, and their children would find fat meadows. Perspiring and at peace, they went on with their work. All honour to the new sons of Zion! (Cohen 1930: 290)

Enthusiasm and hope are certainly there, as well as in parenthetical remarks where the author engages himself, beyond fiction, to reassert the reality of an experience that the novelist's fantasy risked reducing to a game of pure imagination:

> The light awakened the lilies of the field. On the shores of the sea, momentarily amaranthine, palm trees stretched out their fingers. (One day perhaps you will see the country Myriam, my daughter and my love.) (Cohen 1930: 289)

The Cohen who wrote *Solal* is the same, politically, as the one who wrote the Song of Zion: it is the writer who has changed and in this case the novelistic genre that imposes its laws on his politics. Cohen's works highlights contradictions in his *poetic* treatment of the *incarnation* of the Zionist ideals.

The first point to be made: the Zionist utopia does not seem to be compatible with Cohen's novelistic imaginary. Palestine's sedentary character runs the risk of killing the novelist's fantastic characters, who, upon their arrival, are transformed into "Unskilled Labourers,'—the Gallants' new name" (Cohen 1930: 289). Saltiel and Solomon are only resuscitated in the following novel, when establishing themselves in the Promised Land is no longer a possibility. As for Solal, he will never set foot in the land of his ancestors. The Valeureux's aborted settlement in Palestine seems to symbolize the exclusion of the Zionist utopia from the process of literary creation.

What is the explanation for this? With *Solal* and his project *Geste des Juifs*, Cohen is in the process of inventing a novelistic universe that is beginning to perceptibly distance itself from the epic/theological model of *Paroles juives*. The five members of the Valeureux family are quintessential Diaspora Jews, capricious and inoffensive, who have nothing to do with the "new man" that Zionist project calls for. In *Solal*, "Pollakstine" is a land of Eastern European Jews from "lands of mist" (Cohen 1930: 291), far from the maternal warmth of Salonican ghettoes and Mediterranean shores. Should one be surprised at the results of the adventure? Who dies in Palestine? Saltiel, the maternal uncle, and Solomon, the man-child. The return to Zion means the death of both the maternal and childlike elements of Judaism. Who survives? Mattathias, Mangeclous, Michael, Maimon (the one hundred-year-old Kabbalist). That is: the businessman, the cunning one, the half-pagan and the incarnation of Judaism's mystical and timeless essence. All of them too undisciplined, too estranged from the logic of history, to share the fate of Russian and Polish Jews. To take on the Palestinian adventure also means breaking with, if not the values, then at least the affects, schemas and images left by the mother. When in *The Valeureux* Cohen opposed the "Israeli Israel" with his valorous fantasies, his pathetic ghetto dwellers, he linked these creatures to their origin: "j'écrirai donc encore sur eux, et ce livre sera mon adieu à une espèce qui s'éteint [. . .] mon adieu au ghetto où je suis né, ghetto charmant de ma mère, *hommage à ma mère morte*" [I will write about them again, and this book will be my farewell to a dying breed, my farewell to the ghetto where I was born, my mother's charming ghetto, *a tribute to my departed mother*].[7] From the 1930s, Cohen's Zionism is condemned to remain a *cosa mentale*: an essential and nourishing idea, an inspiring one, but one that must stay at a healthy imaginary distance. Good, certainly, but for other Jews. This is the first identifiable tension: between political will (which is stated in the Zionist diction) and the imagination's reticence (expressed in Zionist fiction), the gap between thought and the imaginary, between politics and their effects.

The Palestinian episode is devoted in large part to the story of the attacks made by the Arabs against the small colony of "Kfar-Saltiel." It is necessary to guard oneself against a naïve reading, overestimating the meaning of an adventure written in a mode that is less epic than it is burlesque. One finds nevertheless:

(a) An overall Manichaeism in the story, conforming to the literary code adopted by Cohen and to the Zionist "meta-narrative" of the interwar period, in which the brave and clumsy pioneers confront faceless enemies. As one could expect, none of the Arabs are individualized. In conformity with Orientalist imagery, the Arab is both the "ass-driver" who in passing shouts "a love call to a Bedouin girl, who fled burying a laugh of confusion into a watermelon," and the man who "drew near the Jews and cried that tomorrow their heads would be hanging on the trees [. . .]" (Cohen 1930: 292). The Arabs are a deaf and invisible threat, transmitted by "disturbing rumours" (Cohen 1930: 292). And if the narrator seems to make fun of Salomon's childish terror, it is also to underline that his fears are not pure chimeras:

> He then saw that the meadow was deserted. The little man, prey to violent panic, took to his heels with all the strength of his simple, cowardly heart, imagining Bedouins behind him thirsting for his blood.
>
> And, hidden in the eucalyptus wood, Arab spies were watching the colony's movements (Cohen 1930: 292).

Conversely, the image of the Jew is invariably incarnated (all the Jewish characters have a name and distinct personalities) and positive. *But this image is only positive because it does not fit within the strict rules of the warrior epic.*

(b) A problematic representation of the Jewish combatant. One constant in the novel is that the Jews exhibit a reluctant heroism, fighting in spite of themselves. "The last religious festival seemed to have intoxicated the Arab peasants" (Cohen 1930: 292), and they attack the colony at the moment when the Jews are singing and dancing (Cohen 1930: 294). Forced to fight, "three students of philosophy, five doctors and two fair anti-militarists sallied from the camp in pursuit of the vitriolated foe" (Cohen 1930: 295). When these pacifist intellectuals—destined to become the new Israeli nation—are forced to fight, they are infinitely more effective than the Valeureux. In turn, Solomon and Saltiel become heroes despite themselves. Solomon having, almost by chance, hit an Arab horseman and mounts on his horse, "with a cry of triumph and mortal terror in his heart," and puts his enemies to flight "hardly knowing what he was doing" (Cohen 1930: 295). "Laughter broke out in the camp and the little gallant was cheered" (Cohen 1930: 295).

Saltiel similarly displays a touching awkwardness when the narrator describes how "he prepared a lasso, threw it adroitly and captured himself" nearly strangling to death (Cohen 1930: 295). In this Chaplinesque image one sees the Gordian knot that Cohen takes on in confronting the Zionist rite of passage. Having "neatly killed the colony's one camel" by accident, "in despair and shame" of this innocent death, Saltiel seizes a sword, throws himself toward an Arab, and:

> summoned him to recognize the omnipotence of the God of Israel. The Arab loaded his gun, and Saltiel, considering himself in a state of legitimate defense, lifted his saber. But he was afraid of hurting his opponent and seeing the blood flow. So, shutting his eyes, he contented himself with dealing a deft and heavy blow on the heretic's head with the back of his weapon. The Arab dropped to the ground. Having thus done battle, Saltiel retired (Cohen 1930: 296).

In a malicious parody of the *chanson de geste* (the struggle against "the heretic" seems to be out of place here!), the passage relies on a simple mechanism: on the one hand, it incites the reader to sympathize with Saltiel, to wish for his victory against the "giant" (Cohen 1930: 296); on the other hand, it presents the prowess of the little uncle not as the product of powerful aggression, but rather as the fortunate consequence of his pacifism and humanity.

If one must still not accord a disproportionate ideological importance to this episode of fantasy, it nevertheless testifies to the tensions that sustain the Cohenien imaginary in the 1930s. It is necessary to tell the Zionist epic while peopling it with characters such as the Valeureux, who are pure products of a diasporic imaginary. It is also necessary to show Jewish fighters while assuring the reader that they fight against their will. From these considerations emerge the restrictions imposed by the narrative format (to only show peaceful pioneers confronted by senseless attacks) and the choice of a paradoxal narrative founded on the denial of violence, oscillating between the comic (burlesque) and the emotional registers (the deaths of Saltiel and Salomon).

(c) The presence of the Arab, in the case of this episode in stereotypical form, is revelatory. The necessity to give a realistic human form to the Zionist utopia imposes at the same time the presence of a diasporic counterpoint absent from Cohen's poetry and political declarations[8]: warfare, the presence of the Other and an Enemy. The very logic of fiction—revealed as much in its internal constraints of representation (to give an idea of historical reality) as in the imaginary constructions that it puts to work—lead Cohen to simultaneously invoke and distance himself from the Zionist epic.

AFTER THE WAR: THE CONTRADICTORY INJUNCTION OF ISRAEL

A final turn in Cohen's work takes place in the postwar period. What has happened? Something akin to an ideological about-face.

As could be expected, the Hitlerien persecution and genocide of European Jews gave Cohen's Zionist engagement its definitive legitimacy, its tragic confirmation. The illusions of a certain assimilationism, the optimism born out of the emancipation of European Jewry, die at Auschwitz. Cohen no longer has to demonstrate the necessity of a Jewish state, which becomes the majority view among the European public, still in a state of shock. Two parameters, however, will determine the meaning of this event.

Cohen's meditation on genocide will radically transform his Jewish metaphysics, by adding (if not substituting) the paradigm of the Passion to the paradigm of national renewal. From being a pariah people, the Jews become, during the Nazi regime, a martyred people. This historical fact necessitates a paradigm shift, which takes place during the war. Cohen does not write about the genocide (except for a few lines), but he did write in 1945 "Jour de mes dix ans" ("My Tenth Birthday"; taken up again and reworked, twenty-seven years later, in *Ô vous freres humains*), which can be read as a kind of archeology of European anti-Semitism where the exclusion from which the Jewish child suffers functions as a euphemistic anticipation of genocide. "Jour de mes dix ans" is the Passion of the young Albert Cohen. *The child's identification with Jesus* is overwhelming in this work. In *Paroles juives* (1921), Jesus had been the figure from which it was necessary to liberate oneself, because he incarnated Jewish renunciation, political defeat, alienating spiritualization; in *Solal* (1930) Jesus is the ambiguous double of the dead and resurrected Solal. In the postwar period, Cohen's reconciliation with Jesus is definitive: the prophet from Galilee becomes the fraternal representative of Jewish values carried out to the point of martyrdom. More generally, the themes and ordering of the story themselves are largely attributable to Christian narrativity and thematic: the unjust suffering of the innocent and pure child, a scapegoat given over to the public condemnation of a hostile mob (Camelot serving as an excellent devil figure), the *via dolorosa* of the humiliated child, the call for compassion. Thus history, in its violence, leads Cohen not only to reread his own childhood, but also more generally to bring together Judaism and Christianity, which he had only done before this point in an episodic way, in "Christianizing" the Jewish destiny.

The second parameter is even more directly related to the lexicon and to the political philosophy that underpin Albert Cohen's combat.

In the 1920s, this combat consisted of, on a personal level, thinking of himself as a Jew in opposition to Christians, while at the same time reflecting, on a collective level, on the necessary conditions for Israel's survival among the nations. This project is straightforward in a world where Nazism does not exist. As we have seen, it was possible throughout the 1920s to speak of a "Jewish race" without reference to racism. The realities of the debate changed after fascism had bored its way *ad naseum* into all the currents of postromantic metaphysics, which had been up to that point constructed on the diffuse bases of varying political philosophies. In other words, fascist ideology's usage of vitalist references, crypto- or pseudo-Nietzschean, its obsessive invocations of blood and soil, of races, of organic communities, of energy and nature, had definitively "discredited" these ideas, and even the words that they had been incarnated in. Cohen drew serious conclusions from this ideological polarization that led fascism to identify itself with the cult of force. From the end of the 1920s, Cohen began to elaborate what would become his vision of the world: an antinaturalist morality, founded on the absolute opposition between human law and instinct, on the denunciation of the cult of force and "baboonery." As such, Cohen pushes the radical rethinking of his intellectual project to the point of abdicating all reference to a romantic ideology that had earlier nourished his vision of Judaism and his conversion to Zionism.

From here, one can understand the new *crux* of Cohen's thought and imaginary. Never had the cause of Zionism been so justifiable as after the war; but at the moment when it becomes a necessity, Cohen finds it more difficult than ever to think of Israel's existence and vocation in Zionist terms, to translate them from the language of romantic nationalism, which had been literally confiscated by fascist ideologies. How could Cohen reconcile his personal myth of "a people against nature," a people of the mind, with the celebration of an "Israeli Israel"[9] made of pioneers, farmers and soldiers?

The risk of a rupture is nowhere clearer than in *Belle du seigneur* (1968) at the moment when Solal's hope is announced in a prophetic mode:

> O my Christian brothers you will see how my people will regain their youth when they return in freedom to Jerusalem and they will exemplify justice and courage they will be a witness for other nations who will look and stand amazed and beneath the sun in that sky there will be no more boors my lovely pathetic boors the luckless offspring of

centuries of pain and you will see how the sons of my people restored to the land of Israel will be serene and proud and handsome and noble in bearing and brave in war if need be and when at last you see our true face Hallelujah you will love my people . . . [10]

What does this passage invoke? Even though it is written after the creation of Israel, it draws on the old strata of Cohen's Zionist imaginary, describing the pure utopia of a resurrected and regenerated Israel. In response to image of the imaginary Jews of anti-Semitic propaganda, shaped by diasporic tribulations, Cohen offers up one of a young nation of citizen-soldiers having returned to the normal conditions of a national existence (very much in conformity with the image of Jewish state that prevailed at the time of its founding). Up to this point, one finds nothing that would seem to differ from Cohen's early ideas. From now on, the problem comes from the strange dissonance of this evocation at the heart of fiction. To integrate the Zionist utopia into his novel, Cohen seems suddenly constrained to betray his new axiology: that of a Jewish antinaturalist moral in open struggle with the pagan mythology of energy, force and youth. Certainly, the Israelis celebrated by Cohen work in the service of humanity and justice; but they are also "calm and proud and beautiful and of noble presence and hardy warriors when necessary." So even if the novelist (through his main character) never ceases to assail the cult of youth, beauty and virility—understood as masks of "the power to kill,"[11] in *Les Valeureux* the renewed Israel seems like an "adolescent sprung forth from an august past, an ancient spring, a virile beauty revealed to the world." The tension is palpable: a few lines after having celebrated the "noble presence" and the beauty of these "hardy warriors," Solal denounces the "strong naked bodies tanned by the sun [. . .] beauty and youth which are might the might which is the power of life and death all alone!" (Cohen 1968: 877). The valiant youth of a renewed Israel cross over into the pagan register denounced by Solal, through the imaginary of military heroism.

An act of renunciation, a contradiction? The truth is without doubt more complex. Cohen felt obligated to make a place for the resurrection of Israel in Palestine, and it seems logical that a part of him understood that the antinaturalist ideal, the ideal of the "sublime deformity,"[12] was unable to pave the way for the Jewish entry into history. If there had only been men like Solomon, Saltiel and Jeremiah, there would never have been a Jewish state. Zionism only becomes possible by virtue of a vital egoism, without which neither the individual nor the nation would be equipped with the means of survival. There is in Zionism an assent to life, a consent given to the logic of vital interests and consequently a submission to the political order and to force, to which the writer must reconcile himself, but for which he did not have the means to think through. If the Jewish state must submit itself to a contradictory injunction, to a double bind, to be at the same time in the real world and a utopia, to be a homeland inhabited by citizens who are "serene and proud and handsome and noble in bearing" but also "builders" of "justice," then it is better not to look too closely at it. If Israel must exist in this way, then it is better to love it from a distance, as one loves an idea, and not to make policy or history based on it: both of them are in essence demystifying.

It becomes impossible then to make Cohen's (diasporic) model of the defenseless Jew—which tends asymptotically toward an antinatural ideal of integral nonviolence—and the image of the citizen-soldier, of the new man that Zionism attempts to forge. A trace of this predicament can be seen in *Les Valeureux*. The tribute to the "frères en Israël [. . .] adultes et dignes, sérieux et de peu de paroles, combattants courageux, bâtisseurs de patrie et de justice" [brothers in Israel [. . .] mature and dignified, serious and of few words, courageous combatants, builders of the homeland and of justice] is accompanied straightaway by a personal justification, in the form of an excuse: "Mais qu'y puis-je si j'aime aussi mes Valeureux qui ne sont ni adultes, ni dignes, ni sérieux [. . .]" [But what can I do if I also love my Valeureux who are neither mature, nor dignified, nor serious], "representatives of a dying breed" (Cohen 1969: 94). The Jewish ethical model and imaginary that Cohen had praised is revealed to be incompatible with the Israeli political adventure. Hence the celebration of rediscovered homeland in Solal's monologue appears as a foreign graft that does not take: fixed in a messianic vignette, it cannot give life to a story, to history. Certainly, Cohen is less interested in painting a portrait of a country which, in the temporality of his fiction, does not exist, than he is in restoring a salvific dimension to the Zionist adventure. The upshot of the monologue is that the European Jews are on the way to extermination and that it is necessary to counter this catastrophe with the enunciation of the good news of Israel's rebirth. Nevertheless, Cohen, forever a Zionist, does not after this moment consecrate anything more than a few lines, repeated from one book to the next, to a project that had for a long time preoccupied him.

One can distinguish, therefore, two phases in Cohen's Zionist writings, both traversed by tensions and contradictions. The first phase, during the 1920s and part of the 1930s, where via his poetry and articles in the *Revue de Genève* or the *Revue juive*, Cohen espouses the Zionist cause and makes himself its cantor, grounding his images in the Bible and its prophets as well as in the romantic depths of national energy, collective myths, the mystique of people, between Barrès and Peguy, between the thought of rootedness and universalist ideals. To this ideologically heterogenous construction—in no way original, since it is nothing but the redistribution of elements commonly found in the diversity of Zionist doctrines—novelistic fiction adds, in the 1930s, its modulations, if not its reticence and its fears: reticence to melt and dissolve oneself in a collective undertaking; an affective and imaginary difficulty in appropriating a pioneer ideal decidedly hostile to the (maternal) poetry of (Solal's) exile and the ghetto (the Valeureux).

The second phase, going from the latter part of the 1930s to the postwar period, years during which Cohen, under the pressure of history—the rise of fascism, war, genocide—breaks almost completely with the political romanticism of his youth, with his vitalist mythology, and illuminates the contours of a metanarrative where Jews are the witnesses (and sometimes the martyrs) of a "human principle" elevated to the sublime, in its essence incompatible with the political order. Henceforth, the status and meaning of Zionism are different: never was Cohen more ill at ease in reconciling Israel's political necessity (uncontested) with his new vision of Judaism, inspired by a victimized, diasporic, spiritual and moral model (the unarmed Jew). Israel would only ever occupy a marginal place in his new works: a utopian space of the improbable reconciliation of force and right, a maternal and hospitable land, faraway, a place that one may dream of, on angst-filled and melancholy nights, in Geneva.

ACKNOWLEDGMENT

This article is a slightly reworked and abridged version of the author's more in-depth study, "Les tête-à-queue de l'Histoire: Fiction et diction sionistes dans l'oeuvre d'Albert Cohen," in *Les Cahiers Albert Cohen*, 13 (2003). Where possible the translator has used the available English translations of Cohen's works. Also, translations have been given in brackets following the original French for all citations from works that have not been translated into English.

NOTES

1. Albert Cohen, "Déclaration," *La Revue juive* 1(1925): 5–13, for the following citations.
2. As the recent issue of *Archives juives* on the "Jewish renaissance in the 1920s" has established: "Les Belles Lettres" 39 (2006).
3. Albert Cohen, "Cantique de Sion," *Revue Juive* 3(1925).
4. Cohen, "Cantique de Sion," 343.
5. Albert Cohen, *Solal* (Paris: Gallimard, 1930). *Solal*, trans. Wilfrid Benson (New York: E.P. Dutton, 1933), 288.
6. Cohen, *Solal*, 287. Subsequent references to this volume will be indicated parenthetically in the text.
7. Albert Cohen, *Les Valeureux* (Paris: Gallimard, 1969), 94. The italics are Phillipe Zard's.
8. If only very allusively in the "Cantique de Sion," in a roundabout verse: "Land bought at the price of blood," 344.
9. Cohen, *Les Valeureux*, 94. Subsequent references to this volume will be indicated parenthetically in the text.
10. Albert Cohen, *Belle du Seigneur* (Paris: Bibliothèque de la Pléiade, 1968), 900. *Her Lover (Belle du Seigneur)*, Trans. David Coward (London: Penguin Classics, 2005), 876.
11. Cohen, *Her Lover*, 338.
12. Frederich Nietzsche, *Beyond Good and Evil*, Trans. Marion Faber (New York: Oxford University Press, 1998), § 62, 57.

3 "One Nation (In)divisible?"
Sartre and the Jewish Question
Lawrence R. Schehr

After the defeat of France in 1871 in the Franco-Prussian War, the country bore an open wound, the predictable result of the amputation of Alsace-Lorraine. The subsequent foundation of the Third Republic, the legislation of the Ferry Laws in 1881 and 1882 and a generalized *Zeitgeist* together pointed toward both the belonging that is proper citizenship and the core set of republican values that have lasted and evolved through the present: a universalizing and secular discourse, the importance of the Republic and a rejection of identitarianism are at the heart of this mentality. But these values were partly founded on that amputation; the appeal to the universal and to the Republic was to some extent a response to the wound: the idealistic values were not necessarily generated from pure idealism.

No better illustration exists of this than the famous primer on citizenship, *Le Tour de la France par Deux Enfants. Devoir et Patrie*, written by G. Bruno (the pen name of Augustine Fouillée).[1] This 1877 novel is the story of two boys, André and Julien, who leave Lorraine after the defeat and travel throughout France, eventually they wind up in Paris. In each location, they learn about local history, production and important sites; they meet local people proud of their "pays," and through these encounters, they learn their own obligations as citizens of the Republic, the ideals of the nation—"patrie"—that supersede those of the "pays," and the means by which they must become good citizens of this newly formed and newly articulated country. Their road trip is never a *Heimkehr*; there will be no return home to Lorraine, which would remain part of Germany until the Treaty of Versailles (1919); it is thus significant that they wind up in Paris, centralized locus of French ideals, head and heart of the Republic and command center for the country. They learn their double allegiance: to the local and to the universal, if by universal we understand the Hexagon.

Jean-Paul Sartre's *Réflexions sur la question juive*, written in the fall of 1944, after the Liberation but before the discovery of the extent of the Final Solution, as Arlette Elkaïm-Sartre notes in her preface to the French edition, came on the heels of a second wound to the integrity of France, not an amputation of one part, but rather, the split of France into two distinct political units, an action that nullified the integrity of the nation-state that had been one of the bases of French identity for centuries.² This split was followed by an occupation of the whole country by Germany that would not come to an end until the recapture of France by the Allies after June 6, 1944, the defeat of Germany and the liberation of Paris by Leclerc in August 1944. Sartre is writing in the wake of five years of trauma, but before the discovery of Auschwitz and the understanding of the Holocaust.

For him, the question of the Jews in France is one of domestic politics, and he focuses on the internal repercussions and consequences of anti-Semitism for France as a contradiction of republican and universalist ideals, as a set of prejudices based on a complex ideology of the local and the national and as an ongoing divisive force within France that is both a nostalgic return to a past that never existed and a wish for a France of the future that is an impossibility. At a metalevel, Sartre's prescient text seeks to understand the problematics of belonging, of "being" from somewhere; it is a meditation on national identity, on citizenship and on egalitarian rights. In that, the first part, originally published as "Portrait de l'anti-sémite" ["Portrait of the Anti-Semite"], is not without a generic conception similar to those portraits by Albert Memmi, who wrote portraits of the colonized and the colonizer in the following years; this work also seems to be asking, in the nascent and jejune vocabulary of what will become a critique of colonialism, "Who is French?" Thus Sartre's reflections, understood both as meditation and as what is perceived in a mirror is the double portrait of the other who is not "franco-français" and that of the "franco-français" necessarily morphed by the presence of that other, those others, be they Jews, Maghrebians, sub-Saharan Africans, or Southeast Asians.³

The fundamental problem for all parties—the anti-Semites, the liberals and democrats, the Jews, Sartre—is the maintenance of the "indivisible totality of the country" ["totalité indivise du pays"] (Sartre 1954: 29, 32).⁴ In light of the trauma of the war, this totality and indivisibility take on primary importance, for this nation, both amputated and recently divided, is at risk of dissolving into an amalgam of disparate localities, with no unity and no republican spirit of the whole. For Sartre, this indivisibility, also a desideratum, becomes the hallmark of anti-Semitism in a rhetorical move that marks the anti-Semite as possessing whole and part at the same time. Master of metonymy and synecdoche with a flowing field of signifieds, the anti-Semite needs a double logic to stake out his position: "True [vrais] Frenchmen, good [bons] Frenchmen are all equal, for each of them possesses for himself alone France whole and undivided [la France indivise]. Thus I would call [Aussi nommerais-je volontiers] anti-Semitism a poor man's snobbery" (Sartre 1954: 26, 28). In using free indirect discourse (*discours indirect libre*) with morality- and value-laden words such as "vrais" and "bons," Sartre is attacking the deontological code of anti-Semites who, in his eyes, believe themselves superior to Jews, even when qualities of Jews may far outstrip their own, since for them "intelligence is Jewish" ["l'intelligence est juive"] (Sartre 1954: 23, 25). But at the same time, the troping of France as indivisible creates a fantasmatic France of purity for Sartre's anti-Semites, a fantasyland in which there is a seamless floating between whole and part, for that part not only is a synecdoche of the whole, it is the whole, both in extent and through time: "The true [vrai] Frenchman, rooted [enraciné] in his province, in his country [dans son pays], borne along by a tradition twenty centuries old, benefiting from ancestral wisdom, guided by tried [éprouvées] customs, does not *need* intelligence" (Sartre 1954: 23, 25–26).[5]

Citizenship and the nation then, for the anti-Semite, are not questions of action, participation, intelligence or abstraction, but rather of a belonging to or a rooting (*enracinement*) in an atemporal chronicity and an antigeographic topography subtended not by a defense and illustration of the French language, but by a dogged adherence to an essence of Frenchness that no amount of intelligence and erudition can undo. For the anti-Semite, language is innate and inherited and no amount of book learning can take away what he owns, the combination of the French language, the land and its culture natively intertwined: "I *possess* Racine—Racine and my country and my soil" ["je *possède* Racine. Racine et ma langue et mon sol"] (Sartre 1954: 24, 27). Not technically a zeugma, this is still a kind of yoking together that corresponds to the rhetorical metonymy and synecdoche already discussed: the anti-Semite takes as his credo that is an essential relation among these diverse categories (land, language and culture), and this yoking of the disparate reinforces the aberrant nature of the situation. Thus does the individual anti-Semite become a metonymy or synecdoche of himself, of the French nation and of all French citizens—all, of course, except the Jews: "He has spoken this language for only twenty years and I, for a thousand years" ["Cette langue, il la parle depuis vingt ans seulement et moi depuis mille ans" (Sartre 1954: 24, 27). In Sartre's mind then, the position of the confirmed anti-Semite exceeds time and space, moment and place and local and global. The position of the anti-Semite outstrips any grounding in the actual, so that he sees himself as the metonymical (and tautological) equivalent of France.

Let us pause to consider what this might mean for the question of citizenship. The confirmed anti-Semite whose portrait Sartre is painting is adamant in his beliefs in a birthright that transcends the moment to veer toward an achronic eternal. One is French because one has always been French; I am myself, but I am not distinct from the thirty or forty generations of French citizens who preceded me. At the same time, for the anti-Semite, it little matters how long the Jew has been in France—twenty years or two hundred years—he will always be other, a noncitizen even when the state or the Republic has decreed that he has all rights as a citizen.[6] Together, the rhetorical moves of this impossible chronology and the ideological underpinnings make the Jew other in a different fashion, not so much just different from "us," but a different species entirely. Whereas the "real" French are grounded, palpable, tangible people, the Jew fades into the "*idea* of the Jew that one forms for himself which would seem to determine history, not the 'historical fact' that produces the idea" (Sartre 1954: 16, 18); the "Jew" is someone or something—*golem*, *dybbuk* or *horla*—that crosses space and time in an unacceptable fashion.[7] And in describing this idea, Sartre uses a word key to his vocabulary: "it is *the idea of the Jew* that appears to be the essential" (Sartre 1954: 19).

Now, even if "essential" is an everyday word, it is not the case for Sartre, and he seems to be projecting his own thought categories into (or onto) the anti-Semite who is in bad faith in believing that he (the anti-Semite) has some essential *en soi* tied to the land, the language and a transhistorical position of always having been there. Thus the anti-Semite is in bad faith, but he is also in bad faith in seeing that it is not the *en soi* of any individual Jew that is problematic, so much as the nebulous idea, not grounded in any here and now, not tied to any bit of land, except the phantom imaginary nation of Israel/Palestine "out there." For the Sartrean anti-Semite, the Jew becomes this soulless essence occupied by some transcendental idea that destabilizes the system and its orders. And thus, this ungroundedness can easily be translated into a morality play of good and evil, simply because the demonized Jew is not restricted by his body, place and time: "There is only one creature, to my knowledge, who is thus totally free and yet chained to evil; that is the Spirit of Evil himself, Satan. Thus the Jew is assimilable to the spirit of evil" (Sartre 1954: 39–40, 43). The Jew is reinserted into the dualism of a Manichean universe (Sartre 1954: 148, 157) in which his religion and nation are akin to those of the devil, but characterized, not as evanescent, but as transcendentally impalpable except in their negativity (the demonized version metonymized in each individual Jew) and in which those of the anti-Semite are erected as the only true possibilities: "a concrete historical community is basically [d'abord] *national* and *religious*; but the Jewish community, which once was [fut] both, has been deprived [s'est vidée] bit by bit of both these concrete characteristics" (Sartre 1954: 66, 72). If, from the period of the Babylonian captivity (Sartre 1954: 64, 70) onward, the Jews have become a wandering nation, it is, at least since the Revolution, the fault of the Gentile nations not to have known how to integrate—Sartre uses the word "assimilate" (Sartre 1954: 67, 73)—them and thus the deontological question one must ask of "Christian conscience" (69, 74). Here, Sartre is going beyond the position of averred anti-Semitism, again using the metonymical pattern that is foundational for the rhetoric of this essay, to ask *"What have you made of the Jews?"* [*"qu'as-tu fait* des Juifs?"] (Sartre 1954: 69, 74).[8]

Early in the essay, Sartre writes that "the anti-Semite asserts the equality of Aryans" (Sartre 1954: 29, 31). Ostensibly, the equivalence among "Christian conscience," technically the addressee of the question, the "anti-Semite," who certainly does not characterize himself, essentially as such, but rather as French, and "Aryan," is meant to imply the thinking of those whom Sartre targets, who, at least implicitly, ally themselves not only with the racist invective of Drumont, but also, and more importantly, with the myth of Aryan superiority (i.e., that of all non-Slav Western Europeans) that was the mainstay of Nazi propaganda. Later, in discussing the difficulty for Jews to assimilate to the Gentile majority, Sartre uses the phrase "the security [la sécurité épaisse] of the 'Aryan'" (Sartre 1954: 133, 142), and this, from the point of view of the Jew. In so doing, he repeats his major trope, the use of synecdoche and metonymy: he has moved from anti-Semite to Christian and now to Aryan; these are associated ideas, somewhat overlapping circles in a Venn diagram, but not at all identical. So do Jews and anti-Semites share the same rhetorical trope? Does Sartre as well? It is not clear whether Sartre ever fully distinguishes his troping pattern from that of his targets or their victims. So we cannot know what "you" did with the Jews without knowing who "you" are, beyond the vagueness of Christian conscience.

For that, it is useful to turn to another model in the early pages of the volume. As I have already indicated, from the projected position of bad faith, Sartre seems to be saying that all anti-Semites must have read *L'Être et le néant* in their spare time, and thus, they seem to have arrived intuitively at the idea that there are two races (in the very old-fashioned sense of the word), or better yet two species. Early on, however, Sartre lays a biochemical groundwork, as if to say that for the anti-Semite, the difference in races is physically essential as well. The anti-Semite seems to be a free radical (in the chemical sense): "Thus anti-Semitic opinion appears to us to be [apparaît comme] a molecule that can enter into combination with other molecules of any origin whatsoever without undergoing alteration" ["susceptible d'entrer en combinaison sans s'altérer avec d'autres molécules d'ailleurs quelconques"] (Sartre 1954: 8, 10). That is one biochemical position: unchanging essence, free to combine with other attributes, to create a multiheaded monster of anti-Semitism still true to its roots. Sartre takes this notion of the free radical and denies its validity for anyone, Jew and Christian alike: "There is not *one* virtue of courage which enters indifferently into a Jewish character or a Christian character in the way that oxygen indifferently combines with nitrogen and argon to form air and with hydrogen to form water" (Sartre 1954: 34, 37). So the laws of science may indeed obtain in the Sartrean solution: there are universal laws of combination to be followed, not two sciences, two species, two races, but singularities whose individuality is unique but whose aggregate qualities need to be measured according to the same metrics and assessed according to the same rules: "each person is an indivisible totality that has its own courage, its own generosity, its own way of thinking, laughing, drinking, and eating" (Sartre 1954: 34, 37). But this is more a Sartrean desideratum for a future in which assimilation will have been accomplished with the preservation of uniqueness. Let us return to the here and now of the moral question, "What did you do with the Jews?" because, even if the extent of the Final Solution is not known, there are hints and glimmers, and the position of the anti-Semite, which Sartre describes most of the time as despicable, somehow has gone beyond the merely human.[9] And even if he describes the stories in Drumont's *La France juive* as being "ignoble or obscene" (Sartre 1954: 45, 49), we realize that there is a position beyond obscenity: "A destroyer in function, a sadist with a pure heart, the anti-Semite is, in the very depths of his heart, a criminal. What he wishes, what he prepares, is the *death* of the Jew" (Sartre 1954: 49, 53).

Before deciding what Sartre means, let us go to the heart of the problem, for there is certainly a problem. The scene is set in the months after the Liberation and a note (Sartre 1954: 71n, 76n) tells us that "today" means October 1944, and a precise reference is made (Sartre 1954: 71, 76–77) to General Leclerc's troops (i.e., the divisions that entered Paris from the south in August 1944), who accomplished the final liberation of the city from German occupation:

> Now all of France [la France entière] rejoices and fraternizes in the streets; social conflicts seem temporarily forgotten; newspapers devote whole columns to stories of prisoners of war and deportees. Do we say anything about the Jews [Va-t-on parler des Juifs]? [Will one praise the return among us of those who escaped].[10] Do we give a thought to those who died in the gas chambers of Lublin? Not a word. Not a line in the newspapers. That is because we must not irritate the anti-Semites; more than ever, we need unity [Plus que jamais la France a besoin d'union] (Sartre 1954: 77).

Buried in this quotation and unglossed is the phrase "gas chambers," and, even if the full extent of the destruction of the Holocaust is not yet known, the hint is there: there is no reason to think that the gas chambers of Lublin are epiphenomenal. Why does Sartre not expand on this?[11] Why is the phrase just said in passing? Why does he have recourse twice to words—"la France entière" and "union"—relating to indivisibility? It is difficult to say. Part of the passage seems ever so slightly to hint at free indirect discourse, as if Sartre were mocking the position of "well-intentioned" people and media. But it seems to me that his role would have been to question that expression, "gas chambers" and to leave mockery and irony to one side. What has stayed his hand, I would argue, is the looming of the unspeakable events and discourses of the Holocaust, the prescience that there is something bigger just down the road and the recognition, perhaps, that the discourses of humanism and existentialism, and of existentialism as a humanism (to use a later title), will be inadequate to assess, describe, digest and process the specter looming over the face of Europe.

So how does France go forward? In the short run, how will France deal with the integration or assimilation of the Jews, while retaining its own sense of identity and indivisibility, its commitments to the Declaration of the Rights of Man and its uniqueness as the "French exception"? In the long run, what does this integration do to the status of the individual? Clearly, Sartre rejects what he perceives to be a failed American model, but he does so through the creation of a straw man argument and an implicit tropic jump—for this is the only plausible explanation from religion to race. At first, he seems to be talking about the position of the liberal democrat in French society relative to the question of anti-Semitism and he argues that this progressive position is not successful because the democrat, in order to reach the goal of assimilation, "wants to separate the Jew from his religion, from his family, from his ethnic community" (Sartre 1954: 57, 61). The democrat thus wants to put him into the "democratic crucible" ["le creuset démocratique"] (Sartre 1954: 61).[12] Now while Sartre may indeed be correct in assuming that many liberal democrats, or what we would call universalist republicans nowadays, might think that this is the ideal, they also know that we do not and cannot live some utopian universalist republican ideal, and that is where the separation of public and private spheres comes in: in public, one is not a Jew (or a Beur or a gay or a woman, etc.); in private, that liberty is steadfastly maintained. And I believe that Sartre knows he is on shaky ground, because he sets up the U.S. "melting pot" as the straw man, but not without first having recourse once again to his chemistry lesson: there is the melting pot "whence he will emerge naked and alone [seul et nu], an individual and solitary particle, like all the other particles" (Sartre 1954: 57, 61). There is a fear of the loss of an individual's singularity, which has been a *leitmotif* throughout the essay. But let us return to the United States: "This is what, in the United States, is called a policy of assimilation; immigration laws have registered the failure of this policy, and [. . .] of the democratic point of view" (Sartre 1954: 61). But the question in the United States was seldom a religious one, except in secondary fashion: even if Jews were refused entry into certain upper strata of WASP aristocracy (think of *Gentleman's Agreement*), the relative integration of Jews and other religious groups in the United States was, by and large, a great success (with the exception more recently of Muslims, some fringe groups practicing polygamy and certain "cults"). What was not successful (to this day) was an integration of "races," be it laws aimed at controlling Chinese entry into the western United States around 1900, the current problem of "illegal aliens" (i.e., Latinos) and, of course, the largest question, the integration of the African American population into the larger U.S. community.[13] Sartre has made a subtle rhetorical shift by implicitly substituting one category of difference for another and later, in arguing his "solution" to the problem of anti-Semitism—and the word "solution" begins to take on a creepy adumbration in 1944, he makes explicit the shift between the Jewish question in France and the racial question in the United States: "But *we* who are not Jews, should we share it [the repugnance that certain Jews have for joining the anti-anti-Semitism fight]? Richard Wright, the Negro writer, said recently: 'There is no Negro problem in the United States; there is only a White problem.' In the same way, we will say that anti-Semitism is not a Jewish problem, it is *our* problem" (Sartre 1954: 151–52, 161).

Even if there is only "one Truth" (Sartre 1954: 111, 119), with the capital letter indicating its transcendental nature, there is perhaps no solution, not here, not now. And Sartre indicates as much: "The preceding remarks of course make no pretense of providing a solution to the Jewish problem. But perhaps they do give us a basis for stating [préciser] the conditions on which a solution might be envisaged" (Sartre 1954: 143, 152). And that solution is, one might expect, "the socialist revolution" that is "necessary to and sufficient for the suppression of the anti-Semite: it is for the Jews *also* that we shall make the revolution" (Sartre 1954: 150–151, 160). And yet the problem still seems to be in the rhetoric: the pronouns and possessive adjectives that leave "you" and "we" as undefined subjects, except insofar as this "you" is troped in its semantic contents and as it morphs from one figure of the Gentile to another. And the "we" and "our" in the quotations above are also problematic, for this is never a "we" of the whole, never a "we" undivided, indivisible; it is a "we" always already divided, just as France was in 1871 or Vichy France and Occupied France were during the Second World War. No amount of molecular chemistry can heal this wound, especially in the face of the additional factor, the rumors swirling at the time about gas chambers and more. Time has told us of another solution, the Final Solution that was not one.

ENVOI

I have focused on a few aspects of Sartre's thought in this chapter, rather than recapitulating or paraphrasing the argument, and have left to the side much of his commentary on the "anti-Semite" as essentialist category. This was done to develop an alphabet and syntax of the conjunction of figures in the rapidly changing landscape, real and ideological, topographical and human, in the autumn of 1944.[14] It also allows me to speculate, albeit briefly, on the future of this past. How can France, more than a half century later, engage the question of the assimilation or the integration of the other? And how can those others be integrated with the nation as a whole and with each other? Abandoning certain words—labeling some as politically incorrect (as opposed to blatantly racist or obscene)—does not indicate that "we" (and by that I mean an inclusive "we") have abandoned the underlying thought processes.

Perhaps in a postmodern world, one in which, as Jean-François Lyotard has so presciently shown, there are no longer any master narratives, the possibility for this "we," multiple and cohesive, tesselated yet united, in a molar, as opposed to a molecular, chemistry, will be the solution.[15] And in France, as everywhere else in the West, it involves a renewed commitment to individual and collective freedoms, to a sense of the public and the private and to a sense of the inclusive "we" in a nation or a European Union indivisible. It is only then that the question of the other can be put to rest, I think, an other who is both "other to the others," to use an old phrase, and "same to the same."

NOTES

1. G. Bruno, *Le Tour de la France par Deux Enfants: Devoir et Patrie* (Paris: Librairie Classique Eugène Belin, 1877, rpt. 2000).
2. Arlette Elkaïm-Sartre. "Préface," in *Réflexions sur la question juive* (Paris: Gallimard [Folio], 1954, rpt. 1970), i. For the English translation, see Jean-Paul Sartre, *Anti-Semite and Jew*. Trans. George J. Becker (New York: Schocken Books, 1954). For an overview of Sartre's opposition, see Alain Finkielkraut, *L'Humanité perdue: Essais sur le XXe siècle* (Paris: Seuil, 1996). 41–51.
3. The terms "franco-français" and "français de souche" refer to French citizens who have been French for many generations. The ethnicity or the "race" figured in the famous expression used in grammar school books to teach French history, "nos ancêtres les gaulois" ["our ancestors, the Gauls"].
4. For the quotations from Sartre, I am putting the page for the translation first, then that for the original French text. The French word "indivise" is ambiguous, as it means both "undivided" and "indivisible."
5. The expression "dans son pays" is ambiguous, as it can mean "country," as the translator suggests, but it also had the meaning of "in his neck of the woods."
6. With few exceptions, most of which relate to feminine beauty or sexuality, Sartre, as is his wont, seems to conceive of the individual subject as male. I have thus decided to opt for the masculine third-person pronoun in this essay because it seems to translate Sartrean thought better. Two notable exceptions to this male universe are a discussion of "the beautiful Jewess" (48, 52) and a surreal scene in a bordello in which a Jewish man finds himself with a Jewish prostitute, during which the man is stricken with "intolerable sense of humiliation that expresses itself in spasms of vomiting" (106, 113), and this because it is "he and the whole Jewish people" who are "prostituted, humiliated" (106, 114).
7. A "golem" is an animate creature created out of inanimate matter (clay). In Yiddish folklore a "dybbuk" is an evil spirit that escaped from hell and that haunts a living person. A "horla" is an invisible creature who possesses the protagonist/narrator in the Maupassant story of the same name.
8. I have chosen explicitly to use the word "Gentile," a word that has fallen out of favor, in order to underline the historicity of the Sartrean discourse and, at the end of this modest essay, to underline the fact that even if we have abandoned certain words—Sartre would have used "Indochinese" ["indochinois"] instead of the "southeast Asian" I have elected to use—we have yet to abandon the underlying thought processes. I have also used the word "Gentile" to render strange (in the Russian formalist sense of the word), the concepts of self, same, Christian, French, etc., in the discourse Sartre attributes to the anti-Semite. The translation itself also seems dated, as it uses words like "Jewess" and "Negro," which have also fallen out of favor.
9. I am using a somewhat more literal translation of "Qu'as-tu fait des Juifs?" than the one offered by the translator.
10. This phrase was not translated; I have inserted my own translation.

11. In his critique of Sartre's text, Traverso (73) notes that he mentions the gas chambers at Lublin, but does not talk about Auschwitz. He does note that much of the essay was written in 1944, i.e., before the information was known, but he reproaches Sartre implicitly for not having taken this into account for the 1946 publication. Galster mentions that the current critical position is that Sartre could have brought his text up to date. Hollier (142) also mentions this absence, but modifies it to include the deportations as well; Sartre's silence on the matter is interpreted as being "of a technical, linguistic order" and not "a moral one." And for Hollier, I think rightly, the question is of the rhetoric of "breaking a silence" (143). By the time Sartre gives his speech, "Reflections on the Jewish Question, A Lecture," on June 3, 1947, he is aware of the extent of the Holocaust and calls the event "the catastrophe you know all too well" (34). See Enzo Traverso,"The Blindness of the Intellectuals: Historicizing Sartre's *Anti-Semite and Jew*," Trans. Stuart Liebman. *October* 87(1999): 73–88; Ingrid Galster, "Sartre and the Jews," *Journal of Romance Studies* 6(1–2; 2006): 93–104; Denis Hollier, "Mosaic: Terminable and Interminable," *October* 87 (1999): 139–60; Jean-Paul Sartre, "Reflections on the Jewish Question, a Lecture," Trans. Rosalind Krauss and Denis Hollier. *October* 87 (1999): 33–46.
12. Given the reference to the United States that immediately follows, a more accurate translation would be "the democratic melting pot."
13. This is clearly not the place to develop a theory about the failed politics of U.S. assimilation, or the relative successes of affirmative action. My point is that Sartre had to shift categories in order for his paradigm and polemic to function. On the immigration of Chinese women in the late nineteenth and early twentieth centuries, see Eithne Luibhéid, *Entry Denied: Controlling Sexuality at the Border* (Minneapolis, MN: University of Minnesota Press, 2002).
14. For a wide variety of historical and interpretative approaches, see the excellent issue of *October* 87 (1999) on the subject, edited by Denis Hollier.
15. Jean-François Lyotard, *La Condition postmoderne: Rapport sur le savoir* (Paris: Minuit, 1979).

Part II
Francophone Literature and Cinema on the Conflict, 1957–2000

4 Slimane Benaïssa, or the Voice of Dissidence

Cyril Aslanov

In the Arab world, the rejection of Israel is a commonly accepted preconception. This opinion is almost never challenged, either in the individual discourse or in the public sphere, so that any attempt to express an independent opinion is doomed to be considered as reflecting an idiosyncratic point of view, if at all. However, the specific situation of postindependence Algeria, where the mass media are strongly controlled by the state and/or by the army, has brought several intellectuals to contest the official voice of the power and the monistic thought of the mainstream. Since the Algerian government relentlessly condemned Israel, a few opponents have adopted a subversive viewpoint based on an attempt to reassess the allegedly generally accepted truth.

In other Maghreb countries, the liberal intelligentsia is usually quite radical in its anti-Zionism. This may be due to the fact that in Morocco, and to some extant in Tunisia, the strong powers of Hasan II/Muhammad VI and of Zine al-Abidine ben Ali, respectively, tend to be in favor of normalization with Israel. Thus, contesting of the power involves the rejection of any idea of compromise with Israel. In Algeria, on the contrary, both the clique in power and the Islamic opposition are so fanatically hostile to Israel that the intellectuals who are among the main victims of both the dictatorial power and of the Islamic opposition sometimes feel some sympathy for Israel. In this attitude, they probably follow the principle according to which the enemy of my enemy is my friend. However, there may be also a positive reason for their diffuse sympathy at stake. It is quite understandable that freethinking people who suffer every day from governmental oppression, as well as from the threat of fundamentalist obscurantism, cannot remain indifferent to the fact that Israel is objectively the unique genuine democracy in the Middle East.

Thus it is the dynamic of dissidence that may explain why the Francophone Algerian writer Slimane Benaïssa has chosen to deal with the issue of the Israeli-Palestinian conflict from an unconventional perspective. The most obvious examples of such a staging of the conflict from Benaïssa's dissident vantage point are two of his plays, published in the same year (1999): *Prophètes sans dieu* (*Prophets Without God*),[1] a subversive dialogue between Moses, Jesus Christ and the author, and *L'avenir oublié (The Forgotten Future)*,[2] a polyphonic confrontation of divided identities.

I would like to analyze the place of the literary discourse displayed in both plays from a pragmatic/sociolinguistic perspective that might allow us to elucidate the strategies deployed by Benaïssa in order to express unconventional points of view. Like many other Algerian authors,[3] Benaïssa used French as a fecund alternative to the politics of re-Arabizing that characterizes the Algerian sociolinguistical horizon since the independence.[4] One can also consider it a way to escape auto-censorship. It is highly symptomatic that the five plays that Benaïssa wrote in Arabic before his exile in 1993 are composed in the spoken dialect and not in Standard Arabic. From a sociolinguistic perspective, it is possible to explain this implicit equivalence between French literary discourse and the Algerian dialect as a result of the asymmetry between French and Algerian diglossias. Whereas in Algeria the dialect is almost a distinct language compared to Standard Arabic, the gap between written and spoken French is not sufficient to allow us to suggest that they are different languages.

Thus, the ability to transfer the literary discourse to the French/Francophone stage was instrumental in Benaïssa's struggle toward universality and intellectual freedom. However, Benaïssa's location within the French/Francophone discourse is certainly far more complicated than the mere adoption of the language and culture of the former colonizer. First of all, Francophony is no longer synonymous with universality. In many respects, the Francophone world appears as a remote neighborhood of the global village.[5] Second, Benaïssa tried somehow to short-circuit the mediation of the Christian/ post-Christian world in his attempt to bridge the gap between Jews and Arabs. Does this mean that Benaïssa is going back to the colonial past of French Algeria where Jews and Arabs coexisted with more or less harmony? And did fraternization and friendship with Algerian-born *Pieds-Noirs* Jews (like the late André Chouraqui, for instance) exert a significant influence on the way Benaïssa represented the Israeli-Palestinian conflict or the Jewish-Muslim theological dissents in his militant and dissident theater?[6] In my crossed reading of *Prophètes sans Dieu* and *L'avenir oublié* I will try to show that his attempt to stage the Muslim-Jewish theological controversy or the Arab-Israeli conflict oscillates between an abstract vantage point and a more concrete and specific framing of the debate.

DECONSTRUCTING BENAÏSSA'S WAY OF DECONSTRUCTING THE ISRAELI-PALESTINIAN CONFLICT

In *L'avenir oublié*, Benaïssa tries to denounce the absurdity of the conflict between the Israelis and the Palestinians by deconstructing the opposition between the two camps. The technique he uses consists in imagining two characters who are in a relation of dissidence toward their own peoples. This dissidence is focused on the question of military duty. Although the Israeli Arab hero Antoine-Nasser is not supposed to serve in the Israel Defense Forces (IDF), he tells his family that he has the intention to fulfill the military duty, to which a Jewish, Druze or Bedouin citizen of the state of Israel is obligated. This decision to enroll willingly in the ranks of the IDF provokes a deep reprobation among the members of his family. At the end of the play, however, Antoine-Nasser reveals to his Jewish friend Joseph that this decision is only a lie intended as a strategy to prepare his family for another shocking revelation, his decision to marry Yaël, an Israeli Jewish woman.[7] From the vantage point of the playwright, this *deus ex machina* is a way to recuperate an apparently Romeo and Juliet-like situation according to Terentius' tradition in which a young man and a young woman have to cheat their own families in order to get the authorization to marry. The paradox is that in order to succeed in this stratagem the hero is able to pretend to betray his nation.

Antoine-Nasser's mirror image on the Jewish side is Joseph, a thirty-two-year-old leftist who, not unlike many young pacifist Israelis, is reluctant to serve as a reservist in the occupied territories. He finds an alibi in alcohol, which helps him assume divergent positions toward the values of the Israeli consensus. The fact that Joseph's mother, a caricature of the hysterical and intrusive *yiddishe mame*, represents the voice of the consensus is an important psychological ingredient of the plot. The aggravating presence of the mother is also stressed by the fact that Joseph bears a name that is the masculine counterpart of Josette. He is named after his mother. However, the "anti-hero" Joseph is not so willing to identify with values that are so aggressively advocated by this *pasionaria* of his mother. Hence he escapes to an alternative way of behavior and thinking.

The mirrored symmetry between the affronted camps is enhanced by another range of parallelisms and analogies: the widowed mothers Josette and Fatima are both intransigent in their discourses; the uncles Yahou and Abou-Daoud are both fanatic, each in his own way; the uncles Isac and Brahim are both skeptical and disillusioned, but still part of their respective national consensuses.

The emphasis put on the divisions within each camp (to the extent that Joseph and Antoine-Nasser almost leave their respective camps in order to join the camp of the other) is a way to relativize the bipolarization between Israelis and Palestinians. It is also highly significant that the Palestinian family actually belongs to the jurisdictional category of the Israeli Arabs and that Fatima's late husband was a Christian. The fact that the only Christian is a deceased person may be an allusion to the diminution of the Arab Christian component of the Palestinian population as a result of the migration of the elites and of the rise of intransigent Islamism within the Arab populations of Israel and Palestine. It may also be a way to suggest that the solution to the conflict between Jews and Arab Muslims does not pass through the mediation of the Christian world.

Lastly, the blurring of the identities of the converging figures Antoine-Nasser and Joseph is comically expressed at the end of the play when Antoine-Nasser reacts to Joseph's highly moralistic discourse by assuming that Joseph has been a Catholic priest in his former life. To this Joseph answers with no less humor that Antoine-Nasser has probably been a Jew in a previous avatar (*L'avenir oublié* 1999: 46). Lastly, Antoine-Nasser concludes with an even more blurring generalization when he says that in another life, "on a tous été juifs" ("all of us have been Jewish").

Besides the creation of a grey zone between the bipolarized camps, Benaïssa's deconstructionist approach is also manifested by the fact that each of the speaking characters (actually, speeches hold a disproportionate place within the play) proposes his own narrative both of the Israeli-Palestinian conflict and on the inner conflicts within each camp. Thanks to this pluralistic polyphony, the convergence that brings Joseph and Antoine-Nasser toward each other's camp is more understandable.

However, if we go deeper into the reading of the text, we might find hidden strata that suggest considering that this convergence is less symmetric than it appears at first sight. In the final scene, the Arab Antoine-Nasser and the Jew Joseph cooperate in the boring of a well (this itself is an allusion to the acute water problem common to both Israelis and Palestinians; *L'avenir oublié* 1999: 42). Yet while performing this task, Antoine-Nasser remains above, while Joseph goes down to the bottom of the well. This situation is an obvious reminiscence of the Biblical story of Joseph who was thrown down a dry pit by his brothers.[8] The homonymy between the hero of the Genesis and the character of the play is certainly not fortuitous. Moreover, this unequal situation between friends is explicitly underlined by Antoine-Nasser who asks: "Et là-haut vu d'en bas, qu'est-ce que ça donne?" ("What does the bottom look like seen from above?"). Such a dialogue may echo La Fontaine's fable "Le renard et le bouc" ("The Fox and the Ram")[9] or another reverberation of this Aesopian motive. In the apologue of the Fox and the Ram, the latter (who is actually a billy goat in La Fontaine's reworking of the motive) remains at the bottom of the well, while the former manages to escape. As a matter of fact, Joseph eventually emerges from the well, so that a happy end overcomes the disturbing subtext.

The comparison of La Fontaine's intertext with his reworking by Benaïssa requires us to decipher the author's position on the Palestinian question. According to the morality of the fable, there is always a winner and a loser. Applied to the Israeli-Palestinian conflict, this conventional wisdom could reflect the pessimistic stand according to which the resolution of the Jewish question by the creation of the state of Israel brought the Palestinians to a condition of stateless displaced persons that is quite similar to the condition of the Jews before 1948. However, Benaïssa's happy end in his discrete rewriting of the apologue of the Fox and the Ram hints at the fact that the happy end of one side of the conflict does not preclude the possibility of a happy end for the other. In other words, Benaïssa discretely advocates the idea of two states for two nations, which was part of the political agenda of both Israelis and Palestinians when the plays were first staged in March 1999.

However, *L'avenir oublié* has deeper implications than yet another plea in favor of a fair resolution of the Israeli-Palestinian conflict. The author uses the mediation of his Jewish character Joseph in order to express a bold paradox about God's atheism (*L'avenir oublié* 1999: 42–43). Joseph's self-contradictory axiom echoes *Prophètes sans Dieu*, Benaïssa's almost contemporaneous play published a month before *L'avenir oublié*.

A PIRANDELLIAN TREATMENT OF THE THEOLOGICAL DEBATE BETWEEN THE THREE MONOTHEISMS

In *Prophètes sans dieu*, Benaïssa stages the encounter of Jesus and Moses as related in the New Testament episode of the Transfiguration.[10] However, Benaïssa dropped the name of Elijah, who is said to have appeared together with Moses on the top of Mount Tabor. Indeed, from a Muslim perspective, Moses and Jesus are two perfectly symmetrical[11] prophetic figures, far more important than the Prophet Elijah (Ilyas in his Qur'anic reverberation). The author is also represented in the dialogue, once as a child,[12] and again as an adult playwright (*Prophètes sans dieu* 1999: 22–47). His position as a kind of arbiter between the discussing figures is reminiscent of the function of the Gentile in Ramon Llull's *Book of the Gentile and the Three Wise Men*. However, for reasons that are commented on at length throughout the play, Muhammad (in fact, his Gallicized name "Mahomet" is used) never joins the meeting. The reason given for his absence at the meeting is that Islam prohibits representing the Prophet. Therefore, the implicitly Muslim author is compelled to speak in Muhammad's name notwithstanding his refusal to play the role of the Prophet.

Toward the end of the fourth and last scene of the play (*Prophètes sans dieu* 1999: 40–45), the actors who are supposed to embody the characters of Moses and Jesus begin to be explicitly designated as "l'acteur Moïse" ("the actor Moses") and "l'acteur Jésus" ("the actor Jesus"). This shift can hint at the fact that the space of the confrontation between the characters is no longer theological, but merely theatrical. The turn toward reality is all the more impressive since at the very beginning of the play, Jesus and Moses were supposed to talk with each other on the occasion of the Transfiguration, the Greek term of which (μεταμόρφωσις, or "metamorphose") expresses a change of appearance that reveals the ontological superiority of the metamorphosed/transfigured person. The abolition of the theatrical distance is tantamount to an anti-Transfiguration in that the empirical beings of flesh and bones that were supposed to play the noble roles of Moses and Jesus prove to be nasty complainers.

As long as Moses and Jesus were presented as such, the author was a marginal figure in the dialogue. However, once the prophets admit that they are no more than actors, the status of the author becomes central. He is actually the only one whose ontological status has not been affected by the downgrading from theatrical illusion to a metatheatrical reflection on theater because, since the very beginning of the play, he never ceased to be the author. As a result of this self-reflexive cancellation of theatrical illusion, theater becomes the main object of debate between the dialoguing characters. Since theater turns to be dealt with for its own sake, it appears as a kind of substitute for religion that is orchestrated by the author. This transition from theology to theatrology is all the more natural in that theater was born in a religious context, though not in the context of monotheistic religions. The ceremonial dimension of theater as a ritual may justify the cancellation of the established religions from a para- or meta-religious perspective. Nonetheless, some features of religion are preserved because of the Dionysian origin of the theater as a whole.

Furthermore, the attempt to neutralize antagonisms from the universalist perspective of theater may be considered an attempt at creating something totally new, which could be defined as a post-Muslim secularism. Since secularism is never an abstract *a priori* move but rather the sublation and transformation of a specific religious background, Western secularism may be considered a post-Christian secularism. Jewish secularism, on the other hand, is a specific blend of secularism within the Western world. First of all, its roots are irreducible to the Christian substrate of the West. Second, the history of the Jewish people makes it a living bridge between East and West. Third, the ethnic-national dimension of Jewish identity somehow compensates for the trend toward secularization. However, in spite of the complexity involved in the crystallization of a post-Jewish secularism, it does exist nowadays, albeit as a result of individual assimilation to Western societies or thanks to the process of collective normalization, which is the essence of genuine Zionism, as it was conceived by its founding fathers in the late nineteenth century.

Whereas post-Christian and post-Jewish secularism are clearly defined entities, there is a degree of indeterminacy as far as post-Muslim secularism is concerned. Actually, secularism in a Muslim context is mainly represented by Arab nationalism, born at the end of the nineteenth century among superficially secularized Christian Syrians and continued throughout the twentieth century by dictatorial secular regimes: Nasser's ideological legacy in Egypt, Algeria and Palestine; Ba'ath in Syria and Iraq. In all these cases, secularism has been confiscated by hard-line politics and nationalism instead of constituting an area of freedom and dialogue.

Moreover, what may explain the difficulty of the emergence of a post-Muslim secularism is that the order of appearance of the three different monotheisms on the stage of history (and not only on the scene of the little theater where the première of *Prophètes sans dieu* has been played) allows the Muslims to view their religion as the ultimate one. Islam does not only overcome the two previous monotheisms. It also may be considered a dialectical sublation of the secular criticism that emanates from post-Christian secularism or post-Jewish secularism. Since Islam is allegedly the last Prophecy and the ultimate religion, the average Muslim may encounter some difficulty in conceiving of the mere possibility of an ideological vantage point that could constitute a post-Muslim perspective. It seems that this latter position is precisely what Benaïssa wants to promote, thanks to the translation of theological debate to the neutral space of the theatrical stage.

The fact that during the play the quotations from the Bible, the New Testament and even from the Qur'an are given according to André Chouraqui's translation of those sacred books hints at Benaïssa's debt to the legacy of this Algerian-born Francophone Israeli who tried to transcend the rivalry between the three monotheisms when he translated their respective foundational texts into French (*Prophètes sans dieu* 1999: 6, 9–10, 18, 20–21). The secular horizon of Francophony is, therefore, the common instance where otherwise irreconcilable particularisms may be brought together.[13] It is the linguistic space where an Algerian Jew and a Muslim Algerian can communicate and quote each other. However, since the French used by Chouraqui is deliberately far away from the smoothness of academic French, Benaïssa's adhesion to the Chouraquian model, which is hinted at by his use of the translation by his old friend, is a way to imitate the creative way this translator adapted the French standard to the foreign aesthetics of the Hebrew text of the Bible and to the even more exotic beauty of the Qur'an. Stimulated as he was by the convention-breaking boldness of his Jewish friend, the Algerian playwright felt sovereign to modulate the French-speaking literary discourse according to the palimpsest of his Arabic linguistic identity.

THE CULTURAL ROOTS OF BENAÏSSA'S SYMPATHY FOR CHOURAQUI

Even before Algeria fell victim to French colonialism, the Muslims often perceived the Jews as bearers and propagators of cultural devices prohibited by the puritan tradition of Maghrebian Islam. As in many other Muslim countries, Algerian Jews were often professional musicians in a context where intransigent Islam forbade the cultivation and performance of music.[14] Throughout the Maghreb, Jews were also known for their ability to prepare alcoholic drinks from dates or figs (*mahya* in Morocco; *bukha* in Tunisia). The Jews were also far less oppressive with their wives or daughters. They allowed them to leave their homes without concealing their faces. Moreover, the Iberian or Italian origin of many Maghrebian Jews made them more receptive to the Romance languages spoken in the western Mediterranean. Thanks to their knowledge of Spanish, Catalan, Portuguese or Italian, the Sephardic Jews settled in the harbor cities of North Africa were able to communicate with the Christians in a way that was certainly more elaborated than the *lingua franca* or *petit-mauresque*, a rudimentary pidgin in use in the intercourse between Muslims and Christians. More generally, Maghrebian Jews fulfilled the role of intermediaries and middlemen, no matter whether they were wealthy merchants or humble peddlers. This ability to make contact between worlds that would have been otherwise isolated from each other bestowed on the Jews the reputation of being innovators and even a little like magicians.[15]

Broadly speaking, the mere fact that Jews were not Muslims transformed them into the ultimate Others in an otherwise homogenous Islamic society. The perfect correspondence between Jewishness and Otherness in the Maghrebian cultural horizon was all the more accentuated in that, except for Christian slaves and captives and the ex-Christian renegades, there was not any constituted Christian community that could have relativized the confrontation between the Muslim majority and the Jewish minority, as it was the case in the Levant.

However, with the arrival of the colonial power of Christian France,[16] the situation changed altogether. Since Algerian Jews were Arabic-speaking until the first decades of the twentieth century at least, their Otherness was relativized in comparison with the absolute Otherness of the Christian colonists. After the bestowal of French citizenship on the whole Jewish community of Algeria in 1870, Algerian Jews constituted a kind of grey zone in the bipolarity between the colonizers and the colonized. Due to this fundamental ambiguity in the perception of the Jews in Muslim eyes, the Algerian Arabs developed mitigated feelings toward the ex-dhimmis. These feelings could range from envy and hatred to admiration and affection. The gamut of all these nuances is clearly expressed by the fact that in the Algerian dialect as well as in the local variety of colloquial French, *yahudi/ juif* became a generic insult meaning a treacherous and dishonest person. And yet, some of the uses of *yahudi/juif* are paradoxically loaded with a positive content.

Nowadays, there are almost no Jews left in Algeria. Nonetheless, Jews are still very present in the Algerian collective memory, albeit by virtue of the simultaneously and paradoxically derogative and positive use made of the words *yahudi/juif* in the everyday discourse. In 1993, Benaïssa was compelled to leave Algeria because of the threats he received from Muslim fundamentalists and because of the ambiguity of public powers. From then on, he found himself in a situation of exile that he might have perceived as somehow similar to what had been experienced by Algerian Jews. Like them, he was the object of a fanatical hatred to the extent that he was reduced to the status of the Other and rejected by his own country. Once turned into an exile, vomited by his fellows and his native land, he could identify with the experience Algerian Jews suffered thirty-one years beforehand when they were forced to accept expatriation camouflaged as repatriation. Joined to the coefficient of familiar Otherness and relative freedom associated with the figure of the Jew in the Algerian cultural context, this sense of identification may explain Benaïssa's self-identification with the Jewish Other and his commitment to the dialogue between Jews and Arabs from a perspective that is definitely different from the monolithic stands of the Arab mainstream.

And yet neither *Prophètes sans dieu* nor *L'avenir oublié* stage reconciliation between Algerian Jews and Algerian Arabs. To be sure, Joseph comes from a French Jewish background, as shown by the fact that his Uncle Isac comes from Paris to visit his relatives in Israel. However, Joseph's family does not have any particularly Algerian characteristics apart from the name of the mother Josette, which is quite frequent in the *Pied-Noir* onomasticon. As for the Arab Israeli Antoine-Nasser, he has absolutely nothing to do with the Algerian specificity, which was the theme of Benaïssa's novel *Les colères du silence (The Wrath of Silence)*. In this partly autobiographical fiction, the only mention of Jews appears only in the framework of a hypothesis *ad absurdum* about the alleged power of a pseudo-marabout.[17] It seems, therefore, that Benaïssa is able to deal with the issue of the Arab-Israeli conflict or of the Muslim-Jewish religious controversy only on the condition that the framework has no connection with the Algerian background. This situation may be due to the fact that Benaïssa's sympathy toward the Jews and his implication in the reconciliation process is the consequence of his situation as a dissident, an outsider and an exile. One can ask here whether this ability to adopt such an alternative stand toward the monistic attitudes of the Arab world is not part of the phenomenon of "nomadic thought," which has proved to be an important ingredient of modern Maghrebian literature.[18]

At this point, I would like to propose a bold assumption as to the role of Benaïssa's personal experience of exile in his understanding of the historical tragedy of two nations doomed to a restless wandering: the Jewish people, and especially the Algerian Jews who were compelled to leave their ancestral land as a result of their unwilling complicity with the French colonizers; the Palestinian people exiled from their homeland by the end of the long exile of the Jewish people. This connection between the experience of exile and the sharpening of the poetical consciousness reminds of the revelation of Edmond Jabès' talent as a Jewish poet. Before his exile out from Nasserian Egypt, Jabès was perceived as a French poet. However, *Je bâtis ma demeure*, the collection of poems and aphorisms he wrote between 1943 and 1957 while he was still a sedentary bourgeois in Cairo, lacks the deep originality and poetical strength of *Le livre des questions* and Jabès' subsequent poetical production, which is a good example of nomadic thought.

One of Jabès' *leitmotifs* is precisely the equivalence between the poet and the Jew.[19] Applied to the case of Benaïssa, the loss of territorial roots was tantamount to the revelation of the essentially stateless nature of literature. From this aesthetic-centered perspective, the national dimension of the Israeli-Palestinian conflict or the theological implications of the controversy between the three monotheisms can be staged with distance and humor. Moreover, it allows the author to adopt a post-religious perspective, which means in this case an ability to play with the reference of Islam from an overtly non-pietistic and almost irreverent vantage point.

What makes Benaïssa's voice quite unique in the panorama of the Francophone reverberations of the Israeli-Palestinian conflict is that his universal perspective does not erase the cultural specificities, neither his own Arab Muslim one nor the specificity of his Israeli Jewish interlocutors. This ability to combine a universalistic struggle for justice and truth with the preservation of a cultural specificity is perhaps the main lesson Benaïssa owes to his friend and mentor, André Chouraqui.

It is Benaïssa's personal friendship with the Algerian-born writer and translator, André Chouraqui, that allowed him to give a positive content to the vague sense of sympathy he felt toward Jews in general and Maghrebian Jews in particular. The resolution of the contradiction between the two points—on the one hand, biographical contacts with Algerian-born Jews, on the other hand obliteration of the Algerian context on the stage—may lay in a dialectic of coexistence between the rich concreteness of the context and its sublimation on the stage. After all, Benaïssa's plays are more philosophical sketches than realistic *tranches de vie*. Since he strives to give a minimalist representation of the problems at stake—the theological one and the political one—the author does not indulge in a depiction of the specific Algerian horizon that is common to him and to his spiritual mentor, André Chouraqui. However, it is precisely the existence of such a common background that may have triggered the dialogue between them (perhaps more than their common belonging to the category of French-speaking intellectuals).

The common Algerian background that functions as an implicit horizon to Chouraqui and Benaïssa is by itself rooted in a deeper layer of representation related to the legacy of Al-Andalus. Throughout his years of activism for a political and religious reconciliation between Arabs and Jews, Chouraqui always referred to the memory of Arab-Jewish coexistence in pre-Almoravid Muslim Spain as a kind of lost paradise, the recuperation of which could eventually lead to the solving of all the misunderstandings between Israel and Ishmael. This retrospective utopia may have influenced the choice of the title *L'avenir oublié*, where *oublié* is paradoxically used in reference to the time to come. In order to resolve the riddle contained in this apparent nonsense, one has to keep in mind that what is forgotten is not a colorless future but rather the possibility of renewing an idealized past.

The implicit reference to al-Andalus that used to function as a kind of mantra whenever Sephardic Jews and Muslim Arabs tried to bridge the gap between themselves is doomed to remain a chimerical myth as long as al-Andalus remains an abstract set of representations. In Chouraqui's and Benaïssa's case, however, the meaning of the adjective *Andalusi* is rooted in a personal experience connected with the specific Algerian context wherefrom both of them originate. For Chouraqui, born in the Western Algerian town of Aïn-Temouchent, the memory of al-Andalus was still very tangible, as he repeatedly used to stress. More specifically, the word *Andalusi* corresponds to a very precise meaning in the cultural horizon of North African Jewry. It is the term which Jews from Morocco and Oranais (Chouraqui was born in the department of Oran) use to refer to the specific tunes of their liturgical tradition considered a direct continuation of the Andalusi past. Interestingly enough, the same term *Andalusi* is also used in Eastern Algeria (Benaïssa was born in Guelma, east of Constantine) in order to refer to the classical musical lore of *maalûf,* which is sometimes coined "Arabic-Andalusi style" (*style arabo-andalou*).

As mentioned previously, the best performers of music in traditional Algeria were precisely local Jews. By the way, one of the last representatives of this eastern Algerian musical style performed by Jews is Gaston Ghrenassia, better known under his pseudonym of Enrico Macias, as far as his singing in Arabic with the accompaniment of traditional *'ûd* (Arabic lute) is concerned. Born in Constantine, not far away from Guelma, Benaïssa's birthplace, Enrico Macias received his musical training from Sheikh Raymond Leyris, a Jewish musical master whose title of sheikh is a borrowing from the fields of sacredness recycled in the context of art. This blurring of the boundaries between sacred and secular reflects that in Algeria, the ability to transmit the secrets of traditional singing was held in a quasi-religious esteem or conversely that art could function as a substitute of religion where Jews and Arabs could forget for a while the differences between their established confessional affiliations.

Thus for both Chouraqui and Benaïssa, the Andalusi reference was something more than a bookish reminiscence. It was a world of beautiful sounds that bridged the gaps between Western and Eastern Algeria, between the sacred and the secular, between Jews and Arabs. This resort to art in order to restart an interrupted dialogue between Muslims and Jews, between Palestinians and Israelis, is precisely what is at stake in Benaïssa's dramaturgy. If prosaic reality does not leave any hope of reconciliation between the brothers-enemies, so at least the theatric stage (and art in general) may be the locus where the end of warfare is dreamed. It is perhaps not fortuitous that in Israel itself, theater professionals from both the Israeli side and from the Israeli Arabic/Palestinian side used to stage shows in common in order to promote peace. This is exactly what Benaïssa intended to do when he staged *L'avenir oublié* in March 1999 in the Parisian suburb of Bobigny, a place where many North African Arabs and Maghrebian Jews coexist with more or less harmony.

CONCLUSION

Benaïssa's resort to theater as an artistic medium allowed him to put in perspective the desperate concreteness of the Israeli-Palestinian conflict. The use of a minimalist dramaturgy with a Pirandellian twist may be a way of suggesting some important truths obliterated by eighty years of warfare between Arabs and Jews in Palestine/Land of Israel (the very name to give this country is a matter of contention between the conflicting sides). One of these truths is the mirrored symmetry between the families of Joseph and Antoine-Nasser in *L'avenir oublié*. It is a way of suggesting that as far as the immediate experience is concerned, people react in the same way, no matter what deep differences separate them in terms of political, nationalistic, or religious agendas. This process of abstraction of an urgent political situation thanks to a sharp *vis comica* continues the best tradition of the father of comedy, Aristophanes, who dedicated four of his eleven surviving plays to the purpose of advocating peace between Athens and Sparta during the Peloponnesian War. As for *Prophètes sans Dieu*, it is a way to come back to the religious/Dionysian origin of theater in order to put in doubt the ontological status of the three monotheisms.

In this use of the art of playwriting in order to free himself from heavy allegiances and solidarities, Benaïssa is following the path of his old friend, André Chouraqui, who chose to consider the sacred texts of the three monotheisms as aesthetic objects and to convey their beauty in a highly original and artistic blend of French writing. However, neither Chouraqui nor Benaïssa remained isolated in their respective ivory towers. Their commitment to their respective forms of aesthetic expression is far from being an *art pour l'art* stand. It seems that the apparently autotelic cultivation of art—dramaturgy in Benaïssa's case, artistic translation in Chouraqui's case—is only a strategy used in order to instrumentalize art toward the promotion of a clear ideological message: the reconciliation between the three monotheisms and more specifically the relaunching of the dialogue between Arabs and Jews in spite of the Israeli-Palestinian conflict. The fact that Benaïssa and Chouraqui are united by a whole set of concrete references to their common Algerian background as well as to the reminiscence of the glorious days of Jewish-Arabic coexistence in Al-Andalus allowed them to counteract the danger of superficiality involved in this disengaged distance by a rich and dense existential dimension. May I suggest here a rereading of the earlier-mentioned episode of the boring of the well in *L'avenir oublié*? Perhaps what Joseph and Antoine-Nasser were looking for in the deepest stratum of the ground was not the water table but rather the common substrate of both Arabs and Jews, especially when both come from the same countries and share the same Andalusi legacy.

ACKNOWLEDGMENT

This chapter is dedicated to the blessed memory of André Chouraqui (1917–2007).

NOTES

1. Slimane Benaïssa, *Prophètes sans dieu* (Brussels: Lansman, 1999).
2. Slimane Benaïssa, *L'avenir oublié* (Brussels: Lansman, 1999).
3. See Belinda Jack, *Francophone Literatures: An Introductory Survey* (Oxford: Oxford University Press, 1996), 7; Farida Abu-Haidar, "Inscribing a Maghrebian Identity in French," in *Maghrebian Mosaic: A Literature in Transition*, Mildred Mortimer, ed. (Boulder, CO: Lynne Riener Publishers, 2001), 13–25 (especially 13–17).
4. About the role of French in Benaïssa's writing, see the metalinguistic reflections that the author put in the mouth of one of the characters (Bouâlem Souhil) of his novel Les colères du silence (Paris: Plon, 2005), 201–202: "Quand je parle en français, je me demande parfois ce que la langue est en train de me faire dire parce que je sens qu'elle m'échappe, elle me traîne vers des libertés que je ne connaissais pas" ("Whenever I speak French, I sometimes wonder what the language makes me say because I feel that it is running away from me and is drawing me to take liberties which were unusual for me"). Shortly after this confidence Bouâlem Souhil explains that he bestows on the French language the same function he used to bestow on the Algerian dialect (see 202).
5. This may explain why it took time until postcolonial studies were applied to the research on Francophone literature. On this late encounter between those fields, see Kamal Salhi, *Introduction to Francophone Post-Colonial Cultures: Critical Essays*, Kamal Salhi, ed. (Lanham, MD: Lexington Books, 2003), xi–xiv.
6. The subtitle of *L'avenir oublié* mentions André Chouraqui's contribution to the writing of the play: "Avec la complicité de André Chouraqui" ("With the complicity of André Chouraqui").
7. Benaïssa, *L'avenir oublié*, III, 2, pp. 44–45 (subsequent references to this edition will be indicated parenthetically in the text). The choice of the name Yaël for this absent character may be motivated by the fact that one of André Chouraqui's daughters bears this name. It can also be considered an intertextual link to Edmond Jabès' *Yael* (1967).
8. Genesis 37: 24; Qur'an 12: 10, 15.
9. Jean de La Fontaine, *Fables*, III, 5.
10. Matthew 17: 1–3; Mark 9: 2–4; Luke 9: 28–31. This episode is quoted almost verbatim in *Prophètes sans Dieu*, I, 1, p. 9 in André Chouraqui's translation of Matthew's version of the narrative.
11. As reflected by the rhyme that unites the name of Moses (*Musa*) with the name of Jesus (*'Isa*).
12. Benaïssa, *Prophètes sans dieu*, 1, pp. 5–22. Subsequent references to this edition will be indicated parenthetically in the text.
13. See Cyril Aslanov, *Pour comprendre la Bible: la leçon d'André Chouraqui* (Monaco: Éditions du Rocher, 1999), 209–210.
14. See Amnon Shiloah, *Jewish Musical Traditions* (Detroit, MI: Wayne State University Press, 1992), 199–205.

15. See André Chouraqui, *Histoire des Juifs d'Afrique du Nord* (Paris: Hachette, 1985), 100.
16. From a traditional Arab-Muslim vantage point, even republican secularized France is a Christian power.
17. Slimane Benaïssa, *Les colères du silence* (Paris: Plon, 2005), 77.
18. See John D. Erickson, "Nomadic Thought, Postcolonialism, and Maghrebian Writing," in *Postcolonial Theory and Francophone Literary Studies*, H. Adlai Murdoch and Anne Donadey, eds. (Gainesville, FL: University Press of Florida, 2005), 68–86 (especially 79–84).
19. Actually, he seems to have borrowed this idea from Paul Celan, who himself put Marina Tsvetayeva's incipit "All poets are Jews" as an epigraph to his poem *Die Niemandsrose*.

5 The Israeli-Palestinian Conflict in France
A Conflict in Search of Novelistic Representations

Anny Dayan-Rosenman
(Translated by Rachel Nisselson and Robert St. Clair)

Curiously, though the Israeli-Palestinian conflict is above-the-fold news in French media and serves as a frequent debate topic among the French public, this issue is less commonly found in French-(language) novelistic production. It's as if this inflammatory and ever-current event has had the paradoxical result of paralyzing of the literary imaginary, or as if the ever-growing number of history books, essays, documentaries and contradictory debates surrounding the topic have in some way dried up the wellspring from which the production of fiction and novels is drawn.

Indeed, in France nothing resembles the militant tone or tenor of Leon Uris' *Exodus*, or the playful critique of Philip Roth's *Operation Shylock*.[1] There are certainly a handful of novels and films by French Jewish authors that make reference to Israel, some clearly linked to the Israeli reality, others less so. However, to the extent that these texts and films attest to a certain ambivalence with regard to this reality or, more recently, to the extent that they evoke the effects and consequences of the current violence as experienced by France's Jews,[2] these works rarely manage to explicitly depict what is at stake in, or portray the agents/main actors of, the present conflict.

In this chapter—which can admittedly only be as partial as it is subjective, I will investigate three time periods and three modalities of this writing. The works I will treat all bear the ideological trace of the moment in which they were written. The first, *Terre d'amour et de feu*, is a passionately written account of the birth (pangs) of Israel by Joseph Kessel.[3] Next I will examine novels written by the young Sephardic writers starting in the 1980s that portray a critical bitterness toward the *land of milk and honey*, a criticism that is often more social than political. Finally, I will explore a couple of recent films that at first glance seemed destined to fail—films that attempt to create a dialogue of echoes between two conflicting narratives of a single conflict while revisiting the key historical moment of the war of 1948.

JOSEPH KESSEL, OR THE TIME OF THE MIRACLE

Rereading the texts that Kessel dedicates to Israel—grouped under the heading *Terre d'amour et de feu*—means going back, in a certain sense, to those early descriptions that gave birth to France's positive representation of Israel. It's like returning to a sort of archaeology of France's initial relationship to the image of Israel.[4]

Terre d'amour et de feu is made up of three large accounts produced by Kessel during three different trips to what was at the time called Palestine and then to Israel. The first, entitled *Les pionniers*, was written in 1928. The second, entitled *Les guerriers*, was completed in 1948. The third, *The Judges* (which this chapter will treat only in part), was written in 1961 while Kessel was covering the Eichmann trial in Jerusalem.

The work as a whole bears witness to the qualities of empathy and the power of the pen that make Kessel a great "reporter." But his reports also convey the journalist's relationship to his Judaism, a relationship that is undoubtedly expressed in these reports with strength and emotion like nowhere else in his oeuvre.

What is striking from the very first lines of the initial text is the extraordinary fusion of past and present that the wide-eyed visitor has the sense of witnessing. For him, indisputably, the Jews returned to their ancestral land in a sidereal temporal short circuit. One could cite entire pages expressing the feeling that a miracle is taking place while time has stopped: "It is the land of the past and the future. It seems that one never conjugates the verb 'to be' in the present there."[5] The term "return" is present in every line, as a way of qualifying the Jewish presence in Palestine.

Another theme affirmed with just as much insistence is the wonderment at the physical and cultural diversity that constitutes the gathering of exiled peoples: the extraordinary diversity of the types of human beings constituted by and over centuries of Diaspora that the fascinated traveler continually points out, comments on and describes. Yemenite Jews; Parisian or New York Jews; Jews from Russia, whose faces wear, Kessel says, "the ineffable imprint of hardiness, of roughness that distinguishes those who were born or grew up under the Bolsheviks"; Jewish officers who are *prodigiously English*; and the Jewish Afghani, a "large man whose beard was completely embalmed in benzoin oil, with magnificent eyes made up with kohl and nails that had been stained red by henna" who arrives with a jewelry box straight out of *A Thousand and One Nights* (Kessel 1965: 35, 36). Despite their tremendous diversity, these exiled peoples succeed in unifying as one people.

A third dimension that is palpably present in the text is that of the triumph of will. Kessel expresses his admiration for these pioneers, many of whom have fled lands of pogroms, who forge ahead without a look behind them at the Old World.

One of the most enthusiastic chapters is entitled *La République des enfants*. Kessel relates here his visit to *Kfar Yeladin* and his encounter with Pougatcheff, a famous Russian pedagogue who immigrated to Palestine. It was there, in this former orphanage/village, that Pougatcheff devised a new pedagogy founded on the autonomy and full responsibility of children. The narrator is aware that he is reporting hard-to-believe facts when he evokes this collective life among children between twelve to fifteen years old who govern themselves, who provide almost entirely for themselves, who have their own constitution, press and electoral system (Kessel 1965: 65). The reader cannot help but think of Janusz Korczak, who around the same time developed a very similar pedagogical theory in the Warsaw orphanage of which he was the director. But the reader might also understand that what seduces Kessel throughout his journey is the innovative social dimension, the construction of a world that seeks to embrace new models and to implement a certain number of values. Kessel is impressed by the dimension of "holiness" that is conferred on work, by the constant projection into the future and finally, by the mix of utopia and obstinacy that he sees at work and which he qualifies as an absolutely unique adventure in the history "of human perseverance and bravery" (Kessel 1965: 98).

Thus, from the agricultural colonies to the cities under construction, the author depicts a fertile land in labor; one of feverish activity and an almost miraculous growth that is metaphorically interpreted as a profound germination. "In Tel Aviv, the streets take shape amongst the dunes that are still intact; the houses arise in the middle of a deserted moor. A mute germination of brick and concrete is at work in this land. The city continuously breaks limits that one believed to be stable . . ." (Kessel 1965: 49) The images of trees, of roots, of seeds multiply, evoking the agricultural context of these *Jewish farmers,* but above all emphasizing the almost natural dimension of a return which, albeit miraculous, seems to Kessel to be inscribed in the cyclical dimension of nature and seasons. "And the winds of all the countries, of all the horizons, had brought back here the seeds of this indestructible people, and they had taken root with a prodigious speed and force. And the tree had grown again and the Jewish people was home once again, rooted, in the state of Israel" (Kessel 1965: 97).

What's more, conscious of both his enthusiasm and the exalted nature of his reports, the journalist feels the need to confirm the authenticity of what he writes: "I am not exaggerating. I am not carried away by simple lyricism. What I write, I saw; I witnessed these events" (Kessel 1965: 66).

Thus, for Kessel, at the time of this first visit, there doesn't seem to be a conflict, nor does there seem to be the possibility of an eventual or justifiable war, between the Jews and the Arabs. Inscribed in the ideology of his time, he sees in Palestine only a confrontation between what he believes to be the forces of the future (characterized by the efficacy of the people, their relationship to technology and hygiene that makes them able to drain the desert and to fight against malaria) and what he presents as the forces of the past, even though he recognizes within these forces an incontestable aesthetic and architectural superiority: "Two civilizations, one afflicted with what seemed to be an eternal sleepiness, the other still somewhat diffuse, but which gathered up all the weapons of the future," he writes (Kessel 1965: 39).

It is necessary to note, however, that at the time he wrote these accounts, Kessel had no precise goals or political vision and that he perceived none among the pioneers whom he described:

> What will this building be? What territorial, moral, and social shape will it have? How many Jews will be able to live here? None of those who currently, with a fervent, febrile sense of sacrifice, place the first stone of its edifice will be able to tell and I doubt even that they ask themselves this question. The imprecision of their dream is equaled only by its intensity (Kessel 1965: 87).

At this stage, the future remains open and coexistence possible.

The second textual account is more political and more dramatic. Indeed, Kessel arrives on May 15, 1948, onboard the *Petrel*, a small plane rented in Paris—the first to touch down in the new state of Israel on its first day of existence and its first day of war. This second account is a militant one that takes the form of a journal and of chapters hastily written to the rhythm of expeditions in trucks and half-tracks, from one front to the next. Kessel has the impression not of witnessing a war, but of being on the field of an immense guerilla combat unfolding on multiple and moving fronts. "Several notes thrown together without any linear order would give the most accurate portrayal of events. The Palestine War: the most disordered of all and somehow amorphous" (Kessel 1965: 110). This account outlines, however, a certain number of underlying themes that seem essential to understand the situation that he describes, the war-torn country that he crisscrosses, the feelings that he shares with the Jewish combatants.

There is first of all the sentiment of an absolute disproportion of the forces in conflict—a disproportion that renders the sole act of resisting a miracle in itself. This disproportion extends from the number of actual armies in conflict to the number of weapons used by and available to both sides. He thus evokes the image of a practically unarmed, new-born state. "Betrayed by England, attacked from every direction, in geographic and strategic conditions that are materially untenable, in a space that the armored division could cover in a few hours" (Kessel 1965: 157). This explains the frustration of the combatants who had few, if any, arms. Kessel echoes these complaints that reappear page after page, like a *leitmotif*: "'Oh! A plane, a plane,' he murmured. 'It was a South African Jew who had served as a fighter pilot for the duration of the 1940 war. He trembled with fury and powerlessness'" (Kessel 1965: 99). In a similar vein, the journalist cites another combatant who bitterly exclaims: "What's the point? What's the point of recognizing the State of Israel if the foreign governments refuse us weapons!" (Kessel 1965: 99).

The text also expresses a very strong hostility toward the British. Kessel denounces British partiality and a systematic ill will which drives them to give back to the combatants of the Arab legion every one of "the forts, with fortifications, arms, munitions and supplies" that could determine the outcome of the current battle (Kessel 1965: 157). Also apparent throughout the work is the exhilarating feeling of living a series of *first times*. The pride of having obtained the *first* visa that the new state issued, the feeling that "it's the *first time* in 20 centuries" that the Jews wage their own war and take their destiny into their hands. This certainty could not help but intoxicate a fighter drunk on liberty and adventure.

What emerges from Kessel's report is the description of a war for survival. It is also the affirmation of the absolute legitimacy of the Jewish people to return to their land, the legitimacy of a long history, but even more, the legitimacy conferred upon those who have survived so much suffering. "Through what migrations, what expulsions, what invalidations, through what massacres, what auto-da-fés, what pogroms. Through centuries and centuries of terror, ghettos, contempt, tortures . . ." (Kessel 1965: 97). Curiously, however, Kessel sees only one side of the situation. He seems completely indifferent, impermeable to the suffering caused to the *other* of this battle. He cites without commentary the name of an Arab village that was captured, lost, recaptured and burnt. He seems incapable of distinguishing the fate of Palestinian villagers from the fate of the combatants of the Arab League, and speaks in a paradoxical manner of the reinforcement brought to the enemy by "Arab groups recruited in Palestine" as if these groups were merely the backup forces in a war that was not their own (Kessel 1965: 156).

It would be unjust not to recognize the exactitude and precision of Kessel's descriptions, but, at the same time, one must not forget that he only portrays one side of the events, from an Israeli perspective. His accounts evoke the reality of a country at war, whose survival is threatened, but the text also forges the doxa to which Israel and the Jewish world would adhere until 1967. He evokes a mix of fear, happiness, recognition, admiration and almost motherly distress that characterizes that link between many Jews throughout the world in reaction to this country and this history, as well as the happiness and the desire to believe Israel to be just and egalitarian, essentially governed by moral values.

For Kessel, as for some of his contemporaries, there are no Palestinians. There are only Arabs. It would be several decades before the other half of the story is heard, before other voices made their account—that of the Palestinians or of Israel's New Historians—heard.

THE TIME OF BITTERNESS

A few decades later, accounts of the region take on a less lyrical tone. In the works of a series of Sephardic writers, who start writing at the end of the 1970s, Israel is less idealized, though still very present.

In the wake of the decolonizations and displacements that tore the Jewish communities of Northern Africa and the Mediterranean away from an environment in which they had lived for centuries, writing has had the function of expressing loss, the violence of history, the pain of exile, but also the hope constituted by the Promised Land—the long-awaited, dreamed-of country; the land found anew. *Un baiser froid comme la lune,*[6] *Les jours innocents,*[7] *Le cri de l'arbre,*[8] *Un été à Jérusalem,*[9] *La fortune du passager.*[10] All of these texts express the waiting, the nostalgia for a fraternal society, the desire to invest Israel with a healing function; then comes the time of disappointment, of love scorned, the confrontation with a society that harmed the immigrants in their very dreams.

Some, such as Ami Bouganim, write their accounts in the form of a collective epic, describing the departures in the middle of the night, in the context of *Alya-Beth*, the clandestine emigration that led thousands of Jews inspired by a messianic impulse and an immense hope from Morocco to Israel. For others, like Paula Jacques, the matrix of remembrance is constituted by the moment of expulsion, which is in turn linked to events in the Middle East or to the decolonization movements. This moment of expulsion is then relived obsessively. She describes collective expulsion, with its lines of emigrants carrying one lone suitcase jostling each other about at the Cairo airport. For other writers, such as Shoshana Boukobza or Jean-Luc Allouche, the departure from France to Israel seems to be a personal adventure, the answer to a question of identity, to a malaise, to the nostalgia for the land of one's childhood fed by the grayness of suburbs like Sarcelles.

In each case, Israel is a dreamland of recovered identity, a land of togetherness and unity. It is a motherland, but also a kind of identitary matrix that these writers believe will allow for an individual and collective (self) fulfillment despite the danger, despite the wars and despite those whom North African Jewish emigrants collectively call "The Arabs."

In most cases, the encounter with reality is harsh. The Promised Land doesn't keep its promises, it doesn't welcome its children with the love they were expecting, it is not equal in kind to their fervor. Whereas Kessel was amazed by the cultural diversity of the immigrants and by the egalitarian character of the society he discovered, the newly arrived only see disparity and segregation. In text after text, the reader discovers Jerusalem's sordid suburbs jam-packed with families with ten children. He sees "developing cities," a coded euphemism for dormitory-towns that surround the country like a security belt,[11] where the majority of immigrants from North Africa were sent. He discovers the hegemony of European culture, which, for a long time, leaves scant or no room for mutual recognition or for cultural exchange.

If coming to terms with this discrepancy between dream and reality engenders so much pain and bitterness, it is not due to the day-to-day realities of poverty, but rather because of the fact that these harsh conditions are not the result of a choice freely made, like the choice made by the pioneers. It is due to the feeling that these conditions were imposed, frequently just because of one's origins, or, whatever the case may be, with a sort of indifference as to the outcome.

From one page to the next, the grand myths of the Israeli ethos, so dear to the Israelis and to the Jews of the Diaspora, are questioned (especially the myth of a fraternal society). For Naïm Kattan's narrator, an immigrant from Iraq, it is the injurious segregation that elicits a destructive irony:

> Operation Ali Baba. We left by the thousands to construct a new country . . .
> He was expected. He would be welcomed like the prodigal son. He wasn't aware that he possessed an ancient and forgotten country. It was being returned to him.
> His friends were sending letters from London, from New York, from Tehran. His very own, brand new capital was named Pardess Hanna.
> An undefined plot of land where, each week, wooden huts were raised. The Baghdad Jews were all cooped-up in the same lot. Each morning and evening, they went to get water in the fountains spread out through the paths and passages.[12]

In this passage the juxtaposition of paragraphs highlights the opposition between the sheer magnitude of what seemed possible in Diasporic existence and the true limits of an integrated village. It conveys the shock at the disparity between the fraternal dream and reality, the bitterness of the prodigal son transformed into a migrant worker who is *cooped up/penned in (parquer)* with other Iraqis.

As for Paula Jacques, a more iconoclastic and ironic writer, it is the ethos of the kibbutz and of community life that are derided. This communal life seems to be a never-ending nightmare to the young Egyptian immigrant. The adolescent rebels against all of the values that her elders try to teach her. She remains attached to French while refusing Hebrew and the songs and dances that are supposed to socially inscribe her within her new culture. She refuses to renounce her individualism even though it is viewed as a defect. In *Un baiser froid comme la lune*, Paula Jacques, who spent many of her childhood years in Israel, settles the score. The militant Zionist who organized the young protagonist and her father's emigration is depicted with a particular ferocity. He is given a ridiculous name, Zoltan Gadol, as well as a glass eye, and a pompous and grandiloquent discourse that turns out to be untruthful. Even the attack and defense of the kibbutz where they ended up because of Zoltan Gadol is described more like a war waged in a Marx Brothers film (or like a citation of the hilarious attack of Kfar Saltiel[13]) than an act of tragic heroism. Finally, Tobias del Burgo and his daughter, aristocratic crooks lost in the sunflower fields of the land of pioneers, are ready to lie and cheat their way out of paradise and the kibbutz. They manage thus to leave the Promised Land for France, with Tobias leaving hidden in a coffin belonging to Pierre Levy, a tourist who died of a heart attack at the port of Haifa. The homage to Albert Cohen is stressed: the similarities between these unconvinced pioneers and *Les Valeureux*[14] is underlined by the collective escape, by the irreverent discourse about the Promised Land and the Ashkenazi pioneers and by Tobias's coffin/hideaway that recalls the coffin where the old Maïmon, Solal's ancestor, sleeps.

Ami Bouganim's account is, without a doubt, the most bitter and most desperate. No one character is singled out as heroic in this work; rather, it is a collectivity that is the hero, the *mahabara* (the village made of tents and patched-together huts, with a few water sources, intended to be temporary, although the depicted immigrants have already spent more than ten years there). *The Tree's Cry* depicts a *mahabara* inhabited by Moroccans, where life unfolds between an arid countryside and the road to Haifa, between picaresque eloquence and hopelessness.

The reader witnesses fathers deposed of their authority, crumbling patriarchal structures, rabbis who have become mute, artisans turned to sweepers, children who learn to be ashamed of their parents and their birthplaces, and the neglect and negligence of the authorities who appear only for political visits during election cycles.

The overriding feeling is one of humiliation, anger and degeneration. First the shock of the spraying of DTT powder when the boat arrived: *"They certainly weren't expecting an official reception with trumpets and fanfare; but a DTT shower!!"* (Bouganim 1983: 5).

Then there is the melancholy description of a former man of influence who was the symbol of an entire culture. In effect, the narrator puts an end to his provocative pranks when Yechiel Lombroso, the *mahabara*'s spokesman, discovers, in a hovel in the heart of Waddi Salib (Haifa's poorest neighborhood), Saltiel Cohen, who was Greece's consul to Mogador, reverently referred to as *consul of consuls*. At this point, a space for meditation on exile opens up in the text—for meditation on the pain of all exile, on the loss of social status, but also on oblivion, on the erasure of what one was, a fact that is here aggravated by *a priori* contempt and unfamiliarity.

But to focus entirely on such a desperate account would be to undervalue the humor of these narrators who chose to laugh and to make others laugh, despite their circumstances. Take Salitel Cohen, the deposed consul, for example, who declares that he comes from the line of Solals, which he explains with rediscovered chattiness:

> Saltiel Cohen's clandestine son, of the elder branch of Solals, native of Cephalonia, whose tribulations led him to Morocco, where for a certain time he sold harps to the Berbers. And it was a sumptuous stay,

in that he had the luminous idea to deposit his seed, without authorization and without the knowledge of his savior and master, Rabbi Albert Cohen, in the entrails of my loose and yet no less saintly mother, R'Becca Knafo.[15]

Like Paula Jacques, Ami Bourganim is clearly writing in the vein of *Rabbi Albert Cohen* with his epics of the trivial, his crazy wandering knights, his characters armed only with the power of the verb and iconoclastic diatribes that are leveled at everything—even the causes nearest to his heart. For despite the bitterness and the anger that often make the *mahabara* rumble, there is still the power of love that the inhabitants carry in their hearts for this country, their country, there despite all odds. "Despite their disappointment and their resentment, they never doubted the legitimacy of this war in which their spirit was engaged: the defense of Israel suffered no hesitation, no compromise, no questions" (Bouganim 1983: 66).

A survey of other works written during the same time period would no doubt reveal the same themes and the same contradictions.[16] However, one can notice that, beyond the social dimension, most of these works express unflattering opinions, however timid, of the politics of Israel's successive governments, creating a distance between the declaration of community leaders and the positions of writers.

We note that in *Les jours innocents*, the narrator, Jean-Luc Allouche, makes a lucid judgment about the consequences of the Six-Day War and on the blindness of his Israeli interlocutors:

> A new cult has seized the country since the recapturing of Jerusalem and the occupation of ancient biblical territories; and when one opposed to this cult's arguments the no less imperious rights of the other people, they would retort without hesitation.[17]

This fear-of-tomorrow is shared by Yehiel Lombroso, the tragic character who embodies the failure at the heart of Ami Bouganim's gesture, and who, after spending years planting trees, gives up the role of the pioneer, in which he had invested all the values of the past and the future, in favor of the diasporic role of the prophetic madman: "What kind of future does this victory assure us? What hate will it stir up? What exactions will it make us commit? The milk of hospitality has soured; the honey of coexistence has fermented. Yesterday we were propitiatory victims, today we are victors, tomorrow we will be oppressors" (Bouganim 1983: 220).

The same anguish and repudiation regarding the political choices of Menahem Begin's government can be found in Shoshana Boukhobza's narrator who, in *Un été à Jérusalem*, returns to the city in the midst of the Lebanese War. She describes a country whose life is dictated by the rhythm of *communiqués* (press releases), families who await the return of their sons who have been drafted. The severity is mitigated as always by the cries of mourning mothers and by the feeling of being besieged. If the Arab Israelis are depicted as anonymous and mute in Shoshana Boukobza and Jean-Luc Allouche's work—simple silhouettes of haughty gardeners or taciturn students enrolled at the University of Jerusalem—then we cannot maintain that the causes or the solutions of the Israeli-Palestinian conflict have been conceptualized nor have they been broached by any meaningful protagonist.

WELCOMING THE MEMORY OF THE OTHER?

The golden legend that claimed that Palestinian leaders ordered the Palestinians to leave Israel despite calls to stay from Israeli leaders has been debunked. The war that Kessel describes is challenged by a competing narrative, that of the Palestinians, which is confirmed in part by Israeli New Historians.

Deir Yassin[18] has become, rightly so, an unforgettable date of the war of 1948, but also of *Nakba*, the Palestinian mourning of men and land, inscribed in the collective memory. And yet, long-hidden or denied, certain massacres, once revealed and denounced, can eclipse others with their long shadows. Thus the scandal of the Deir Yassin massacre progressively overshadowed the massacre of a convoy of Jewish doctors which took place, four days later, during the siege of Jerusalem,[19] and the Kfar Etsion massacre, which took place five weeks after Deir Yassin, and left behind 128 Jewish victims.

The goal of these historical reminders[20] is by no means to justify one massacre by another, to establish a sordid book-keeping of suffering or to hide the reality of the expulsion and the suffering of Palestinians. But these reminders are necessary in order to prevent myths from being turned or inverted into other myths, given the intense desire on both sides to see only torturers or victims. This is all the more urgent given the fact that, in this region of the world, myths are deadly to any hope of peace.

Indeed, a golden legend was succeeded by a nightmare of mythic proportions, which in French far-Left culture begins to take on the appearances of doxa. The images of fearless and irreproachable Haganah soldiers were replaced by representations of child-killing Israeli soldiers thirsty for Palestinian blood[21]; the same holds for the retroactively constructed images of a super powerful and abundantly/overly armed army (in the image of the current Israeli army) which supposedly exercised its invincible force against unarmed Palestinians in 1948. From this *tableau*, the presence and power of the Arab Legion, the Iraqi, Egyptian, and Jordanian armies have little by little disappeared, to say nothing of the number of deaths on the Israeli side (losses which for this war represented about 1 percent of the Jewish population at the time). Indeed, these historical elements are simply incompatible with the vision of an all-powerful Israel/Israeli army.

If French novels seem to have in some way abdicated the powers of fiction, and have given up portraying this unsolvable conflict, a number of films seem to have taken up the challenge. Is it possible to use the power of the image without exacerbating hate and prejudices in a way that makes one hear as well as see elements of two antagonistic narratives, of two contradictory legitimacies?[22] These are the questions that seem to pose to us films that, in their attempt to return to the 1948 war with some sort of equity, were undoubtedly destined for failure. One example of such a film is *Kedma* (2002) by Amos Gitaï, an Israeli director whose films often have a substantial impact on French audiences. This film—coproduced in part by Marin Karmitz—is a courageous, perhaps the most courageous, film by Amos Gitaï and yet it was met with a more or less resounding silence. Likewise, *O Jerusalem!* (2006), a film by Elie Chouraqui adapted from Larry Collins and Dominique Lapierre's bestseller, was much anticipated by an advertising campaign before its release, but only remained on the big screen a few weeks, disappearing as a victim of the simultaneous discontent of a Jewish audience who found it too ecumenical and the hostility from a pro-Palestinian audience who considered it to be a Zionist propaganda movie. Were the technical quality and writing of these films not up to the task? Were they lacking a certain epic force? Perhaps. But we would do well to ask if those films that were clearly, violently partisan were any better in this regard.

Several images from these films will nonetheless remain etched in public memory. In *O Jerusalem!*, the explosions of Jewish and Palestinian attacks that follow each other in an infernal cycle, the chiasmatic litany of mourning and tears, the confrontation between the Haganah and the militants of the Stern group: a confrontation between realists and extremists that was never truly resolved in Israel. In *Kedma*, there are those Palestinians who walk behind the donkey carrying their belongings and who encounter, on their path of exile, Jewish immigrants. Of these haggard, freshly debarked immigrants who managed to escape the English soldiers patrolling the beach, many will die before the end of the day.

These are films that reexplore a conflict whose complexity, contradictory legitimacies, intricate refusals and violence are both difficult and vital to express. For if these stories are not told, we risk venturing into the territory where founding myths get elaborated.

NOTES

1. Léon Uris, *Exodus* (Paris: Laffont, 1961). *Exodus* (Garden City: Doubleday, 1958).
2. Nathalie Azoulay, *Les manifestations* (Paris: Seuil, 2003); Michael Sebban, *Lehaïm. A toutes les vies* (Paris: Hachettes Littératures, 2004).
3. Joseph Kessel, *Terre d'amour et de feu* (Paris: Plon, 1965).
4. It is also necessary to cite reports such as Albert Londres's *Le Juif errant est arrivé* (Paris: A. Michel, 1930). [*The Jew has come home*, Trans. William

Ewart Staples (New York: R.R. Smith, 1931)], republished in the collection "Motifs," *Le serpent à plumes*, as well as Jean-François Armorin's *Des Juifs quittent l'Europe*, Préface de David Rousset (Paris: La Jeune Parque, 1948).
5. Kessel, *Terre*, 86. Subsequent references to this edition will be indicated parenthetically in the text.
6. Paula Jacques, *Un baiser froid comme la lune* (Paris: Mercure de France, 1983).
7. Jean-Luc Allouche, *Les jours innocents* (Paris: Lieu Commun, 1983).
8. Ami Bouganim, *Le cri de l'arbre* (Tel Aviv: Stavit, 1983).
9. Shoshana Boukobza, *Un été à Jérusalem* (Paris: Balland, 1986).
10. Naïm Kattan, *La fortune du passager* (Montréal: Hurtubise, 1989).
11. See Haroun Jamous, *Israël et ses Juifs. Essai sur les limites du volontarisme* (Paris: F. Maspero, 1982).
12. Kattan, *Fortune*, 21.
13. Albert Cohen, *Solal* (Paris: Gallimard, 1930), 425. *Solal* (New York: E.P. Dutton, 1933).
14. Albert Cohen, *Les Valeureux* (Paris: Gallimard, 1972).
15. Bouganim, *Cri*, 89 (subsequent references to this edition will be indicated parenthetically in the text). Indeed, at the end of *Solal*, he is reminded that before going to Palestine, "Saltiel était allé dans le Rif marocain pour y placer des harpes," 423.
16. See Marco Koskas, *Destino* (Paris: B. Grasset, 1981); Claude Kayat, *Mohamed Cohen* (Paris: Le Seuil, 1981); *Mohamed Cohen: The Adventures of an Arabian Jew*, Trans. Patricia Wolf (New York: Bergh, 1989).
17. Allouche, *Jours*, 80.
18. The Deir Yassin massacre occurred on April 9, 1948, during the War of Palestine. It was carried out by the combatants of Irgoun and Lehi. Today, historians estimate the number of deaths to be between 100 and 200 people, made up mostly of civilians, women and children.
19. On April 13, 1948, a medical convoy heading to the Hadassah Hospital on Mont Scopus in Jerusalem was attacked by Arab combatants. Eighty doctors and nurses were massacred, undoubtedly as revenge for the Deir Yassin massacre. On May 15, 1948, 128 defenders of the Kfar-Etzion colony were massacred by soldiers from the Jordanian legion and by paramilitary forces after they had surrendered.
20. Historical Sources: Charles Enderlin, *Paix ou guerres. Les secrets des négociations israélo-arabes 1917–1995* (Paris: Fayard 2004); Benny Morris, *Victimes. Histoire revisitée du conflit arabo-sioniste* (Bruxelles: Editions Complexe, 2003).
21. See the film by the Egyptian director, Yousry Nasrallah, adapted from the novel by Elias Khoury, *La porte du soleil* (Arles: Sinbad/Actes sud, 2002) [*Gate of the Sun*, Trans. Humphrey T. Davies (Brooklyn: Archipelago Books, 2005)], released in 2004, which shows countless images of "Nazified" Israeli soldiers.
22. Take, for example, Costa-Gavras's film, *Hana K*, released in 1983, which attempts to "objectively" read the conflict. This near-impossible task undoubtedly explains one of the few failures of his career as a filmmaker.

6 When *"L'Essence Arrose de Haine"*
The Reinvention of Identity in Francophone Tunisian Literature[1]

Lamia Ben Youssef Zayzafoon

Revisiting Hegel's argument that Islam is the "universalization" of Jewish monotheism," Slavoj Zizek wonders if "the time has not come, especially with regard to the Middle East conflict, to talk about the Jewish-Muslim civilization as an axis opposed to Christianity."[2] Reproducing Hegel's opposition between the polytheist trinity in Christianity and the pure monotheism encountered in Judaism and Islam, he concludes that if there is so much "anti-Semitism" in Islam, it is "because of the extreme proximity of the two religions." What is relevant to this chapter is Zizek's de-Semitization of Arabs-Muslims and his transfer of Hegel's anti-Semitism (which targeted Jews and Muhammadans)[3] into some abstract Islamic essence. As Gil Anidjar has pointed out, what "differentiates Judaism from Islam" in nineteenth-century anti-Semitic literature is the *verbreitung*[4] or "spatio-political" location of the enemy: the Semitic Jew is the theological enemy within, the Semitic Arab-Muslim is the political enemy without. If anti-Semitism is to be understood as a historical discursive practice, then what Islam, what century and what part of the Muslim world is Zizek referring to? If, as a solution to the Middle Eastern conflict, Zizek reinvents Islam as anti-Semitic and proposes to read its alleged anti-Semitism as proof of the proximity between Judaism and Islam, then would he entertain the counterargument that Judaism is anti-Semitic because of its proximity with Islam? After all both Jews and Arabs-Muslims were invented as Semites by nineteenth-century European anthropology! It is such discursive cul-de-sacs that this chapter attempts to address—for, unquestioned, language hinders rather than facilitates our understanding of the Israeli-Palestinian conflict. This chapter examines in particular how, in response to two specific historical conjunctures (the Israeli-Palestinian conflict and the rise of Islamism), Tunisian left-wing intellectuals have reshaped and reinvented the Eurocentric categories of the Semite, the anti-Semite, the Jew and the Arab-Muslim to reconstruct themselves and others. While Albert Memmi reproduces in his work these discursive categories, Gisèle Halimi, Hédi

Bouraoui and Fethi Benslama attempt to subvert them through both feminist and Sufi humanist aesthetics.

Memmi's view of the Israeli-Palestinian conflict has been shaped by many factors: namely, his involvement with the Third World anticolonial struggle, disillusion with the rise of the postcolonial Islamic nation-state and support for Zionism as a legitimate nationalist movement like Arab nationalism. In his semiautobiographical novel *The Pillar of Salt* (1955), written one year before Tunisia's independence and seven years after the first Arab-Israeli War of 1948, Memmi tells the coming-of-age story of Alexandre Mordechai Benilouche, who goes to French school only to be irreparably alienated from his uneducated and poor Jewish family. Benilouche recalls feeling alienated from everyone: from the French because he is a native African and a Jew, from the European Jews because he is a poor African, from the Muhammadan kids because he is a Jew and from his fellow native Jews because he makes "the guttural speech of a Mohammedan."[5] In Memmi's first novel, Tunisian Muslims are referred to as Muhammadans, not Arabs. Benilouche has learned this derogatory medieval slur from his French colonial education, in the same way he has internalized European anti-Semitism and learned "to resent all Jews who dared engage in business."[6] While he is conscious of the danger of interiorizing European anti-Semitism against the Jew, Benilouche remains unaware of the anti-Semitic rhetoric in which the concept of the "Muhammadan"[7] race is couched.[8] Contrary to Memmi's assumption that only the Jew is the target of European anti-Semitism, French colonial literature shows that that the borderlines between anti-Semitism and Orientalism are often blurred. In *Loin des Icônes* (1920), officer Ermolaïve (a Russian expatriate in Tunisia) blames Muhammad for the fall of Tzarist Russia and lists him as one of the Israelites who have conspired to control the modern world along with Karl Marx, Freud and Jesus.[9]

In *The Pillar of Salt*, the narrator confesses that it is in French schools that he truly discovered anti-Semitism: "It was in high school that I discovered how painful it is to be a Jew" (Memmi 1992: 255). At a movie theatre, Benilouche remembers being harassed and called "kiki!" by a group of Sicilians and Maltese (Memmi 1992: 101). Even though he admits that relations between Muslims and Jews were not always rosy, as the attack of the Muslim infantry on the Jewish quarter in the Tunisian South attests to, Benilouche does not read this attack as evidence of Arab anti-Semitism against Jews, but rather as a French colonial tactic pitting natives against one another. Standing between "two walls," "[Benilouche] had to choose between repulsive hypocritical anti-Semitism (European), which had probably been the instigator of the massacre, and these murderous explosions [by Muslims] which, like letting blood, periodically relived the pressure of so much accumulated hatred" (Memmi 1992: 268–269). While in 1956 Memmi constructs anti-Semitism as a European racism that targets exclusively the Jew, he argues in *Juifs et arabes* (1974)—a book he wrote one year after The Yom Kippur

War of 1973—that "it is not European anti-Semitism which is at the origin of Arab-Anti-Semitism as Arab nationalists argue, but the opposite"[10] (i.e., it is Arab anti-Semitism which created Zionism). In his later works, Memmi refutes the hypothesis that the current anti-Semitism in the Arab world is a European import and, attacking Jewish occidental historians who view the Nazi Genocide as a unique experience of Jewish oppression,[11] he argues that the only reason why the Holocaust is seen as the most horrifying experience for the Jews is that Jewish history has so far been written by occidental Jewry. In the 1970s, Memmi constructs Arab-Jewish identity as a linguistic aberration, a political ploy invented by Arabs like Kaddafi to conceal the historical oppression of Jews in Arab lands for the purpose of delegitimizing the creation of Israel (Memmi 1973: 57, 60–67).

By de-Arabizing Jews[12] and de-Semitizing Arabs in the 1970s, Memmi reinvents the traditional conflict between Tunisian Muslims and Jews as a racial conflict: non-Jewish Tunisians are no longer referred to as Muhammadans, but as Arabs (even when they happen to be Berbers). To the denativization of Jews in postcolonial North Africa, Memmi responds with the denativization of Palestinians, even though by his own admission Arabs and Jews descend from the same Middle Eastern racial stock (Memmi 1973: 14). "True," he writes, "the Arabs of Palestine live a tragedy like us; but it should not be forgotten at the table of negotiations that they are not more numerous than us; and that, they too, come from elsewhere like us" (Memmi 1973: 65). If Jews and Arabs descend from the same indigenous populations of the Middle East, then where does Memmi locate the "mystical" elsewhere from which the Palestinians come? Who were the Palestinians before they became "Muslim converts" (Memmi 1973: 14)? If the expression "Arab Jew" is a misnomer, then what should we call those Jews who converted to Islam? Is it accurate to call them Muslim Jews or Hebrew Muslims? Since Memmi occludes the historical différance intrinsic to the word "Semite"—a racial and religious epithet that historically includes the Jew, the Arab, the Muslim, the Negro and the Italian (because tainted with Oriental or African blood)—then when does Memmi's monolithic Semite cease to be one? Memmi's discussion of the Israeli-Palestinian conflict is not only mediated through the Eurocentric binarism of the Jew and the Arab, but also based on a self-centered androcentric notion of the Semite, whom he equates with his own portrait (i.e., that of a Jewish man; Memmi 1973: 28). Memmi reads Jewishness not only in essentialist terms, but also through the perspective of the male subject who contemplates the history of Jewish oppression through what Hélène Cixous would call the logic of the same or *"repérage en soi."*[13] "To be a Jew," for Memmi, "is to undergo the same objective destiny of a group of men," not women (Memmi 1973: 40).

Retracting his indictment of French colonialism and anti-Semitism in *The Pillar of Salt*, Memmi now argues that the colonial period "was more secure" for Tunisian Jews than the postcolonial period.[14] Like their Moroccan and Algerian neighbors, after independence the Tunisians have "liquidated their Jewish communities" through economic sanctions, favoritism to their coreligionists and discrimination in civil service and "Kafkaesque charges" (Memmi 1975: 3). What Memmi refers to as anti-Semitism (the objective condition of being Jewish, of being subjected to oppression and discrimination in a hostile environment; Memmi 1975: 31) ought to be related to a larger crisis of state accountability, that of a new nation-state which has failed to protect all of its citizens, Jews, Muslims, Christians and atheists.[15] The 1962 Kafkaesque trial and assassination of Salah Ben Youssef in Germany and the forced exile of Ahmed Ben Salah, the mastermind of the Tunisian Socialist Experimentation in the 1960s, indicate that oppression was not the exclusive condition of the Tunisian Jew. The massacres and forced expulsion of the Harkis, those hundreds of thousands of Muslims in Algeria who fought with the French against their coreligionists in Algeria, shows that the forced departure of Algerian Jewry who sided with France during the Algerian Revolution is part of a specific historical process that is related to colonialism and nation building in the postcolonial period, not simply an Arab or Islamic anti-Semitic essence, as Memmi of the 1970s has argued.

A lawyer by profession, a feminist and a political activist, Halimi became famous not just for defending the Front de Libération Nationale (FLN), but also for acting as counsel for victims of French torture in the Algerian Revolution. Halimi's involvement with the Algerian and Palestinian nationalist movements shows not only that the Semite is gendered, but more important, that oppression is a nonexclusive human condition that is not restricted to a particular ethnic, racial or religious group. Looking back at the status of women in French colonial Tunisia, she observes that segregation and social and legal subordination were the common lot of all Tunisian women, Jewish or Muslim.[16] In contrast with Memmi's argument that oppression of the Jew comes from the outside world, Halimi shows that the oppression of the gendered Semite comes from within and without. If Memmi has come to deny in the 1970s the existence of "Arab Jews" because of the Israeli-Palestinian conflict, after her father's death, Halimi has embarked on a reverse journey to retrieve a denigrated Judeo-Arabic identity denied to her by both her French colonial education and the Israeli-Palestinian conflict. In her first autobiographical novel *Le Lait de l'oranger* (1988), she revisits Jewish-Arab relations in colonial and postcolonial Tunisia to examine what remains of her North African roots ten years after her father's death, the only umbilical cord that has ever attached her to her Tunisian origins. In an interview, Halimi confesses: "I have told in *Milk for the Orange Tree* (1988) in the original how some French have gunned down young unarmed Tunisians who were demonstrating. I was about twelve or thirteen and I couldn't help make the parallel between the situation of the Arab that was scorned and that of the woman that I was, also deprived as I was of my rights and the means to express myself."[17] Halimi's confession establishes a correlation

When "L'Essence Arrose de Haine" 97

throughout her novel between the inferior status of women and the colonized Arab as a scorned, silenced and castrated male subject.

In Halimi's memoirs, it is the Arab, not the Jew, who dwells at the bottom of the social/racial hierarchy in French colonial Tunisia. It is through the privilege of citizenship that French colonialism pitted the Jew against the Arab and was able to "reign."[18] As a child she was unable to reconcile the French ideals of "liberty, justice, and fraternity," which she never ceases to hear from the mouth of her Gallicized father, with "this blood which soaked the pavements" of Tunis on 9 April 1938. To Bourguiba's demand for a parliament, "civil liberties" and a responsible "government," the French military responded with submachine guns firing at disarmed students, women and children (Halimi 1988: 69–70). Because he was now French, her father Édouard "puffed" at the Neo Destour's nationalist aspiration for independence. In contrast with her communist uncle, Jacques, who, like Memmi, supported all forms of anticolonial struggle, Halimi's mother, Fortunée, reproducing General Hubert Lyautey's policy of "pacification," wonders: "What evil did we do to these Arabs? Why are they making up these stories? . . . If they are not happy, they have to leave!" (Halimi 1988: 74).

During the German occupation of Tunisia in World War II, the young Halimi wonders at first how "victims of racism [Arabs] ally themselves with Hitler and *Mein Kampf*," but she quickly learns from her Uncle Jacques that this was part of a geopolitical game, in which the colonized finds himself forced to "utilize to his advantage the game of contradictory objectives, in a given power struggle situation" (Halimi 1988: 71). Rather than seeing Arab sympathy for Hitler in North Africa as evidence of Arab anti-Semitism against Jews as many contemporary historians have argued, it is French racism against Arabs which made Hitler seem attractive to the colonized Arabs. After relocating in Paris to pursue a law degree, Halimi discovers the hidden anti-Semitism of those communists who make "generous big speeches on equality, colonialism and racism" (Halimi 1988: 82). From Mme Delrue, the friend of her landlady in Paris, she learns that neither Jews nor Arabs are native to North Africa; "Semites from elsewhere" (Halimi 1988: 87)—the same "elsewhere" Israelis and Palestinians use today to denativize and delegitimize each other's national claims.

In the 1950s, Halimi's French citizenship and professional training as a lawyer have allowed her to enter politics and be *femme-sujet* (i.e., a woman-subject who is not afraid of entering the male world of politics, whether in France or North Africa; Halimi 1988: 240). Because she was associated with the French intellectual Left, Halimi has been able to cross gender boundaries and be the interlocutor of Messali Hadj, Habib Bourguiba and Mehdi Ben Barka. Swimming with President Bourguiba in Carthage, she discovers to her dismay that he did not approve of her involvement with the Algerian cause. Enraged, he shouted: "Enough of Algeria! . . . After all you are Tunisian . . . Do not forget it! *Enti tana*, you belong to us" (Halimi 1988: 219). What is important here is not Bourguiba's lack of Arab solidarity with his Algerian neighbors—after all this is a well-documented fact which was the cause of his rift with his political rival Salah Ben Youssef in Tunisia and the Egyptian leader Gamel Abdul Nasser in the 1950s and 1960s—but rather the ambiguity in his statement "you belong to us." In Halimi's text, *"enti tana"* is translated in French as a patronizing or patriarchal reminder that as a woman she is the property of the Tunisian man/nation. From Bourguiba's perspective, however, Halimi's involvement in the Algerian Revolution is a form of national betrayal! Only Tunisia as a nation-state exists, this is why he reads Halimi only as a Tunisian, not even as a French citizen. In the postcolonial context of the 1960s, only allegiance to the nation-state is recognized as a form of responsible citizenship: if Halimi's involvement with the FLN—a fellow "Arab" and "Islamic" nationalist movement (on the strategic level at least)—did not win the approval of President Bourguiba, then Memmi's Frenchness and especially his support for Israel and the Zionist movement can only be constructed as a betrayal of his Tunisianness. In contrast with the current Tunisian intelligentsia, the political leadership of the 1960s had unwillingly repressed the complex ethnic and religious identities of its citizens in the name of secularism and unique allegiance to the nation-state. In the first years of independence, Bourguiba's preoccupation was with nation building through education, economic and social reforms only; minority rights, constitutional reform, or what we call today global citizenship did not figure in his political agenda.

The duality of Halimi's roots is expressed through the metaphors of milk and the orange tree. While milk is the symbol for her forced Frenchification through a matrilineal line, the orange tree is the umbilical cord which connects her to her African and Judeo-Arabic Tunisian roots through an exclusively agnatic line. She still remembers how her paternal grandfather Babah "drags her for a walk under the orange trees" (Halimi 1988: 25) to which he bestowed all the "possible virtues" from the "incomparable perfume" of their leaves to their *"maazar"* (orange blossom). Deprived of the "sun" and "the warm soil" of her doting father, Halimi, like a transplanted orange tree, can no longer claim to grow "solid roots." Settled in France since 1945, what remains of her Arabitude except "the couscous [that] ties [her] to [her] childhood" (Halimi 1988: 379) and the few Arabic words of endearment she learned from her father? In contrast with Memmi who defines Jewishness as an immemorial objective condition of oppression, Halimi's novel presents Tunisian Judeo-Arabic identity as a historical process, and as such, it is born, renewed, transformed and terminated according to the laws of historical change.

Bouraoui's work is part of the new postmodern Francophone Tunisian literature that is deeply rooted in Sufi philosophy. A secular Muslim poet and critic who lived in Tunisia and France before settling in Canada, Bouraoui's political commitment is geared toward a global crusade against all originary narratives including the myths of Arabism, Tunisianism and Islamism. Against the Tunisian nationalist myth of Elissa, he locates national identity in the very notion of *émigressence* (i.e., in change, renewal or the very act of border crossing). In contrast with the Tunisian political leadership which deployed political Islam and Arabism as ideological tools to gain legitimacy during the anticolonial struggle, Bouraoui deploys Sufi Islam to call for political pluralism in the postcolonial era. As the pun on *Je* and *Jeu* suggests in an untitled poem, the *tawhid* (God's oneness and uniqueness) is only a trick of the eye/I, for only through the ninety-nine names of the Divine (i.e. multiplicity) is the essence of the One made visible.[19] This Sufi *émigressence* from the human to the Divine, from the self to the other, from the visible to the invisible realm is what informs Bouraoui's views on the Israeli-Palestinian conflict and his antinationalist reading of Tunisia's identity.

In "Attachment," neither the Palestinians nor the Israelis are "castrated."[20] The Promised Land appears as an "illusion," a "propaganda," with no spiritual salvation, for the blind chant the "psalms of God," while behind, in their "sand castles," they pour the oil of hatred. Because in French the word *"essence"* refers to both oil and origin, it can be inferred that it is in this originary and essentialist thinking that Bouraoui locates the roots of the Israeli-Palestinian conflict, as each side believes themselves to be the chosen ones, the only legitimate heirs to the land God promised Abraham. In replacing the originary narratives underlying the discourses of Zionism, Arabism or what Benslama calls *islamessence*[21] with the postmodern notion of *émigressence*—a migratory subjectivity that derives from the Sufi destabilization of the sign—Bouraoui rewrites the Israeli-Palestinian conflict as a question of justice that has been thwarted by the originary myths of identity. *"Paysure,"* the title of Section III in *Émigressence*, constructs the Israeli-Palestinian conflict, not as a racial or religious strife as Memmi has argued, but as a land dispute as the pun on the French words *"pays"* (land/home/country), *"paix"* (peace), and *"sure"* (certain/guaranteed) suggests.

Bouraoui's experience of exile and marginalization undermines Memmi's claim that only the Jew was subjected to discrimination and oppression in postindependence Tunisia. What Memmi constructs as discrimination or anti-Semitism is what Bouraoui refers to ad nauseam as the despair of postcoloniality. The "supreme Father[s]" of the nation moved neither by "prayer" nor the cries of "injustice."[22] Building on Aimé Césaire's famous pun on negritude as phallic (*debout*) and castrated (*de boue*),[23] he suggests that the dream of postcoloniality has turned into mud ("*âge de boue*"; Bouraoui 1992: 84) as the "Governors of Nausea have betrayed the miracle of the word" (Bouraoui 1992: 77) and transformed the dream of "the communal we" into *"perforated cards of Com-pétences."* The French puns on *"com"* and *"con"* and *"pétence"* and *"pétance"* dismiss postcoloniality as the magnified farts of an idiotic and incompetent political leadership. In "Maghreb Dream,"[24] the narrator is confronted with "two giant swords" barring his "path." While his father retires from the outside world to review his life "behind a window pane," the son feels that some "invisible hands" have placed on his "shoulders a white burnous" and pushed him into exile and symbolic death in Europe's "snowy land." Bouraoui's experience of exclusion and marginalization in postindependence Tunisia shows that Muslims Arabs were subjected to the same mechanisms of oppression as the Jews. If Jewishness is an objective condition of oppression as Memmi argues, then Bouraoui's literature of exile, discrimination and marginalization in postcolonial Tunisia is prototypical of Tunisian Jewish *écriture*, a statement which is paradoxical only if we hold on to the essentialist racial and ethnic values underlying Memmi's theory of Jewishness.

A psychoanalyst by education and training and a self-declared secular Muslim, Benslama is a politically committed writer who is engaged on multiple fronts: against "le circus Islamicus of the theo-scientific jugglers" (Benslama 2005: 18–25); "the modernity of the ignoramous"; "religious intoxication" bent on "hate, romantic sacrifice and self-destruction"; violence of the Islamic nation-state; and the political opportunism of Western governments who support Islamic despotic regimes while posing as apostles of human rights (Benslama 2005: 93). In *Déclaration d'insoumission*, Benslama calls for the imperative need to distinguish Islam, as the name of a religion, from Islam as an entire civilization that is "constituted of multiple cultures and of an irreducible human diversity" (Benslama 2005: 23). In contrast with secular Arab Muslim leaders who adopted state policies which opposed secularism to Islam, Benslama, to face the increasing threat of Islamism, finds it "urgent" that that the disciples of secularism organize and place themselves within an "Islamic reference" to signal their "break-up with the logic of mythical religious identity" (Benslama 2005: 66–67) claimed by Islamists. Rather than originating in Islamic scriptures, the "causes of Islamic extremism" are rooted in a catastrophe on the level of language, which can no longer translate for the people their immediate historical experience.[25] One way of combating Islamic extremism and establishing a free society is to question and challenge through historicization of language the four constituent parts of the Islamic self claimed by Islamists: one religion (Islam), one language (Arabic), one text (the Quran) and the national.[26] Excavating the historical archives of Islamic memory, it is in Ibn 'Arabi's mystical "dessentialization" of the term "Muslim" that Benslama finds a precedent of Muslims who refused to submit to the religion of submission, as Islam is reductively understood in Islamist and Orientalist narratives. Contrary to Orthodox explanations which translate it as "submission" to the will of God, the word Islam derives from *slm*, a root with three consonants and endless ramifications such as "to save," "to cure," "to greet," "to make peace," "to receive/welcome," "to reconcile" and even "to give a kiss" (Benslama 2002: 29). In "*Désir Ardent*," a poem by Ibn Arabi, a Muslim is not one who submits to *islamessence*—submission to the will of God—but one whose religion is love, whose faith is accommodating of all forms of otherness: heathen images, the tables of the Torah, Christian convents, pagan temples and even prairies for gazelles. Against the mainstream Muslim narrative which holds Ishmael as the sacrificial lamb, Ibn 'Arabi holds in his *Bezels of Wisdom* that Isaac was the son that Abraham saw in his dream, not Ishmael.[27] It is from the interchangeability of Ishmael and Isaac in Sufi mysticism and from the linguistic "arborescence" (Benslama 2005: 28–29) or différance rooted in the etymology of the word "Islam" that Benslama tackles the Israeli-Palestinian conflict and revisits the Holocaust (Benslama 2002: 28). In European history, "the Mussulman"[28] of the Nazi concentration camps came to "designate" not Muslims but paradoxically those Jews who give themselves up to their "executioners" and lose all "sparkles of humanity" (Benslama 2005: 29).

For Benslama, both the Semite and the anti-Semite are gendered. While Nazi anti-Semitic propaganda focused on protecting the non-Semitic German woman from the Jewish male, in the Bosnian genocide, the Serbs raped the Semitic Muslim woman to humiliate the Semitic Muslim male. Because "woman" is often perceived as the female body of the nation, she becomes "the genetic code or 'genos' that the enemy tries to take over" (Benslama 2005: 37–39). If the Serbs in Bosnia-Herzegovina held hostage the Muslim women they raped until an advanced stage of pregnancy, it is for the purpose of inflicting humiliation on the Muslim male enemy by making his genealogy impure.

In contrast with Memmi, who invented an immemorial Islamic anti-Semitism in the aftermath of the the Yom Kippur War, Benslama makes a distinction between traditional anti-Judaism (exemplified in the *Israeliyat* narratives told by Medieval Muslim chroniclers[29]) and the contemporary European anti-Semitism which has recently become part of Arabic nationalist rhetoric, as illustrated in the recent controversy in Morocco over the *Mudawana* reforms that Islamists dismissed as a Zionist conspiracy to victimize the Muslim woman (Benslama 2005: 38). For Benslama, anti-Semitism is both a gendered and a historically situated discourse that gets reinvented, passed on and internalized even by those who have been dubbed Semites by others.

For Benslama, the Israeli-Palestinian conflict is not an ethnic problem, but rather a question of justice (Benslama 2005: 42) that has been thwarted by modern "nationalist pathologies" (Benslama 2005: 41) and the games of monotheist identity characteristic of Christianity, Judaism and Islam. Initially, the Palestinians had their share of responsibility as they have refused the existence of the state of Israel and rejected the partition plan of 1947. However, things changed in 1988 when the Palestinians recognized and conceded to Israel 78 percent of historical Palestine. The failure of the Oslo Accords, for Benslama, cannot solely be attributed to Palestinian violence, but also to the continued construction of new settlements in the Palestinian occupied territories. Rather than reading Palestinian martyrdom as an intrinsic part of their faith, Benslama argues that it is Palestinian nationalism which deployed the language of religious sacrifice to justify and sublimate death and "despise for the other" in the name of the nation-state (Benslama 2005: 44–45), not the other way round. The resolution to the Israeli-Palestinian conflict and the battle with Islamic extremism are to be held not just within the civic context of free society, global responsibility and fair application of international law, but also through a careful examination and historicization of language.

In conclusion, the Israeli-Palestinian conflict did have a strong impact on the politics of self-identity in the Francophone literature of the Tunisian diaspora. Even though situated on the Left of the political spectrum and former eminent figure in Tunisia's anticolonial struggle, the Arab-Israeli Wars of 1967–1973 and Memmi's disillusionment with the rise of the postcolonial Islamic nation-states, which recognized only Arabic and Islam as the official state language and religion, made him reinvent and transform the religious tensions between the Jewish minority and Muslim majority in precolonial, colonial and postcolonial Tunisia as an immemorial racial strife between Arabs and Jews; thus, obfuscating the Ottoman colonial context in which both the "Jew" and the "Arab" were inferior native Others. Obliterating the French colonial policies which contributed to denativing North African Jews by giving them French citizenship,[30] he now argues that it is Arab/Islamic anti-Semitism that led to the departure of the Algerian Jews (Memmi 1973: 12, 53), not their fighting along French colonial forces in the streets of Algiers during the fight for independence, as he formerly argued in *Colonizer and Colonized*.[31] In contrast with Memmi's androcentric reading of the Semite/anti-Semite, Halimi and Benslama locate the latter in a gendered nationalist Eurocentric discourse which oppresses both the Arab and the Jew, male and female. In the very act of claiming an Arab Jewish identity, Halimi paradoxically declares it obsolete with the death of her father. While Memmi constructs Arabitude and Jewishness as binary opposites, Halimi, resisting the racial and ethnic essentialism characterizing originary narratives, views Tunisian Judeo-Arabic culture identity as a historical process (i.e., in terms of fluidity, transformation, renewal and death). Rather than being an ethnic or religious problem as often presented in the Eurocentric, Zionist or Islamo-centric accounts, the Israeli-Palestinian conflict is constructed by Bouraoui and Benslama as a crisis of justice and language. No long-term peaceful solution to the Israeli-Palestinian conflict can be finalized without a historicization of language, its symbols, its fissures, its absences and presences.

NOTES

1. I am keeping the original French text because the English translation "oil pours hatred" does not fully capture Hédi Bouraoui's pun and critique of racial essentialism. In French, *l'essence* has the dual meaning of combustible fuel and ethnic origin. The pun implies that the quest for pure origin is what is inflaming the current conflict in the Middle East. Otherwise indicated all subsequent translations from French texts are mine. See Hédi

Bouraoui, *Echosmos* (Oakville: Canadian Society for the Comparative Study of Civilizations and Mosaic Press, 1986), 156–57.
2. Slavoj Zizek, "A Glance into the Archives of Islam," *The Antinomies of Tolerant Reason*, page 1. par. 3, available at http://www.lacan.com/zizarchives.htm (Accessed July 14, 2008).
3. For this subject see Gil Anidjar's chapter "Muslims (Hegel, Freud, Auschwitz)," in *The Jew, the Arab: A History of the Enemy* (Stanford, CA: Stanford University Press, 2003).
4. Anidjar, *Jew*, 131.
5. *The Pillar of Salt*, Trans. Edouard Roditi (Boston: Beacon Press, 1992), 30.
6. Memmi, *Pillar*, 49. Subsequent references to this volume will be indicated parenthetically in the text.
7. See Anijdar's discussion of European anti-Semitism in *Semites: Race, Religion, Literature* (Stanford, CA: Stanford University Press, 2008).
8. The "Semitic Spirit," for Ernest Renan, has in fact only two "pure forms": "the Hebraic or Mosaic form, and the Arabic or Islamic form." Ancient and vengeful, both Muhammad and Solomon are incapable of maintaining a state. See *Histoire Générale et système comparé des langues sémitiques* (Paris: Calmann Lévy, 1877), 94.
9. Étienne Burnet, *Loin des Icônes*, in Dugas's *Tunisie: Rêve de partages* (Lonrai: Omnibus, 2005), 997.
10. *Juifs et arabes* (Saint-Amand: Gallimard, 1973), 12.
11. Memmi, *Juifs*, 13. Subsequent references to this volume will be indicated parenthetically in the text.
12. I am using the available English translation of chapter 2 in *Juifs et arabes*. "What is an Arab Jew?" *Jimena: Jews Indigenous to the Middle East and North Africa, February 1975*, available at http://www.jimena.org.memmi.htm (Accessed June 18, 2008).
13. Hélène Cixous, "The Laugh of the Medusa," in *New French Feminisms*, Elaine Marks and Isabelle de Courtivron, eds. (Amherst, MA: The University of Massachusetts Press, 1980), 206.
14. Memmi, "Who is an Arab Jew?" 1. Subsequent references to this volume will be indicated parenthetically in the text.
15. For this subject, see Waciny Larej's call for state responsibility in his post-civil war Algerian novel *Balconies of the North Sea* or *Shurufat bahr al shamal* (Beirut: Dar al Adab, 2002).
16. Halimi, *Le Lait de L'oranger* (Paris: Gallimard, 1988), 108–109.
17. Extracts from a published interview, "Femmes et citoyennes, du droit de vote à l'exercice du pouvoir," Patricia Latour, Monique Houssin and Madia Tovar (Les éditions de l'atelier/Le temps des cerises, 1995), available at http://www.amiens.iufm.fr/amiens/histoire/femmes/biblio/Biographie_Halimi_Gisele.rtf (Accessed September 13, 2009).
18. Halimi, *Lait*, 68. Subsequent references to this volume will be indicated parenthetically in the text.
19. Bouraoui, *Émigressence* (Ottawa: Les Éditions du Vermillon, 1992), 61.
20. Bouraoui, *Émigressence*, 156–157. Subsequent references to this volume will be indicated parenthetically in the text.
21. See Benslama, *Déclaration d'insoumission: à l'usage des musulmans et de ceux qui ne le sont pas* (Paris: Flammarion, 2005).
22. Benslama, *Déclaration d'insoumission*, 77. Subsequent references to this volume will be indicated parenthetically in the text.
23. Aimé Césaire, *Notebook of a Return to My Native Land* (Paris: Présence Africaine 1968).

24. *Echosmos* (Oakville: Canadian Society for the Comparative Study of Civilizations & Mosaic Press, 1986), 81.
25. Benslama, *La Psychanalyse à l'épreuve de l'Islam* (Mayenne: Aubier, 2002), 22.
26. Benslama, *Psychanalyse*, 32. Subsequent references to this volume will be indicated parenthetically in the text.
27. Ibn 'Arabi, *The Bezels of Wisdom*. Trans. R.W. J. Austin (Mahwah, NJ: Paulist Press, 1980), 98–99.
28. For Anidjar, the figure of the Mussulman stands for the stage where the Eurocentric categories of the Jew and the Arab overlap and collapse. See, *The Jew, the Arab: History of the Enemy*.
29. See Anidjar's Chapter 4 "'Eber va-'Arab (The Arab Literature of the Jews), in *Semites*, 91.
30. In contrast with Memmi, Richard Ayoun and Bernard Cohen maintain that neither the creation of Israel nor the rise of Arab nationalism caused the denativization of Algerian Jews. It was rather their acceptance of *la Francité*, i.e., belief in the superiority and virtues of French civilization. See *Les Juifs d'Algérie: 2000 ans d'histoire* (Paris: Lattès, 1982), 142–152.
31. Memmi, *Colonizer and Colonized*, Trans. Howard Greenfield (Boston, Beacon Press, 1967), xiv.

7 Otherwise Occupied
The Israeli-Palestinian Conflict in the Francophone Cinema

Lincoln Z. Shlensky

An argument advanced in the mid-1970s by Jean-Luc Godard in his provocative essay film *Ici et ailleurs* is that Europe and its historically romanticized or demonized Others, such as the Palestinians, are linked—as he puts it, "chained"—together by the images they produce of and for one another. The problem, as the film indicates, is that the makers and consumers of these images fail to recognize that such fantasized constructions of the Other tend to conceal disavowed representations of themselves. Implicating his own earlier representational praxis, Godard suggests that Europe's fascination with, and projection onto, the Other reveals a narcissistic belief in its own capacity for objectivity; it is this Western fantasy of detachment that forecloses critical self-scrutiny and, even more importantly for Godard in his Dziga Vertov Group years, the possibility of revolutionary action informed by active political engagement with ideas that seem to come from "elsewhere." More than thirty years have passed since Godard and his collaborator, Anne-Marie Miéville, made *Ici et ailleurs*, but arguably public discourse and the visual media rely ever more heavily on the distancing effect of screen memories—visual shortcuts that seal off here and now from there and then—to truncate critical historical analysis and cultural self-reflection. In the Francophone context, it is instructive to return to the example chosen by Godard to illustrate his point. For France, and more generally for Francophone Europe, the outbreak of the Palestinian Second Intifada has reactivated a set of social conflicts whose historical and geopolitical connection to the Israeli-Palestinian conflict is only indirect, but whose ramifications in the media and the public sphere indicate a complex symbolic linkage between Middle Eastern politics and Francophone culture. This linkage remains largely unarticulated, and its meaning veiled, in Francophone public discourse and particularly in the visual media, where screen memories and graphic snapshots of historically disjointed *événements* often substitute for analysis.

The effect of the screen memory is evident in what is perhaps the most enduring imagery of the Second Intifada—the death of a Palestinian boy named Muhammed Al-Durra at the Netzarim junction in Gaza in 2000, apparently a victim of Israeli crossfire—captured by a Palestinian camera operator employed by the France 2 television network. As this imagery circulated nationally and internationally, few observers posed questions about its status as an image. How was French television in a position to capture the image in the first place, why did the incident so quickly achieve popular notoriety and media staying power, why has its historical veracity been the subject of such vehement ensuing controversy, and what do the images of Al-Durra's death say about the society for which they have become so memorable? Those who have raised questions about the incident, such as Philippe Bensoussan and Jacques Tarnero in their polemical film *Décryptage* (2003), focus on it as evidence of the Francophone media's putative bias against Israel. While that claim is weakly supported through inference, what is more telling is that in analyzing the Al-Durra imagery, Bensoussan and Tarnero fail to consider the contributing historical causes for the French fascination with the incident or the reasons for the growing polarization of the Francophone Jewish and Muslim communities since the Intifada's onset. The Al-Durra episode thus continues to serve as one among a series of historical screen images widely remembered but little interrogated, in its signifying reticence like "un flot d'images et de sons qui cachent du silence" ("a flood of images and of sounds that hide silence"), as Godard's early film remarks of the Palestinian corpses exhibited in the French media following Black September.[1]

The Francophone cinema has offered some important correctives to the decontextualizing and ahistorical tendencies within public and media culture, and a number of recent films that touch on or directly address the Israeli-Palestinian conflict can be counted as among the most provocative of these revisionist works.[2] Filmmakers of the generation following Godard's, including Karin Albou, Philippe Faucon and Michael Haneke, have recently directed dramatic films that address the topic of the conflict tangentially but with an acute awareness of its cultural significance in the Francophone context. In addition to these recent dramatic features, productions by three renowned French auteurists—Chris Marker, Claude Lanzmann and Jean-Luc Godard—address the Israeli-Palestinian conflict explicitly in a remarkable series of essay films made between 1960 and 2004. The common thread among these dramatic and essay films is that in recalling to public awareness the Israeli-Palestinian conflict, each aims to reveal the symbolic overlays and displacements with which narratives of national identity are constructed and collective history is codified. The Israeli-Palestinian conflict serves as a reference point for these filmmakers, I argue, because it distills while displacing many of the internal contradictions that Francophone culture, and the French Republic in particular, historically have expressed in defining the nation as a stable and unproblematic unit of collective identity.

These contradictions reached a point of crisis in the aftermath of the Second World War, when liberation struggles in colonies long considered French, and Vichy participation in sending Jews to the Nazi death camps, similarly indicated that the self-evident meaning of French national identity and the moral bulwarks of republican egalitarianism could no longer be assumed.[3] The overthrow of the Vichy regime and the nominal end of colonization, however, did not resolve these tensions. On the one hand, as Marcel Ophüls elaborated in his documentary *Le Chagrin et la pitié* (1964), it was only belatedly that France came to recognize the extent of popular support for the Vichy government and also the casual anti-Jewish discrimination in which ordinary French citizens participated.[4] In a recent television documentary, *Comme un juif en France* (2007), Yves Jeuland updates Ophüls's critique by showing how even postwar cinema participated in the purging of French memory regarding the deportation of French Jews, and that this forgetting arguably continues in dismissive official and public responses to recent anti-Jewish incidents. On the other hand, as Todd Shepard perceptively points out, the liberation of Algeria also marks the onset in France of a newly racialized conception of the essential differences between "Algerians" and "the French."[5] This racialized conception of otherness undoubtedly informs much of the current discourse on Muslim difference within Francophone Europe and conditions the surprising volatility attaching to representations of the Israeli-Palestinian conflict in France.

The dramatic and essay films under examination here locate the indelible traces of these historical social dilemmas in Francophone representations of the Israeli-Palestinian conflict. The dramas convey a stark recognition that the public discourse on the Israeli-Palestinian conflict in Francophone culture remains preoccupied with the clash "over there" because it so closely mirrors, while displacing and thus sealing off, unresolved anxieties and antagonisms of Francophone identity in Europe. In the essay film lineage, the Middle East conflict has been addressed more directly but, for Marker and Lanzmann, the connections between it and the predicament of Francophone identity are much more attenuated and must be worked out by the viewer. Godard is alone in having tackled the conflict as an explicit theme twice in the course of thirty years; his approach is to create formal disjunctions in the film work itself that implicate filmmaker and film viewer in a series of political intertexts and citations that never resolve into a consoling cultural whole. Using a variety of strategies, each of these films suggests that the Middle East conflict remains a fetishized cultural flashpoint because it evokes, in distorted form, an inarticulate memory of intimate betrayals in Francophone Europe. The problem of traumatic memory, as Joshua Cole points out in his analysis of the meaning of torture in the Algerian War, is that it implies an "unspeakable" intimacy, rather than an irreconcilable distance, between a conflict's agonists.[6] These films acknowledge the betrayal of that as yet unavowed intimacy and, in doing so, they suggest a means of reconciliation—if not between the antagonists themselves, then perhaps nonetheless between the Francophone world's present and its past.

The Israeli-Palestinian conflict is little more than a background theme for the dramatic films this chapter examines. When they address the Israeli-Palestinian conflict, they generally do so, like Philippe Faucon's *Dans la vie* (2007) does, as a cautionary tale of political intransigence and senseless enmity that symbolizes the extreme limits of strained intercommunal relationships and failed national coherence. For these narrative films, the increasingly globalized film narrative itself is a problem because it tends to equate cultural identity with political commitments, rather than challenging such a simplistic linkage. As Faucon's film suggests, however, narrative representation can also be part of a socially reparative solution if suppressed cultural *histoires* are addressed in a dialogical, nonhierarchical relationship. In *Dans la vie*, such a relationship develops between two Algerian émigrés in France—a disabled elderly Jewish woman and a devout Muslim housewife with whom she forms an unlikely friendship. What Esther and Halima bond over is their ability to discuss their family histories in Algeria and thereby to nurture a tenuous mutual understanding that is the antithesis, in Faucon's film, of the intractable fighting between Palestinians and Israelis that forms a noisy quasi-documentary background to the film's intimate drama. The explosive symbolic resonance of the Israeli-Palestinian conflict in France, in Faucon's presentation of it, amplifies the silence of the still unspoken history of shattered relationships between Jews and Muslims in the Algerian colonial context.

Whereas Faucon's film refers constantly to the Israeli-Palestinian conflict as an extreme case of collective social dissolution, Karin Albou's modest and nuanced narrative about a Sephardic Orthodox Jewish family living in the Paris suburbs, *La Petite Jérusalem* (2005), barely references the politics of the Middle East. The film does, however, elucidate some of the cultural and political dilemmas facing French Jews, and it questions whether the political reconciliation that Faucon envisions may ever be possible in the context of France's cultural wars. Albou, herself the daughter of Algerian-born parents, sets her film in Sarcelles, a dreary *banlieue* of Paris that is home to a large number of North African immigrants, including many Jews. The film's eighteen-year-old protagonist, Laura (portrayed by Fanny Valette), struggles to balance the tensions between her observant Jewish family and her own passion for Kantian secular rationalism. A series of crises erupt that unsettle the precarious equilibrium between faith, passion and rationality that Laura maintains, including her unexpected attraction to an undocumented Muslim immigrant and an assault on her brother-in-law, Ariel (portrayed by Bruno Todeschini), that evokes similar attacks on Jews, mainly by young North African Muslim men, in the early 2000s. In *La Petite Jérusalem*, the crises Laura and her family face pose questions not only for the cultural identity of Jews in France but also for republican political values. The Orthodoxy practiced by Laura's family sequesters them within a community of like-minded religious adherents who seem to reject the traditional role Jews have played as a nonnational cultural group in the Republic since Napoleon I enfranchised them in 1808. The increasing untenability of such a cultural solution is suggested when, at the end of the film, Ariel and Mathilde (portrayed by Elsa Zylberstein) decide to emigrate to Israel. Their quasi-national conception of an ideal Jewish community has become impossible in France, and their decision raises the implicit question whether the term "French Jew" can be anything but an oxymoron.[7]

Albou's film does not suggest any resolution to such conflicts, but it does offer one subtle comment—if, in fact, a comment it is—on the kind of cultural-nationalist resolution to which the family is drawn in emigrating to Israel. In one of the final scenes of the film, as Ariel and Mathilde are preparing to leave their apartment, their children play a game of house on the apartment floor, trying to imagine what it will be like to live in their new residence in Israel. The youngest son plays with a toy airplane, which, to the dismay of all, he uses to suddenly destroy the house his sisters have built. Though only possibly intended as such, this brief scene concatenates the breakup of the family's French home with the house demolitions in the occupied Palestinian territories that have inflamed so many Arab immigrants in the Parisian suburbs. In my reading, this scene offers the provocative comment, otherwise unvoiced in Albou's film, that political quandaries raised by French ethno-religious tensions cannot simply be resolved by displacing them onto another context in which, as the young boy unwittingly indicates, a different set of political struggles and forms of violence prevail.

Michael Haneke's 2005 thriller, *Caché*, considers similar questions from a different perspective in suggesting that cultural minorities may not be the sole victims of France's unresolved conflicts of national identity. His film interrogates the consequences of collective forgetting in a way that Albou's film does not. In recalling to memory the events of October 17, 1961, when French police beat and killed hundreds of Algerian protestors taking part in a political demonstration in Paris, Haneke's film shows how accreted layers of historical denial increasingly distort the present as long as collective guilt and responsibility remain unacknowledged.[8] *Caché*'s plot concerns the disruption of the comfortable lives of a celebrity television journalist, Georges (portrayed by Daniel Auteuil), and his family by a haunting secret that Georges thought he had left behind about his childhood rejection of an adopted Algerian brother whose own parents, in turn, had been killed in the 1961 massacre. In addition to its thinly veiled allegorical denunciation of France's collective forgetting of the inconvenient past, the film also critiques the nation's present-day disregard for its North African immigrants and their children. It was completed in the year following France's passage of the *laïcité*, or secularity, law of 2004, which banned Muslim headcoverings from public schools, and at a moment when tensions between French Muslims and Jews was at its highest.

Yet Haneke's film intimates that the volatile present can only be understood as an oblique reflection of the unresolved past. In one of the film's most tense scenes, Georges and his wife Anne (portrayed by Juliette Binoche) become fearful when they realize they have inexplicably lost track of their teenage son. As Anne frantically telephones their son's friends and Georges impassively broods, Haneke places a television set conspicuously, but not disruptively, in the center background of the film's frame, from which vantage we, along with Georges, watch the day's foreign events newscast. The news broadcast proceeds from reports about the continuing Iraq War to the Abu Ghraib trial; the reports continue with news of an air attack by the Israeli military on Palestinians in Gaza, resulting in the deaths of twelve Palestinians, including several children, and the wounding of fifty others. The bloody face of a Palestinian victim is carried into the view of the television news camera—the first actual image of physical violence in Haneke's film (see Figure 7.1). In this short but densely staged sequence, Haneke manages to link France's colonial history, and what he obviously views as its bourgeois self-preoccupation, with the contemporary global map of violence in which Europe is implicated, including the Israeli-Palestinian conflict. Very few other recent films have so suggestively extended the chain of culpability from the European context, and the West generally, to local conflagrations which, as Haneke's film indicates, all too easily come to appear as mere background noise barely noticeable in the midst of domestic national and personal dramas from which such events appear to be dissociated.

While the dramatic films discussed above concern themselves with the lacunae or repressions of narrative representation, the essay films I will discuss next are more directly concerned with the question of citation. These

Figure 7.1 Michael Haneke's film, *Caché*.[9]

films tend to treat the problem of memory as one whose complications stem from the authority claimed by prior textual instances that overlay the present, constraining its meanings but also offering the potential for transgressive historical rereadings. The earliest of these essay films is Chris Marker's *Description d'un combat* (1960), which notably appeared in the same year as Hollywood's historical melodrama about the birth of Israel, Otto Preminger's *Exodus*. Despite the radical differences in form, Marker's film bears a minor resemblance to Preminger's in its thematic emphasis on the heroic successes of the new state in creating a living nation out of a broken people, the Jews, upon a barren and empty landscape, against daunting odds and at great human cost. Camels and modern road signs; an Arab youth, Ali, to whom Marker attributes the wish to think of his humble rolling cart as a race car; a young Jewish art student, whom the film presents as an appealing cipher of a future Israeli identity—each of these, for Marker, is a visual sign of the radical break *and* continuity with the past that the young Israeli state symbolizes.

Aside from cart-rolling Ali on the Haifa hillside, and an impoverished Arab girl in Nazareth, who represents for Marker the social inequalities Israel has just begun to address, there are almost no other mentions of the Palestinians. They are an absent presence signified only synecdochally by these two youths, and by the runes of ruins displayed in the first scene of the film: a burnt out tank, framed by Marker as if it were an abstract modernist sculpture, set on a sand dune, pointing to Israel's birth pains but not directly to an Arab counternarrative, let alone a Palestinian Other. Like most other Europeans prior to the discursive shift linked to the 1967 Arab-Israeli War, Marker considers the indigenous Arab inhabitants of Palestine to be incidental to the European historical narrative in which the founding of a Jewish state in the biblical Land of Israel only can be seen as the redemptive answer to Europe's moral fall. The film does, nevertheless, articulate an ideological perspective that implicates Europe in Middle Eastern history, arguing that the various Western nations, including France through its "indifference," are responsible for the flight of Jewish refugees to Palestine and the consequent need for a Jewish state. "This is what *we* [Europeans] have done," Marker intones, and he identifies a corresponding moral conundrum in the aftermath of Israel's establishment: "[t]he greatest injustice," he concludes, "is the denial of [Israel's] right to be unjust, because injustice weighs more heavily [on the Jews after the Holocaust]." Marker thus almost prophetically sounds a theme which insistently would come to haunt the wider Francophone discourse on Israel and the Palestinians: that Israel's moral rights derive from Europe's legacy of anti-Jewish oppression, and not from the colonial problematic in which it has since become embroiled with the Palestinians. Marker's statement presupposes a question he does not pose: can Israel ever be an "ordinary" nation, and Israelis a "normal" people? This is the question that Claude Lanzmann would ask more directly, although his films do so with what seems, in retrospect, to be more than Marker's merely anachronistic affirmation of Israel's political claims.

Lanzmann's *Pourquoi Israël* (1974) and *Tsahal* (1994) are the bookends of his triptych of essay films, the centerpiece of which is *Shoah* (1985), his monumental nine-hour treatment of the Holocaust. Lanzmann has said that he does not consider *Shoah* to be a documentary, and the other two films in the trilogy, which deal with the phenomenology of the Jewish state, are not either.[10] *Pourquoi Israël* (the absence of a question mark in the title is intentional), although it was completed before *Shoah*, is Lanzmann's effort to explain why, in the wake of the Holocaust, Jews so greatly desired a Jewish state to restore a sense of normalcy to themselves as a people, and how the effort to achieve such normalcy is both necessary and impossible. He does this through interviews with Israelis of all stripes, from policemen to dockworkers, from Russian immigrants to Sephardic "Black Panther" activists and from leftist kibbutzniks to Orthodox Jewish settlers. *Tsahal* (the title is the Hebrew acronym for the Israeli military) effectively covers the same ground but focuses on the Israeli military's achievements and burdens, with the benefit of a twenty-year interval to bolster the state's sense of selfhood as less culturally tied to the past but no less haunted by its legacies of fear, isolation and cynicism.

Lanzmann's overriding concern for Jewish national identity in Israel may be explained, to a degree, by his participation in the political regrouping of 1960s Jewish activists on the French Left, who underwent what Yaïr Auron has described as a "processus de transition de 'radicaux juifs' en 'juifs radicaux.'"[11] This shift is linked in turn to their belated awareness of the specificity of the French Jewish experience during the Shoah.[12] It is difficult to say, of course, whether such collective dynamics can help explain Lanzmann's intense interest in the young Israeli state (and the "new Jew" evolving there), but the arc of his twenty-year oeuvre suggests the extent to which he construes Israel as the appropriate answer to, if not a consolation for, the trauma of the Holocaust. This may help to explain his strange, but also, as Auron's comment should remind us, commonplace, political trajectory: in 1960, Lanzmann was one of the principal authors, along with Maurice Blanchot and others, of the "Declaration on the Right to Insubordination in the War in Algeria," which announced French leftist intellectuals' solidarity with the rebellious Algerians, and with those French citizens who refused to participate in suppressing them.[13] Just over a decade later, Lanzmann began the first of his films about a place and a time when a formerly repressed group of people was in open rebellion against the past and against new enemies with whom it dubiously associated its historic subjugation. In these films, the insubordinate ones are the Jewish Israelis, who answer Europe's murderous legacy of xenophobia and scapegoating with a surprisingly vigorous national resurgence; the Palestinians—a people who, despite this redemptive narrative, are themselves insubordinate toward Lanzmann's anointed insubordinates—remain mute.

The director perhaps most renowned for his essay films, Jean-Luc Godard, would comprehend the intersection between the Middle East conflict and

French history entirely differently. In 1970, four years before Lanzmann's *Pourquoi Israël* ignored or discounted the question of Palestinian identity, Godard and his collaborator in the Vertov Group, Jean-Pierre Gorin, were commissioned by the Arab League to create a documentary about the Palestinians. The resulting production, *Jusqu'à la victoire*, documented the political aspirations and guerilla warfare tactics of the Palestinians, but it was never released because Godard and Gorin abandoned the project. They ended their collaboration two years later, but Godard decided to use the footage for a restructured film, *Ici et ailleurs* (1976), which launched a sharp critique of the idealism of the Vertov Group's political and aesthetic tenets. The film also offered an elaborate analysis of the problems entailed in Western representations of Third World liberation struggles, and captured the ironic perspective with which Godard viewed Israel's new dominance in Middle Eastern politics after the 1967 War. Godard and his collaborator on the film, Anne-Marie Miéville, were also intent on showing ideological connections between the alienated French working class and the marginalized Palestinian peasant fighters. They aimed to deflect the instrumentalizing gaze and idealist politics of liberal Europe, which projected the need for a revolution *ailleurs* but not *ici*. Such a politics, their film suggested, failed to account for the ways that modern media representations had reified the Palestinian struggle in discrete and digestible images produced for Western consumption. At the same time, the Western liberal romance with foreign struggles failed to appreciate how the French working class was similarly over-mediatized by the spectacles promulgated by television and consumerism.

Godard does not efface the images of armed struggle and the fervent revolutionary rhetoric that he had captured on film four years earlier, but he attempts to show in *Ici et ailleurs* why these images and sounds need to be treated with greater distance—as citations. This process of rethinking or rereading screen images never presupposes a direct relation between representation and political activism in the way that the Vertov Group might have done; there is no assumption that to show the revolution is to materially aid it. Instead, "en repensant à cela" ("in rethinking that," a phrase that reappears in a number of variations throughout the film), Godard argues against the internal coherence of any representational system, whether verbal or imagistic, in favor of the continuous slippage of textual citation.[14] "*Presque tous les acteurs sont morts*" ("almost all the actors are dead"), one of many didactic yet ironic intertitles that flash on screen during the film, ostensibly refers to Black September, but more subversively challenges the ways in which these "*acteurs*" come to be understood as representatives of a cause, as role-players in a film spectacle and as autonomous political agents. How, the film asks, can death itself be acknowledged in the context of cinematic representations or political discourses that can do nothing but appropriate it?[15] These epistemological problems are at the center of Godard's rhetorical and political project in *Ici et ailleurs*, and they point to his central concern: that filmmaking unaware of its own participation in the production of history is fundamentally deceptive. Godard's constructivist essay film technique is so startling precisely because the connections it draws between different historical events and times are so consciously artificial. There are also moments, however, when such tactics go badly awry, as when the film juxtaposes Hitler and Golda Meir, Israel's prime minister from 1969–1974, in a historically manipulative analogy (see Figure 7.2). The iconographic inversion is disquieting, as Godard intends it to be, yet it also slips all too easily into the traditionally Judeophobic rhetoric that simply inverts, this time with a negative valence, the claim for special treatment of the Jews. Perhaps just as problematically, by simply replacing the politically sanctified victimology of the Jews with a new mythos of the Israeli state as a perpetrator nation comparable to the Nazis, Godard's film fails to acknowledge the historical logic in which France and other nations were willing to grant the Israeli state a politically hallowed status in the first place as a form of atonement for unresolved French guilt. In seeking to interrogate the cinematic production of historical screen images, Godard thus needlessly obscures the Francophone historical role in fomenting conflicts such as that between Israel and the Palestinians.

It is surprising that Godard does not draw connections in *Ici et ailleurs* between the political disclaimers with which the Israeli-Palestinian conflict has been represented and France's involvement in the Algerian

Figure 7.2 Godard's film *Ici et ailleurs*.[16]

War, which he had dealt with as both a metaphorical culture war and an actual proxy war in *Le Petit Soldat* (completed in 1960 but banned in France until 1963). Godard may be attempting to correct this oversight in his most significant subsequent treatment of the Israeli-Palestinian conflict, *Notre musique* (2004). *Notre musique* is structured in three sections or "kingdoms," Hell, Purgatory and Heaven, in allusion to Dante's *Divine Comedy*. The first segment, Hell, presents a montage of sequences culled from cinema history that seem to echo Walter Benjamin's famous comment in the *Theses on the Philosophy of History* about the linkage between civilization and barbarism.[17] Godard's hallmark gesture of self-implication is reiterated in the film's second section, set during an artists' peace conference in postwar Sarajevo. In this present-day purgatory, the film becomes a quasi-narrative of missed encounters, in which, among other events, a young Israeli journalist, Judith Lerner (portrayed by Sarah Adler), attempts to arrange a conversation about "morals" between her grandfather in Israel and the man who had hidden him during the war, a Maquis who now serves as a jaundiced French ambassador (portrayed by Simon Eine). Meanwhile, a young Russian Jew also attending the conference, Olga Brodsky (portrayed by Nade Dieu), plans an act of violence that she will carry out in Tel Aviv. The film freely crosses genre lines; Godard himself appears at the conference to give a lecture on the imagery of violence, and the Palestinian poet Mahmoud Darwish and other literary figures read from their works and offer heady pronouncements on the failures of contemporary society and politics.

Notre musique's narrative humanizes Israelis and Jews—in addition to Judith and Olga, Godard's translator at the conference is a polyglot French Jew (portrayed by Rony Kramer)—in a way that *Ici et ailleurs* failed to do, and this is both the film's strength and its weakness. The humanizing gesture succeeds insofar as the film works against polarizing political discourses to reinscribe the Israeli-Palestinian conflict in a global historical framework that implicates Europe in the exemplary violent struggles within and beyond its hazily defined borders. Yet there lies a contradiction that the film cannot work out between its desire to humanize Jews and its corresponding acknowledgment that the West's historical fascination with the Palestinians continues to *de*humanize them. Citation is not in itself subversive, as the poet Darwish suggests during Godard's film in reading from the transcript of an interview he had actually given elsewhere comparing the Palestinians to the Trojans, whose claim to fame resides in losing the fabled war. Speaking apostrophically to Israel, Darwish laments, " . . . because Jews are the center of interest of the world . . . you defeated us, but you gave us renown. We are your propaganda ministry. The world is interested in you, not in us." The problem appears to be that Godard's humanizing gesture works against itself because he continues to speak of *the* Jews and *the* Palestinians, rather than simply Jews and Palestinians shorn of their archetypal symbolism. Godard, in short, cites the very historicism he had rejected in *Ici et ailleurs*, and in doing so he reintroduces in *Notre musique* the dehumanizing constructions he had sought to renounce. The film closes in the mode of lyrical mourning, with Olga, in the final Heaven sequence, playing the role of a ghost whose desperate act of (self-)representation—she has been shot dead by the police after issuing an empty threat to blow up an empty Tel Aviv film theater in the name of peace—has failed. Godard seems to acknowledge here the failure of his own project as well; even radical representation cannot actually deliver its own metatextual critique. Against expectation, the Israeli-Palestinian conflict suggests this perspective. The incommensurate historical narratives that this conflict activates form an aporia through which, paradoxically, Francophone public discourse can engage in the inconsolable—and in that sense ethical—mourning initiated by Godard's *Notre musique* and other recent Francophone films.

A number of successful younger filmmakers, mainly Israelis and Palestinians, have revitalized the essay film as a genre that can address the Israeli-Palestinian conflict without dehumanizing its antagonists. Their productions thus have offered new ways of thinking through the conundrums of collective memory and historical contextualization. Among the most notable of these directors are Elia Suleiman, Simone Bitton, Dan Geva and Amos Gitai. Perhaps the most obviously "Francophone" work made by one of these directors is a recent film by the Israeli Dan Geva, *Description of a Memory* (2006). Geva's film is not actually in French, but it is structured as a direct response to, and it quotes repeatedly from, Chris Marker's *Description d'un combat*. Geva's response to Marker's film, which he watched repeatedly while growing up in Israel, is to question the veracity and stability of the "signs" Marker had delineated and interpreted. Where Marker's film ingeniously collocates images in such a way as to release their incongruities, ironies and mundane uncanniness, Geva approaches his "much too promised land" with a greater degree of modesty (the exasperating absence of which he notes in Marker's film), and a politically jaundiced attitude that responds to what Geva sees as his own nation's destructive hubris.[18] Geva begins and ends his film with an unsettling shot of the director looking directly into the camera lens and screaming; it is a painful reminder that his film is a form of self-implicating mourning, and that it concerns a history too intimate, and too upsetting, for him to be able to adopt the ruminative and droll distance, much less the optimism, of Marker's film. Geva often shoots using a fish-eye lens, which at once unsettles his viewers in their sense of mastery over the image, and conveys the impression that there is more content and meaning in each framed shot than can be plausibly incorporated into the film's purview without distortion. He spends much of the film focusing on the noxious consequences of Israel's subjugation of the Palestinians and confiscation of their land; when filming around the Israeli-built separation barrier, he wonders whether he would be able to use X-rays in order to see the parallel, yet asymmetrically destructive, effects of these monolithic walls on both sides at once.

A similar such scene occurs in Simone Bitton's film, *Mur* (2004), which also tracks the violence of occupation through the symbolic yet material consequences of the Israeli separation wall. Bitton asks a young girl playing on the Israeli side of the wall—which is painted with a trompe l'oeil scene of bucolic tranquility—whether she is afraid to speak to the filmmaker. She replies that she is not afraid, because she has heard the filmmaker speaking in Hebrew and thus knows that she is Jewish. Bitton's film suggestively emphasizes the series of interpellations in which the young girl is already caught; many Arab Palestinians, of course, especially those among them who are Israeli citizens, also speak Hebrew. Yet Bitton subtly turns the questions around, hinting at her own personal background as a Moroccan-born Jew, and unexpectedly evokes the girl's repressed and ambivalent cultural identity: when Bitton asks her whether it isn't true that some Jews also speak Arabic, the young girl replies, first, that Jews certainly do not speak Arabic, and then, after a moment's hesitation, she admits that her own mother, in fact, speaks Arabic—but only at home. Geva and Bitton are both using the essay film form to trace a relation to history that is different from that articulated in the films of their cinematographic mentors and predecessors. These younger filmmakers are aware of their inability to incorporate history as narrative into their work because the only narratives they can represent are fractured and incomplete. Geva's acknowledgment of these limits is expressed in the visually distorted images of the fish-eye lens. His film indicates, through tropes of absence and failure, the sense that he cannot possibly do full justice to the history he is trying to understand, nor can he adequately convey the tragic loss of that earlier idealism and openness—so compellingly expressed in Marker's film—for which the most authentic means of mourning he can muster is a repeated scream of pain and incomprehension. Bitton, likewise, seems at a loss: her sense of exasperation, or even grief, can be summed up in the failure of language referred to by one of her Palestinian informants, who surveys the strangled city of Ramallah under near-permanent Israeli closure. "What's your question?" he asks of the interviewer, and then, as if in answer, adds, "There is no question. The question is what you see." For the Francophone cinema, the answer "one can see" resides in the awareness—of audiences and filmmakers alike—that the past must be better mourned so that the future may remain unsettled rather than preoccupied.

ACKNOWLEDGMENT

I wish to thank Jeffrey Skoller for his many incisive comments on earlier drafts of this chapter, Jacques Marchand for helpfully debating the topic with me, Yushna Saddul for her proficient research assistance and Caren Zilber-Shlensky for her encouragement.

NOTES

1. John Drabinski argues that in the figure of the "mute and ghostly" Palestinian corpse, Godard's film grapples with the representation of death as figure of representation itself. John Drabinski, "Separation, Difference, and Time in Godard's *Ici et ailleurs*," *SubStance* #115 37, no. 1 (2008), 148–158: 151. Black September is the name given to the confrontation between Jordanian forces under King Hussein and Palestinian militants in 1970 that resulted in thousands of Palestinian mortalities and the expulsion of the Palestine Liberation Organization (PLO) and many Palestinians from Jordan to Lebanon.
2. The difficulty of defining the term "Francophone cinema" has been much discussed. My own definition, for the purposes of this brief essay, will be narrow: my discussion is confined to films made with primarily French dialogue or narration, and films that have been produced with a specifically Francophone audience, and Francophone cultural references in mind. For a helpful discussion of some of the difficulties entailed in defining the Francophone cinema, see Carrie Tarr, "French Cinema and Post-Colonial Minorities," in *Postcolonial Cultures in France*, Alec Hargreaves and Mark McKinney, eds. (New York and London: Routledge, 1997), 59–83.
3. For a thumbnail history of these conflicts, see Peter Fysh and Jim Wolfreys, *The Politics of Racism in France* (New York: St. Martin's Press, 1998): 37–39, 90–93.
4. Joan Wolf points out that French Jews, too, arrived at a full recognition only in the 1960s that their community's suffering during the war had been fundamentally different from that of the rest of France. Joan B. Wolf, "'Anne Frank Is Dead, Long Live Anne Frank': The Six-Day War and the Holocaust in French Public Discourse," *History and Memory* 11, no. 1 (1999), 104–140: 107–108.
5. Shepard places the terms "Algerians" and "the French" within inverted commas to indicate the process of continuous redefinition that characterized their usage in French discourse. Todd Shepard, *The Invention of Decolonization: the Algerian War and the Remaking of France* (Ithaca, NY: Cornell University Press, 2006): 7–8.
6. Joshua Cole, "Intimate Acts and Unspeakable Relations: Remembering Torture and the War for Algerian Independence," in *Memory, Empire, and Postcolonialism: Legacies of French Colonialism*, Alec Hargreaves and Mark McKinney, eds. (New York and London: Routledge, 1997), 125–141.
7. For a discussion of the turn by French Jews toward a "nationalist" conception of culture in the late 1960s, see Judith Friedlander, *Vilna on the Seine: Jewish Intellectuals in France Since 1968* (New Haven: Yale University Press, 1990).
8. For a scholarly study of the 1961 incident, see Jean-Luc Einaudi, *Octobre 1961: Un Massacre à Paris* (Paris: Fayard, 2001).
9. *Caché*, dir. Michael Haneke, copyright 2005 by Les Films de Losange, distributed in the USA by Sony Pictures Classics.
10. In response to an interviewer's question, Lanzmann admits that he would like to destroy footage that he filmed but did not include in *Shoah*; "This, at least, would prove that *Shoah* is not a documentary." Claude Lanzmann, Ruth Larson, and David Rodowick, "Seminar with Claude Lanzmann: April 11, 1990," *Yale French Studies*, no. 79 (1991), 82–99: 96.
11. Yaïr Auron, *Les Juifs d'extrême gauche en mai 68*, trans. Katherine Werchowski (Paris: Albin Michel, 1998); quoted in Sven-Erik Rose, "Mathieu Kassovitz's *La Haine* and the Ambivalence of French-Jewish Identity," *French Studies* 61, no. 4 (2007), 476–491: 488.

12. Wolf, "The Six-Day War and the Holocaust in French Public Discourse": 107, 111–113.
13. Maurice Blanchot, Claude Lanzmann, et al., "Declaration on the Right to Insubordination in the War in Algeria" (September 5, 1960), trans. Mitch Abidor, Marxists Internet Archive, http://www.marxists.org/history/france/algerian-war/1960/manifesto-121.htm (accessed August 16, 2008).
14. Nicholas Paige argues that this instability also extends to the question of genre and visual codes, which Godard "vampirizes" in his films. Nicholas Paige, "Bardot and Godard in 1963 (Historicizing the Postmodern Image)," *Representations*, no. 88 (2004), 1–25: 4.
15. On the theme of death in *Ici et ailleurs*, see Drabinski, "Separation, Difference, and Time."
16. *Ici et ailleurs*, dir. Jean-Luc Godard, copyright 1976 by Gaumont and Sonimage, distributed in the USA by Facets Multimedia Distribution.
17. Walter Benjamin, *Illuminations* (New York: Harcourt, 1968): 256.
18. I borrow the phrase "much too promised land" from the title of David Aaron Miller's useful recent account of the failures of American efforts to broker peace in the Middle East. Aaron David Miller, *The Much Too Promised Land: America's Elusive Search for Arab-Israeli Peace* (New York: Bantam Books, 2008).

Part III
Violence, Martyrdom and Terrorism, 1970–2007

8 The Agony for Justice

Fethi Benslama
(Translated by Robert St. Clair)

The title of this chapter, "The Agony for Justice," comes from an expression that I've borrowed from a 1951 article by Ernest Kantorowizc entitled "Pro Patria Mori (in Medieval Political Thought)."[1] It comes toward the end of the text, when the author evokes the moment—around the thirteenth century—at which a mutation takes place in the West's attitude toward death and war. Because of this mutation, the Western, Christian world passes from the holy wars of the Crusades to a secularization (of war)—an essential point indicated by the preposition "for"/"pro" in "pro patria mori," dying *for* the fatherland. "For" condenses, in effect, the "for *what*" (pour*quoi*) as well as the "for *whom*," both the cause and the ends. In a word, it expresses that entire order which calls out for a reason for war, that justifies war and that gives it the appearance of being just. Let us note that, in French, we can draw two separate meanings from the word "just": one that refers to justice, and another that refers to a state of conformity to a rule and/or a given reality. In the first case, the contrary of "just" is the "unjust"; in the second case, its opposite is that which is false or erroneous, and it is only in the contemporary era that the two meanings have melded, with justice coming to designate the conformity to a positive rule of law. There are indeed languages, such as in Arabic, in which these two semantic currents are designated by different words: "adl" or "insâf" mean justice as a moral value, and "çahih" or "haq" designate the conformity to a rule, reality or truth.

I took an interest in Ernest Kantorowicz's article because for several years I had been seeking to understand the recent mutation that has taken place in the Muslim world's relationship to war and death—a mutation that has made possible on a large scale what we call "suicide attacks," a phenomenon subtended by a widespread martyropathology, to use the expression employed by Farhad Khosrokhavar in a remarkable sociological study on the subject.[2] More precisely, I was looking to identify the mechanisms at the discursive level that, at a given point in time, allowed for the emergence of the type of act designated by the expression "suicide attack." This expression, it should be noted, is itself problematic to the extent that, on the one hand, we aren't dealing with persons who kill themselves solely to put an end to their own lives, but rather who do so in order to take others with them in an act of war. The aim of this "self-sacrifice" is an act of heterocide in the service of a cause. On the other hand, the persons in question are convinced that they will not die, but rather that they shall live on beyond a physical and apparent demise. Perhaps, then, another term is called for: a sui-heterocide, or a self-putting-to-death-of-the-other (*auto-hétéro-mise-à-mort*), would be a more appropriate, if more unwieldy, term. By "putting-to-death" a will to perform a *mise en scène*, or a staging of destruction that is simultaneously directed toward the self and the other is signified.

I came to the subject of this research because although the reasons invoked in order to explain this recourse to "suicide attacks"—reasons such as situations of extreme oppression and humiliation—are not necessarily false, they do seem to me to be insufficient, if only when compared to historically similar situations. The colonial regime in Algeria, for example, used ferocious means of repression that led to tens of thousands of deaths, founded a long period of humiliation for the native Algerian population and, toward the end of its reign, systematically used torture on its enemies. And yet, despite the disproportion of power in question, the Front de Libération Nationale (FLN) never relied on said "suicide attacks," even if numerous civilian attacks were carried out at its instigation. The same holds true when one evokes Islam as a theological corpus authorizing such acts: the Algerian struggle for liberation was also carried out in the name of Islam, only that name did not, at that time, authorize "suicide attacks." In fact, generally speaking, the liberation movements in the Muslim world during the first half of the twentieth century did not carry out such attacks. But were we to suppose that the theological corpus of Islam did include passages that justified recourse to "suicide attacks," we would then have to ask ourselves why it is that it has only been in the last twenty years or so that they have become both possible and frequent beyond the confines of zones of full-blown conflict. I was therefore progressively led to the hypothesis that a historical change had taken place in this civilization's posture concerning death and war, and that the configurations of this new attitude was to be grasped in the element of discourse, where one often locates the trace and trajectory of such shifts.

The interest, then, of Ernest Kantorowicz's article is that it follows a similar path, albeit in a different context, revealing to us the linguistic operations at work during times of historical change and whose pivot is the reference to a collective identity.

The article begins by evoking the pastoral letter that Cardinal Mercier, the Primate of Belgium, addressed to his parishioners on Christmas 1914, during the occupation of Belgium by the German army. The title of the letter was "Patriotism and Endurance," and in it he established a certain number of connections between the "fatherland" (*patrie*) and "religion." These connections appeared unacceptable to some of his colleagues at the *Sacré Collège*, such as Cardinal Billot in France, who was nevertheless just a patriotic as Cardinal Mercier. In his letter, Mercier attempted to respond to a question that had been put to him concerning whether or not a soldier who fell while serving a "just cause" could be considered a martyr. He first replies that a soldier who dies in combat is not a martyr since he dies with his weapon in his hand, whereas a martyr surrenders himself without resistance to his executioner. On this point, he was calling to mind the strictly Christian theological stance concerning martyrs. We will note here that such is not the case for the theological conception of the martyr in Islam, which conforms on this point with the Koranic text according to which a soldier that falls in combat is indeed a martyr, as is designated by the term "châhid."

However, once he gets this doctrinal point out of the way, Cardinal Mercier introduces a "but." He writes:

> But if you ask me my opinion on the eternal salvation of a brave man who consciously gives his life to defend the honor of his country and to avenge violated Justice, I do not hesitate to reply that there is no doubt whatsoever that Christ crowns military valor, and that death Christianly accepted guarantees the salvation of the soldier's soul . . . The soldier who dies to save his brothers, to protect both their hearths and the altars of his country fulfills the highest form of love . . . We are justified in hoping for him the immortal crown that girds the brows of the elect. For such is the virtue of an act of perfect love that, of itself alone, it effaces an entire life of sin. Of the sinner, it instantaneously makes of saint.[3]

And here is the objection formulated some months later by Cardinal Billot: "To maintain that the sole act of consciously dying for the just cause of the fatherland 'suffices to guarantee salvation' means that one has substituted the Fatherland for God . . . , it means that one has forgotten what God, sin and divine forgiveness are" (Khosrokhavar 2002: 131).

While reading this exchange from the opening of Kantorowicz's article, I was struck by the fact that this divergence of opinion between two cardinals at the beginning of the last century reminds one, in certain respects, of the debate taking place today among Muslim theologians around the question of whether or not those who carry out "suicide attacks" can be considered as "châhid." The importance of this *disputatio* need hardly be labored; it suffices to say that, generally speaking, what is in question here is the theolegal and moral justification of self-putting-to-death-of-the-other (*auto-hétéro-mise-à-mort*) as a just act of war, and its consequences on the individual and collective levels: does the candidate go to heaven, or to hell; is the holiness of war a legitimate or illegitimate postulate?

In the case of Cardinals Mercier and Billot, the debate reveals the entire shift that would take place in the West—which Ernest Kantorowicz would go on to unfold—ending in the passage from holy war to the secularization of war. Indeed, Cardinal Mercier's position consists in a movement from the church to the fatherland, and in conferring upon the soldier who dies for the former the same status and value as one who dies for the latter (i.e., the status of martyr whose sins are forgiven, implying salvation and saintliness). For Cardinal Billot, even though the fatherland constitutes "a just cause," dying for it does not suffice to guarantee salvation, and he denounces this substitution of the fatherland for God.

And yet, strictly speaking, this substitution is not the only significant element of the process of secularization of war. For Cardinal Mercier introduces a signifier that did not exist in theological language prior to this mutation when he writes that: "[the soldier] who consciously gives his life to defend the honor of his country and to avenge violated Justice." This new signifier is "Justice," capitalized in the text, and it represented a profound upheaval in what is understood by "to die *for*" and by "just." Indeed, in Christian theology, the soldier who went off to a Christian war—as was the case for the Crusades—did so "out of love for God and his brothers," a love which had the value of *Caritas*. Charity, then, justified and sanctified war and death, not justice. "I go off to die for my God and my Brother," such was the *credo* of the Christian soldier according to the Church.

Hence, what Ernest Kantorowicz demonstrates in this text is that the passage from Church to State forced Western humanity to pass from a conception of the just as saintliness to a conception of the just that coincided with justice. This passage begins when the king himself becomes a saint, a bearer of justice. At—and ever since—that point, the "agony for justice" of his subjects is the same as the agony for the sovereign and his kingdom. To the kingdom of heaven, then, the kingdom of earth—the *terr*itory—was substituted. As Kantorowicz notes, in Jeanne D'Arc's battle cry, "Those who declare war on the holy kingdom of France declare war on the King Jesus"; we already witness this passage from the Church to the fatherland. Nevertheless, there is an element here that is of even greater importance: that is, at the same time that God is displaced in favor of the fatherland—and saintliness in favor of justice—a "transfer" (the term employed by the author) takes place between emotional values and "moral emotions." This expression, "moral emotions," gave me no small amount of pause for thought.

To what are "moral emotions" due, of what do they consist? According to the author, they reside in what he calls "corporatism"—and, here, we begin to approach the theses of Ernest Kantorowicz's brilliant work, "The King's Two Bodies,"[4] published several years after this article—according to which, what is transferred is in fact the body. We move from the Church as the mystical body of Christ—a martyred, sacrificed body that experienced agony—to the body of State, passing along the way through the body of the sovereign. Kantorowicz demonstrates in example upon example how the State becomes, in effect, a *body politic* in which the body of State is a secularized version of the *Corpus Christi*: "Death for the fatherland is henceforth seen in a truly religious perspective; it appears as a sacrifice for the corpus mysticum of the State, which is no less real than the corpus mysticum of the Church." He goes on to add that: "Humanism had its effect, but the quasi-religious aspects of dying for the fatherland clearly derive from the Christian faith, whose forces were at the time at the service of the secular corpus mysticum of the State."[5]

In other words, what didn't change disappear the shift from holiness to justice was the enduring need for a martyred body; the need for someone's (or the One) sacrificed body, a corps of the *dead for* . . . , in order to constitute the corpus of the human community within which the transfer of moral emotions takes place. The just, then, can pass from saintliness to justice, but he will nevertheless remain anchored in his death, or rather, more precisely, in his "dying for" (*pro mori*). "I die for us," "I die for you," "I die for the other," "the other has died for me," such is, in all of its possible declinations, the formula for the moral emotions that represent the source of the shared community. Yet, we are here confronted with an experience of the impossible, for death is the absolute limit of what is sharable. It is impossible to substitute one death for the death of another. The other, by dying for me, can only ever differ from my death, and vice versa. One's own, mine, "mine-ness" in general consists precisely in this limit. That is, in any case, the Freudian point of view (i.e., the death drive is not only destructive, but appropriative as well, as we are reminded by that line of popular verse that Freud cites in his *Reflections on War and Death*): "I had a comrade [. . .] a bullet is whizzing overhead, is it for you or is it for me?"[6] "You" *or* "me": therein lies death's true roll of the dice, death's true denominator; whereas in "me for you," and in "you for me," there is love, sacrifice and the community of "we," the fantasy of a libidinal amplification of the ego. I would remind the reader of Emile Benveniste's precious commentary on this point, according to which the "we" does not simply mark the passage of the singular to the plural or simply imply the pluralization of a verb, but belongs rather to a whole other category—that of the amplified person, or of an "I" in a state of dilation through which the "I," Benveniste informs us, fuses with the "non-I."[7] The hyperparadox, therefore, of the community is this: that death as absolute limit of the sharable becomes a locus of shared experience. Moral emotion, in other words, would be our sharing that which is un-sharable, indivisible. Often enough indeed the *ethos* of the community, its essence (its character or the virtues of its character, its *ethikai*, in Aristotle's terms), refers to a community's dead, and its "home" refers to the final resting places of those departed. Were one to judge, in any case, simply by the names we give to our streets, one would indeed get the impression that we circulate in the arteries of our dead.

As one can plainly see in the clinic (see my *What is a clinic of exile?*), death's inscription into collective space and destiny is one of the more powerful identitary mechanisms, producing the illusion of a stripping away of one's solitude in death and conferring upon the act of dying together the effect of a prolonging of love beyond life. Indeed, *la comourance*, in Montaigne's words, bears witness to the indissoluble passion of two lovers (as is mentioned by the whole Arabic tradition of courtly love) to such a degree that a martyrological status is conferred upon this form of death.[8] It is more than likely that this is simply another formulation of what Freud calls, in his *Group Psychology and the Analysis of the Ego*, the "libidinal constitution of a group,"[9] to the extent that death, here, stands for a power that solidifies, unifies, or indeed amalgamates individual bodies into a commune one. It may even be the case that the process of identifying with a leader only acquires the power of identification if the leader is perceived as being a "master of death," capable of transforming death into life, of making it a force capable of creating bonds and compelling adhesion rather than a force of dissolution. Such is the case in instances of self-sacrifice, of belief in resurrection and in the afterlife.

The conclusions that I have drawn from reading this text by Ernest Kantorowicz have helped me considerably to analyze the difficult question of the "self-putting-to-death-of-the-other" as—for those who carry them out and for those who support such actions—a "just" act of war. To briefly sum up, I would say that the historic change that took place in the West corresponded to a double modification, in both language and the guardian institutions of the community, concerning what was "just": the fatherland was substituted for the church and justice for saintliness, with an accompanying transfer of the same corporatist moral emotion. In other words, one single signifier now refers to new signifieds, serving all the while as a vehicle for the old religious trope that substitutes one body for many. And we know the price that just such a transformation cost Europe in the First and Second World Wars.

While reading the testaments of candidates for "self-putting-to-death-of-the-other" I was at first surprised to find in their discourses justifications for their acts that mingled the fatherland with religion and saintliness with justice—the same justifications were often repeated verbatim by their families after they had carried out their act. The wording of one father (a Shiite Muslim from Southern Lebanon) commenting on the "martyr's" death of his son, is almost stereotypical: "We have lived with injustice and it is a bare minimum to die for justice [. . .] Ever since he was a child, Karim was always moved by the Holy Family and the Imam Hussein. He chose the path of faith and justice."[10] In and of itself, this admixture profoundly disrupts what has heretofore been understood in theological tradition by holy war (referred to by the vocable "jihad"), but the real change lies elsewhere still.

Up until the 1980s, the lexicon of *jihad* was comprised of two principal terms: that of "mujahid," stemming from the same root as "jihad" and designating a combatant, and that of "chahid," which corresponds to "martyr." I would remind the reader somewhat schematically that the Arabic language—that of the Koran and of the Muslim liturgy—is a language founded on consonantal roots that one declines through the use of vowels in order to generate words. With just six vowels and three or four consonants, one has at one's disposal hundreds of possible combinations that are not always exploited. This is so because usage and syntactical forms fix at any given moment what can be considered admissible (or non-admissible) uses of the language. For example, taking the radical "j.h.d." can lead to generating "j*u*hd" (effort), "j*i*had" (holy war) or even "*mu*jah*i*d" (combatant—*mu* is the prefix that designates the agent), to take just three out of many possible words. The most frequent metaphor given to explain how the language functions is that of a body, formed by consonants and animated by vowels. These remarks are important for understanding the analysis to follow, especially in so far as it concerns the important emergence of a new signifier which radically modifies the discourse on war and death in the context we have been discussing.

If the "mujahid" is a combatant, belonging to the same register as that of the warrior or soldier in the service of a holy cause, the term "chahid," the exact translation of which is "martyr," belongs to an entirely other register. It comes from the root "ch.h.d.," designating the act of observing, of being present for and bearing witness to. It gives us the terms: "ch*a*h*i*d" (the witness), "*m*ach*h*ad" (scene, spectacle), *m*uch*a*h*i*d (the spectator), ch*a*h*a*d*a* (testimony, attestation) as well as "ch*a*h*i*d" (the martyr). It is as though the testimonial act could take either the path of the word (*parole*) or that of sacrifice; but the sacrificial potential that resides in the attestation of truth does not on its own make any more intelligible the current recourse to "suicide attacks." We find the same common bond, after all, in the Greco-Latin context: "martyr," borrowed from ecclesiastical Latin, comes from the Greek "marturos" which means "witness." Hence, for Christian authorities, the martyr is "he who bears witness to the truth by his sacrifice."[11] On this point, then, there isn't anything specifically Islamic about martyrs.

In the context of the Koran, "chahid" refers to a Muslim fallen on the battlefield—an act that confers upon him an exorbitant status mentioned in several sura, the most explicit of which is the following: "Do not believe that those who are killed whilst combating on the path to God are dead; on the contrary, the live on and are nurtured in the presence of their lord" (III, 136). In other words, the "chahid" is only dead in appearance; he survives and receives nourishment quite as though he were alive even though this nourishment is of a celestial nature. There is also a strange Koranic passage where the following is said: "Say not of those who are killed on the path to God: 'They are dead!' No, they are alive, but you are not aware of it" (II, 154). In a way, the martyr is the locus of the absence of representation of death in the unconscious. It designates the immortal in each of us. It designates, we might add, the child that never dies.

In Islamic discourse up until the 1980s it is apparent that the two terms "mujahid" and "chahid" do not overlap. The "mujahid" is not necessarily a martyr, and the martyr (chahid) is not necessarily a combatant (mujahid).

The "mujahid," in going off to battle, is of course willing to sacrifice ("fida" or "tadhya"), and can become a "chahid" if he is killed, but his aim is not to intentionally become a martyr, but rather to fight and survive. What's more, the verb "ch.h.d." can only be conjugated in the passive voice, and refers to the unknown ("ustushhida"). There is no willful, conscious act that corresponds to "chahid," which is accidental and unpredictable. The combatant is only a martyr by supplement. This is why the term "chahid" can be used for someone who dies an accidental death, outside of combat—notably if that person is young and especially if he or she is a child. In short, if the subject "mujahid" is active, the "chahid" subject is passive, *a passive subject who only enters onstage when the agent is annihilated.*

An important event takes place, then, toward the middle of the 1980s; an event in the order of discourse in the Arabic language to which neither political sociology nor the more customary analyses have paid any attention (on this point I would add that one needs to lend an analytic ear in order to detect this change). This event is the invention of a new term, which, over the course of the fourteen centuries of Islamic history, had not previously existed in common usage. This word is of course created out of the language's potentiality discussed previously, but it is also a word that was, until now, unheard of in the language. Indeed, from the root "ch.h.d." the term "*istichhadi*" is formed—a term constructed according to the form corresponding, in canonical usage, to what we might call "the pressing demand for/of a thing." It is by using this nominal that one designates the person carrying out a "suicide attack." To put it another way, the category invented through this noun is that of "one who seeks/demands martyrdom." It is here that we have a historical turning point, displacing the horizon of signification of the "chahid" from the order of a passive subject, accidentally subjected to his fate, to that of a subject actively seeking death, the modality of which is the desire to kill and simultaneously be killed.

It is understandable that experts on terrorism fail to take such an invention into account; or, when they do, that they mention it in passing, as a point of limited, secondary interest. For them, the concept of "demand" does not have the same range that we attribute to it in psychoanalysis (i.e., that it is through demand that the Other's hold on the subject is constituted). By making possible in the universe of discourse and in the Arabic language the pressing demand for/of martyrdom, a space of fatal address is opened up toward which certain subjects will orient themselves. But who opened up this space, and how indeed does it become so attractive? Words such as "kamikaze" or "suicide attacks," with all of the horror that they contain hidden below the surface, have managed to obscure the event in the language through which the Other's desire is enounced as the desire to see the subject kill himself while killing others. This is what explains, to my mind, both how, at a given moment, the demand for/of martyrdom was able to spread like the plague and the appearance of "demanders" of martyrdom throughout the world, including in those areas where there are neither battle fields nor wars.

We know that it is with Hezbollah, during the 1983 Israeli occupation of Southern Lebanon, that the first so-called "kamikaze" attack was carried out in the name of Islam. The term "kamikaze" intervened as a reference to the Lod Airport massacre, which was carried out in Tel Aviv on May 30, 1972, by a branch of the Japanese Red Army. Two out of the three members of the group blew themselves up with their own hand grenades. One might be led to think that it was this act that inspired Hezbollah, but both the word and the self-destructive gesture it entails obscure a more important fact, without which we would fail to understand the spread of the phenomenon of suicide attacks: i.e., Hezbollah wasn't just a laboratory where formidable walking bombs were created (a technique that would soon spread throughout the entire Middle East); it was also an ideological laboratory within which the infernal discursive machine that I've been describing was developed.

To grasp the internal mechanics of this linguistic invention, we must take into consideration several historical facts that touch on the creation of Hezbollah. Hezbollah—the "party of God," in Arabic—was founded in June of 1982 and is a Lebanese, Shiite politico-religious movement that has at its command an armed branch (out of which the political branch was in fact born). It was created in reaction to the Israeli invasion of Lebanon. Shiite Islam is a minority branch of Islam (with respect to what we call Sunni Muslims, who represent the orthodox majority), but it nevertheless represents some 15 to 20 percent of all Muslims.

This conflict has its origin in a major historical event that took place in the very beginning of Islam, one that resulted in a bloody civil war over the question of its founder's rightful successor. Indeed, after Mohammed's death, some Muslims considered that power and sovereignty should remain with Mohammed's family. The first to inherit this sovereign power, then, would have been the prophet's cousin, Ali, who, having married Mohammed's daughter, was also his son-in-law. Others believed, however, that in the absence of any testamentary indication as to who should receive power, the succession should take place in/after consultation among the Muslim faithful, and that the successor need not necessarily come from within the prophet's line. This difference led to a civil war that was marked by Ali's murder as well as by the torture of his son Hussein. When I write "torture," I mean that the body of the prophet's grandson was torn to shreds. It seems to me that this tearing-to-shreds of Hussein's body—given its place in the history of Shiite Islam—is not without analogy to the exploding bodies of the so-called "kamikazes" themselves, one of whom wrote the following in his will: "My brothers, I swore to myself that I would only present my body to God and my master the Imam Hussein once it was in pieces, dismembered, without hands nor head so that I should be truly worthy before the King of the mighty, worthy of the Imam Hussein and of his companions who gave their lives for him."[12] Hussein's body was indeed dismembered and its parts dispersed by his enemies. Today, his head can still be found in the Grand Mosque in Damas, built by the descendants of those same enemies and where thousands of Shia pilgrims come to weep—as I was once able to observe firsthand—as though they themselves had just died. In the midst of a disconsolate crowd, it was an old woman, with tears in her eyes and her face racked with pain, who impressed upon me the perpetual present-ness of this martyr who died a millennium and a half ago.

Hussein's torture represents the primal scene of sacrifice that founded Shiite Islam. It gave way to narratives in Islam as a whole and to spectacular rites of commemoration among Shiites during which the faithful flagellate themselves in memory of Hussein's torment and as a sign of penitence, bearing witness, as it were, to the intense sentiment of guilt that these followers have inherited.

Up until the Iranian Revolution, the narrative that leads up to the torment—as well as the one that recounts it—enjoyed a considerable interpretative stability in Shiism. Right up until 1979—that is, for fourteen centuries—this narrative was practically always the same. Schematically speaking, the principal sequences related the story of how Hussein, in his quest to reclaim the sovereignty that was supposed to remain within the prophet's line, received from the denizens of an important city of that day and age (named Koufia, about eighty miles from Baghdad) their assurance that they would be his allies. When he goes off to meet the inhabitants of Koufia—bringing along only a few of his followers—he meets, along the way, his enemies. Greatly outnumbered, a ferocious but unequal battle ensues and the inhabitants of Koufia fail to come to Hussein's aid, despite having given their word to do so. In the end, Hussein is massacred. The symbolic core of Shiism is constituted out of this torture and the guilt of desertion by the inhabitants of Koufia, of whom today's Shia consider themselves to be the descendants—the descendant heirs of a crime. They didn't kill him directly, but through their defection they contributed to his murder.

After Hussein's massacre, the inhabitants of Koufia reacted by carrying out what we could term a series of wars of attrition, which, as the name indicates, were wars of revenge and expiation. All of this can be seen in the commemorations of the Battle of Karbala, as well as in Shiite rituality and spirituality. Whence this faith marked by a cult of pain that in many respects resembles that of Christianity—and for good cause, since it too is marked by the murder of a son whose father was also killed. At the heart of Shiism, then, we find a genealogy of martyrs which, because of the tragic fates awaiting many of Hussein's descendants, would continue to unfold. But, given his surname of "prince of martyrs," it is Hussein who has pride of place in the martyrological institution of Shiism. His sacrifice occults that of his father, a point which seems to my mind to be crucial for developments that were to follow.

Up until the Iranian Revolution, the narrative of Hussein's sacrifice is organized around the classic schema that I have just outlined: Hussein is a combatant (mujahid) who is killed by his enemies at Karbala and becomes a martyr (chahid). The faithful congregate and commune in memory of his agony as a culpable community. Hussein's martyrdom, what's more, is considered inimitable. With the Iranian Revolution, however, a new figure of the revolutionary Shiite emerges, and with it a new reading of the scene of Hussein's death emerges as well. It is this reading that provokes a decisive mutation, one of the effects of which is the opening up of the discursive "space" of "suicide attacks." The reading in question is founded upon an interpretation advanced by an Iranian intellectual close to Khomeini named Ali Shariati (1933–1977). Shariati was a thinker who played a very important role (he translated F. Fanon, obtained a PhD in sociology at the Sorbonne and was so influential that the Shah's secretive services finally assassinated him) in theorizing the intersections of Marxism and Islam. He was the intellectual father of what he himself called "red-Shiism" (red, as in the color of the blood of the martyred, but red also as in the emblem of the proletariat revolution).[13] The novelty of his interpretation of Hussein's martyrdom resides in the following points:

1. Hussein was not only a combatant (mujahid) who met his death unwillingly (i.e., he was not seeking to die), but in fact chose to go to Karbala knowing full well the fate that awaited him. He knew he was going to die and went off all the same in an act of willful self-abnegation for the cause. He was therefore not just a "combatant-martyr," but a "martyr-martyr." In this sense, he was a "demander of martyrdom" (istishhadi).
2. The Shia were not only collectively guilty—*qua* community that descended from the community of Koufa—of having left Hussein to die (as is the case in the traditional interpretation), they are individually and subjectively guilty of having done so. We see here something akin to a *privatization* of the collective sacrificial neurosis—comparable to what Freud diagnosed in cases of obsessive neuroses with respect to religion.
3. This individualization, or privatization, implies that the revolutionary Shiite subject is not only a subject who worships in collective guilt, but one who must totally identify with Hussein by imitating his demand for/of martyrdom. He is no longer simply one of the faithful, commemorating the event of Hussein's martyr, but a conscience actually carrying out that event in the present. In other words, it is no longer a question of commemorating Hussein's sacrifice, but of reproducing it; a question not of remembrance, but of repetition. The subject is compelled to repeat for himself, as though he were in fact Hussein.
4. Martyrdom becomes a general commandment valid in every case where it is a question of dying or putting-to-death ("If you can, kill;

if not, die yourself"[14])—acts through and by which the revolutionary individual subjectively attains purpose. "Subjectivity" is indeed the right term since, for Shariati, it is consciousness that accedes to its own individuality through/in the "self-putting-to-death-of-the-other." In that sense, there is a subversion of tradition: the martyr is no longer subordinate to the combat (jihad), but rather the opposite is true. This subversion—called for by Shariati, who thus invents a "modern martyrological subjectivity"—is furthermore not subject to the traditional rules governing holy war. In a word, the subject arms himself with his own annihilation; he becomes a subject in sacrificing himself.

Hezbollah put all its stock into Ali Shariati's new interpretation of the scene of self-sacrifice. It is not just, therefore, an organization that invented the *practice* of "suicide attacks"—and that conditioned a certain proportion of its members to perpetrate acts of self-putting-to-death-of-the-other, which is in fact possible—but it is also and above all else the laboratory in which a new order of signifying agency was put into operation, one that opened up the trapdoor of the primal scene of sacrifice. How could we not see the importance of a reconfiguration that modifies the rapport of the Shiite subject to Hussein as an ideal? Once inaccessible, the ideal is henceforth what the subject should aspire to be. Hussein becomes the locus of an incitation to come unto him in the act of consciously dying. *The ideal calls out for the Egos to dissolve in and be absorbed by Him, and that is what leads to self-sacrifice.* Each potential attacker combines in his or her body the torn and tattered body of Hussein, not only as a martyr of the faith but also as a revolutionary. The moral emotion of the tortured body circulates henceforth between God and revolution, and the potential attacker incarnates the circulation of the *corpus mysticum* between the former and the latter.

The hypothesis that I would like to propose here is the following: in the new signifier "istichhadi," Hussein no longer has the cultural function of the guardian, of the dead Father taking upon himself the absolute sacrifice that constitutes the community. Or, rather, he no longer serves as a mediating term (to mediate in the sense of making something non-mediate), he no longer "bars the Other," in Lacanian parlance, opening up the possibility of a confrontation with the ideal Father.[15] I would remind the reader that in psychoanalysis the dead Father represents an inaccessible point of origin, a symbolic mooring that tempers the exigencies of the ideal Father, which is a menacing, cruel, persecutory figure demanding sacrifice. What we have here, then, is a reconfiguration of what Freud called the "cultural superego"—a notion that has been insufficiently elaborated and which would merit being looked at again as a way of interpreting, for example, those periods of mutation during which the obligation to give one's body to the community becomes so pressing that the *sacrificer and the sacrificed bleed indistinguishably into one another in an interminable bloodbath*, almost as though the stoppage allowed for by symbolic substitution at the moment of foundational violence is no longer efficient.

Further support for this argument can be seen in the role of the *intercessor* (chafi) that is conferred upon the "demander of martyrdom" in this new signifying arrangement. We come across this designation in the wills of those who carry out attacks, who address (in the first place) their mothers, fathers and brothers by saying: "I go off to intercede on your behalf." In the families' discourse too, these sons are attributed the title of intercessor. What's more, Hezbollah's authorities make this one of their criteria for authorizing which candidates get to become martyrs. Here is what Sayed Hussein Nasrahallah (one of whose sons carried out an act of self-sacrifice) said about his meeting with one such candidate: "I asked him one thing, and it is in fact the sole condition that I impose in order to formally facilitate the arrival of the demander of martyrdom on the terrain and to obtain, with the others, his intercession."[16]

What, then, does this intercession entail? The term (chafi) comes from a radical in Arabic that signifies "amnesty" and "forgiveness." The title of intercessor is accorded to someone who intercedes on behalf of someone else in order to obtain forgiveness from a sovereign or from God in the case of the intercessor being a holy man. It is therefore the function of a third party who relieves the debt and the guilt of a subject, thus sparing him or her a sanction. One couldn't transform the "demander of martyrdom" into such an intercessor if the person to whom he appeals were not a menacing figure, a figure capable of reprisal, and if these young men weren't sons going willingly off to die with the aim of circumventing the terror of the ideal Father.

Thus, in the current state of Islam—just as not long ago in the West—the historical mutation of the relationship to war and death is the correlate of a reconfiguration of ideals that is imperceptible without the production of new signifying agencies in the domain of discourse. The slippage of one vocable to another and the emergence of a word in a millenary montage accompany new forms of putting-to-death. Dying *for* the fatherland, *for* God, *for* the revolution, etc.: One probably doesn't die just because of words, but one doesn't die without them; that is to say, without the thing that comes "before" or "in front of" the cause, the thing that the preposition "for" ("pour" in French, or "pro" in Latin) represents. The thing that comes before the cause seeks to orient death, to trace for it a trajectory of meaning, to give it a site, a destination, in a word, *to refer (to) death*, which is the same thing as giving it a name. And indeed, for that name one kills, one kills oneself, one kills one another—as though the worst thing was that all this death was for naught.

How are we to understand the diffusion of the model of the "demander of martyrdom" beyond Hezbollah, beyond the sacrificial configuration that is particular to Shiism to the Sunni majority—that is to the whole of the Muslim world where candidates for "self-sacrifice" daily feed the "suicide attack" columns in the press? We certainly aren't dealing with the first instance of a minority group's invention spreading beyond the group's borders to reach a larger human community. That may after all be what defines an invention, once it seems to bring the solution to a problem, or appears to respond to some urgent need. More precisely, the emergence of a new signifier, such as "istichhadi," would have been nothing more than an empty language game, it would have remained a dead letter if, along the way, it hadn't met up with and been articulated to a cruel reality. And under what form does this reality manifest itself? In my opinion, it reveals itself in what we call "the worst"; when, in an ongoing situation of oppression and suffering, degradation and shame appear to have no end in sight. Perseverance, living on for some, is equivalent to maintaining the power of indignity they are under. It is as though, in some such cases, these men choose to become the superego incarnate of their community. They take upon themselves the shame of, and become the vicars of, the humiliated. Self-sacrifice is the ascension of the worst of superego-men. We have perhaps failed to register the full force of the incarnation of the superego of a community and the injunctive power of its message: *you are undignified and no longer have the glory required to pull through*. Borrowing Jean Genet's expression from *The Prisoner of Love*, I would say that in this case, glory is "the shattering out of shame." This last book by Genet was written over the course of two years that he spent in Palestinian camps and attests to the captivating fascination of this consubstantial dimension of being. The communication to the whole of the Muslim world of the "demand of/for martyrdom" passed in transit through the Palestinian situation, where it was adopted (by Sunni Muslims) and resonated intensely when the breaking down of the peace process substituted the abyss for the horizon. We must be cautious to not mistake explication for justification. All the more so because if the communication of the "self-sacrifice" model to the youth of the Muslim world—and, in particular, to the Arab Muslim world—has been able to propagate to the extent that it has, it is to the extent that conditions of oppression and shame of being have been regulated by local powers for decades now; the spectacle of bombardments and civilian massacres had already created thousands of vicars ready to flee their conditions through the escape hatch of glory. Spiritual guides and preachers were able to captivate their audiences with offers of substituting the horror of living with the eternal beatitudes of martyrdom, via the explosion of an abject corps into the imperishable body for the community.

On this point, I feel that it is necessary to come back to what Ernest Kantorowicz called "corporatism" in order to better ascertain its full reach through the relationship between sacrifice and the *identitary pairing* that I discussed in the introduction to this chapter. I would remind the reader that according to the developments that I proposed, the primary function of identity is to pair up (*to unite*, in the antiquated sense of the word) the "self" to "self" and the "me" to "us," but that the radicality, or the excess, of identity ends in a polarization of the subject in which he tends to resolve into the singular phase of an id (the magmatic body) or into the single phase of a superego (the solar superiority, the pineal eye).

Ernest H. Kantorowicz introduces the notion of "corporatism" in order to apprehend the transfer of the "same moral emotions" from the Church to the State. And yet, we have seen that this moral emotion gets its emotional character precisely from the operation of transference of a singular body proper to a collective body, and that this sharing operates as a sort of surpassing of the impossible in a shared death. We can no doubt glimpse on the background of "corporatism" the model of the Eucharist, and of Catholic transubstantiation, and perhaps more generally we can see the transformation of the body of Christ into a *corpus mysticum* (i.e., the Church as an institution of the Christian community). Still, the term "corporatism" is in fact fairly deceptive; it certainly belongs to the type of deception which is at the root of identity pairing, for the transfer of a singular body to a collective body necessitates rather an operation of *ex-corporation*, which is first of all a dis-incorporation effectuated through real sacrifice. Then comes the secondary moment of *in-corporation* into a supposed common body, which is an imaginary operation. Perhaps "moral emotion," then, has a double under-girding: on one side is a becoming bodiless, or of the dislocated body invoked by the candidates for "suicide attack" cited earlier, and on the other side is the arrival of glorious body into the collective body that sets loose an emotion of infusion and of confusion, that is to say, of communion. But between dis-incorporation and in-corporation there is the radical interruption of death—a time out of time, a passage through nothingness whose identitary principle is supposed to assure the passage in order to reappear unchanged on the other side. The body, in sum, is of little importance. It is there within that resides the absolute of emotion and, in a sense, the emotion of the absolute: when the impossible is obliged to bend, by the lure or fiction of the appropriation of death (death's surpassing) by a subject or a group. We might call this phenomenon the desire for *transpropriation*, which is what the sacrifice seeks to accomplish.

Transpropriation consists in the partial or total passing of what is particular in a thing or being to the particular of another thing or being—a passage that nothing seems to be able to hinder. What's more, interruptions, gaps, discontinuity—in a word, the frontier—only serve to encourage the energy and force of the passage. The notion of *transgression* might come to mind, but this term designates the moment of a passage beyond a limit, whereas *transappropriation* is a movement of reabsorption of lines and borders. Rather than a *borderline* moment or state, it is an energy of lines overflowed, and of discrepancies inbetween states, spaces, levels and entities that it passes off, desires to pass off and pass on without any consideration for value, time, for the difference between life and death, love and hatred, truth and falseness, self and non-self, etc. When looked at close enough, transpropriation plays on and with every register. Even if in the case of theological incorporation it can be conceived as imaginary, we could just as easily conceive of it as symbolic, if only in virtue of the passage from the real body to the word "body." "What's a word?" asks Nietzsche, "It is the sonorous transposition of a stimulus of the nerves."[17] Transpropriation doesn't operate any less in the real, for eating an apple or transforming grains of sand into crystal is the metabolisation of the particular of a thing into something else. Transpropriation, then, would be the act of identification of the non-identical, and the dis-identification of the identical, in such a way that destruction is not the end, but a passage toward the other thing or side. This is why it aims not only beyond the pleasure principle, but beyond that beyond, for with transpropriation not even death is a limit. In final analysis, transpropriation is man's desire and his primitive powers, both of which proceed from his tense relationship with two heterogeneous polarities and that he resolves with a metaphorical solution concerning himself and everything else.

In *Totem and Taboo*, Freud provides us with an illustration of transpropriation when he writes: "Primitive man would bow down before the surplus power of death with the same gesture by which he seems to deny it."[18] However, if we simply stick to this static dualism, we cannot comprehend how from this contradiction between recognition and denial, he sees spring up: "Man's first theoretical operation—the creation of spirits." Animism appears indeed as a metaphorical solution that moves between recognition and denial of death; and as for the rest, the example that he brings up of Schreber's delirium a few lines further on supports the hypothesis of the desire for transpropriation, seeing as in his delirium he sees himself transformed into God's wife.

"My brothers, I swore to myself that I would only present my body to God and my master the Imam Hussein once it was in pieces, dismembered, without hands nor head so that I should be truly worthy before the King of the mighty, worthy of the Imam Hussein." This presentation of a body dismembered in order to be "truly worthy" reveals the aim of a *jouissance*, in horror, of the appropriation of one's death ("present my body") whose logic is that of the idealization—for the ideal alone allows for disincorporation—or, if you will, the cannibalistic absorption of the Self into the ideal. Of course, the appearance of a dislocated body before the "king of the mighty" is only the prelude to the heavenly reconstruction of the very same body, and to its re-sexualization among the virgin women of paradise (the houris)—still, the moment of self-sacrifice is indeed characterized by an extreme exhaustion in which the ego frees itself of its bonds to the id and enters into a state of ecstasy as pure, overhanging superego. This is one of the reasons that Jacques Lacan's proposition on sacrifice seems to be uncorroborated by the facts when he writes: "Sacrifice signifies that, in the object of our desires, we try to find the proof of the presence of the desire of that Other that I call the *Deus Absconditus* (le *Dieu obscur*)."[19] Idealization, in that it is a superegotistic elevation, is perhaps, rather, an abduction out of obscure flesh, a purifying clarity that signals the presence of the God of light, as indicated by the etymology of the words "sacrifice" and "to sacrifice" in Arabic. In effect, the radical "dh.h.a." from which they stem, signifies the acts of illuminating (something) with a blinding light, of making (something) evident, of appearing, of making something disappear in the shadows, of eradicating opacity; hence lucidity and zenith. There is even an expression for wishing someone's death that goes: "May God annihilate (sacrifice) your shadow." The logic of sacrifice does not permit us to exculpate the desire of the God of Light, nor the ideality of its reason. It is even plausible that obscurity is anti-sacrificial, and that a certain opacity may even be more favorable to the preservation of life. Sacrificial transpropriation may have started in the shadows, but it started there like the solar movement at daybreak, breaking away from the Earth, as is suggested by the etymology of the word "soleil" ("sun"), which is an extension of the word "sol" ("ground").

In a way, Shariati's theory—that of modern martyrological subjectivation as a conjunction of the figures of the proletariat and the martyr—may have appeared to pose a new ideal on the horizon of the youth of the Muslim world as it was plunged into the obscurity of blind modernism, abandoned in the night of ferocious tyrannies; it may have appeared to offer to those without the means of enlightenment at their disposal a way up toward the devastating clarity of self-sacrifice, where they could accomplish total identity with the ideal object[20] by simply shedding the shattered shadows of their bodies.

NOTES

1. Ernest H. Kantorowicz, *Mourir pour la Patrie* (1951), trad. L. Mayali (Paris: Fayard, 2004).
2. Farhad Khosrokhavar, *Les Nouveaux Martyrs d'Allah* (Paris: Flammarion, 2002).
3. Khosrokhavar, *Martyrs*, 129.
4. Ernest H. Kantorowicz, *Les Deux Corps du Roi* (1957), trad. J.P. Genet and N. Genet (Paris: Gallimard, 1989).
5. Kantorowicz, *Roi*, 157.
6. Sigmund Freud, "Actuelles sur la guerre et la mort" (1915), OC (Paris: PUF, 1988), 145.
7. Emile Benveniste, "Structures des relations de personne dans le verbe," *Problèmes de linguistique générale* (Paris: Gallimard, 1966), 235.
8. Raja Ben Slama, *Al-'ishq wa kitaba* (L'amour et la vérité) (Al-Kamel Verlag, Kôln, 2003).
9. Freud, "Psychologie des masses et analyse du moi" (1921), O.C., t. XVI (Paris: PUF, 1991).
10. Cited by Diana Cheaib in her master's thesis on "suicide attacks" in Southern Lebanon entitled: "Mourir pour vivre," Ecole Doctorale de Recherche en Psychanalyse (Paris: Université Paris 7, 2005).
11. *Le Robert, Dictionnaire Historique de la langue Française*, sous dir. Alain Rey, Paris, Dictionnaire Le Robert, 1995. t. 2, 1198.

12. Cited in Cheaib, "Mourir."
13. See, on this point, Farhad Khosrokhavar's exposé on the theory of the martyr developed by Shariati in *Les Nouveaux Martyrs d'Allah*, 72ff.
14. The formula is Shariati's, cited by F. Khosrokhavar, *Martyrs*, 76.
15. This is also Guy Rosolato's opinion. See *Le Sacrifice, Repères Psychanalytiques* (Paris: PUF, 1987).
16. Extract from a Lebanese documentary entitled "The Princes of Paradise," cited in Cheaib, "Mourir."
17. Friedrich Nietzsche, *Vérité et mensonge au sens extra-moral*, N. Gascuel, trad. (Paris: Babel, 1997), 12.
18. Freud, "Totem and Taboo" (1912–1913), O.C. (Paris: PUF, 1998), 303.
19. Jacques Lacan, *Les Quatre Concepts Fondamentaux de la Psychanalyse*, séminaire XI (Paris: Seuil, 1973), 247.
20. Here is what Freud has to say about the issue of self-sacrifice in *Group Psychology and ego analysis*: "[. . .] in the exalted love of the young man; the ego becomes more and more stripped of all demand, it becomes increasingly modest as the object becomes increasingly grandiose, increasingly precious and finally takes possession of the ego's self-love, to such an extent that the self-sacrifice of the latter becomes a sort of natural consequence" ("Totem," 15).

9 Out of Palestine
Jean Genet's Shooting Stars
Bruno Chaouat

Jean Genet's epic memoir of the Palestinian revolution, *Un captif amoureux*,[1] appeared twenty three years ago, in 1986, the year of the author's death. It was only a few years after the massacre of Palestinians in Sabra and Shatila (1982) by a Maronite Christian militia, arguably with the compliance of Israeli military authorities.[2] The book appeared a few years after Genet's brief account of the massacre published in the *Revue d'études palestiniennes*[3] under the title of "Quatre heures à Chatila." It is worth noting that 1986 is also just a few years after the attacks against the synagogue of the rue Copernic and a Jewish restaurant in Paris that occurred as a ricochet of the Arab-Israeli conflict in France.[4] Genet's book, divided into two sections, "Souvenirs I" and "Souvenirs II," evokes the author's experience in the Palestinian refugee camps in 1970, 1971 and 1972. The year 1970 marked King Hussein's brutal expulsion of Palestinians from Jordan, an event known as "Black September." The year 1972 marked the year of the assassination of eleven Israeli athletes in Munich by a Palestinian terrorist group named after this event, "Black September." Genet's Palestinian memories are intertwined with memories of the author's stay among the Black Panthers, who hosted him in 1970. Black Panthers and Palestinians seem to be interchangeable in Genet's *Weltanschauung*. Oppressed by the white or colonial power, they respond with transgression, style, intimidation and, ultimately, terror. Palestinians and Black Panthers, not unlike the poet-thief, are tropes for "nomadism" and subversion of the Law.[5]

Reading Genet's swan song in the wake of the Second Intifada and of September 11, 2001, constitutes an uncanny endeavor. To this global context one should add significant cultural events such as the success of Steven Spielberg's *Munich* and the first nomination of a Palestinian movie, *Paradise Now*, for an academy award.[6] *Paradise Now* confronts the issue of suicide bombing from the perspective of two would-be martyrs—a *jihadist* version of *Schlemihl* and *Schlimm mazzal*. Today's Arab terrorist has gained a status of movie star long anticipated and dreamed of by Genet. Paul Virilio noted just one month after September 11, 2001:

L'imaginaire scientifique . . . rejoint celui . . . des kamikazes islamistes mourant sans doute heureux de devenir les acteurs d'une superproduction mondiale où la réalité basculerait dans le néant électronique, une bonne fois pour toutes. [The scientific imagination . . . merges with that . . . of the Islamist kamikazes dying probably happy to have become the actors in a multinational high budget production in which reality would collapse into electronic nothingness, once and for all.][7]

Read in the light of what Walter Laqueur branded the "new terrorism,"[8] Genet's aestheticizing of terror as absolute artistic performance resonates with the German composer Karlheinz Stockhausen's genuine awe and terrorist envy expressed a few days after September 11, 2001:

What has happened is . . . the greatest work of art there has ever been. That minds could achieve something in one act, which we in music cannot even dream of, that people rehearse like crazy for ten years, totally fanatically for one concert, and then die. This is the greatest possible work of art in the entire cosmos. Imagine what happened there. There are people who are so concentrated on one performance, and then 5000 people are chased into the Afterlife, in one moment.[9]

For Stockhausen, whose avant-garde oeuvre rests on some Luciferian conception of artistic creation, the ultimate performance, next to which any artwork pales, is the suicide of the artist and the ensuing mass murder of the audience. The avant-garde composer longs for this asymptotic point at which the world would be abolished, and, with it, the artist and his art— "*Fiat ars, pereat mundus*," of a sort.[10] Artistic performance as a metaphor for both the poetic and the terrorist, terrorist/poetic act as absolute creation within destruction—this, as we will see, fits Genet's memoir rather well.

The events of September 11, 2001, have generated a cortège of aesthetic and apocalyptic responses by Western philosophers and artists. In France, I surmise that these responses were nurtured by memories of Dadaism and Surrealism, inspired by the avant-garde's fascination with violence and sacrifice, and with the abolition of the distinction between art and life, representation and acting out.[11] In England, the artist Damien Hirst declared that "the terrorists responsible for the September 11 attacks 'need congratulating' because they achieved 'something which nobody would ever have thought possible' on an artistic level."[12]

If Genet's memoir cannot be reduced to yet another avatar of Orientalism, there is little doubt that his vision of the East is informed by nineteenth century Eurocentric clichés, as witnessed by this characterization of Islam as the religion of submission, based on a shallow etymology of the word in Arabic: "Elle-même doctoresse mais musulmane, donc soumise, étymologiquement . . ." ["A doctor herself, yet a Muslim, therefore submissive, etymologically . . ."] (Genet 1995: 395).[13]

My reading of Genet's Palestinian memories is indebted to Eric Marty's landmark essay, "Jean Genet à Chatila," published in late 2002.[14] The essay subsequently became the core chapter of a book that mixes the genre of the diary with literary and philosophical criticism. Marty's essay is twice a tour de force: an unimpeachable textual analysis of Genet's Palestinian writings that sheds new light on the earlier works, the essay is also a piece of polemic meant to denounce the rise of a new anti-Semitism hidden behind anti-Israeli sentiment in the aftermath of September 11, 2001. Marty's essay has renewed Genet studies by engaging in the first serious and systematic exploration of the writer's anti-Semitism. His analysis stands out as the first attempt at rethinking Genet's literary metaphysics since Georges Bataille's 1957 *La Littérature et le mal*, which overlooked Genet's fascination with Hitler.[15]

With friends like Genet, Palestinians do not need enemies. Indeed, one can hardly imagine a more ambiguous supporter of any political or moral cause than the poet of evil and metaphysician of betrayal. According to the legend, Yassir Arafat himself requested that Genet write on the Palestinian revolution. If this reveals in the founder of the Palestine Liberation Organization (PLO) an unsuspected literary eclecticism, it does not speak very well for his political judgment. To date, there has been no official Palestinian distancing from Jean Genet's perverse celebration of the Palestinian revolution.

Fleetingness defines Genet's Palestinians. Genet's attraction to the terrorist and to figures of deception and maliciousness is attuned with his inclination for theatricality and histrionism legible in his earlier novels and stage productions. In 1968, Andy Warhol declared that, "In the future, everyone will be world famous for fifteen minutes." As if to confirm Warhol's prophecy, Genet notes that television turned the Black Panthers into stars:

> Fragile . . . par la quantité d'images de télé, qui étaient par définition fugaces, par la rhétorique à la fois brutale et tendre, non soutenue par une réflexion interne sévère, par une théâtralité inconsistante—la théâtralité en somme—, par la qualité des emblèmes vite effacés. [Fragile . . . by the quantity of television images, which were by definition fleeting, by the rhetoric at once brutal and tender, not supported by an internal and rigorous reflection, by an inconsistent theatricality—theatricality itself, in sum—, by the quality of emblems soon erased.] (Genet 1995: 74).

Genet's terrorist—the Black Panther or the Palestinian *fedai*—must attain the level of inconsistency, superficiality and transience that will literally turn him into a shooting star. Assassination as one of the fine arts, or, as Sartre put it in his *Saint Genet*, "Des belles-lettres considérées comme un assassinat" ["Of *literae humaniores* considered as assassination"][16]: " . . . l'Assassinat peut être considéré comme un des Beaux-Arts, à condition de donner aux mots les majuscules qu'ils attendent" ["Assassination can be considered as one of the Fine Arts, as long as one confers on words the capital letters that they yearn for"] (Genet 1995: 263).[17]

Accompanying the author's slow extinction, *Un captif amoureux* is Genet's *Mémoires d'outre-tombe*. The narrative is woven as a sumptuous and discrete suite of fragments and drifting memories, a sort of fugato or requiem. The musical metaphor holds throughout the memoir, first with an evocation of the Renaissance composer of church music, Palestrina (Genet 1995: 60), an anagram, Genet notes, of "Palestine," then to Mozart's *Requiem*. Funeral or sacred music is, in the memoir's Proustian economy, tied to the Palestinian revolution. Genet's Palestine is musical, and his *fedayeen* are bards who sing their exploits:

> A un moment j'ai chanté en énumérant toutes les villes d'Europe où nous avons fait des coups et je les ai décrites. Tu as entendu que je savais chanter München en allemand sur plusieurs tons? [At one point I sang and enumerated all the European cities we struck and I described them. Did you hear that I could sing München in German in several keys?] (Genet 1995: 71).

Terrorism in every key. Genet's memoir is a polyphony of terror, a rhapsodic embrace of Eros and death. Listening to Mozart's *Requiem* on a Walkman in his hotel room, the memorialist turns Christian music into a Dionysian experience of excess and the loss of individuation, drifts from a fantasy of transsexualism to the epideictic glorification of the suicide bomber or kamikaze. Mozart's funeral music triggers an apology of the counter-natural and of monstrosity à la Sade, revisited by Pasolini. The terrorist is portrayed, by analogy with the transsexual, as a hero who challenges the natural order as the perpetuation of life thus crushing the very foundations of Judeo-Christianity. Christian music, in a scene reminiscent of *A Clockwork Orange* where Alex masturbates to Beethoven's Ninth Symphony, is turned into a debauchery of death and sex, an ode to joy and death or a "Viva la muerte" that echoes the Futurists' celebration of war and the symphony of putrefaction:

> Le transsexuel sera donc un monstre et un héros . . . La terreur commencera par la résistance des pieds refusant de diminuer: les chaussures de femmes, talon aiguille pointure 43–44 sont rares, mais la joie couvrira tout, elle et la gaieté. Le *Requiem* dit cela, joie et crainte. Ainsi les Palestiniens, les Chi'ites, les Fous de Dieu qui se précipitaient en riant vers les Anciens des cavernes et les escarpins dorés du 43–44 se virent sauter avec mille éclats de rire en avant, mêlés au recul farouche des trombones. Grâce à la joie dans la mort, ou plutôt dans le nouveau, contraire à cette vie, malgré les deuils, les morales furent en panne. Joie du transsexuel, joie du *Requiem*, joie du kamikaze . . . joie du

héros. [The transsexual will be monster and hero . . . Terror will begin with the resistance of feet refusing to shrink: women's shoes, stillettos size 43–44 are scarce, but joy will overwhelm all, joy and gaiety. The Requiem speaks that, joy and fear. Thus the Palestinians, the Shiites, the Mad for God who rushed laughing towards the old Cavemen and golden court shoes size 43–44 saw themselves explode with a thousand bursts of laughter forward, mixed with the ferocious retreat of trombones. Thanks be to joy in death, or rather in the new, contrary to this life, despite the mourning, morals broke down. Joy of the transsexual, joy of the Requiem, joy of the kamikaze . . . joy of the hero.] (Genet 1995: 91).

Genet is aware that terrorism pertains to fascist nihilism. He writes of the Black Panthers: "Il faut pourtant des moments saccageurs et pillards, côtoyant le fascisme, y tombant quelquefois momentanément, s'en arrachant, y revenant avec plus d'ivresse" ["And yet one needs looting and pillaging moments, approaching fascism, falling into it at times momentarily, tearing themselves away, coming back to it with more drunkenness"] (Genet 1995: 424). A Dionysian figure who transgresses borders and limitations (genders, life and death, good and evil, self and other, but also geo-political borders), Genet's Black Panther and Palestinian *fedai* also recall Nietzsche's tragic Greeks, who were superficial out of profundity, and conversely, serious out of lightness:

> Le sérieux des révolutionnaires n'est que jouer [The revolutionaries' gravity is just play] (Genet 1995: 345).

> L'expression des Grecs: "Que la terre te soit légère", avant qu'il ne meure le feddai on peut dire qu'à la terre il fut léger [The Greek phrase: "May the earth be light upon you," before dying one can say that to the earth the *fedai* was light] (Genet 1995: 367).

Palestinians point to a theatricality which itself pertains to an ontological regime of spectacularity and spectrality. This spectral regime subverts distinctions between reality and appearance and fosters a ghostly and evanescent modality of being—what Genet refers to as "vapor" and "evaporation." The Orientalist cliché of the ghostly, vaporous indigene is reversed into an ontologically positive attribute. This ontological positivity echoes Georges Bataille's "instant" as opposed to "durée,"[18] a distinction that grounds the other distinction, between the economy of expenditure and play and the bourgeois economy:

> Les feddayin, les responsables, leurs actions, la révolution palestinienne, tout fut un spectacle, c'est-à-dire que je vis les feddayin quand je les vis, sortis de ce qu'on nomme angle de vision, ils n'étaient plus. Pour mieux

les saisir le mot juste serait évaporés. Où partis? Quand revenir? D'où? Qu'y faire? D'être ainsi, spectres apparaissant, disparaissant, leur donnait cette force convaincante d'une existence plus forte que les objets dont l'image demeure, qui jamais ne s'évaporent, ou plutôt l'existence des feddayin était si forte qu'elle se permettait des évanescences immédiates, presque courtoises afin de ne pas me fatiguer par une présence insistante [*Fedayeen*, those in charge, their actions, the Palestinian revolution, all was a show, that is, I saw the *fedayeen* when I saw them, outside of what is called the angle of vision, they were no longer. To grasp them better, the right word would be evaporated. Where gone? When to return? Whence? What to do? Being thus, appearing ghosts, disappearing, endowed them with this convincing power of a stronger existence than the things whose image remains, which never evaporate, or rather the existence of the fedayeen was so strong that it could afford spontaneous evanescence, almost courteous so as not to fatigue me by an insistent presence] (Genet 1995: 493).

Slide, mortals, don't bear down! as Sartre's granny would have it. To the heaviness of being that characterizes the Judeo-Christian civilization, Genet opposes the transient lightness of appearances and gestures that he fancies as the stuff of the Palestinians. Palestinians, like the Black Panthers, are real insofar as their struggle fosters an economy of play, expenditure and simulacrum that recalls Jean-Francois Lyotard's 1975 praise of the Sans Culottes' frivolity.[19] Recall that Genet's stay among the Palestinians and the Black Panthers occurs in the aftermath of May 1968, during the pagan revival of French thought, the emergence of a philosophy of surfaces and simulacra, the time of Gilles Deleuze's and Félix Guattari's *Mille plateaux*, of Jean-Francois Lyotard's *Economie libidinale* and *Rudiments païens*, a neo-Nietzschean era when truth and depth were turned upside down.[20] French thought, jaded by conceptual durability, explores aesthetic and political alternatives. This is the time of "intensities," a rebellion against the heaviness of dialectic. French intellectuals surf not only on the West Coast but also on philosophical concepts and traditional logic. French philosophy, in its post-structuralist, post-1968 moment, rubs the skin of thought. This is also the time of the prohibition of prohibition, according to the proverbially paradoxical and Dadaistic May motto, "Il est interdit d'interdire" ["Forbidding is forbidden"], which turned the Law against itself. The joyful memories of May 1968's festival are superimposed on the Palestinian revolution through multilayered personal memories interwoven with historical events (Genet 1995: 405). The more frivolous the revolutionaries are, the more real. For Genet, the reality test, in revolution, is simulacrum and fugacity. A revolution is real to the extent that it shines for an instant and fades out. The Palestinian revolution is best encapsulated in this formula, in which one easily recognizes Bataille's "instant" that characterizes the economy of evil: " . . . avoir été dangereux un millième de seconde" [" . . . to have been dangerous for a fraction of second"] (Genet 1995: 391). The power of the Palestinian upheaval, like that of the Black Panthers or Baader's Red Army, strikes like lightening and erases itself—as do the poet's words that constellate on the page, as do the black letters that imprint their dark light on the white page of America:

> Fulgurant, Saint-Just savait sa fulgurance, les Panthères Noires leur brillance et leur disparition, Baader et ses compagnons annonçaient la mort du shah d'Iran; les feddayin sont aussi des balles traçantes, sachant que leur trace s'efface en un clin d'oeil [Lightning, Saint-Just knew his fulgurance, the Black Panthers their brilliance and their vanishing, Baader and his comrades heralded the death of the Shah of Iran; the *fedayeen* are also tracer bullets, knowing that their trace disappears in the blink of an eye] (Genet 1995: 97).

Revolt should remain aerial, like a bird's flight, a volt in the air, or the pulverization of a plane with its passengers, lest it monumentalize itself. The more removed from an end revolutionary terror is, the more Genet embraces it. Genet's revolution is, to use Giorgio Agamben's terms, a poetics of means without end.[21] Such is, one could argue, the poet's conception of terrorism. What is a revolution, for Genet? A revolt that failed because it succeeded. Revolution is the name that popular upheaval takes "quand elle dure et se structure, quand cessant d'être une négation poétique, elle se veut affirmation politique" ["when it lasts and structures itself, when, ceasing to be a poetic negation, it aims at political affirmation"] (Genet 1995: 171).

In that regard, the metaphysics of terror with its regime of transgression, speed, pulverization and erasure must crush the *dureté* and the *durée* of the Jewish Law and of the Jewish state as the worldly incarnation of an origin written in stone. Note that while Genet identified with the fate of black Americans and the Palestinians as victims of Western oppression, the group among the former victims of the West that does not benefit from Genet's unconditional love is the Jews. Apparently, the Jews' impairment for Genet lies in that by becoming Israelis, they joined the family of settled nations and betrayed their status of eternal wanderers and metaphysical pariahs. The once oppressed have, in a dialectical reversal often denounced by Genet, imitated their oppressor. The Jews have become the Nazis.[22] Furthermore, Holocaust survivors, by resettling in Israel, have punished the Palestinians rather than the Europeans for their suffering. Arabs, according to Genet, had to pay for crimes and losses inflicted upon the Jews by Europeans. In Genet's worldview, Palestinians have taken up the metaphysical status of eternal wanderers, despite the fact that, as the writer himself admits, they express contempt for the nomadic condition:

> Historiquement: ils se veulent la descendance des Philistins, "peuple venu de la mer", c'est-à-dire de nulle part. Géographiquement: limité par

deux côtes, celle de la mer et celle du désert, il fut longtemps un peuple exécrant le nomadisme. Attaché à la terre, il vivait d'elle [Historically: they claim to be descendants of the Philistines, "people come from the sea," that is, from nowhere. Geographically: confined within two shores, the sea shore, and the desert shore, this was long a people that loathed nomadism. Attached to the land, living off it] (Genet 1995: 343).

To be fair, Genet lucidly admits that his love for the Palestinians was enhanced by their homeless condition and that his unconditional justification of their struggle may stop if and when the Palestinians are established in a nation-state:

Le jour où les Palestiniens seront institutionnalisés, je ne serai plus à leur côté. Le jour où les Palestiniens deviendront une nation comme les autres nations, je ne serai plus là [The day the Palestinians are established, I will no longer be at their side. The day the Palestinians become a nation like other nations, I will no longer be there].[23]

Yet, despite apparent similarities in the fate of the two exiled peoples, Genet's relation to the Palestinians greatly differs from his relation to the Jews. While Genet's relation to the latter is one of anxiety and repulsion, his relation to the former can at worst turn into indifference and forgetting once Palestine becomes a state. Genet's repulsion for the Jews, his early fascination with Hitler, cannot be reduced to a mere rejection of established power and of state terror against disarmed populations. What attracts Genet to the Palestinians and the Black Panthers is less their alleged vulnerability than their virility. As Marty puts it, siding with the Palestinians and the Black Panthers against Israel and the United States amounts to siding with "puissance" against "pouvoir": "Encore au début de 70, le Parti avait souplesse et raideur qui évoquaient un sexe mâle—aux élections ils préféraient son érection" ["Back in early 1970 the Party enjoyed the suppleness and stiffness that evoked a male organ—to elections they preferred its erection"] (Genet 1995: 425).

Genet's attraction for the Black Panthers' and the Palestinians' stiffness is notorious. It is also well known that Jews did not turn him on. Recall Sartre's witty comment on Genet's declaration that he could never have sex with a Jew: "Israël peut dormir tranquille" ["Israel can sleep tight"].[24] If Jews did not attract Genet, it is obviously not out of racial prejudice or repulsion for the color of their skin or the size and shape of their nose. Just as the Jews were an "anti-race" for the Nazis (*Gegenrasse*), for Genet, the Jews are the anti-erotic people insofar as they embody the origin of Judeo-Christian morals grounded on the principle of limitation, sexual reproduction and sexual difference—precisely what the aesthetic and erotic of terrorism strive to subvert. Marty argues that for Genet, the Jews embody anxiety toward the Good and the Law. Genet's Jewish anxiety is both a fear of the archaic and an archaic fear. The Jews, an arch-historic people, emerge from what Maurice Blanchot used to call "l'ancien, l'effroyablement ancien" ["the archaic, the dreadfully archaic"].[25]

Remembering road signs in Beirut written in English, Arabic and Hebrew, Genet writes: "Dessiné plutôt qu'écrit, sculpté plutôt que dessiné, l'hébreu causait un malaise comparable à celui qu'eût donné un troupeau tranquille de dinosaures" ["Drawn rather than written, carved rather than drawn, Hebrew provoked a malaise comparable to the one that a quiet herd of dinosaurs would have provoked"] (Genet 1995: 442). Genet's malaise triggered by the encounter with the Hebrew writing can be traced back to a traumatic childhood memory, a form of archaic terror that only the anarchic violence of Palestinian terrorism can conjure away:

> Mon enfance se souvenait d'avoir vu ces caractères, sans connaître leur sens, ciselés dans deux pierres oblongues, collées l'une à l'autre par les tranches, et nommées Tables de la Loi [My childhood remembered having seen these characters, without knowing their meaning, chiseled in two elongated stones, stuck one to the other by their edges and called the Tables of the Decalogue] (Genet 1995: 442).

Hebrew writing, by synecdoche, points to the threatening and indelible engraving of an incomprehensible Law. Follows a natural depiction à la Buffon of Hebrew writing, perhaps triggered by a confused memory of the letters *shin* and *tsadeh*—not by chance the first letter of the name of the Israeli army, *Tsahal*:

> Un ou deux caractères étaient coiffés de l'aigrette, celle des grues; trois minces pistils soutenant trois stigmates antés[26] sur les trois pistils attendant les abeilles qui poudraient le monde d'un pollen plusieurs fois millénaire, ou, mieux, original; et ces aigrettes de la lettre qui se dit à peu près *ch* en français, n'ajoutaient aux mots ni à l'injonction quelque légèreté, elles disaient le triomphe cynique de Tsahal et les trois points de l'aigrette avaient la majesté un peu sotte de la tête du paon, un peu sotte aussi de la bécasse espérant le sperme [One or two characters were crowned by the egret, the cranes' egret; three thin pistils supporting three holes grafted on the three pistils waiting for the bees who powdered the world with a pollen several thousand years old, or, better, original; and these egrets of the letter pronounced something like *ch* in French, added lightness neither to the words nor to the injunction, they declared the cynical triumph of Tsahal and the three dots of the egret had the somewhat silly majesty of a peacock's head, somewhat silly also of the woodcock yearning for semen] (Genet 1995: 442).

This natural (floral and avian) depiction of Hebrew calligraphy is sexual and political through and through. It expresses, if possible, both contempt ("silliness") and awe ("triumph") for the sovereign power of the Hebrew letter, crowned by an "egret" or crest, and seen as a promise of fertility and regeneration. Hebrew writing, for Genet, is pregnant with reproductive potential (an "original pollen") and sexual difference that Genet's writing strives to avert.[27] *Tsahal*, the Israeli army, in Genet's metaphysics, secures the sovereign triumph of sexual reproduction and seals the victory of weight and durability over the subversive lightness of Palestinian terror. To the Hebrew writing's threatening squares, incised in stone as it were, Genet's poetics responds with aerial and convoluted arabesques. More enigmatically, Hebrew writing is characterized by discontinuity and intervals between letters that point to a multilayered temporality:

> Mais surtout notre surprise, notre dégoût restaient marqués de ce terrifiant discontinu, chaque lettre épaississant entre elles un espace non mesurable et un temps si tassé que cet espace résultait d'un empilement de plusieurs épaisseurs de temps; espace si éloigné entre chaque lettre qu'il méritait le nom de "temps mort", car il était impossible à mesurer autant que l'"espace"—mais est-ce l'espace?—séparant un cadavre de l'oeil du vivant qui le regarde [But above all our surprise, our revulsion remained struck by this terrifying discontinuity, each letter thickening between them an unmeasurable space and a time so compact that this space resulted in a sedimentation of several layers of time; space so removed between each letter that it deserved the name of "dead time," as it was as impossible to measure as the "space"—but is it space?—separating a corpse from the eye of the living who gazes at it] (Genet 1995: 442).

This immeasurable interval between each square letter, Genet fancies, is a "dead time" comparable to the interval that separates a corpse from the eye of the living that gazes at it. The anxiety triggered by this incised and incisive writing is thus a death anxiety. Looking at Hebrew writing amounts to staring at the face of the dead letter as if at Medusa's head. But this petrifying death is distinct from the festive and pagan death that terrorism celebrates, just as Palestinian terrorism is distinct from Israeli state terror, just as "puissance" is distinct from "pouvoir" and anarchy from *arche*. Instead, this petrifying death is the abhorrent cycle of generation and perpetuation of the Jewish race grounded on the transmission of the letter of the Law according to a political and sexual process that echoes that of bee pollination and "swarming": "Dans cet espace incommensurable séparant chaque lettre hébraïque, des générations sont nées, ont essaimé" ["Within this incommensurable space that separates each Hebrew letter, generations were born, have swarmed"] (Genet 1995: 442) (We should heed to the waves of meaning and sounds propelled by this "essaimé": "s'aimer," "semer" and "sémite.")

In his essay on the Sabra and Shatila massacre published in the *Revue d'études palestiniennes* a few years before the publication of *Un captif amoureux*, Genet had already expressed, in a vivid rhetoric reminiscent of traditional anti-Semitism, his anxiety with regard to the perpetuation of the Jewish race. Interestingly, the following excerpts, probably deemed counterproductive by the editors of a journal published by a publisher known for its antifascism and antiracism, were cautiously suppressed from the final version of Genet's account:

> The Jewish people, far from standing out as the most unfortunate among the peoples of the earth, was forcing upon everybody the story of the genocide while in America, Jews, rich and poor, were banking sperm for procreation, for the perpetuation of the "chosen" people.[28]

For Genet, it is less that the Jews have exploited their real suffering than that they have fabricated it altogether. They forged the Holocaust. It is worth noting that Genet writes these lines just a couple of years after Robert Faurisson claimed in French newspapers that the gas chambers never existed.[29] While European Jews were forging this "story" of suffering and persecution, American Jewry, rich and poor alike, more faithful to "race" solidarity than to class struggle, manufactured human weapons—an interesting projection on the Jews of what will become in Palestinian warfare the turning of human beings into literal weapons.[30] Jews reproduce capital and other generations of Jews—Jew as currency and capital as Jewish—at a pace that threatens mankind. Eventually, the true face of the Jews emerged in the creation of the Jewish state. Israel, the state, reveals the essence of the Jew, the eternal Jew, as it were. The Hebrew colonizer and persecutor of Gentiles supercedes the falsely persecuted wanderer:

> Finally, thanks to a sophisticated yet predictable metamorphosis, the Jewish people is now such as it had been preparing itself to become for such a long time: a temporal and abject power, a colonizer as one would no longer dare to be, the Definitive Power that it owes to its long curse as well as to its election (Genet 1991: 408).

It is now clear that Genet's Jews point to a prehistory before prehistory, to the *arche* itself, in the two senses of power and origin, as principle of the Law and of generation. Prehistory is but the trope of an encrypted and repressed archive, of what we may begin to intuit as sexual difference. This figure of the *arche* is given by Genet as an irrevocable *arch-writing*, a primal scene of writing that, I would argue, Genet's own writing attempts to un-write and conjure away:

> Remontée, cette écriture ne l'était pas seulement de l'enfance, mais bien qu'elle fût présentée au monde au sommet d'une montagne elle remontait d'une caverne, profonde et sombre, où étaient emprisonnés Dieu, Moïse, Abraham, les Tables, la Thora, les Ordres, revenus

ici, à ce carrefour d'une préhistoire avant la préhistoire, et sans rien savoir de précis sur Freud, nous éprouvâmes toute l'énormité de la pression qui, en deux mille ans, avait réussi ce Retour du Refoulé [Resurfaced, this writing not only from childhood, but although it had been presented to the world at the summit of a mountain it was resurfacing from a cave, deep and dark, where God, Moses, Abraham, the Torah, the Commandments were imprisoned, resurfaced here, at this crossroads of a prehistory before prehistory, and without knowing anything precise about Freud, we felt the enormity of pressure which, in two thousand years, had accomplished this Returned of the Repressed] (Genet 1995: 443).

With Genet's metaphysical anxiety, triggered by the Hebrew letters seen on the Beirut road signs, we are far removed from a critique of Zionism, colonialism or Israeli oppression. Genet's oeuvre presents the best exemplification to date of the ambiguous contamination between anti-Zionism and the metaphysics and psychology of European anti-Semitism.[31] Most fascinating is the paradox inherent in Genet's critique of the Jewish state: both in accordance with and against the founder of modern Zionism, Israel appears to Genet as both new and old—Theodor Herzl's *Altneuland*. This collision of the new and the old, of the modern and the ancient, turns modern Israel into a Benjaminian historical event, a dialectical image of sorts, which triggers awe and aversion.

To highlight the significance of this primal scene of writing and to stress the insoluble ambiguity of Genet's position vis-à-vis Hebrew letters and thus vis-à-vis Judaism, Israel and the Jews, I will turn to the introit of the memoir, which already contains an elusive reference to Hebrew writing. This elusive reference seems to undo, or at least to nuance beforehand, the characterization of Hebrew writing in terms of anxiety, contempt or revulsion that I have attempted to describe above. To begin, one must state that the first two pages of Genet's memoir, perhaps even more stubbornly than the rest of the novel, resist legibility. Moreover, this grandiose overture stands as an allegory of the resistance of reading and of the limits of translation—reading as translation of writing, writing as translation of the lived experience. This overture stages the untranslatability of the experience of the Palestinian revolution into an epic written in French. Genet begins with a rhetorical question. This question suggests that the spaces between words—the intervals or the voids (i.e., the unwritten or un-inscribed)—may carry more reality than the letters themselves, the black characters on the white page:

La révolution palestinienne fut-elle écrite sur du néant, un artifice sur du néant, et la page blanche, et chaque minuscule écart de papier blanc apparaissant entre deux mots sont-ils plus réels que les signes noirs? [Was the Palestinian revolution written on nothingness, an artifice written on the void, and the blank page, and each tiny space of blank paper appearing between two words aren't they more real than the black characters?] (Genet 1995: 11).

The real or the lived experience hides between the words and ought to be read in the void spaces between them. Then a characterization of reading as an art of interstices follows. This characterization borrows its lexicon from the marine and mountaineering registers, granted that the predicate "étale" (flat, still, quiet) applies especially to the sea: "Lire entre les lignes est un art étale, entre les mots aussi, un art à pic" ["Reading between the lines is a still art, between the words as well, an abrupt[32] art"] (Genet 1995: 11). This double metaphor projects the art of reading between the lines onto two perpendicular axes, the horizontal axis of the sea and the vertical axis of a cliff or a mountain. Reading between the lines, reading the unwritten, is thus described as an art that can potentially trigger dizziness—precisely what is occurring, in a movement of *mise-en-abyme*, to the reader of this introit, myself, and, by hermeneutic contagion, to the reader of this reading. The art of reading is stretched between the meditative serenity of a still sea, and the imminent danger of a fall:

> Si elle demeurait en un lieu la réalité du temps passé auprès—et non avec eux—des Palestiniens se conserverait, et je le dis mal, entre chaque mot prétendant rendre compte de cette réalité alors qu'elle se blottit, jusqu'à s'épouser elle-même, mortaisée ou plutôt si exactement prise entre les mots, sur cet espace blanc de la feuille de papier, mais non dans les mots eux-mêmes qui furent écrits afin que disparaisse cette réalité [Were it to remain in one place the reality of the time spent near—and not with them—Palestinians would be preserved, and I say it awkwardly, between each word claiming to bear witness to this reality whereas it is curling up, even coinciding with itself, carved or rather so exactly caught between the words, on this blank space of the sheet of paper, but not in the words themselves which were written so that this reality could disappear] (Genet 1995: 11–12).

The experience of Genet's stay with the Palestinians can only be preserved, if at all, between the very words that claim to account for it. Again, Genet's metaphor is that of carving, "mortaisée." It is as though the illegible, original experience were carved out between the words, as though the writing were hollowed out by the real (the *Erlebnis*) that it claims to account for. But the participle "mortaisée" also splits into "mort" and "taire," death and silence, as though the writing had silenced and suppressed the lived experience. Not only do the words fail to translate the lived experience, but also they suppress it. Not only do they suppress it, but also they intend to do so. Indeed, Genet tells us that the words were written *in order to* undo this reality, in accordance with the sublating movement of *Aufhebung* that at once preserves and suppresses. The finality of language, legible in the syntactical conjunction "afin que," consists in suppressing the world and replacing it with the word, an argument attuned with Maurice Blanchot's theory of language in his famous 1947 essay on terror and literature.[33] Transposing history into words erases history. Yet, words—letters—exist as the vestige of such an erasure. All in all a Mallarmean or Hegelian cliché about the nullifying essence of language that sublates the thing into a concept thus abolishing it all the while preserving it, Genet's introit would not be especially original or relevant to the current discussion. However, it is at this very juncture that Genet evokes, for the first time in the novel, the example of the Hebrew writing:

> Ou bien je le dis autrement: l'espace mesuré entre les mots est plus rempli de réel que ne le sera le temps nécessaire pour les lire. Mais peut-être l'est-il de ce temps compact et réel, serré entre chaque lettre de la langue hébraïque [Or let me put it differently: the space measured between the words is more pregnant with reality than ever will be the time needed to read them. But perhaps it is so with this compact and real time, folded between each letter of the Hebrew language] (Genet 1995: 12).

The voids between the words are filled with time (experience and reality), just as time is compressed between each letter of the Hebrew language. The reader is thus confronted with a dizzying conundrum: first, writing erases reality which can only be inferred from what is not written between the words; second, the Hebrew writing is threatening because it is filled with time, duration, generations, etc. Hebrew writing, as the medium of the Law, is saturated with time and history. Third, the Hebrew language, to the extent that it opens spaces between letters, is the ultimate witness to history. There is no easy way out of this conundrum. The Hebrew language in fact stands as a trope of reading itself—as the opening of text to different readings throughout time. The irresolution of meaning should press the reader to extreme caution and nuance when it comes to gauging Genet's anti-Semitism.

To be fair, Genet never concealed his metaphysical antipathy for the people that he perceived as the shepherd of the immemorial, as witnessed in the following rhetorical question:

> Si elle ne se fût battue contre le peuple qui me paraissait le plus ténébreux, celui dont l'origine se voulait à l'Origine, qui proclamait avoir été et vouloir demeurer l'Origine, le peuple qui se désignait Nuit des Temps, la révolution palestinienne m'eût-elle, avec tant de force, attiré? [Had it not fought against the people which seemed to me the darkest, that whose origin claimed to be in the Beginning, which claimed to have been and to wish to remain the Beginning, the people which

called itself the Night of Times, would the Palestinian revolution have attracted me with so much force?] (Genet 1995: 239).

If, as Artaud declared in 1947, "Là où ça sent la merde, ça sent l'être" ["Where it smells like shit, it smells like Being"], then by defecating over Japan in the bathroom of the airplane that takes him to the orient of the earth, Genet frees himself from his Judeo-Christian being and expels this encrypted origin:

> Je me levai . . . afin d'aller chier à l'arrière de l'avion, espérant me libérer d'un ver solitaire long de trois mille ans. Le soulagement fut presque immédiat: tout irait bien puisque la délivrance commençait par une nasarde à la bienséance [I stood up . . . to take a shit at the rear of the airplane, hoping to free myself from a three thousand year long tapeworm. The relief was almost immediate: all would go well because the liberation had started with a slap at good manners] (Genet 1995: 78).

Having relieved himself of Judeo-Christian morals, a three-thousand-year-old parasite, Genet anticipates that once in Tokyo, he will be "nu, souriant, prompt, capable de décapiter d'un coup le premier, le second douanier ou de m'en foutre" ["naked, smiling, swift, able to behead in one blow the first, the second customs officer, or not to give a damn"] (Genet 1995: 78). The terrorist act, instead of a violent yet salutary enactment of justice, is coextensive with the eradication of the Law according to the nihilistic motto, "All is permitted." Once landed in Japan, Genet imagines the murder of a Japanese little girl, in a vision soon to be short-circuited by images of Jews in death camps:

> "Tant de fragilité est une agression qui exige une répression." Je me dis cela probablement sous une autre forme et l'on peut supposer que je fus traversé par des images de juifs nus ou presque nus, décharnés dans les camps où leur faiblesse était une provocation ["So much fragility is an aggression requiring punishment." I said this to myself probably with different words and one can suppose my mind was crossed by images of Jews, naked or half naked, emaciated in the camps where their weakness was a provocation] (Genet 1995: 79).

Two modalities of nakedness should be distinguished: (a) the nakedness of innocence regained after the defecation of the Law as a principle of separation and prohibition (*nu comme un ver*, as the French has it), and (b) that of the exposed Jewish flesh whose vulnerability, like that of the Japanese girl, begs for punishment—the body of the Law itself, this tapeworm that hinders anomic *jouissance* and must be crushed or expelled. To conclude, I would argue that condemning Genet as an anti-Semite is as futile as glorifying him as a militant for peace and justice in the Middle East. To construe Genet, as Edward Said attempted to do in a 1990 essay, as the advocate of the colonized and a righteous author, is a misreading, deliberate or not. Here is how Said characterized Genet's political and artistic position:

> Je ne pense pas qu'il soit erroné de dire qu'au vingtième siècle . . . le grand art n'apparaît au sein d'une situation coloniale que dans la mesure où il soutient ce que Genet dans *Un captif* appelle l'insurrection métaphysique des indigènes. L'art plus médiocre fait dans l'élégance, mais finit toujours par donner sa faveur au *statu quo* [I don't think that it is erroneous to say that in the twentieth century . . . great art appears in the midst of a colonial situation only to the extent that it supports what Genet calls in *Un captif* the metaphysical insurrection of the autochthones. More mediocre art plays the game of elegance, but always ends up furthering the status quo].[34]

For Said, the great artist, in a colonial conflict, should choose either political progress (i.e., the people's upheaval and revolutionary terror) or conservative cheesiness. Assuming that the Palestinian side was the right one, I would argue that Genet did not side with the Palestinians out of moral integrity or political progressivism. Said, understandably touched by Genet's political position in the Arab-Israeli conflict, misses the writer's metaphysics and aesthetic so authoritatively analyzed by Marty, after Georges Bataille (who died twenty years before the publication of Genet's Palestinian memoir). By wanting at all costs to put Genet on the side of the good and of political progress, by missing Genet's fascination with evil and with reactionary, at times feudal, forms of community, Said misrepresents precisely what makes Genet a great poet. Genet does not merely side with the oppressed and the colonized but with those who are the most likely to crush the Law and to abject the Jew within the Western self. This does not mean that great art is necessarily anti-Semitic, nor does it suggest that Palestinians are not oppressed, but that, in order to be great, art does not have to be virtuous. This does not suggest either that the Palestinians and the Black Panthers are not the weak in the equation of hostilities, but instead that Genet's literature, as Andre Gide would have it, is not made out of good sentiments.[35]

ACKNOWLEDGMENT

This article is dedicated to Eric Marty.

NOTES

1. Jean Genet, *Un captif amoureux* (Paris: Gallimard, coll. "Poche" 1995). All further references will be to this edition. All translations from the French are

mine. Readers familiar with Genet's work are aware of the difficulties that a translator encounters, especially because of the syntactic ellipses (anacoluthia) and of perpetual shifts in the lexicon. In other words, its elusive and "tropological" quality (as Paul de Man would have it) makes Genet's prose particularly hard to render in another language. Because my analysis rests on close attention to the original signifier, I have chosen to use my translation instead of the official one: Jean Genet, *Prisoner of Love* (New York: NYRB Classics, 2003).
2. On the vexed question of responsibilities in this massacre, see Eric Marty, "Jean Genet à Chatila," in *Bref séjour à Jérusalem* (Paris: Gallimard, 2003). Marty's inquiry weighs in favor of the Israelis and of former General Ariel Sharon, but he is just in recalling that the one who ordered the massacre was the member of the Lebanese Phalange Party, Elie Hobeika. Not long after the event, Hobeika was appointed deputy in the Lebanese Parliament, then became minister of several pro-Syrian governments from 1991 to 1998. Unlike Sharon, Hobeika was never indicted or charged with war crimes. He was murdered on January 24, 2002, by the Syrian secret services.
3. See *Jean Genet et la Palestine, Revue d'études palestiniennes* (Paris : Editions de Minuit, 1997). The *Revue d'études palestiniennes* was founded in 1981 and hosted by the Editions de Minuit. Everything indicates that the Arab-Israeli conflict is as much a French question as a Middle Eastern and international one. Indeed, Editions de Minuit, an underground publisher founded in 1941, was instrumental in circumventing Nazi censorship. There is little doubt that the foundation of *Revue d'études palestiniennes* can be perceived as a continuation of the French communist resistance against fascism. *Mutatis mutandis*, it puts the Palestinians in the place of yesterday's "Résistants" and the Israelis in that of the Nazis or French collaborators. See also "Les Palestiniens," in *Genet à Chatila*, textes réunis par Jerome Hankins (Arles: Babel, 1994), and "Quatre heures à Chatila" in *L'Ennemi déclaré*, (Paris: Gallimard, 1991).
4. On this political ricochet and its repercussions in French memory of WWII, see Joan Wolf, *Harnessing the Holocaust: Politics of Memory in France*, (Palo Alto, CA: Stanford University Press, 2004).
5. Note that Gilles Deleuze and Félix Guattari, the initiators of nomadic philosophy, were also advocates of the Palestinian cause. Guattari authored a piece on Genet's novel in *Revue d'études palestiniennes* devoted to Genet. In 1957, Georges Bataille had identified in Genet, along with Marcel Proust and Charles Baudelaire, a poet of evil; in the 1970s and 1980s, Genet was harnessed by the philosophy of "déterritorialisation," nomadism, schizophrenia and "anti-Oedipus."
6. *Paradise Now* was directed by Hany Abu-Assad and released in 2005.
7. Paul Virilio, *Ce qui arrive* (Paris: Galilée, 2002), 92.
8. See Walter Laqueur, *The New Terrorism: Fanaticism and the Arms of Mass Destruction* (Oxford: Oxford University Press, 2000).
9. Quoted in Frank Lentricchia and Jody McAuliffe, *Crimes of Art and Terror* (Chicago, IL: University of Chicago Press, 2003), 7.
10. This motto was attributed by Walter Benjamin to Marinetti, in the conclusion of his famous essay on fascism, art and technology, "The Work of Art in the Age of Mechanical Reproduction," in *Illuminations* (New York: Schocken Books, 1969). See, on the terrorist, the poet and the European tradition of nihilism, Paul Berman, *Terror and Liberalism* (New York: Norton, 2004).
11. On the flirtation between Surrealism and totalitarian ideologies, see the intriguing and polemical book by the art historian Jean Clair, *Du surréalisme considéré dans ses rapports au totalitarisme et aux tables tournantes*, Mille et une nuits, coll. "Fondation du 2 mars," 2003.

12. See Rebecca Allison, "9/11 Wicked But A Work Of Art," *The Guardian*, September 11, 2002.
13. On the multilayered etymology of the word "Islam," see Fethi Benslama, *La Psychanalyse à l'épreuve de l'Islam*, Aubier Montaigne, 2002. On Islam and submission in Western philosophy since Montesquieu, see Gil Anidjar, *The Jew, the Arab: A History of the Enemy* (Palo Alto, CA: Stanford University Press, 2002)
14. *Les Temps modernes*, Gallimard, No 622, December 2002.
15. Georges Bataille, *La Littérature et le mal*, (Paris: Flammarion, 1990, or 1957 for the original edition).
16. This is the title of a section of Sartre, *Saint Genet, comédien et martyr* (Paris: Gallimard, 1952).
17. On this question, see again Lentricchia and McAuliffe, *Crimes*.
18. See Bataille, *La Part maudite* (Paris: Editions de Minuit, 1949), and again *La Littérature et le mal* for its application to literary theory.
19. See "Futilité en Révolution," in *Rudiments païens*, Editions 10–18, 1977.
20. See proceedings of the Cerisy-la-Salle colloquium, *Nietzsche aujourd'hui*, Editions U.G.E 10–18, 1973.
21. See Giorgio Agamben, *Means Without End: Notes on Politics* (Minneapolis, MN: University of Minnesota Press, 2000).
22. Once again, it is uncanny to read Genet's polemical writings today, at a time when, in the wake of the Second Intifada, Israel has been repeatedly compared to Nazi Germany in Europe and the United States, by Jews and non-Jews alike. See Alvin Rosenfeld's essay "Progressive Jewish Thought and the New Anti-Semitism," in *American Jewish Committee*, December 2006. See also Berman, *Terror*.
23. Genet, *Ennemi*, 282.
24. Marty, *Jérusalem*, 91.
25. See Maurice Blanchot, *L'Ecriture du désastre* (Paris: Gallimard, 1980).
26. The verb "anter" does not exist in French, let alone the past participle "antés." Genet should have written "entés," from the verb "enter," "to graft," but one can assume that his train of thought was haunted ("hanté"!) by the floral motif (hence the homonym "antés" that echoes "anthology," "chrysanthemum," etc., from the Greek *anthemon*, flower.) However, I have not been able so far to verify the spelling on the original manuscript. On Genet and flowers, see Jacques Derrida, *Glas* (Paris: Galilée, 1974).
27. The quasi scientific rigor of Genet's description recalls eighteenth century Naturalists. See for example the scientific prose of the *Encyclopédie ou Dictionnaire raisonné des Sciences, des Arts et des Métiers*, article "Fleurs des plantes" (p. 6: 853): "Le pistil est la partie femelle de la génération; il est composé du germe, du stile, & du stigmate; le germe renferme les embryons des semences; le stile est entre le germe & le stigmate, mais il ne se trouve pas dans toutes les plantes; le stigmate est l'ouverture qui donne entrée aux poussieres fécondantes des étamines, pour arriver aux embryons des semences à traver le stile." (1749.)
28. These sentences shed a new light on Genet's metaphysical reasons for siding with the Palestinians in the conflict with Israel. This excerpt can be found in the scholarly dossier gathered by Albert Dichy, in *L'Ennemi déclaré*, 408 (subsequent references to this volume will be indicated parenthetically in the text).
29. On the Faurisson affair and Holocaust denial in the early 1980s see Alain Finkielkraut, *L'Avenir d'une négation* (Paris: Le Seuil, 1982), and Pierre Vidal-Naquet, *Les assassins de la mémoire* (Paris: Le Seuil, 1995).

30. Arafat is reported to have declared often that "his strongest weapon is 'the womb of the Arab woman.'" (see Fareed Zakaria, "Israel's Best Plan: Build More Walls," *Newsweek*, August 13, 2001.) Such a chilling bio-political declaration echoes the twentieth century militant demographics in totalitarian and fascist regimes. It assumes that the female body ought to be offered on the altar of a nation embodied by a male leader who claims ownership on women.
31. For a psychoanalytic approach to contemporary anti-Semitism and anti-Zionism, see *Psychanalyse de l'antisémitisme contemporain*, in *Pardès*, issue 37 (2004), edited by Shmuel Trigano.
32. "à pic" evokes the peak of a mountain, a nuance lost in "abrupt."
33. See Maurice Blanchot, "La littérature et le droit à la mort," in *La Part du feu* (Paris: Gallimard, 1949).
34. In "Les derniers écrits de Jean Genet," *Revue d'études palestiniennes*, 39 (1991): 91–104.
35. "j'aurais voulu vous expliquer comment c'est avec les beaux sentiments que l'on fait la mauvaise littérature, et qu'il n'est point de véritable oeuvre d'art où n'entre la collaboration du démon" ["I would have wished to explain to you how it is with lofty sentiments that one makes bad literature, and that there is no authentic work of art without the collaboration of the devil"]. André Gide, *Dostoïevsky* (Paris: Gallimard, 1964), VI, O.C. t. XI, 283–284.

Part IV
Muslim-Jewish Relations in France, 1990–2008

10 The War Comes Home
Muslim-Jewish Relations in Marseille during the 1991 Gulf War

Maud S. Mandel

On August 2, 1990, Iraq invaded Kuwait, unleashing the first Gulf crisis. When, by January, the United Nations' economic sanctions had failed to force Iraqi withdrawal, the United States and a thirty-four nation coalition invaded. Although Israel did not participate, this brief war, over by February 28, could not help but intersect with the ongoing Arab-Israeli conflict. Not only did the Iraqi president, Saddam Hussein, choose to drop missiles on Tel Aviv, touching off a secondary crisis over potential Israeli involvement, but calls to resolve the Palestinian question as part of a regional settlement circulated widely. For Muslims and Jews watching developments from afar, the First Gulf War thus became more than a conflict over Kuwaiti independence, oil rights or western imperialism. Rather it became a barometer of Muslim-Jewish relations around the world.

Nowhere was this more evident than in France, the one country outside of Israel where significant Jewish and Muslim populations still live in close proximity. With an estimated 4–5 million Muslims and 600,000 Jews concentrated in a select number of cities, France stood poised for its own crisis. Indeed, as the U.N. withdrawal deadline of January 15 grew near, journalists, communal leaders, police informants, government officials and the "man on the street" worried that the Gulf War was coming to France, and Christian, Jewish and Muslim religious leaders held joint services hoping to stave off interethnic conflict.[1] SOS Racisme, the antiracist association which had famously brought Muslims and Jews together in the mid-1980s, was torn asunder as several founding fathers—well-known Jewish intellectuals—quit over the organization's pacifist stance on the war.[2] "All our work to bring the communities together risks being wasted," lamented the French Algerian comedian, Smaïn, of the mounting tension.[3]

As the war progressed, however, interethnic violence did not increase significantly, leaving commentators to explain why the worst had not come to pass.[4] According to one journalist, a common cultural heritage and "nostalgic memories of warm relations in the Maghreb" may have helped to dampen passions.[5] Others stressed the multiple calls for peace by Muslim and Jewish leaders and the French national culture of promoting citizenship over ethnic particularism.[6] Still others blamed the media for overstating interethnic rivalry in the first place. "French society is not on the verge of civil war," declared the sociologist Adil Jazouli.[7]

How, then, can we understand Muslim-Jewish relations during the 1991 Gulf War? Was civil war imminent, and, if so, what kept passions in check? If not, what accounts for the growing fear? This article will address these questions by focusing on Muslim-Jewish relations in Marseille. A cosmopolitan port city, in 1991 Marseille numbered Muslim and Jewish populations of approximately 100,000 and 80,000, respectively.[8] While Paris housed substantially more of both, Marseille's urban landscape, which brought the two populations into greater contact, and its proximity to the Gulf and to North Africa, which was itself experiencing considerable war-related disruption (and to which many of Marseille's Muslims and Jews had links), led many to believe that interethnic conflict was inevitable.[9] An "army of journalists invaded the city," noted the Chief Rabbi, "[where] they expected a violent confrontation between Arabs and Jews."[10]

As elsewhere, however, such dire predictions proved inaccurate. What prevented the "inevitable"? Perhaps the explanation lies in hypotheses for Marseille's generally peaceful climate, which have focused on everything from the city's sunny weather to its cohesive urban geography.[11] And yet if Marseille's unique social landscape has encouraged peaceful interethnic cohabitation, the Gulf crisis provides additional clues as to why relations remained calm. In particular, the policing of minority populations, and particularly Muslims who, it was feared, sympathized with Saddam, influenced events. By early January fears of international terrorism and violence in immigrant neighborhoods led the Ministry of Interior to implement the Plan Vigipirate, increasing surveillance of airports, official buildings, public gathering places and French Muslims.[12] While various officials, including President Mitterrand, insisted that law-abiding Muslim residents had nothing to fear, insecurity loomed large.[13] In contrast, for Jews, so often accused of dual loyalty, the First Gulf War proved a pleasant change. While nervous about Israel's fate, they supported France's decision to ally itself with the coalition. Thus, as Muslims grew increasingly uneasy, Jews experienced a growing sense of security. These differing stances had a marked impact on intercommunal relations.

Marseille's Gulf War crisis unfolded in two stages. The first began in August and took full shape as the U.N. ultimatum to withdraw drew closer. During this period, Marseille's Muslim and Jewish populations both hoped that war could be avoided and feared that, if not, urban life would suffer. In the second stage, from the war's outbreak to early February, relations grew increasingly tense. Although leaders on both sides called for calm, seemingly stabilizing mounting interethnic strains, the calm hid stark differences. If "civil war" was never likely, interethnic tensions were palpable and had a lasting impact on the city.

MOUNTING TENSIONS

From August until mid-January when war still seemed avoidable, public conversation about Kuwait remained relatively muted in Marseille. To the extent that Muslims and Jews voiced opinions, they not surprisingly differed over possible resolutions and potential repercussions for Palestinians or Israelis. Such perspectives were often secondary, however, to shared concerns that war in the Gulf would have negative consequences at home. In short, Jews and Muslims responded to early events through the prism of their shared urban environment.

The fusion of the international and the local surfaced immediately in Jewish responses as fears over Israel's security were intermixed with concerns over potential violence at home. By early January, Israel had not mobilized its army, leading many Jews in Marseille and throughout the world, to hope that in any war Israel would remain peripheral. As armed conflict seemed evermore likely, however, Marseille's Jews began fearing terrorism and intercommunal violence. Such fears were salient enough that Marseille's Consistoire, the local arm of French Jewry's central religious institution, established a sophisticated security apparatus. In addition, Jewish leaders requested permission from Marseille's prefecture to arm key communal figures. Concern about the local repercussions of war also initially subdued Jewish hopes for French participation in the American coalition. Some Jewish leaders quietly observed that any intervention could be interpreted as support for Israel, providing an inevitable boost to local anti-Semitism. Similarly, local members of the Conseil représentatif des institutions juives de France (CRIF), the umbrella political body for French Jews, worried that anti-Semitism was being stoked by an anti-Israeli media bias. While there had as yet been no domestic or international violence, Jews in Marseille already viewed themselves as potential victims of the international political drama.[14]

Marseille's wider population also responded to the conflict as if their city would be one of its battlefields. As the U.N. ultimatum grew closer, sugar, oil, and pasta began disappearing from supermarkets, and public commentary focused increasingly on the local repercussions of an international conflict. According to one resident, "There are not enough police to protect us." Another commented, "If the Iraqis ever attack Israel, the conflict will ignite and the Arabs will increase terrorism in France."[15] Particularly in Marseille's northern immigrant neighborhoods, xenophobia by non-Muslim residents was palpable. "We buy sugar, the Arabs buy bullets," remarked one police informant. According to another, "if [war] explodes, the police and army won't be able to do anything here."[16] Here fears of imported terrorism merged with longstanding anti-Muslim prejudices to predict violence in Marseille.

Anti-Muslim attitudes alone, however, cannot explain mounting concerns, since Muslims were equally afraid, stocking up on provisions like their neighbors and avoiding peace rallies where they might attract attention. Indeed, as will become clear, Muslims—even more than their Jewish and non-Jewish neighbors—worried about the consequences of a Middle Eastern war on their daily lives (and in their countries of origin). Although some sympathized with Hussein for his anti-American and anti-Israeli stance, most hoped war could be averted.[17]

Given the size and diversity of Marseille's Muslim population, there was no initial consensus on how to respond. The Iraqi attack against another Muslim nation meant that the Arab world more generally disagreed over the conflict's potential resolution; indeed, most Arab states *joined* the American-led coalition. These divisions manifested themselves in France's Muslim population primarily around generational lines. Thus, older Muslims with a longer history in Marseille generally urged support for France's international stance and voiced little public support of Saddam. Younger Muslims and those who had more recently immigrated adopted a harder line, leaving police to predict that 90 percent of Muslim youth would refuse to join their military units in a general mobilization call. Police also fretted over, "a certain arrogance among young Muslims, such as the group that drove back and forth in front of the caserne des marins-pompiers de Plombières making throat-slitting gestures to the soldiers on guard."[18] Reflecting police biases more than any widespread stance by young Muslims, such comments nevertheless point to concerns about the war's domestic impact. Such fears were bolstered when some merchants reported being threatened by young Maghrebians, and on January 12, when a dozen Muslim students assaulted some peers for supporting the United States against Iraq.[19]

If such incidents, however, suggest that some young Muslims felt emboldened by Saddam's Kuwaiti incursion, more dramatic are the lengths to which most religious and associational leaders went to preserve civic peace. Although initially unanimous that Saddam Hussein had provided them with "honor and dignity," most "refused to discuss the merits of the conflict or to offer a clear-cut judgment." Indeed, like those Jewish leaders who feared rising anti-Semitism, Muslim leaders responded to the Gulf crisis by assuming that xenophobia would inevitably result and by working to calm communal passions. Thus local imams used the last Friday before the ultimatum to call for calm, as did the Conseil national des français d'origine arabe on January 16. Although individual Muslims criticized French policies and proclaimed support for Iraq, such appeals remained isolated given communal leaders' fear that they would, "degenerate" and become "a source of embarrassment."[20]

Also calling for calm was Marseille-Espérance, a multi-confessional body created in 1990 by the mayor, Robert Vigouroux. Under its auspices, representatives of Marseille's various religious communities—including Jacques Ouaknin, Chief Rabbi, Mohand Alili, president of the Association culturelle islamique and head of the Grand Mosquée de Marseille, Abdelhadi Doudi, president of the Ligue islamique de Marseille and Bachir Dahmani, president of the Fédération régionale des musulmans du sud de la

France—planned a joint ecumenical service on January 17.[21] While multi-confessional efforts were not unique to Marseille, the fact that Marseille-Espérance had existed prior to the war and maintained an official link with the mayor's office gave it distinctive symbolic power.[22]

Whether as a direct result of such calls or as a reflection of wider fears that Marseille's interethnic fabric was at risk, the city remained calm prior to the invasion. On the charged day of January 15, bars in the *quartiers populaires*, generally frequented by a mixed European and Muslim clientele, remained quiet despite some isolated incidents. Moreover, directors of social housing units in Marseille's northern districts reported no "feeling of exasperation within the Muslim community, including the youth."[23] Insofar as Jews and Muslim held different hopes for the conflict's resolution, these mattered less than maintaining Marseille's ethnic balance.

THE OUTBREAK OF WAR

Immediately following the coalition invasion, most city residents opted to "lay low," continuing to stock up on supplies. If the external environment remained quiet, however, the local landscape had shifted. Jews, often accused since 1967 of dual loyalty for criticizing French Middle Eastern policies, found themselves on the "right" side of the country's international policy. Muslims in contrast felt increasingly insecure as their allegiances were questioned, a shift that inevitably influenced the evolution of Muslim-Jewish relations.

For Jews, the shift was not immediately apparent, since the invasion brought fears of local violence to a head, and communal leaders made no public declarations of any kind. Moreover, attendance at religious services dropped, a stark contrast from Paris where the main synagogue was full to capacity for a pro-Israeli prayer vigil on January 14. Clearly, then, the sense that the war could come home was still salient. Unlike the preceding days, however, Marseille's Jews began drawing comfort from France's international stance. Early fears of increasing anti-Semitism gave way to relief that France had joined the coalition. Still focused on international events and hoping the Israeli army would stay home, Jews nevertheless slowly began to feel more comfortable, a fact that became visible in the day to come.[24]

For Muslims, the invasion was anything but reassuring; the government's decision to join the coalition disappointed many, particularly—as we have seen—young Muslims, and set the stage for unrest. Initially, however, as for their Jewish neighbors, all that was evident was the marked tension accompanying the outbreak of war. Associational and religious leaders made no public pronouncements. In Aix, prayer services were poorly attended, and the university was notably absent of flyers or meetings. In Marseille, market streets in Muslim areas were virtually empty, and according to police, the "climate [was] very tense."[25]

Anger at the turn in international events, however, was palpable. "Muslims are attentive to the evolution of events," reported police, "and skeptical of the western media's objectivity in reporting news."[26] This skepticism was driven by a tacit support for Saddam among young Muslims who took pride in his willingness to challenge the world's most powerful nations. As one Parisian high school student remarked, "Saddam is an Arab who is ostracized by everyone—like us in our cities. For once, we do not feel humiliated, but rather defended. We are holding discussions on an equal footing with the big powers." For many young French Muslims, then, Hussein's stance provided a potent symbol for their own struggles for civic inclusion. The early 1990s had been marked by a growing interest in the Palestinian cause, as a generation of French born Muslim youth sought outlets to express their own sense of oppression. As Kader Selmet, president of the sociocultural organization Emergence in Nanterre, noted, "Today, the beurs' cause is Palestine. It even overtakes issues of racism, employment and housing."[27] Given that Yasser Arafat had been one of the few Arab leaders to support the Iraqi invasion and that Saddam Hussein's attacks against the West included strong denunciations of the Palestinian plight, the link between the war and Palestinian oppression was all the more palpable.

In Marseille, pro-Palestinian sentiment also characterized youth culture and became entangled with Hussein's war. As one twenty-three-year-old Muslim resident remarked, "We do not stand behind him 100%, but we have found in him the best defender of the Palestinian people." Here hopes of finding a champion merged with support for Saddam and the Palestinians—support that was manifest in sales of the Algerian singer Mohamed Mazouni's song "Vas-y Saddam," the cover of which replaced Pascal with Hussein on the 500 franc bill. According to one local merchant, three hundred cassettes had been sold in fifteen days, a record for the distribution company.[28]

Not surprisingly, mounting support for Hussein among Muslim youth led to tension with French Jews. Thus teachers reported rising interethnic conflict in schools with mixed populations, and the number of violent incidents increased. On January 20, for example, Muslim students attacked some young Parisian Jews while yelling "Saddam Hussein." On January 16, members of the right-wing Zionist youth movement, Betar, attacked a Tunisian student for distributing tracts at the université de Paris-Tolbiac, and a handful of Jewish religious institutions were vandalized following the invasion. In the first fifteen days of the war, there were approximately thirty anti-Muslim and forty anti-Jewish incidents throughout the country.[29]

In Marseille, such tension was particularly marked. According to one reporter, "Marseille, an open, diverse, and lively city, has suddenly witnessed a change in atmosphere. She has become contorted before the war's coming storms: fear of attacks and confrontations between communities."[30] In this environment, anti-American and anti-Zionist rumblings began to link American policy in the Middle East to the influence of Jews.

"Nothing differentiates an American Jew from an Israeli Jew," remarked one Muslim informant to police.[31] Most notably, on January 18, the Imam of the mosque of Madrague Ville, Abdelhadi Doudi, called on Muslims to unite against the "the Jewish lobby that dominates the west, the USA and France." More worrisome, he insisted that "peaceful co-existence" between Muslims and Jews was impossible and that it was necessary to "persecute them until they disappear."[32] Likewise, a circulating tract declared Muslims and Jews to be eternal enemies. While such tracts were atypical and surfaced mostly outside of Marseille proper, police reported that, "the situation is such that the smallest incident could lead to intra- and even extracommunal confrontations."[33] Muslim observers feared that if Israel entered the war, "there would inevitably be additional tension and some risk of loss of control [derapages]."[34] In this atmosphere, the joint ecumenical prayer service previously scheduled for January 17 was cancelled. In its place, key religious leaders met privately to call for fraternity throughout Marseille's population, standing arm in arm for a photo that was published in local papers that day.[35]

Worried about the tense environment, national Muslim leaders stressed the multiplicity of views in the Muslim community, insisting (correctly) that French Muslims were a heterogeneous population. Thus Daniel Youssouf Leclercq, president of the Fedération nationale des musulmans de France, for example, noted that, "This is not [just] a Muslim issue. There are Muslims on both sides."[36] Locally, such responses were echoed by second generation French Muslims, such as Said Merabti, representative of France Plus, who urged his coreligionists not to demonstrate and to trust the French president to respond to Muslim hopes for justice.[37] Such comments were a reflection of a complex social reality in which generational rifts led Muslims with roots in France for many years to support the government's decision to join the coalition. Even more interestingly, however, were those communal leaders who had previously taken a hard line on France's stance in the war, and who now began shifting tone. Thus during services on January 18, for example, Alili, who had previously condemned America's presence in the "Holy Land," defended France, urged calm and turned his attack against "the Arab governments implicated in this conflict."[38] Similarly trying to tamp down on rising tensions, Radio Gazelle, a community-based radio station directed at French Muslim audiences, refused to play Mazouni's song supporting Saddam, a choice that was echoed by Radio Soleil in Paris.[39]

It was in this tense environment that Iraq dropped Scud missiles on Tel Aviv. Given the heated rhetoric of previous days, one might well have expected televised images of Israelis in gas masks and euphoric Palestinians to ignite the long-feared interethnic war in Marseille. Interestingly, however, there was little public response. Nevertheless, the impact of the shifting political environment was clearly evident. Jews not surprisingly expressed deep pain over the attack. Given that many had family in Israel, calls for revenge circulated widely, but privately, and the directors of CRIF called for moderation regarding all discussion of Middle Eastern affairs. Widespread Western support and Israel's choice not to retaliate made such advice easier to follow, even though, according to police, most Jews did not support any measures that would hinder Israel. Rather, anger at the bombing evolved quickly into pride that Israel had not responded to provocation and to substantial fundraising efforts. Subsequently, leaders of Zionist associations began organizing a pro-Israel rally for January 28 at the Consulate General. In the short run, then, outrage over the attack and a sense that French and Jewish concerns finally coincided returned confidence to Marseille's Jewish population, symbolically evident in the willingness of young Jews to wear *kippot* in the streets.[40]

Muslims felt no such security. Following the Scud attack, public support for Saddam certainly increased, and the "man on the street" displayed visible relief that the Iraqi leader would regain respect after humiliating war losses. Annoyance over media representations of Iraqi versus Israeli destruction under bombardment was also rampant. Generally speaking, however, the Scud attack did not disrupt the malaise that blanketed Marseille's Muslim population. If anything, people became more discreet, glued to radios and televisions inside their homes. Police noted very few North Africans in Marseille's streets, a 60 percent drop in market activity, and low attendance at religious gatherings, a pattern that continued for weeks. Moreover, Hussein's call for a Holy War on January 20 fell on deaf ears.[41] As one Moroccan resident wrote in a letter to the prefect after expressing concern about "the climate of uncertainty that has been stirred up," by the war, "holy war must never be used to carry out an attack or a crime."[42] In this environment, some French Imams criticized Hussein for tearing apart the Muslim world.[43] While Radio Islam France announced a blood drive for Iraqi victims and played Arab nationalist songs and while departure rates for Algeria increased somewhat, public demonstrations were notably absent. Rather, the Grand Mosquée in Marseille planned a day of mourning and contemplation for January 21 during which merchants were invited to lower their blinds and Muslim children were asked to stay home from school. While, according to police reports, 95 percent of North African merchants in the city center participated (as did local Jewish merchants who feared altercation with their neighbors), this muted demonstration was much more subdued than the march planned for January 28 in front of the Israeli consulate.[44]

Given the fear of civil disruption, it is notable that communal life remained calm. The coalition's rapid victories certainly disappointed those hoping for rapid Iraqi success and any public support for Hussein diminished. By late January, a national poll indicated that 56 percent of Muslims viewed Hussein critically with only 22 percent expressing sympathy for him, statistics that suggest that early predictions of mass support for Iraq among French Muslims were misplaced. Moreover, and perhaps more importantly, a series of domestic decisions put France's Muslim population on high alert. As noted previously, the Plan Vigipirate had already increased surveillance to an alarming degree. Then, on January 22, the French government expelled a well-known Algerian activist along with fifteen other Iraqis, Moroccans, Algerians and Lebanese, increasing precipitously the feeling that French Muslims were at risk. According to the same poll, 73 percent of the 582 Muslims interviewed feared a rise in racism and new difficulties finding work, 57 percent feared expulsions and 58 percent worried about their future.[45]

Such fears began reigning in communal radicalism. Abdelhadi Doudi, for example, previously notorious for his incendiary discourse, began calling for the conflict's peaceful resolution. As a declaration from the Ligue islamique de Marseille, of which he was president, proclaimed: "[We] appeal to all Muslims to work toward peace and fraternity among all of the ethnic groups that form one single family . . . We are all brothers."[46] This was a radical change from his previous week's preachings. Fear also kept Muslims away from the large peace demonstration on January 26. As local police noted, "the expulsions' psychological impact are much greater than one might have imagined . . . it is thus a sense of fear and an attitude of discretion that dominates."[47] Anti-French tracts circulating in the city's northern districts and signed by the Amicale des Algeriens en Europe (ADAE) also caused distress. The latter, an Algerian compatriotic organization, disclaimed responsibility, insisting that French extremists were circulating such tracts to foment anti-Muslim attitudes (an assertion that was backed up by newspaper reports that month). ADAE officials instead called for calm.[48]

Some Muslims, of course, insisted that fear should not determine communal priorities. In particular, those representing a younger, more politicized generation, angrily decried efforts to paint French Muslims as a menace. Namane Saada of the Nouvelle génération, for example, condemned the Plan Vigipirate for its repressive monitoring of Arabs, "who are not all terrorists." This organization participated enthusiastically in Marseille's peace demonstration on January 26 and raised relief funds for Iraqi civilians.[49] Tahar Ramani, representative of Perspectives et solidarité arabo-musulmane de France, railed on Radio Galère against accusations of double allegiances, asking rhetorically: "Are three million Arab immigrants foreign agents in France?" Sympathy with the "Arab nation" and particularly with the conflict's civilian victims, was no different he argued, than Jewish loyalties toward Israel. Lest this reference be misunderstood, he finished by saluting "the harmony of the Arab and Jewish populations who are going through a difficult time." Arguing that the call for calm was exaggerated, he nevertheless underscored that cohabitation among all communities was essential: "The French Arabo-Muslim community, particularly in Marseille, desires to maintain its identity with respect and dignity. We therefore call on all communities to remain calm in the face of this psychosis and for the respect of everyone in their diverse opinions."[50]

Ramani's anger over accusations of double loyalty and double standards nevertheless emphasized the value of peaceful interethnic relations. Indeed, despite differences within the Muslim population over how best to respond to the new domestic challenges, such calls for cooperation soon became pervasive. On January 23, for example, the director of Radio Islam France, Kheila Safia, invited Muslim, Jewish and Catholic mothers to jointly call for peace.[51] Not to be outdone, Radio Galère called for "social peace in Marseille among all co-habitating communities and for the end to the war" so as to ensure that "war does not cause interethnic confrontations in Marseille."[52] Likewise, Club Mergence, an organization promoting Franco-Maghrebian integration, established dialogue groups in Marseille's schools.[53] Nationally, a delegation of Jewish and Muslim leaders, brought together by the associations Identité et dialogue and Dialogues juifs et arabes en France, visited the prime minister, to proclaim their opposition to "all uses of the current conflict to incite racial hatred and intolerance."[54]

This environment had an impact on local Consistoire and CRIF representatives who began working evermore closely with Muslim leaders to reduce intercommunal tensions. In fact, by the end of the month, interethnic cohabitation had begun taking precedence over other communal priorities, a point most clearly underscored by the fate of the pro-Israel rally on January 28. As noted earlier, when bombs first fell on Israel, several Jewish organizations in Marseille, including the Consistoire and CRIF, agreed to sponsor a rally. As the date approached, however, leaders of both organizations put pressure on local Zionist organizations to cancel the event. While the Fédération des organizations sionistes and Betar refused, other Jewish organizations chose not to send representatives and only 250 activists turned out, at least half of whom were between sixteen and twenty-five years of age. Like their Muslim counterparts, Jewish youth displayed greater militantism than their elders. Nevertheless, the rally was significantly reduced in a region well known for large pro-Israel demonstrations.[55] Thanks, then, to the caution of leaders of both groups as well as to the profound sense of insecurity hovering over Marseille's Muslim population, urban tension diminished. According to police, despite periodic circulation of incendiary tracts, interethnic conflict was on the decline. By January 25, streets had taken on their "normal appearance" and no incident had disturbed the public order.[56]

The peaceful nature of communal interactions are perhaps most evident in one of the moments that broke the calm. On January 27, an unknown Zionist organization claimed responsibility for a small explosion at an immigrant workers' hostel in Marseille. Interestingly, little public outcry followed. Behind the scenes, Jewish and Muslim leaders coordinated their response, helping to keep tempers calm.[57] Alili insisted that the event was not significant enough to mobilize the community, and Radio Galère, a local station stressing Marseille's multicultural heritage, issued a new call for peace.[58] Meanwhile, the Chief Rabbi, Jacques Ouaknin denounced the act by a "pseudo" Zionist group designed "to pit the two communities against each other."[59] The regional press also downplayed the event—in *Le Marseillaise* the only article appeared on page seven—noting that the same building had been attacked before with greater force. The violence, thus, had no visible social repercussions, and police reported that Marseille Muslims viewed it as "a marginal provocation."[60]

And yet if peaceful coexistence continued, the atmosphere remained strained. In early February, police reported that while all was still calm in Marseille, North African youth were again becoming impassioned about the Gulf. In one elementary school, for example, several Muslim children attempted to conduct a prayer for Hussein.[61] Militant Zionists, as we have seen, went forward with their pro-Israel demonstration despite local political costs, and while intercommunal dialogue was widely supported by spokesmen of both communities, Muslim leaders were quick to note that such relations were often "tinged with hypocrisy," given Jewish unwillingness to recognize the acuity of the Palestinian problem.[62]

As such comments suggest, Muslims and Jews continued to view international events from opposing perspectives, the most notable example of which came on February 13 when two American "smart bombs" destroyed an Iraqi civilian air shelter, killing hundreds of civilians. In response, Muslim youth began once again expressing anti-Western sentiment and declaring themselves ready to take up arms for the Iraqis. Jewish residents, in contrast, manifested indignation over the bombardment's sympathetic portrayal in the media. Stopping short of accusing the French media of treason, Jewish observers nevertheless complained of a consistently anti-Israel bias. Such differences had consequences. Thus, on February 20, the Jewish Agency for Israel in Marseille received an anonymous call in Arabic accented French warning of reprisals if Israel attacked Iraq.[63]

And yet, despite such disturbances or perhaps because of them, communal leaders tamped down on all political expression, maintaining calm throughout Marseille's integrated neighborhoods. By mid-February, Muslim religious and associational leaders were meeting weekly with their Jewish and Christian counterparts to ensure peace. All too aware that Hussein would soon lose the war, Muslim spokesmen began calling for a ceasefire over local radio stations. Turning to the war's aftermath, they argued that Muslim neutrality had been a sign of successful integration that the government should reward with increased efforts to fight unemployment and improve living conditions. Whatever tensions remained were thus quickly subsumed under the priority of channeling war "losses" into potential political gain.[64]

CONCLUSION

Despite dire predictions, then, Marseille side stepped the crisis and the Gulf War remained in the Gulf. The question is why. Did preexisting interethnic understanding restrain communal passions? Such perspectives certainly have played a role in Marseille's cultural self-image. As one cab driver recently commented, "I'm a Jew, my neighbors, they're Arabs, we understand each other fine."[65] In 1991, however, the tension was palpable and this mutual respect was far from evident.

Were communal leaders responsible for navigating Jewish and Muslim populations through stormy seas, preventing what would otherwise have been violent altercations? Undoubtedly the existence of Marseille-Espérance and its multi-confessional appeals for calm was significant in its symbolic demonstration that dialogue and peaceful coexistence were possible even in the most trying times. More importantly, the affiliation with the mayor's office opened lines of communication from the municipality to the religious leadership, allowing the latter to react quickly and cohesively when any conflicts arose.

And yet, while those affiliated with Marseille-Espérance celebrated their role in maintaining calm, a focus on leadership alone marginalizes another pervasive force that shaped social choices.[66] As we have seen, Muslims—much more than their Jewish neighbors—experienced the Gulf War through a prism of tremendous insecurity. Increased surveillance, expulsions and a sense that their future in France was in peril, did much to quell public activism. Indeed, one could argue that the Gulf War was a turning point for Marseille's Muslim population and particularly for young French Muslim citizens. For many, the 1980s had seen rapid political integration as unprecedented numbers had participated in traditional electoral politics to fight racism and the Front National.[67] The sense of rejection that came in 1991 was thus profound. As Alili commented bitterly in an interview in *Le Meridonal* on February 25, there was a gap between the inclusive message being promoted by national leaders and its "every day transcription, lived poorly by Muslims."[68] Likewise, police reported that Muslims in Marseille were "disappointed" with authorities, believing they had earned greater trust and "the official removal of all ambiguity regarding their citizenship."[69]

A recent study has argued that Muslim youth in Marseille feel significantly more "Marseillaise" than French, a case the study's authors make by focusing on the role of urban geography in shaping local identities.[70] While the city's unique layout, which alleviates the social tensions of other French cities due to its lack of *banlieus*, has been powerful in integrating generations of immigrants, the material presented here suggests that the Gulf War may very well have alienated a generation of Muslims on the cusp of national integration. Furthermore, while the sense of insecurity engendered by the war explains the root of this alienation, it is also clear that comparisons with their Jewish neighbors played a part in this transition. Indeed, by early March, police reported a sense of bitterness among Marseille's Muslims of having been considered "citizens of a second order ... sacrificed to the Jewish community that had the benefit of a reassuring public discourse."[71] As we have seen, this perception was largely accurate.

During the war, Jewish connections to Israel were rarely questioned and, more importantly, public policy reflected their concerns. For Muslims, in contrast, accusations of double loyalties emerged in force. Tensions between Muslims and Jews, then, reflected this relationship to the French context as much as they reflected differing perspectives on the Middle East, setting the scene for intercommunal relations into the new millennium.

NOTES

1. H.T., "Veillées de prières en France," *Le Monde*, January 16, 1991, p. 10.
2. Bernard Philippe, "Le recentrage de SOS-Racisme," *Le Monde*, February 2, 1991, p. 7.
3. Bernard Philippe, "Les beurs entre la fierté et la crainte," *Le Monde*, January 17, 1991, p. 9.
4. "Selon la Commission nationale consultative des droits de l'homme les violences racistes n'ont pas augmenté en France depuis le début de la guerre," *Le Monde*, February 9, 1991, p. 7.
5. Henri Tincq, "Juifs et musulmans sur la réserve," *Le Monde*, February 6, 1991, p. 1.
6. Arezki Dahmani and Robert Sole, "Une entretien avec M. Arezki Dahmani," *Le Monde*, February 8, 1991, p. 2.
7. Philippe Bernard, "Un rencontre de SOS-Racisme," February 15, 1991, p. 8.
8. For Muslims in the early 1990s, see Jocelyne Cesari, "Les Modes d'action collective des musulmans en France: le cas particulier de Marseille," in *L'Islam en France: Islam, état et société*, Bruno Étienne, ed. (Paris: Éditions du Centre national de la recherche scientifique, 1991), 284–285. The figure for Jews is the commonly cited statistic.
9. More than half of Marseille's Muslims were foreign born and from Algeria, Tunisia or Morrocco. Cesari, "Les Modes d'action collective," 284–285.
10. Robert P. Vigouroux and Jacques Ouaknin, *Laïcité +Religions: Marseille-Espérance* (Marseille: Transbordeurs, 2004), 41.
11. Jocelyne Cesari, Alain Moreau and Alexandra Schleyer-Lindenmann, *"Plus marseillais que moi, tu meurs!"* in *Migrations identités et territoires à Marseille* (Paris: L'Harmattan, 2001), 11–26.
12. Articles by Dominique le Guilledoux, *Le Monde*, January 16, 17, and 24, 1991.
13. "L'Entretien télévisé du chef de l'État," *Le Monde*, January 22, 1991, p. 13.
14. "Crise dans le Golfe Persique: réactions de l'opinion publique des Bouches-du-Rhône," December 14, 1990; "Réactions de l'opinion publique des Bouches-du-Rhône à la tension dans le Golfe Persique et aux perspectives de guerre," January 8, 1991; "Crise du Golfe—État de l'opinion publique des Bouches-du-Rhône," January 16, 1991, 1693W239, Archives départementales, Bouches-du-Rhône. Unless otherwise noted, all subsequent archival notations are from this file.
15. "Crise du Golfe—État de l'opinion publique des Bouches-du-Rhône," January 15, 1991.
16. "Crise du Golfe—État de l'opinion publique des Bouches-du-Rhône," January 16, 1991.
17. "État d'esprit de la communauté musulmane à l'approche de l'expiration de l'ultimatum du 15/1/91," January 14, 1991.
18. "Crise du Golfe—État de l'opinion publique des Bouches-du-Rhône," January 16, 1991.

19. "État d'esprit de la communauté musulmane à l'approche de l'expiration de l'ultimatum du 15/1/91," January 14, 1991; "Crise du Golfe—État de l'opinion publique des Bouches-du-Rhône," January 15, 1991; "Premier bilan de la confrontation armée dans le Golfe pour la communauté musulmane," March 6, 1991.
20. "État d'esprit de la communauté musulmane à l'approche de l'expiration de l'ultimatum du 15/1/91," January 14, 1991; "Crise du Golfe—État de l'opinion publique des Bouches-du-Rhône," January 16, 1991.
21. Despite references to a "Grand Mosquée" in police documents, there was no such formal structure. Indeed, Marseille has a long history of failed attempts to build a central mosque that have only recently been addressed. Marcel Maussen, "Islamic Presence and Mosque Establishment in France: Colonialism, Arrangements for Guestworkers and Citizenship," *Journal of Ethnic and Migration Studies* 35 (6), August 2007: 981–1002.
22. Vigouroux and Ouaknin, *Laïcité +Religion*; "Crise du Golfe—État de l'opinion publique des Bouches-du-Rhône," January 15, 1991. *Le Monde* reported joint prayer services on January 9, 16, 24, and 31, and February 6.
23. "Crise du Golfe—État de l'opinion publique des Bouches-du-Rhône," January 15, 1991.
24. Jean-Michel Dumay, "La communauté juive invité à participer à un voyage de soutien en Israël," *Le Monde*, January 16, 1991, p. 10; "Conflit du Golfe—Réactions de l'opinion publique des Bouches-du-Rhône," January 18, 1991; "Conflit dans le Golfe—Réactions de la communauté juive dans la région Provence, Alpes, Côte d'Azur," January 19, 1991; "Conflit du Golfe—Réactions de l'opinion publique de la région Provence-Alpes-Côte d'Azur," January 21, 1991.
25. "État d'esprit de la communauté musulmane," January 17, 1991; "État d'esprit de la communauté musulmane," January 18, 1991; "Premier bilan de la confrontation armée dans le Golfe pour la communauté musulmane," March 6, 1991.
26. "État d'esprit de la communauté musulmane," January 18, 1991.
27. Bernard, "Les beurs."
28. Bernard, "Les beurs"; "État d'esprit de la communauté musulmane," January 17, 1991; "Premier bilan de la confrontation armée dans le Golfe pour la communauté musulmane," March 6, 1991.
29. Bernard, "Les beurs;" "La guerre du Golfe: incidents en France," *Le Monde*, January 23, 1991, p. 12; "Selon la Commission nationale consultative des droits de l'homme."
30. Porte Guy, "L'Inquiétude dans les communautés musulmane et israélite Marseille, crispée devant les orages," *Le Monde*, January 21, 1991, p. 8.
31. "État d'esprit de la communauté musulmane," January 18, 1991.
32. "Premier bilan de la confrontation armée dans le Golfe pour la communauté musulmane," March 6, 1991.
33. "Conflit du Golfe—État d'esprit de la communauté musulmane," January 22, 1991.
34. "Conflit du Golfe—État d'esprit de la communauté musulmane," January 23, 1991.
35. "Conflit du Golfe—Réactions de l'opinion publique des Bouches-du-Rhône," January 17, 1991.
36. Jean-Michel Dumay, "Dans la communauté musulmane Dieu aura le dernier mot," *Le Monde*, January 17, 1991, p. 9.
37. Note á l'attention de Monsieur le Préfet, "Associations dèpartementales ayant pour objet la lutte contre le racisme," November 16, 1990, 1693W223;

"État d'esprit de la communauté musulmane," January 17, 1991; "Conflit du Golfe—Réactions de l'opinion publique des Bouches-du-Rhône," January 18, 1991; "Premier bilan de la confrontation armée dans le Golfe pour la communauté musulmane," March 6, 1991.
38. "État d'esprit de la communauté musulmane," January 19, 1991; Dumay, "Dans la communauté musulmane."
39. Bernard, "Les beurs."
40. "Conflit dans le Golfe—Réactions de la communauté juive dans la région Provence, Alpes, Côte d'Azur," January 19, 1991; "Conflit du Golfe—Réactions de l'opinion publique des Bouches-du-Rhône," January 23, 1991; "Conflit du Golfe—Réactions de l'opinion publique des Bouches-du-Rhône," January 25, 1991.
41. "Réactions françaises à la guerre du Golfe," January 21, 1991, Le Monde, p. 22; Jean-Michel Dumay and Henri Tincq, "Un Entretien avec le recteur de la Mosquée de Paris," Le Monde, January 23–24, 1991, p. 20; Jean-Michel Dumay, "Dans la communauté musulmane."
42. Amar Boudchar to the Prefect, February 4, 1991.
43. J.-M. Dy., "À la mosquée Omar de Paris: pleurs, désarroi et tracts," Le Monde, January 20–21, 1991, p. 8.
44. "État d'esprit de la communauté musulmane," January 18, 1991; "Conflit dans le Golfe—Réactions de la communauté musulmane dans la région Provence Alpes, Côte d'Azur, January 19, 1991; "Conflit du Golfe—État d'esprit de la communauté musulmane," January 21, 1991; "Conflit du Golfe—état d'esprit de la communauté musulmane," January 22, 1991; "Conflit du Golfe—État d'esprit de la communauté musulmane," January 23, 1991; "Conflit du Golfe—Réactions de l'opinion publique des Bouches-du-Rhône," January 23, 1991; Guy, "La guerre du Golfe".
45. Henri Tincq, "Selon un sondage de l'IFOP incertitude et peur chez les musulmans en France," Le Monde, January 30, 1991, p. 9.
46. "Crise du Golfe: État d'esprit de la communauté musulmane," January 31, 1991; "Crise de Golfe—Réactions de la communauté musulmane," January 24, 1991.
47. "Crise du Golfe—Réactions de la communauté musulmane," January 26, 1991.
48. "Crise du Golfe—Réactions de la communauté musulmane," January 29, 1991; "Crise du Golfe: État d'esprit de la communauté musulmane," January 31, 1991; "Premier bilan de la confrontation armée dans le Golfe pour la communauté musulmane," March 6, 1991. "Un tract d'extrême droite appelle les musulmans français à combattre le 'sionisme mondial,'" Le Monde, February 12, 1991, p. 10.
49. "Conflit du Golfe—Réactions de l'opinion publique des Bouches-du-Rhône," January 22, 1991; "Crise du Golfe: État d'esprit de la communauté musulmane dans la région Provence-Alpes-Côte d'Azur," February 5, 1991.
50. Direction général des renseignements généraux, "Activité des radios locales émettant en direction de la communauté musulmane," January 25, 1991; "Premier bilan de la confrontation armée dans le Golfe pour la communauté musulmane," March 6, 1991.
51. Direction général des renseignements généraux, "Activité des radios locales émettant en direction de la communauté musulmane," January 23, 1991.
52. Direction général des renseignements généraux, "Activité des radios locales émettant en direction de la communauté musulmane," January 24, 1991.
53. "Crise du Golfe—Réactions de l'opinion publique des Bouches-du-Rhône," January 24, 1991.

54. "M. Rocard a reçu une délégation juive et arabe," *Le Monde*, January 21, 1991, p. 22. For other efforts, see Patrick Jarreau, "Un Entretien avec le président du CRIF," *Le Monde*, January 22, 1991, p. 14; Patrick Jarreau, "Des Associations arabes et juives luttent ensemble pour prévenir des affrontements," *Le Monde*, January 29, 1991, p. 11; Philippe Bernard, "Un Dialogue juifs-arabes à Sursesnes: 'Ne nous retranchons pas dans nos ghettos!'" *Le Monde*, January 31, 1991, p. 7; Salem Kacet and Eric Ghebali, "La Guerre des communautés n'aura pas lieu," *Libération*, January 31, 1991; and Joseph Sitruk, "Ce n'est pas une guerre israélo arabe," *Actualité Juive*, January 30, 1991. Several Pieds-Noirs organizations also sought to create links between Jews and Muslims. Alain Rollat, "Les Pieds-Noirs proposent leurs bons office aux communautés juive et musulmane," *Le Monde,* January 26, 1991, p. 9.
55. "Crise du Golfe—Réactions de l'opinion publique des Bouches-du-Rhône," January 24, 1991; Direction centrale des renseignements généraux, "Crise du Golfe—Manifestations des organisations sionistes, le 28.01.1991, en soutien à Israel," January 29, 1991.
56. "Conflit du Golfe—Réactions de l'opinion publique des Bouches-du-Rhône," January 23, 1991; "Conflit du Golfe—Réactions de l'opinion publique des Bouches-du-Rhône, January 25, 1991.
57. "Crise du Golfe—Réactions de l'opinion publique des Bouches-du-Rhône," January 28, 1991; Vigouroux and Ouaknin, *Laïcité +Religions*, 42.
58. "Crise du Golfe—État d'esprit de la communauté musulmane," January 28, 1991; Direction général des renseignements généraux, "Activité des radios locales émettant en direction de la communauté musulmane," January 27, 1991.
59. "Crise du Golfe—Réactions de l'opinion publique des Bouches-du-Rhône," January 28, 1991.
60. "Crise du Golfe—État d'esprit de la communauté musulmane, January 28, 1991.
61. "Réactions dans les établissements scolaires et universitaires durant la crise du Golfe dans le département des Bouches-du-Rhône," February 1, 1991. For other schools, see Philippe Bernard, "La Guerre au programme: ils croyaient à un truc de bouquins d'histoire.'" *Le Monde*, January 31, 1991, p. 17.
62. "Conflit du Golfe—État d'esprit de la communauté musulmane," February 1, 1991; "Premier bilan de la confrontation armée dans le Golfe pour la communauté musulmane," March 6, 1991.
63. "Guerre du Golfe—Réactions de l'opinion publique des Bouches-du-Rhône," February 14, 1991; "Premier bilan de la confrontation armée dans le Golfe pour la communauté musulmane," March 6, 1991; Telegram to Cabinet du préfet régionale, "Menaces anonymes de représailles envers la communaté juive de Marseille," February 20, 1991.
64. "Crise du Golfe. État d'esprit de la communauté musulmane," February 12, 1991; "Crise du Golfe. État d'esprit de la communauté musulmane de la région Provence-Alpes-Côte d'Azur," February 20, 1991; "Crise du Golfe. État d'esprit de la communauté musulmane de la région Provence-Alpes, Côte d'Azur," February 23, 1991; "Premier bilan de la confrontation armée dans le Golfe pour la communauté musulmane," March 6, 1991.
65. Claire Berlinski, "The Hope of Marseille," *Azure* 19 (Winter 5765/2005), p. 38.
66. Vigouroux and Ouaknin, *Laïcité +Religions*, 53.
67. Cesari, "Les Modes d'action collective."
68. "Communauté islamique de Marseille: État d'esprit des responsables associatifs," February 25, 1991.

69. "Premier bilan de la confrontation armée dans le Golfe pour la communauté musulmane," March 6, 1991.
70. Cesari, Moreau and Schleyer-Lindenmann, *"Plus Marseillais que moi,"* 27–52.
71. "Premier bilan de la confrontation armée dans le Golfe pour la communauté musulmane," March 6, 1991.

11 Hung Up on Being Fair and Left Hanging between the Israeli-Palestinian Conflict and the "Banlieues"[1]

Johann Sadock

Let me save us some time: I may well be in the process of becoming what, in a recent issue of the journal *Controverses*, has been called an "alterjuif" ("alterJew"). It is not entirely clear what an alterJew is, but the alterJews portrayed in *Controverses* are diasporic Jewish intellectuals who have grown less and less comfortable with Israel's treatment of Palestinians and who publicly say so. Today, as much perhaps as in 1982 (the date of Israel's invasion of Lebanon), I also find it hard to be "Jewish" in relation to what the Jewish state has shaped that to mean and to feel good about myself.

The "realJews" will say: "One more reason not to defect to the enemy! It's not supposed to be easier than it already is for us diasporic Jews!" Maybe. The thing is I don't see Palestinians as my enemies or even as the enemies of the virtual Israeli in me. Thanks to Israel's law of return, I *am* a virtual Israeli; but really, what return? Not only don't I come from there, but, as I will explain, it is not like I have done anything to deserve the favor. That the same favor is denied to Palestinian refugees who do come from there may be necessary in order to preserve the Jewish identity of the state of Israel, but it does not make me feel better about myself as a Jew.

I have to add, not out of affectation but for full disclosure, that I am probably not wholly comfortable in my Frenchness, either. You cannot be comfortably French and make a documentary, as I did in 1999, in which most of the blacks and Arabs Kabyls interviewed highlight the discrimination they were up against in France.[2] My original intent with this documentary was not to indict France or the French governments that had let the actual "banlieues" rot in the past twenty years. Rather, I wanted to interview young people from various ethnic and cultural backgrounds to give a sense of France's cultural and ethnic diversity to an American audience. It turned out that my interviewees had some complaints.

This documentary may have been partly about myself as well, though. Or as *Controverses*' director, Shmuel Trigano, puts it somewhat perceptively in the issue on alterJews: "Alteridentity is surreptitiously accusatory and always virtuously enunciated on behalf of the Other. But, at the other end of the 'alter' paradigm, or behind it, one can see the ego reign with majesty."[3] As a Jew born in France to French Jews born in Algeria, I did identify with my interviewees, all these young people who were not seen as real French even when they were born in France.

There is nothing really surprising about that. In more than one way, I am also a child of my generation, the "Touche pas à mon pote" ("hands off my pal") generation, a younger brother of the founders in 1984 of the antiracist movement, SOS Racisme. SOS Racisme seems to have been a more contentious affair than I realized at the time, but I experienced it as a common front against racism and anti-Semitism and I still tend to look back at those years with rose-colored glasses. That is probably another reason why in 1999 I took up my camera: because I could not stand that Jews and Jewish intellectuals who had been involved in the antiracist fight of the eighties would give up the fight for visible minorities in the nineties. The date (1999) is also significant in that I conducted the bulk of these interviews before the Second Intifada (September 2000), at a time when everything was rather quiet on the Israeli-Palestinian front and there was some optimism about the Clinton-led negotiations. It allowed my interviewees and me to talk about something else: mostly their lives, but also interethnic relations in France. Many of my interviewees may have guessed that I was Jewish, but I did not feel I had to tell them before interviewing them. For those who guessed, as for myself, it may have been the proverbial elephant in the room, but we pretended that it didn't matter and mostly managed to ignore it.

I usually think, though, that I cannot ignore my background when discussing certain subjects such as the Israeli-Palestinian conflict or interethnic relations. I even believe that when one is marked ethnically or religiously on one side or the other, there is a very limited number of discursive positions that one is bound to adopt (or will be thrown into) when discussing these issues. This is partly why I am interested in—and will also be touching on here—the escapist possibilities that fiction offers when one negotiates the Israeli-Palestinian conflict and interethnic relations with oneself and others.

Someone who did not buy what I thought was my attempt to remain fair about the conflict is Shmuel Trigano.[4] We had met face-to-face for the first time and we were having dinner in the fall of 2006 after a lecture he had just given at Brandeis University. In reaction to a comment I had made about Israel's bombing of Lebanon a few months earlier, he said to me: "I don't pretend to be a judge from on high. If we don't root for ourselves, who will? Nobody will defend us and nobody will rescue us." I was familiar with some of Trigano's positions on the conflict since an article he had published in *Le Figaro* in 2001, "Le péché originel des pays arabes" ("The Original Sin of Arab Countries").[5] In this article, as well as in a special issue of the journal *Pardès* dedicated to the exclusion of Jews from Arab countries published a few years later, Trigano had sought to establish some equivalence between the hundreds of thousands of Jews who had had to leave Muslim lands after World War I and World War II and the hundreds of thousands of Palestinian refugees.[6] On that evening at Brandeis, therefore, I was expecting him to go historical on me. Or at least, in one way or another, to bring up rationales and facts to support his position. But he simply forced me to take a good look at a mirror he placed in front of me.

At first, I did not recognize myself in Trigano's mixed metaphor of a judge from on high—half King Solomon suggesting that the Israeli-Palestinian baby be cut (evenly?) in two and half Messiah, appealing to brotherly love from the Mount. But it got me thinking and I came to see what Trigano meant, how I could come across as hung up on being fair. Not that I wanted to be the judge of anything, but it is important to me to be just and fair, or at least to come across as trying to see, and even feel (!), things from both sides. I wish I could say that I fired something back though, something along the lines of what Israeli author and peace activist Amos Oz wrote in *Help Us To Divorce*:

> I don't believe in a sudden mutual burst of love between Israel and Palestine. I don't expect that, once some miraculous formula is found, the two antagonists, will suddenly hug one another in tears in a Dostoyevskian scene of lost-long brothers reconciled . . . I don't expect a honeymoon either. If anything, I expect a fair and just divorce between Israel and Palestine. And divorces are never happy, even when they are more or less just. They still hurt, they are painful. Especially this particular divorce, which is going to be a very peculiar divorce, because the two divorcing parties are definitely staying in the same apartment.[7]

And if as a result of this peculiar divorce, Jacob gets a better room, it may even be harder for Ishmael (or Filistina), to enjoy his own room with a view—especially if, behind the thin wall, Jacob seems to be enjoying life and himself a little too much. Sure, Ishmael needs to try to *not* focus on Jacob getting the better room. This mental self-discipline may be the spiritual resistance Palestinian poet Mahmoud Darwish had in mind when he asserted: "The occupier expects us to talk about our suffering. Being a Palestinian is not a full time job; moreover, it is to assert that, even in hardship, a human being can love the dawn and blooming almond trees."[8] For almost anyone though, it is a challenge to focus on the world's beauty (the dawn on Gaza beach, a blooming almond tree in Ramallah) when someone next door seems to have a better deal.

Midway through *Un billet aller-retour*, a documentary by Chochana Boukhobza on the relationship of French Jews to Israel, Jacques Attali (the former special adviser of President François Mitterrand), recalls a Talmudic commentary about a biblical episode that deals precisely with King

Solomon's inauguration of the Temple. This commentary warns us that Jews will not be happy as long as the seventy peoples around them are not happy.[9] All neighborly and brotherly love aside, these words seem to me a useful warning to keep in mind. Not only for Israelis but also for French Jews.

Look, I am no Mandela. I know too well how hard it is to forget, let alone forgive, and to make peace or even enjoy a dawn or a sunset when someone sticks it to you and breathes down your neck. "To make peace," I once wrote in an e-mail I felt compelled to hold on to, "one does not have to forgive, just to inject oneself with a little dose of voluntary amnesia." The truth is that it is easy for me to talk about forgetting in regard to the Israeli-Arab conflict, because it has never been too personal a story for me. My attachment to Israel has always been sketchy, sporadic. It probably has something to do with the fact that I have never been there.

For many Jews around the world, going to Israel has been and remains a token of solidarity, especially in times of crisis. I have many excuses for not going there. First and foremost, probably, the buses. I never felt comfortable with the idea of vacationing in a country where I could explode anywhere, any time. As much as about bombs and suicide attacks, I was also concerned that if I did not explode, I would have to tell non-Jews where I had vacationed. And for a long time I wanted not to be disliked by non-Jews.

Then, I had the feeling that I would not like Israelis. I had heard how tough, even ruthless they could be. And I had heard that Israelis were not fond of the French, even of French Jews. Of course, I always understood that one had to be tough to live in Israel. Israeli author and peace activist David Grossman recently helped me better realize what this kind of life does to people:

> I feel the heavy toll that I, and the people I know and see around me, pay for this ongoing state of war. The shrinking of the "surface area" of the soul that comes in contact with the bloody and menacing world out there. The limiting of one's ability and willingness to identify, even a little, with the pain of others; the suspension of moral judgment. The despair most of us experience of possibly understanding our own true thoughts in a state of affairs that is so terrifying and deceptive and complex, both morally and practically. Hence, you become convinced, I might be better off not thinking and opt not to know, perhaps I'm better off leaving the task of thinking and doing and establishing moral norms in the hands of those who might "know better."
>
> Most of all, I'm better off not feeling too much—at least until this shall pass. And if it doesn't, at least I relieved my suffering somewhat, I developed a useful numbness, I protected myself as best I could with the help of a bit of indifference, a bit of sublimation, a bit of intended blindness and large doses of self-anesthetization.[10]

Grossman helped put Israelis' collective psyche in context for me. But, back then, who would have put the diasporic French Jew that I was in context for them?

I do not want to give the impression that I took for granted what Israel did for me. I was always very aware that Israel could be a refuge and that in serving as a backup option, it strengthened diasporic Jews—and therefore strengthened me as a diasporic Jew—in all sorts of ways. This function was displayed in the eighties when many French Jews threatened each other about leaving France if things got worse—by which they meant if Le Pen and his far-Right Front National (FN) kept getting higher electoral scores.[11] I never panicked in that sense and I had no intention to live there myself, but I did realize early on that Israel played an important psychological role for me as well, as one desperate last option. For a long time then, I had it both ways: a backup option and a virtual refuge, without the commitment.

I am not really concerned about defending myself here in the court of Israeli public opinion, but, if I had to, I would probably say that there may well have been a generational factor at play: I was too young to have sensed the threats to the state of Israel. I was not yet born in 1967, was only two years old during the 1972 Munich Olympic Games and only three during the first hours of panic in the 1973 Yom Kippur War. I believe that my first memory of Israel in the news is Sadat's 1977 visit to Israel (people my age do not have any memories of the younger Sadat). Among the images that swirl in my mind immediately after that: Israel's invasion of Lebanon (June 1982); the face of Arafat and his checkered keffieh fleeing Beirut with his fedayin; Sabra and Shatila (September 1982); the images of Palestinians in refugee camps; and the First Intifada in the occupied territories. There were also frequent terrorist attacks against Israelis, but all the years I was growing up, Israel was the bully. That the bully was on my side probably reassured me, but who really likes bullies? And it did not make me feel better that during the First Intifada, Israeli soldiers were close to my age and not trained to deal with young Palestinians throwing the kitchen sink at them.

Along with the memory of Sabra and Shatila, what may have definitely turned me into an alterJew was a certain rhetoric. It is embarrassing to report here on what you could hear on the (French) Jewish side at the time, but I have to. People said things like: "See, the Palestinians put their children in front of guns; they don't even value their children's lives." Another version was: "Their mothers do not suffer the way ours do when their children die." And let's not forget: "They are ready to do anything to influence and manipulate international opinion." I did not like this type of comment.

Something worth adding here is that I started studying at Paris X-Nanterre in 1987, the same fall that the First Intifada began. Because of Nanterre's own association with the May 1968 students' revolt and its enduring mythology, one might think that I would have been sensitive to the aesthetics of what photo reporter Jean-Claude Coutausse poetically called "la danse des pierres" ("the dance of stones"), but I don't remember being into that brand of nostalgia.¹² A few informal panels about the First Intifada were being held on campus and it was easy enough to slip anonymously into a lecture hall and listen to what other students had to say. Of course, I must have thought that I was being open-minded, but no, I did not take pleasure in the experience. I was curious and I wanted to learn more, and I did. In the first place, I absorbed the feelings of rather well-contained indignation sweeping the lecture hall.¹³ Sitting there and simply listening was informative in a way that watching TV news was not. I came out with the feeling that things were not right in the only democracy in the Middle East.

In 1991, though, the year I left France for the United States, something happened that shocked me. It could be what four years at Nanterre had done to me, but, when the Gulf War was launched, I remember feeling relieved for Israel. The war meant that Tsahal (Israel's army) would not have to face Iraq's army on its own and that Israel would have fewer or no casualties. So yes, in 1991, when the First Gulf/Scud War started, like older generations of diasporic Jews during previous Israeli-Arab wars, in a reflex that I had not experienced before and that I have not really experienced since then, I all of a sudden felt closer to Israelis.¹⁴ For a while after that, I kept my mouth shut. I had internalized the "Wiesel doctrine"—a diasporic Jew does not pass judgment on a country fighting for its survival.

To sum up, my relation to Israel has been one of words, most of which I was reluctant to utter for one reason or another.

Around that time, 1990–1991, two texts helped me fine-tune my moral vision and "geopolitical thinking" on the conflict: an essay by French Jewish author Alain Finkielkraut and an American Jewish novel written before the First Intifada. In 1991, Alain Finkielkraut published a text called "le risque du politique" in which he commented on French Jewish philosopher Emmanuel Lévinas' position on the conflict.¹⁵ Lévinas, who is known for his reflection on each man's inescapable responsibility toward the Other, had always been a supporter of Israel, but in reaction to the massacres of Sabra and Shatila he felt compelled to give an interview later published in the journal *Les nouveaux cahiers*. In this interview as well as in two texts republished in *L'au-delà du verset* in 1982 (but written in the seventies after the altered balance of power that followed the 1967 War and the subsequent occupation by Israel of new territories), Lévinas stresses the need to reconcile Israel's right to exist with the ethical demands made on the Jewish state and the Jews throughout history.¹⁶ Here is Finkielkraut's commentary:

> With the practicality of its postage stamps and the might of its army, Israel does not betray the ethical demand represented by Jews throughout history, since an ethical life is for the other and those close to me are also others for me; my closest ones are also my neighbors: this, in and of itself is sufficient to provide a basis for the State [of Israel]. But not, of course, to justify any action from the State: those closest to

me are not my only neighbors. "Peace for you who were far away and peace for you who were near" says the Bible; and it is even the essence of the message of humanity, which is naturally inclined to sacralize the division between the local people and foreigners. The Jews paid so dearly for this message that there is a difficulty specific to the Jews in seeing the neighbor in the foreigner and in thinking that one could owe him something. Such Jewish centeredness, such a pretense of innocence must imperatively be overcome.[17]

As Finkielkraut reminds us in his conclusion, Lévinas' position is that a Jewish state is a necessary political experiment and "un beau risque à courir" ("a beautiful risk to run")—not unlike each man's ethical relation to another man.[18]

The second text that had an impact on me was one of Philip Roth's novels. Not *Operation Shylock*, with its absurdist plot in which Roth's impersonator, Moishe Pipik, advocates "Diasporism," or the return of all Israeli Jews to Europe (I don't believe Pipik had a plan B for non-Ashkenazi Jews).[19] The novel I am referring to is The *Counterlife*.[20] The book was published in 1987, before the First Intifada, and a central chapter took place in Israel.

I partly mention this to stress that at that time (around 1990), after I first read *The Counterlife*, my understanding of Israel and the Israeli-Arab conflict became less French-centered. But the other reason why I mention all of this is that, to my dismay, the book that I spent the most time on at the peak of the Intifada, the book that shaped my vision of Israel, the Israelis and the Israeli-Arab conflict more than any other, the book that taught me almost all I knew on the subject and made it really come alive for me, has many Jewish (and non-Jewish) perspectives, but not a single one voiced by a Palestinian or Arab Israeli character.

I realize that a novel does not have to follow the strict guidelines of a political debate: equal amount of time for all participants. In fiction, not everybody needs to have the same number of lines and a writer does not have to ensure equal representation of points of view and perspectives. But in this specific case, Palestinians and Arab Israelis are just not there, they are out of the picture, and I did not really take the time to look for them somewhere else. So, although Roth's novel finally did it for me, although it partially hooked me to Israel and the conflict, I realize that it was not fiction operating as a way to see through the eyes of the (real) Other. In other words, as they say about portfolios, it may be wise to diversify one's exposure (novels, documentaries, fiction films, essays, etc). Whatever helps you empathize or at least better understand what is going on on the ground.

Having said that, what still puzzles me is that in one case, the "banlieues," I felt the need in the nineties to actually talk to people to understand what was really going on in their lives, and that in the other, Israel/Palestine, I had the impression for so many years to have heard and seen it all with that one novel, the Finkielkraut's essay and a few movies, articles and conversations here and there.

In the case of the "banlieues," I wanted to get as close as possible to people, their experiences, and to what they had to say. This meant short-circuiting any other medium and the media. In the other case, I obviously did not want to get too close and personal. I would like to think that it is because I would not visit one side and *not* the other. But let's face it, I could have gone to the other side, especially before the Second Intifada. The real question for me is, therefore, what it would have meant, as a Jew, to go to one side and not the other. In a book published in 2006 under the title *La discorde: Israël-Palestine, les Juifs, la France*, it is a question that is debated by Alain Finkielkraut and former president of Doctors Without Borders, Rony Brauman (one of the alterJews targeted in Trigano's *Controverses*):

> RB—I go very regularly to Palestine. It is a very singular experience. I do not understand why you haven't gone to the occupied territories. Each time I go there, I come back angered not only by the destruction of a land and a society, by the constant harassment of a population—which one can observe all the time there—but also and above all by hypocritical comments of the type "but what do they want?" or "These people are inherently violent . . . ." Why don't you go to Palestine?
>
> AF—I have been there, but not since the beginning of the second Intifada and for a very simple reason: if one knew that I am Jewish, I would be treated as an enemy. However, I put myself in the shoes of Palestinians and I know that the controls, the checkpoints and [road] closures make their life unbearable. Hence, my plea for a separation of the people. *Archav*, now. As for thrill-seekers who, pumped up by their trips to the West Bank or to Gaza, justify mortar attacks on Israel, they may have been on the ground, but they don't see clearly. They are blinded by emotion as others can be blinded by their indifference.
>
> RB—There is no doubt that emotion can blind you and "the ground," as they say, is in no way a guarantee of truth. But it is as certain that the absence of experience on the ground is a denial of reality. If you had gone to Palestine you would know, for instance, that a Jew is very well received. [This part of the dialogue took place in 2004, before Tsahal's withdrawal from Gaza in 2005]. You would see what biblical love for this land has made of this land and I believe that some of your convictions would not go unaltered.[21]

I agree with Brauman and it troubles me to have been in Finkielkraut's indefensible position. But of course, I was not exactly in his position because I had gone neither to one side nor to the other. Up to this day, I have managed to keep some physical neutrality. I can convince myself that there is one last reason, one last bad excuse why I have not been there: not only could I not sunbathe or even educate myself in Israel while young Jews and Palestinians were fighting each other a few miles away from me, but it would be inappropriate and even obscene to be a Jewish tourist on one side when the other side lived under the occupation and unjust policies of the Israeli government.

This explanation would be more believable if I had shown a real curiosity about Palestinians, their perspectives and viewpoints. No. The bottom line is that I did not make it a priority to go there because I probably did not care enough about one side and the other. And I had found a convenient way to remain in what seemed to me to be a legitimate position not to talk and take a stand about the conflict (i.e., not to denounce Israel's policies publicly). It was more convenient to stay away and just censure myself about this conflict as one is so easily and so commonly inclined to do when one is Jewish.[22]

Which does not prevent me—and I am not making any claim of consistency here—from being angry at French Jewish intellectuals who not only stayed away from the "banlieues" in the nineties but ignored their decay until it exploded in the French Jews' faces after the Second Intifada and the so-called transposition of the Israeli-Palestinian conflict to France. Before going further, I should restate that one should not minimize the failure of the French state as well as of French officials and institutions to fight ghetto-like exclusion and ethnic discrimination in France. I also know that, as Michel Wieviorka underscores in *La tentation antisémite*, questions of what Jews could have done differently are hard to raise and even harder to answer because history has taught us that whatever Jews do, their behavior will elicit anti-Semitism. As Wieviorka (following many others) also reminds us, anti-Semitism is always somewhat fantasist and disconnected from reality.

That being said, I am still left with a couple of perhaps fruitless but nagging questions: could altruistic Jews and especially altruistic Jewish intellectuals have done more for their not so distant French and non-French neighbors from the "banlieues"—and in particular for "visible" minorities? And why didn't they do more to help their former pals overcome the lethal cocktail of socioeconomic exclusion mixed up with ethnic discrimination?

I was not expecting much from hardcore defenders of the French republican (read: "secular") faith like Alain Finkielkraut, whose refusal to acknowledge the specific issues faced by visible minorities within the French nation was in line with his lack of support for SOS Racisme in the eighties.[23] I am referring to someone like the author of *Left in Dark Times*, Bernard-Henri Lévy, Finkielkraut's cofounder of the Institute for Lévinassian Studies in Jerusalem, and one of SOS Racisme's godfathers.[24] There is no doubt that Lévy has done more than his share to alert public opinion to the suffering of distant neighbors and victims from far-off and slightly less far-off lands. So even though the "banlieues" may not be his favored turf—and in no way do I deny Lévy's physical courage—why didn't he do more about his closer neighbors from the French "banlieues"?

This is a question that I asked Lévy, a year and a half before the October 2005 French riots when I sneaked up on him as he was promoting his book about some of the world's forgotten wars on National Public Radio's *On Point*.[25] (These were the riots during which, fueled by the accidental death of two young men chased by cops and several declarations from then interior minister Nicolas Sarkozy, many "banlieues" exploded almost simultaneously throughout France.)[26] I wanted to know, I told him, whether after fighting racism and anti-Semitism in the eighties, he had given up on the "banlieues," our forgotten territories. I know. It's funny that I asked him why he had not saved the "banlieues." But remember: I had believed in SOS Racisme. And he had just come back from reporting on some of the world's forgotten wars. Couldn't he and a few others have used a little of their influence and visibility to shed light on some of the issues that came to the world's attention a year and a half later? Couldn't he have made it to the "banlieues" since he explained on that day that he liked to go "on the ground" when he became too "drunk on words"?

And yes, I know that in a French context, all of that was made almost impossible by divisions on so many issues and even words and concepts (secularism, "communautarisme," multiculturalism, affirmative action, visible minorities, national identity, collective memory, competition of victims, the Israeli-Palestinian conflict, etc.). But as I said, I am a child of my generation, the "Touche pas à mon Pote"/Benetton generation. As the show was coming to an end and the concluding music started covering his voice like a well-timed gong, Bernard-Henri Lévy reassured me/us: "Do not despair! . . . I don't give up! . . . Be sure! . . . I don't give up! . . . My idea is that racism and anti-Semitism are not exactly the same, but it would be another theme of conversation."[27] He was maybe right; it was a theme for another show. And to be fair to him and to a few others, there are probably many reasons why they did not do more for the "banlieues"—the first one being that they had been accused of patronizing others (blacks and Arabs) and of stealing the show back in the eighties, the heyday of SOS Racisme. Many other historic and sociodemographic reasons may have made it tricky for French Jewish intellectuals to engage with and speak up on behalf of their close, often Muslim, neighbors. Chief among these reasons was the Israeli-Palestinian/Arab conflict, which was probably always on everybody's mind and may have held Jewish intellectuals back long before the Second Intifada and the subsequent wave of anti-Semitic acts that washed over France.

Yet I also keep thinking about what Nicolas Sarkozy said at the Knesset on June 24, 2008—three days after a Jewish teenager, dubbed "Rudy H." by the French media, was lynched in Paris' 19th multiethnic arrondissement, in one of these French streets where it is becoming harder and harder to walk wearing a kippah. After issuing an official statement upon his arrival in Israel to denounce anti-Semitism as "a stain on the tricolor flag," Sarkozy delivered a speech very similar in tone to the one, less well received, in which François Mitterrand advocated a two-state solution back in 1982. Sarkozy also advocated the sharing of Jerusalem and stressed that peace depended on a solution to the problem of Palestinian refugees. There was one more thing, though, that Sarkozy said to the Israeli Parliament, almost at the very end, that struck me: when one is strong, one must extend a hand.[28]

I concur. And, at the risk of committing myself the "crime" of transposing the Israeli-Palestinian conflict to the French stage, I will add that in the nineties, quite a few public Jewish figures were in a position of far higher influence than black and Arab Kabyl leaders in France. It is, perhaps, as simple as that: when they could have extended a hand, they did not.

That having also been said, I am still not sure what I will do next. Will I keep going to the "banlieues" and not to Israel? Does it have to be one versus the other, when there is really no connection between the two? Will I make my first visit to Israel-Palestine conditional to a real and fair deal between Israelis and the Palestinians and the creation of a Palestinian state? I am not convinced that I want to get too close, but we will see. Of course, there may be some misplaced pride at this point.

Watching *Un billet aller-retour*, the documentary that I mentioned earlier, it did cross my mind that if Chochana Boukhobza had interviewed me by mistake, I would have been the only one of her interviewees out of ten, perhaps, not to have been there. Ten interviewees, as many different Jews with as many different relationships to Israel, but who had all been there. I will not show off about it though! And I will not try, like Roth's Moishe Pipik, to convince any other Jew to follow my brand of Diasporism. You won't see me advertise "Boycottism" soon. I won't be touring with "Alter-Jewism." Still, I wonder. Could all of this mean something? Will I be called to do more?

ACKNOWLEDGMENTS

Many thanks to Nathalie Debrauwere-Miller for her editorial comments and to Patricia Brennecke, Rob McKean and Bob Irwin for their stylistic comments on a first version of this essay. Unless otherwise noted, all translations from the texts appearing under a French title are my own.

NOTES

1. A code word here for all of those who live in ghetto-like conditions and suffer from socioeconomic and geographic exclusion as well as ethnic discrimination in France.
2. Johann Sadock, *Black, Blanc, Beur: parlons-en*! (Cambridge, MA: MIT Press, 2000).
3. Shmuel Trigano, "Alter-Ego," *Controverses* 4(2007): 8.
4. The author of many works in the fields of philosophy, political thought, and Jewish Studies, Shmuel Trigano has always been a supporter of Israel. Back in the seventies though, Trigano was no stranger to criticizing the Israeli

Ashkenazi elite for its treatment of Sephardic Jews as second class citizens (what he termed " le second Israël" in the 1979 special issue of Les Temps Modernes he edited). This discriminatory treatment had to do in his own analysis with the perception of Sephardic Jews in Israel as primitive and culturally too close to Arabs.
5. Shmuel Trigano, "Le péché originel des États arabes," *Le Figaro* (Paris), June 4, 2001.
6. Shmuel Trigano, ed., "L'exclusion des Juifs des pays arabes: Aux sources du conflit israélo-arabe," *Pardès* 34 (2003). A similar position, advocated by the JJAC (Justice for Jews from Arab Countries), found an official translation on April 1, 2008, when "the U.S. Congress passed *House Resolution 185*, which grants first-time-ever recognition to Jewish refugees from Arab countries. Prior to the adoption of *H.Res.185*, all resolutions on Middle East refugees referred only to Palestinians. This resolution affirms that the U.S. government will now recognize that all victims of the Arab-Israeli conflict must be treated equally. The related resolution in the Senate, *S. Res 85*, is currently before the *Senate Committee on Foreign Relations* (*http://www.justiceforjews.com/resolutions.html*) (accessed on August 28, 2009).
7. Amos Oz, *Help Us To Divorce: Israel & Palestine—Between Right and Right* (UK: Vintage, 2004), 21–22.
8. Mahmoud Darwish, "Je suis malade d'espoir," *Le Nouvel Observateur*, 16–22 February 2006.
9. Jacques Attali, *Un billet aller-retour*, interview by the author Chochana Boukhobza, DVD, dir. Georges Goldman, Paris-Barcelone Films, 2005. A return ticket, 2008.
10. David Grossman, "Writing in the Dark," *The New York Times*, May 13, 2007.
11. In 2004, Ariel Sharon tried to capitalize on this type of fear when he called on French Jews to move to Israel in order to flee (Muslim) anti-Semitism.
12. Jean-Claude Coutausse, *La danse des pierres* (Paris: Denoël, 1990).
13. I should mention that I don't remember seeing many Muslim students in that lecture hall and, at the time, in Nanterre. For a sociological assessment of the impact of the conflict in French universities post Second Intifada, see Michel Wieviorka, *La tentation antisémite: Haine des Juifs dans la France d'aujourd'hui* (Paris: Robert Laffont, 2005), 335–380.
14. Perhaps events at the time also contributed. After gaining some credibility for declaring the Palestine Liberation Organization (PLO) charter "caduque" (null and void) in Paris, Arafat had sided with Saddam Hussein. It was hard to empathize with Arafat. And despite the Intifada and Jean-Claude Coutausse's pictures of young Palestinians throwing stones on the front page of *Libération* and in the news, Arafat was still for me the face of the Palestinians.
15. Alain Finkielkraut, "Le risque du politique," *in Les cahiers de l'herne: Emmanuel Lévinas*, Miguel Abensour and Catherine Chalier, eds. (Paris: Editions de l'herne, 1991), 468–476.
16. Emmanuel Lévinas, *L'Au-delà du verset* (Paris: Editions de Minuit, 1982), 209–228.
17. Finkielkraut, "Risque," 473.
18. For more on Lévinas's position on the relationship between ethics and politics in Israel, see *Difficile justice: Dans la trace d'Emmanuel Lévinas, Actes du XXXVIe Colloque des intellectuels juifs de langue française*, comp. Jean Halpérin and Nelly Hansson (Paris: Albin Michel, 1998), 109–156.
19. Philip Roth, *Operation Shylock: A Confession* (New York: Simon & Schuster, 1993).
20. Philip Roth, *The Counterlife* (New York: Farrar, Straus and Giroux, 1987).

21. Rony Brauman and Alain Finkielkraut, *La discorde: Israël, les Juifs, la France* (Paris: Mille et une nuits, 2006), 221–222.
22. On the subject of self-censorship among Jews in relation to Israel and the Israeli-Arab conflict, see Judith Butler's essay, "L'accusation d'antisémitisme: Les Juifs, Israël, et les risques de la critique publique: Un éclairage américain," in *Antisémitisme: l'intolérable chantage: Israël-Palestine, une affaire française?* (Paris: La découverte, 2003), 97–119.
23. Beyond this consistency though, many have pointed out the contradictions in Finkielkraut's positions, and no one better than Guillaume Weill-Raynal, *Une haine imaginaire? Contre-enquête sur le "nouvel antisémitisme"* (Paris: Armand-Collin, 2005). Here again, Finkielkraut's disconnect from the reality on the ground, and his dismissal of the works of sociologists in the banlieues, seems to have made it harder for him to see his neighbor in the Other. With the increase of anti-Semitic attacks in France—often by young blacks and Arab Muslims—it was therefore, not surprising, only ironic, to see a fine reader of Lévinas link the wave of anti-Semitic attacks to the prevalent antiracist ideology. See for instance, Alain Finkielkraut, *Au nom de l'Autre* (Paris: Gallimard, 2003).
24. For Bernard Henri Lévy's position on the conflict, see "Le sionisme, la guerre, la paix," in *Le sionisme expliqué à nos potes*, Union des étudiants juifs de France, ed. (*Paris:* Editions de la Martinière, 2003), 13–26.
25. Bernard-Henri Lévy, interview by Tom Ashbrook, *On Point*, National Public Radio, May 25, 2004.
26. For more on the main characteristics (age, ethnicity, etc.) of the young people who took part in the 2005 riots, see Gérard Mauger, *L'émeute de novembre 2005: Une révolte protopolitique (*Broissieux: Editions du Croquant, 2006), 63–71.
27. Lévy's position on "new anti-Semitism" in France and the so-called "Intifada des banlieues" is much more nuanced than the one of Finkielkraut and a few other Jewish intellectuals. See for instance his chapter on the 2005 riots in Bernard-Henri Lévy, "Note on a Fire," in *Left in Dark Times: A Stand Against the New Barbarism* (New York: Routledge, 2008), 41–46. In this chapter, he distances himself from the assessment made by a few other Jewish public intellectuals (Finkielkraut most notably) as to the religious nature of the 2005 riots. For a journalistic investigation on "new anti-Semitism" in France, read Sylvain Attal, *La Plaie: Enquête sur le nouvel antisémitisme* (Paris: Denoël, 2004*)*. On France's self-made problems, read Farouk Mardam-Bey and Elias Sanbar's final chapter, "France: Les dérives communautaires" in *Etre arab*e (Paris: Acte Sud, 2005), 277–306.
28. Nicolas Sarkozy, Discours de M. le président de la République à la Knesset, Jerusalem: June 23, 2008 (http://www.elysee.fr/documents/index.php?mode=cview&cat_id=7&press_id=1537&lang=fr) (accessed on August 28, 2009).

12 Jews and Arabs in Postcolonial France, a Situated Account of a Long Painful Story of Intimacy

Nacira Guénif-Souilamas

At first sight, I might look Arab; on second glance, I might start to exceed the seemingly obvious markers of identity, though never to the point of fully escaping the being-belonging-becoming frame I'm caught in and relate to. One could assume reading an essay written by someone who happens to be of Arab North African *indigène* descent that it intends to tell the story of the struggle through the always lurking accusation of Arab and Muslim anti-Semitism which has become part of the predictable political staging in postcolonial France and more widely in Western countries involved in the war on terror. It would be all too expected for me to defend myself from being one of them, simultaneously Arab and anti-Semite, as the case has been made and discussed over and over again in the media. The identification of the main culprit shifts from the Judeophobia in France supposedly expressed only by Arabs and Muslims (and recently blacks) to the surreal debate over whether criticizing Israel's colonialist policy has an intrinsically anti-Semitic subtext. My purpose will not be to avoid the ways I am implicated in this subject and rely instead exclusively on my academic background to analyze such a situation; rather, I may, imprudently perhaps, use myself and my experience as an instrument to explore a situated epistemology that points out some of the motivations of new expressions of the hatred of Jews in France. Without exhausting the question, this attempt aims at providing an abbreviated illustration of such a highlighted and daunting topic.

THE HIDDEN RACE RELATION

Up until now, France has remained an unscrutinized nexus of racial conflicts, especially regarding one of its most volatile tensions: Arab-Jewish relations. One could object to such a statement by pointing out that Arabs and Jews are not races and that, furthermore, if ever the race issue was to be raised in a constructivist perspective, it wouldn't focus on these two "people" who since time immemorial have ironically been bound together in the same ethnic and mythological group, the Semites. Perhaps since there was never any sign of a merging of the two groups for historical and political reasons, the discussion still goes on, using the same old terms, occasionally reframed and refreshed. In addition to the persistence of the entangled and universalized myths of the Israel/Ishmael enmity, and the symptomatic episodes of betrayal and mutual hatred that still shape the common imaginary of European culture and polity, one could stress that at a local level, while both groups have been part of the French landscape for a while, one should not ignore that these presences were neither simultaneous nor equivalent in their political and symbolic dimensions. The 1789 Revolution, the colonization of Algeria which closed the era of French slavery and opened the Imperial one, the collective naturalization of Algerian Jews episode by the "décret Crémieux," the Dreyfus affair, the interlude of the Vichy collaboration, the Holocaust, the creation of the Israeli nation-state, the Palestinian *Naqba*, the Algerian War and, finally, the wars in the Middle East trapped in the colonization of the occupied territories as well as the impossible and always deferred peace process: all these events work as episodes of an intimate history of Arabs and Jews in France. The French postcolonial moment has brought to coincide two histories, the one of the French and North-African Jews and the one of the new French of *indigene* descent, and their specific embodiment of otherness that so far have excluded one another in the French mythology. This scheme is informed not so much by mutual hatred, a false idea and decoy put into curency in the service of reasserting a post-Holocaust orientalist European frame. Rather, this obliviousness can be explained by the fact that their close and long-lasting encounters were staged at a distance from metropolitan France and its blinding Enlightenment before a "repatriation" triggered by decolonization. Stories that long belonged to the Oriental scene recently became part of the Western one. Actors and figures who were scattered all over both the wide and narrow paths of history are now gathered together on a crowded multicultural and multiethnic local stage. Unheard secrets and invisible wounds of former *dhimmis* (protected and subaltern non-Muslim minorities living in the Muslim Umma) and *indigènes* (subaltern local status of natives under the colonial law) suddenly burst onto the contemporary scene while accelerated changes affect, in one of the strongest modernity gestures since the Revolution, the cultural and political weave and fabric of France.

But how can an unfamiliar reader picture the scenes at stake in France and its margins for the past two decades? To abbreviate, I will focus on vicissitudes and words that underscore the quality and flavor of the unresolved hatred following from these once close and unequal Semitic cousins separated by the colonial power and reunited by its successors, now living on the same French soil. The Empire dismantling caused the settlement of the two most important minorities in France coming from the south Mediterranean: Sephardic Jews exiled from North African former French colonies and Muslim natives, later renamed migrants workers, from African and North African background. Such a configuration fomented the conditions for a new anti-Semitism, outsourced to the new, visibly different French, Arabs, Muslims and blacks, that plays as the substitute fuel to a historical Christian blend of anti-Semitism conveniently cut from its European roots. Simultaneously, the reverse of anti-Semitism has been reloaded and relabeled anti-Arab racism and Islamophobia; both sides of the same racist coin are used alternately against one another to fuel a mutual and circular hatred.

THE WHITE (JEWISH) WOMAN AND THE ARAB CULPRIT

One of the most unusual and thus most telling encounters of this intricate process of hatred took place during a mid-2004 event that was largely and, to some extent, overly reported and commented upon by the media and political pundits. On a late June weekend, there was reported the alleged assault on a young white mother with her baby in a stroller by black and Arab youth while boarding a morning train serving the suburban underclass housing projects. When stating the facts and details to the police, she showed Nazi signs on her belly which, she asserted, had been drawn by her assaulters who, she added, had torn her clothes with knives and insulted her, saying she "deserved it because [she] was a Jew since [she] lived in the 16th arrondissement" [a wealthy section in Paris]. She also mentioned that they hurled her baby stroller when exiting the train, and left her in the midst of an indifferent crowd. Her name was Marie L., a fact that exacerbated the violence of the situation, the implication being that she bore the weight of a suffering mother of Christ who needed no last name to assume her stigma. The woman was received by the government official charged with protecting the rights of victims, who happened to be Jewish herself. This representative offered assurances of the government's support and promised that the police forces would work diligently to find the culprits responsible for what was hastily declared to be an anti-Semitic, rather than sexist, deed. Nevertheless, prior to the arrival of any confirmation of the facts, and during that same weekend, I was called by a journalist from *Le Monde* who described to me the details of the events, and asked me whether I would accept to comment on what at first sight appeared totally incredible. The quick and troubling conjunction of signs and speeches that all converged towards presuming the Jewishness of the supposed victim epitomized the special blend that forms the signature of any moral panic episode (anti-Semitism, sexism, class hatred, physical and psychological violence). An avalanche of commentary and denunciation in articles and editorials strongly backed up the reports on the scene and yet, no police evidence of the facts so far. When I discovered the veritable scandal that had emerged (since I had been ignorant of the details and even the headlines of the prior two days), I wavered between incredulity and astonishment. The descriptions fit so perfectly the ideal type of the anti-Semitic and sexist assault that it required a double-checking of every reported detail. I asked the journalist as a precondition of the interview to first confirm the facts of such story. He did so, confirming every detail four hours later. He then asked me to interpret the scene described by the woman who, if she was believed to tell the truth, had experienced the epitome of hate speech and hate crime. I commented on what seemed to be an unprecedented convergence of various forms of violent barbaric behavior at the scene, insisting on a fact that seemed to have drawn no attention by commentators. The metonymic effects of the description resonated oddly after the prior weeks' reporting, as flowing images showed the ill treatment imposed on inmates at Abu Ghraib's prison. It seemed to me that the ongoing display of other images incessantly commented upon could explain why the renewal of such scenarios in ethnic colored suburbs may have become plausible. In both cases the twists and turns of entangled race and gender relations seemed to echo similarly in Middle Eastern countries as well as in the postcolonial French underclass. The whiteness of the French female victim corresponded to one of the female *torturer's (Lynndie England)* in the photographs and videos of Iraqi prisoners taken by soldiers. Before the revelation that the assault was in fact a fabrication, the story took hold because of a ready-made frame, an attraction to excess, the easy presumption of a sexist, anti-Semitic culprit had precluded any other possible explanation. The next morning the masses awoke from their trance: it was revealed that the young woman had lied. The debunking of the event, which was sure to raise the statistics of anti-Semitic incidents in France, must have been a bitter disappointment to the self-proclaimed friends of the Jews. Aside from the obvious increase of anti-Semitic incidents since 2000 documented by various reports, this episode didn't so much deal with such facts than it did with their torsion by a common imaginary fed with anxiety and fear. Suddenly the issue shifted: all the participants (including me, to some extent) were caught up in debates that presumed fantasy representations of the wars between the "eternal enemies"—or so they were regularly labeled in the media—and between the sexes in suburbs "overwhelmed by archaic behaviors," both of which effectively staged the same crucial figure: anti-Semitic, violent, heterosexual Arabs, joined by blacks.[1] Not only did the young woman appear to be a fragile character who made up a terrible story to cope with her collapsing marriage, but one had to observe that she did this by drawing the stigma of others' suffering on her body. In the wake of such an excessive and trivial story, the whole French society had, once again and not for the last time, to face its phantasmal obsessions. The next steps included apologies from *Le Monde*'s journalists to the readers and, incidentally, to me, proposing that I elaborate on my interpretation of the *Affaire de Marie L. et du RER D* and that I reflect on how the incident said something about French society's identity disorientation. Which I did under the title: "Genealogy of a Social Fact."

DISTANT ARAB-JEW INTIMATE RELATIONS

In this article I tried to recapture what I thought had too easily been set aside in the rush to believe and victimize the mythomaniacal woman: the French story of the Arab-Jewish Other. The story gained in credibility as it now included the white woman acting simultaneously as victim of the victimization of the Jews and the scapegoating of the Arab. So to understand the shift of the woman's body bearing falsified use of images floating in the air since the early 2000s, one has to unpack the common story of the pattern of enmity between cousins, as it took place away from the gaze and control of the former colonizer and current domesticator. I stressed in that article the contempt in which Jews used to be held by the dominant if not hegemonic group, Muslims, whether Arabs or Kabyls, and focused on the way language held the traces of such a negative figure since naming someone a "Jew" was a way to discredit a person or a group. This was less pejorative than it was the mere translation and reminder of a relation of subordination. The same contempt soon expressed against Muslims by the colonizer once settled in the land of the defeated former power: the Ottoman Empire. An enduring shared feeling of mutual familiarity, similarity, complicity and yet mistrust and resentment was the stamp of Jews and Arabs mutual relations in the North African colonies. The naturalization granted to Algerian Jews (though they never requested it) would not do enough to uproot those taken-for-granted conceptions; maybe it actually made daily interactions worse, since it may have been difficult for Muslim natives to understand how this proximate subaltern had become the equal of the colonist while they themselves were subjected to the enforcement of a code of *indigénat* that deprived them of fundamental rights within the new legal framework. The submission to a process of civilization and modernization of tremendous magnitude was to follow divergent paths for the *Indigènes* in Algeria and in other parts of North Africa, whether Jew or Muslim, as the Empire drew to a close. Episodes of the colonial period told from this point of view are scarcely mentioned, retrieved in native spaces of the madina, traditional city, or the douar, small scattered villages on the remote land, and withheld in the shadow of the dominant narrative: the one of relations between the natives (the Muslims, Jews or Christians who shared the same roots) and the European colonial population. The official history long elided details about the former colonial hierarchy and maintained this light version after its dismantling, thus rendering almost invisible the immense fleeing crowds of "Europeans" torn between leaving their native land and seeking refuge in an inhospitable homeland where they often ended up sharing the same segregated neighborhood with former natives, the newly renamed immigrants from Morocco, Algeria and Tunisia. Again the former hierarchy was overturned along with its deep effects on minds and memories. French literature rarely evoked these relations and when by chance it did, it located them as the background of a plot involving white Western European protagonists. A notable and very recent exception is a popular comic series called *Le chat du rabbin*, or "The Rabbi's Cat," illustrated by Joann Sfar, a French-born son of North African Jewish repatriates, which takes place in early-twentieth-century Algiers and from there travels in all directions. The successive stories wandered either northbound in metropolitan France or southbound towards Rimbaud's Africa in an initiatic voyage that speaks to the contemporary reader of a deeply embodied past erased from the collective French memory. Indeed, the vividness and closeness of the love/hate relation between Jews and Arabs never caught the attention of the colonizer. Both were embedded in the then French conception of clear boundaries between the citizen and the native summarized and sustained by Renan's apparently disjoined definitions of the nation on one hand and of the Semite on the other, so insightfully recalled to our attention by Gil Anidjar.[2] Hence, they were both contained *outside* the nation and as such functioned as figures by which the nation asserted its boundary. Napoleon's declaration about granting Jews their rights as individual citizens but none as a people had long made such a stance clear. Hence, this relation remained in the background of the French Republic's official history as long as the unequal status for both was needed to guarantee the sustainability of the Empire and of an exceptionnalist Algeria, as the only French colony to become part, as a *département*, of the sovereign state. Once the sovereignty of France was cut back to its former continental territory and its symbolic imaginary was deprived of its quintessential colonial dependencies, the elucidation of relations between the two former subaltern groups became impossible since the encounter now took place in the very center of the postcolonial reconfiguration: the suburban lower income housing projects and new transitional housing developments. This largely ignored relation, in its complexity and contrast, became increasingly obvious as all sorts of unnoticed actors emerged in the public sphere, recently reshaped by de Gaulle's new constitution.[3] Once in France, the only flavorful leftovers of the shared multi-secular table of Jews and Arabs were food and music, as they both were invented and elaborated together in an endlessly stimulating and emulating interaction that was to remain underground until *couscous* became one of the French national dishes and orchestras from Oran or Constantine could again perform on stage, emerging from their exclusive domain of the wedding and the Bar Mitzvah.

Meanwhile, the colorblind French Republic had awoken from its frozen heights and fell down back into a racialized world. Not only because its immigrant minorities introduced all kinds of ethnic and racial nuances into the French complexion, but also and most unexpectedly because its Sephardic minority, ignored in the aftermath of the Algerian War of Independence, expressed a colorful and salient Jewishness repudiated by predominantly Ashkenazi Jews assimilated to colorblind republican universalism. The usual analysis of the local identity shift points only to the growing *visibility* of Muslims, Arabs and blacks that has compelled a white France to acknowledge its multicultural and multiethnic component. Rather, part of this identity shift lies also in the coming together of an unthinkable *racial* France with the symbolic erasure at the highest level as well as in trivial encounters of historical facts involving the Vichy regime, that still need to be understood in relation to the episode of the Algerian War and the Empire dismantling. Hence, understatement and invisibility remain the prerequisites of these postcolonial identities' presence.

THE JEWISH-ARAB HIDDEN LINKS INSIDE THE FRENCH FRAME

Thus, since the early 1960s, there was a tacit consensus between the new French, the Sephardic Jews, the Muslims and Arabs, to avoid spreading the news about their long-time intimate relations. Their successive stages were only recently tied to France: first under Mediterranean meridians where they shared the same roots and history while experiencing an asymmetric status, then under the French colonial power which separated them, and, at least in the Algerian case, reversed their respective status and, then again under the French Republic's universalist rule. This latter experience was cast into a suitable oblivion in line with the recently renewed amnesty era, and echoing strangely with the precedent of post-Vichy amnesia. The confrontation between the two minority groups on the French soil, in the aftermath of the Six-Day War and the Yom Kippur War, which coincided with the first oil crisis, remained anecdotal and was never acknowledged as part of an ongoing political shift related to the remnants of the Algerian War of Independence. Hence, the post-empire backlash is still ahead. It is prompted by the diffuse contempt either for Sephardic Jews not quite erased by the Holocaust, falsely called *Pieds-Noirs* before they would rename themselves *Juif Tun'* or *Feuj*, or for Arabs, still caught in the web of racist labels such as *bicots* or *bougnoules* to be replaced later by the civilizing argotic *Beurs* and other idiomatic labels such as *Rebeu*, *Blédards* or recently reclaimed *Indigènes*. After the burst of the early 1980s riots in suburban housing projects, the seismic effects of an unexpected political and cultural earthquake spread out, despite or because of the arrogance of civil servants and politicians, often repatriated from the deceased empire with the troops and the family. Then took place the first episode of a long series, including the unrest of the fall of 2005. For the first time, such repeated events brought to the forefront the postcolonial immigrants' offspring's continuing anger when recounting the humiliations and unpunished murders of Arab and black youngsters.[4] Alongside the periodical display of burning cars, which could be interpreted as an agency of fire part of the political landscape, demands emerged for equality from those who were bound, sooner or later, to become French citizens. Soon after and then for a long time, such political claims would be dismissed and their advocates relegated to a subaltern status once experienced by their parents. At a distance, the First Lebanese War and the Sabra and Shatila massacre were revealing the worst chapters of the Palestinian tragedy which, in turn, brought about future radicalizations. The First and Second Intifada also produced reactions in France, but these reactions were dwarfed by the scale of reactions to 9/11. Everything gradually fell into place for staging the oversimplified binaries in which Jews and Arabs were to play the key roles. And indeed these roles were displayed by the media in the most tantalizing orientalist way: victim and culprit, faithful and disloyal, civilized and barbaric. The politics of enmity frame was quite different in France because of local and residual historical issues such as the haunting Vichy betrayal of the Jews, the unresolved amnesia of slavery and French colonial past, all of which came into play in the Algerian War of Independence and the gradual visibility of the unexpected French Muslim. In that respect, 9/11 was not the hinge moment in France, since France has an older relation with terrorism. Beginning with the resistance in the Second World War to the Nazi occupiers and their collaborators, the use of unlawful targeted attacks ranged from clandestine militants of the Front de Libération Nationale (FLN) on the mainland soil as well as in Algeria, to Organisation de l'armée secrète (OAS), a later movement of dissident officers and far-Right *Pieds-Noirs*, opposing the independence of Algeria, that spread disorder and death on both sides of the sea. The next French terrorist stage was hosted by far-Left French activists, including pro-Palestinian Carlos among others, in the 1970s and 1980s, and the next by the Kurdish minority resistance action and above all radicalized Islamist Algerians who not only struck French targets during the 1990s but recruited young Muslim immigrant children, sending them from forgotten suburbs to promised lands in ex-Yugoslavia and Afghanistan. Everything about the politics of terror was learned and experienced in these places and moments, culminating in the arrest and execution live on TV of a son of Algerian immigrants, Khaled Kelkal, who, once a brilliant student, turned to radical Islam and active terrorism after leaving prison where he was converted.

THE TROUBLING SPECTACLE OF SHIFTING FRENCH NATIONHOOD

Illustrating the turmoil generated by these tremendous events, the past half-century has become a particularly accurate stage about the morphing of French ethnic identity when both Jews and Arabs have rejoined the continental metropole either as repatriates, as former *indigènes* or new migrants. The decolonization process, invented to reduce the Algerian War of Independence to a peripheral disturbance[5] of a long and glorious narrative is narrowly related to the growing numbers of immigrants generated by the former colonies. Not only did they slowly but steadily become more and more visible in the public space, but their visibility included alterations of color and language to which a traditional republican French mind could not easily adjust. Whether one thinks of the religious minorities such as Muslim French and their recent experience of a reactive ethnicity to racism and discrimination that has become the grammar of a borderline citizenship, or of the assertive ethnicity of Sephardic Jews, now French, compared to the assimilation of European Jews, one observes that the classical frame of ethnic blindness has reached its exhaustion point with the recombined and hybridized ways of belonging that these former natives have imported in their suitcases to France. Shifting French nationhood brought about by these new French speakers, highlighted by previously unheard singing accents and broken French, epitomizes ways to escape the local nation-state frame and, by never quite adjusting to it, exposes its weakened foundation. Stand-up performances of Arabs, like Djamel Debbouze, or Jews, like Gad Elmaleh, both of Moroccan descent, or comedies like *La vérité si je mens*, which popularized the North African Jewish culture of a talkative, jocular conception of life, show the bright side of the ancient relation of complicity and intimacy. Simultaneously, the other side of the coin portrays the new eternal enemies especially after the Second Intifada and the growing anxiety of the return of anti-Semitism supposedly expressed in contemporary form only by French Arabs. Far from being just a fiction, the mutual tensions between the two communities existed alternately under the guise of solidarity and/or nuanced wariness; they led to deep friendship or to strong dislike. But besides these mutually combined relations which are neither predictable nor one-way oriented, a subtext to the so-called universalist republicanism, including an unconscious staging of Christian redemption, has gradually polluted the two groups' relations by triggering the suspicious stance still at play. Under the inverted scenario of current circumstances, the Arabs (and their alter ego, the Muslims) assume the role of the Christians who recently aimed at annihilating the Jews as a race and almost succeeded in their destruction. Too numerous and too close, the Arabs who recently settled in the former colonial state soon became the convenient locus of a reengineering, reshaping of the Jew-hatred map, by placing at its center, the recently invented old enemy of the Jew, namely the Arab in place of the Christian.[6] In such a racial war game, the Arabs of France are exported to a larger scene, namely the Middle East war on terror, where they are expected to embody or at least stand by the threatening enemy. Just because the destructive position of a certain local leader may reverberate in Israel, doesn't mean that all those physically or religiously confused with him follow the same ideological path. The surprising openness to other minorities, including Jews, by Muslims or Arabs in France reported in a 2006 Pew Institute survey contradicts the vision of intolerant, disloyal citizens who are denounced as taking advantage of liberal laws on migration to break into the polity in Trojan horses. The everyday life of both groups sheds a different light on the phantasmal vision of two people bound to hate each other while one is supposed to be aggressively in favor of the destruction of the other. It helps understand how the public discourse, particularly the official political discourse, fuels resentment among children of immigrants who feel abandoned and scorned by a state so quick to demand proof of compliance to norms of assimilation while forgetting its obligations to vulnerable inhabitants. Research from 1993 in Sarcelles, a multiethnic, popular suburban city north of Paris where a large Sephardic community settled in the 1960s, showed that supposed anti-Semitism was more likely to be interpreted as a strong identification of local minorities to the apparently successful one among them, namely the Jews, combined with the diffuse resentment against the latter due to a lack of consideration on the part of local and national civic actors. Then, like now, the Israeli-Palestinian conflict informed the frame of local interaction and representation. Nevertheless, French society did not pay much attention to growing tensions until the Second Intifada followed by 9/11 attacks burst onto a falsely calm sky and imposed an international new agenda.

COMING OUT FROM ASSIGNED IDENTITIES

My personal account crosses these paths and at the same time diverges from them. During the Marie L. moral panic episode, I was involved in a private conversation with a French Jewish retired scholar. The winter before, while the law banning all conspicuous religious signs from public schools was passionately discussed and unanimously passed by the parliament, he wrote to me after reading a piece in a newspaper where I expressed the hope of gathering all *métèques* in a common movement towards mutual understanding. He recognized himself in the multi-secular emblematic figure I proposed, and suggested to exchange our experiences in a conversation that was interrupted late 2004 when he died of sudden and aggressive cancer after he had vainly attempted to have a manuscript including our exchanges published. He explained how shocked he was, a few months before, when, during a heated debate, pro-Palestinian militants accused him of Islamophobia and contributing to the repression and colonization process in occupied territories when not unequivocally opposing Israel's politics of peace. He wished to understand where the misunderstanding between Jews and Arabs in France came from. He led me to recall memories of my childhood from which any mention of the Algerian War was erased under the French light and to recollect some anecdotes where the intimate relations between his cousins (he was Ashkenazi), and my family's community were balancing between tacit acceptance and sharp rejection. I translated to him the idiomatic expression in which the use of the word Jew in Arabic was the equivalent of an insult and had to be immediately followed by a formula of excuse. I realized by sharing with him such an expression (*yahudi hashak*), so deeply rooted in everyday life, how strikingly telling it was of intimate and contemptuous relations between Sephardic and Muslim groups in North Africa. We realized along our conversations that hatred and false images were never far in our Semitic relation from mutual understanding and spontaneous complicity. Our contribution to this highly problematic aspect of contemporary French tensions will remain unshared but through this chapter, it may help unpack the many settings where controversies and disputes are being debated between supposedly irreconcilable enemies.

THE HIDDEN JEW

Unexpectedly, this uneasy story has taken a sudden and fascinating turn as well as finding a tentative conclusion that may read as the closing act of an era when, for the first time in France's history, a president of Jewish descent has been elected. Jewish prime ministers are part of French history: ranging from Léon Blum's Popular Front government in 1936–1937 to Pierre Mendès-France, who during his six-month government period ended the Indochina War and signed the Tunisian independence treaty that were to start the French decolonization process, and more recently Laurent Fabius, Mitterrand's youngest prime minister in the 1980s. But no candidate to the French presidency ever came from a known Jewish background. The "Jewishness" of the former presidential candidate, according to certain sources his mother has a Jewish father from Thessalonica, remained a taboo throughout the campaign and even after: often mentioned in the press and on blogs, never precisely established, but alluded to by close friends as well as his latest cosmopolitan wife in the same sentence mentioning his "immigrant" background. Nothing has been formally stated or discussed about the invisible revolution of having, as head of the state, a political leader whose ambiguous personal identity plays on/with identity troubles experienced by the whole society. Easily referred to as being of Jewish descent by others, he strongly works on asserting in official venues and occasions his Catholic faith in a country where anti-Semitism has continued to fuel hatred, and where he has contributed to reopen wounds and divisive scars in the *laïque* nation-state narrative by challenging its local secular law. The never quite explicit disclosure of his religious ties and belongings points at the way the president lets rumors flow with no denial while loudly referring to a traditional Christianity revived by the European debate on the origins and roots of the Union. This embodies a special meaning in times when anti-Arab and Muslim stereotypes have entered into the long tradition of the necessary Other in the common imaginary. It seems that the unresolved relation to the Vichy past, the stain of turning over Jews to the Nazis, as well as the failure to acknowledge persistent Arab segregation, whether as indigene or as migrant, both played into the silencing of such unheard and inconceivable news: one religion thus alluding to another. By considering the possible reward of a Jewishness recalibrated by Nicolas Sarkozy for a precise political and ideological aim, one may simultaneously measure the difficulty for a larger Christian French society to accept him as such and the benefits he may find in performing its euphemized version towards a wide audience. Hence, for the current president, far from any genuine identity, acting Jewish is predominantly a performance exempted of any authenticity proof. His performativity accounts for various versions of the Semites past and present encounter that today mainly fall under the Arab category. Thus, when stigmatizing the young deviant Arab visibility in the periphery of the French Republic, Sarkozy hardly manages to extirpate himself from this accused group with whom he shares an unsophisticated and harsh behavior stereotype. Once again, the shadow of the Semites is stretching over the French land, adding a new episode to a fecund narrative. Such a move unveils the possibility that the relation to and inside the Semite group was indeed deeply rooted in an unconscious autochtony[7] that has yet to be revealed. Hence, the sensation is still strong that officially acknowledging such a presence at the head of the state could trigger troublesome and uncontrolled reactions among moody French people. One could thus discern in this tendency of the regular French to overlook the troubling part of a French president's identity, the reluctance usually expressed to recognize any religious or ethnic identity of any public official any difference especially when it has something to do with religion and in such case, a Janus face related to a build up race long held under suspicion. The usual French decoy politically addressing racialized relations is the reduction of such multilayered relations to a strict social class issue that points to a withdrawal in the colorblind posture. Thus, seen under such a race and class (one may add gender) light, the Jewishness of the president appears tightly linked to the Arabness (itself connected to the blackness) of the suburban underclass young males he many times called under suspicion and trial as "scum," so as to distinguish his own behavior and situation from theirs. All of these essentialized belongings are local inventions and all of them are tied to each other by the longstanding story of a Frenchness in search of its opposite. In that sense, the current president does not escape the trap he has built for young racial and ethnic minorities. This invention of a local, oppositional, hatred based on phantasms, between the supposed two Semitic people which would draw on a one-sided longstanding experience, exclusively led under the light of a biblical curse, unearths the commodification process of a stranger's intimate story that escapes the scope of the French political cultural influence.[8] The urgent need to keep alive and effective the convenient scenery of enmity by using the closest enemy at hand tells less about the nature of the supposed enemies and of their relations than about the craving for an undisputed biopower that, by any means, must extend its rules over marginal humans and groups. Indeed it seems that such a fiction and its all too real settings are far more convenient to an ambiguous ally, as France pretends to be with the Jews in France and in Israel, on the current geopolitical scene than would be any attempt to locally reduce hatred and fear so effectively fuelled, not to mention affordable and reachable peace in the close and remote scene of the conveniently called Holy Land.

In the perspective of a real peace process there, a new blend of Semitic stories could be reclaimed and overcome by the offspring of the double-sided brotherhood, doomed by biblical and mythical figure. The enemy of the Arabs would simultaneously become the enemy of the Jews before leading to the dilution of the very figure of the enemy itself as the first step towards a mankind extended to all humans and less complacently reduced to its humanistic party. Such a party, so far interestingly located in Western world, stands at the forefront of the Land of the Human Rights so apt to betray its ideals and promises in the past as well as in the present. Multiracial France has still to be invented and freed from its past demons, ranging from former slavery and colonialism to state betrayal of the Jews, by a crossover figure that would simultaneously speak for all identities and all belongings as the Philadelphia speech pronounced by Barack Obama, the future first African American president of the United States, did by designing a language of recognition and of humility.

ACKNOWLEDGMENT

I am deeply grateful to Judith Butler who took part in an initial conversation so to design this chapter and dedicated time and sharp interest to reading it, commenting on certain arguments and making it more readable to an American audience. This chapter was completed before the Gaza war started, at the end of December 2008.

NOTES

1. On the young heterosexual violent Arab see: Nacira Guénif-Souilamas and Éric Macé, *Les féministes et le garcon arabe* (La Tour d'Aigue, L'Aube, 2004). The connection between Arabs and blacks became almost inevitable when, in 2006, the torturer and murderer of a young French Jew proved to be the leader of a "gang of barbarians" of Ivory Coast immigrant descent. About this event: Ahmed Boubeker, "Strangers in the French Melting Pot: The Public Construction of Invisibility of Visible Minorities," in *Frenchness and the African Diaspora: Identity and Uprising in Contemporary France*, Peter J. Bloom, Didier Gondola and Charles Tshimanga-Kashama, eds. (Bloomington, IN: Indiana University Press, 2009).
2. Gil Anidjar, *The Jew, The Arab: A history of the enemy* (Stanford: Stanford University Press, 2005); "Réflexions sur la question," in *Juifs et musulmans: Une histoire partagée, un dialogue à construire*, Esther Benbassa and Jean-Chirstophe Attias, eds. (Paris: Editions La Découverte, 2006).
3. Nacira Guénif-Souilamas, "L'ombre portée de l'exception," *Cosmopolitiques, Une exception si française*, n°16, 2007 p 29–39.

4. About the unpunished murders of Arab and black youngsters of immigrant descent during the past four decades, see *Histoire politique des immigrations (post)coloniales*, Abdellali Hajjat and Ahmed Boubeker, eds. (Paris: Éditions Amsterdam, 2008).
5. See Todd Shepard, *The invention of decolonization* (Ithaca, NY: Cornell University Press, 2006).
6. This issue is unfolded in: Joëlle Marelli, "Usages et maléfices de l'antisémitisme" in *La république mise à nu par son immigration*, Nacira Guénif-Souilamas, ed. (Paris: La Fabrique, 2006).
7. To read more on autochtony and the contemporary belonging patterns: Peter Geschiere, *Perils of Belonging* (Chicago, IL: Chicago University Press, 2009).
8. Two books on such topic are particularly enlightening: Edgar Morin, *Mes démons* (Paris: Stock, 1994); Pierre Birnbaum, *Géographie de l'espoir: l'exil, les Lumières, la désassimilation* (Paris: Gallimard, 2004).

Part V

Judeocentrism, Anti-Semitism and French Intelligentsia, 2000–2008

13 A New Judeocentrism?
On A Recent Trend in French Thought
Jeffrey Mehlman

Let me begin with a word on my title. One sense of Judeocentrism might be the following: given any case of a fairly universal foible or shortcoming, Judeocentrism is the attitude that consists of focusing on and being enraged above all by *Jewish* instances of it. In this sense, Judeocentrism might be characterized as another name for anti-Semitism. This, for instance, is the position taken by Alan Dershowitz on the double standard applied to Jews.[1] On the other hand, the notion that the Jews are to be held to a higher standard points to nothing so much as the key notion of a "chosen people," a people "unlike the others," according to the liturgy, which would make of Judeocentrism another name for Judaism itself. There are things to be said of the contradiction between the two senses, a people longing for normalcy (one sense of the Zionist project), but imbued with a sense of its abnormal calling.[2] (And indeed from, say, Freud to George Steiner, writing about the intolerable psychical pressures entailed by that higher standard, much ink has been spilled meditating an articulation between the two senses of the word—one defining anti-Semitism, the other defining Judaism itself—I have evoked.)[3]

My own use of the word here is more pedestrian, the comment of someone struck, during a recent trip to France, by just how much reflection the condition of the Jews has provoked—at a time of what has been called "a new Judeophobia"—in France, and it is that phenomenon that I'd like to address in this chapter.

Now one of the most consistently provocative figures in the development I will be discussing is Alain Finkielkraut. (These thoughts, I should mention, were originally intended for an exchange with Finkielkraut at the University of Minnesota in October 2004.)[4] Indeed, perhaps my best entry into the subject might be by way of recounting a series of personal encounters with his thought since they will allow me to bring a measure of temporal depth to this chapter, a sense of the "newness" of the "new Judeocentrism" of my title.[5]

Some years ago, while writing a preface for a translation of *Assassins de la mémoire*, Pierre Vidal-Naquet's interesting book about Holocaust negationism (and above all the support it was then receiving on the far Left in France), I had the mixed pleasure of discovering that there was a considerably more rigorous treatment of the subject, titled *L'Avenir d'une négation* and published in 1983, by Alain Finkielkraut.[6] His argument was that the existence of the Nazi gas chambers allowed one to make a crucial distinction between two different capitalist entities, Nazi Germany, on the one hand, and the liberal democracies on the other, and thus to envisage the ethical or political imperative of siding with one—say, the United States—against the other. Since this was precisely a fight the far Left was uninterested in waging, might it not be more expeditious to convince oneself, on whatever spurious grounds, that the gas chambers did not exist (i.e., that there was no *essential* difference between fascism and liberal democracy)? And that thus there was no need to imagine allying oneself with a liberal democracy against what was no longer a qualitatively different regime? What interests me in this context is the sense that Holocaust denial or revisionism was a danger that had to be staunchly resisted. The good fight, however belated, was on behalf (or in memory) of the victims of the genocide. That in 1983.

Consider now another title, from the following decade, that of the final chapter of an important book on Vichy historiography by Henry Rousso and Eric Conan: "L'Avenir d'une obsession."[7] The obsession, in a word, was the wartime genocide of the Jews, and in particular French collusion in the process, and the message of the book was a warning as to how "perverse" an effect on historical understanding the "Judeocentric" view of the French experience of World War II had had. In eleven short years, we go from the "future of a negation (or denial)" in Finkielkraut to the "future of an obsession" in Rousso and Conan. Somewhere in the course of those years the French had come to think that the turning point of World War II was not, for France, November 1942, when Pétain failed to leave Vichy for newly liberated Algeria, but July of the same year when René Bousquet, Vichy's chief of police, entered into formal agreement with the Germans to assume principal responsibility in rounding up Jews for deportation. Not intelligence with the enemy but participation in a crime against humanity, the destruction of European Jewry, became the exemplary crime of the war. And for a number of years it was as though this were the intellectual theme of discussion in France *par excellence*. Pierre Nora, a historian, called the generation in the grips of this obsession the "Bousquet generation," as though the center of the war were the Bousquet accords with the Germans and the central ignominy of contemporary France the ongoing friendship of Mitterrand with Bousquet.[8] The backlash, exemplified by Rousso's warning about Judeocentrism, was not long in coming. But there were other instances as well. Pierre-André Taguieff, borrowing a line from Leo Strauss, began referring to a *reductio ad Hitlerum*, a kind of anachronistic moral exhibitionism, obsessed with the Holocaust in order the better to overlook contemporary horrors such as those then being perpetrated in the Balkans.[9] The intellectual and ethical rot of this "hyperesthesia" or oversensitivity to the Jewish question in *fin-de-siècle* France, eventually became of particular concern to Alain Finkielkraut himself, who wrote eloquently on the subject.[10]

Allow me to zoom in for a close-up in the form of a personal recollection. The scene is the summer of 2000 in Paris, the very height of the principled backlash I have referred to. Call it "anti-anti-anti-Semitism." I was lunching with Régis Debray at a terrace on the rue de l'Odéon, when Alain Finkielkraut, a friend of Debray's (whom Finkielkraut had only recently criticized, with all due cordiality, for muddling the Kosovo question by invoking the benign role of the Serbs in the Holocaust), came lumbering down the street, looking, Debray suggested, as though he had just been run over.[11] What was the matter, he asked. Well, Finkielkraut had just seen the first page of the following day's issue of *Le Monde*, where he was roundly lambasted by none other than Claude Lanzmann, author of the film *Shoah*, as a crypto-supporter of the anti-Semitic far Right. And the worst, said Finkielkraut, was that the next day was his birthday. Whereupon Debray responded, unforgettably, I thought: "C'est vrai, *Le Monde* a toujours eu de ces délicatesses" ("It's true. Considerateness has always been *Le Monde*'s strong suit"). It is for comments like that, the *art de vivre* they embody, that one never tires of returning to France.)

Now the pretext for Lanzmann's attack is of significance here. Renaud Camus, a minor writer, had recently published his journal of 1994. To summarize: one day, switching on his radio, he found himself musing that there was regularly a large preponderance of Jews on the French cultural program called *Panorama* and they seemed compulsively drawn to discuss—sometimes rather well, sometimes less well—topics of Jewish interest. Was it not a bit disproportionate? he asked. More interestingly, he found himself questioning the riskiness of his own observations. Did this make him, prepared as he was to believe that the genocide of the Jews was "probably" the single most catastrophic event of the twentieth century, an anti-Semite? And what if he had referred instead to a preponderance of Bretons disproportionately inclined to discuss Brittany? Would that make him anti-Breton? I will not elaborate the Camus text further (although it did contain one truly objectionable line, worthy of Maurras, about the number of generations in France one needed to truly savor French literature). Suffice it to say that there was a media frenzy around what were quickly qualified as Camus' "criminal opinions." *Le Monde* opined that the adverb "probably"—as in the Holocaust was "probably" the single greatest catastrophe of the twentieth century—was a sure sign of anti-Semitism. Camus' book was removed from circulation by the publisher and the passages deemed offensive duly excised. And Finkielkraut saw in the entire episode a luminous example of the "oversensitivity" to the Jewish question he had come to lament. It was in making that attitude public that he had incurred the wrath of Lanzmann.[12]

Now one reason the media storm over Camus and the denunciation of Finkielkraut's contention that there was something a bit insane about the qualifying of Camus' musings as "criminal" (four times in an open letter signed by Derrida among others) is significant is that not very long after there was a genuine case of anti-Jewish violence in France that went virtually unnoticed by the chattering classes.[13] On September 2, 2001, about a week before 9/11, a group of young North Africans with baseball bats descended on a Häagen-Dazs ice cream parlor on the Champs-Elysées known to be a hangout for Jewish adolescents and began attacking them to cries of "Juifs, on va vous tuer." There was a bloody battle on the Champs-Elysées.[14] This was an early instance of widespread anti-Jewish violence that eventually came to be much commented on, but which an intellectual class obsessed with or still brooding over the musings of Camus found little inclination to notice at the time.

The circumstance is not without its comic aspect. Just as the French intelligentsia imagined it could see its favorite adversary, the anti-Semite, making his protracted exit stage right, indeed as it luxuriated, almost operatically, in prolonging that exit, there entered *stage left* a new variant of the very same nemesis and whacked it, the intelligentsia, on the back of its collective head. There is, that is, something profoundly disorienting in what transpired in France and the much rued silence of the French commentariat over the growing danger faced by French Jews—who did not need to wait for a law to tell them to curtail their use of skullcaps since their rabbis cautioned them that they risked physical assault in the streets of France if they did not—was no doubt an effect of just such a disorientation.

And yet that anomaly—the arrival *stage left* of what was being pursued *stage right*—strikes a note that is not without precedent in French discourse. Consider two statements. The first is Simone Weil's remark on the German army's entry into Paris, declared an open city, on June 14, 1940, that this was "a great day for Indochina."[15] The question raised is, of course, that of the articulation of the intra-European tragedy of the fall of France and the fate of the Jews, on the one hand, and the worldwide iniquity of colonialism, on the other. A local injustice, it was being implied, may be part of a broader justice (as Pangloss might have put it). Or consider the remarks of Jacques Vergès, defense attorney for the ex-Nazi "butcher of Lyon" Klaus Barbie and, it was reported, at one point a prospective attorney for Saddam Hussein as well. Vergès, who was the son of an Indochinese mother, remarked during the Barbie trial: "My mother didn't have to wear a yellow star; she was yellow from head to toe."[16] Again, the question is that of the relation between an intra-European tragedy and the more global tragedy of colonialism.

And it is within that question that the Israel-Palestine question, it has been decided by much of Europe, is to be understood and resolved. Europe having opted to dissolve the shame of its Holocaust in the guilt of its colonialism, appears to have opted to subject the guilt of its colonialism to the salutary acids of its antiracist anticolonialism. It is a process that is no less flawed by its questionable assimilation of Zionism to a form of colonialism than by the blind spots of its dogmatic anticolonialism.

What is at stake is the articulation between the German-Jewish question that so exercised, say, Gershom Scholem, on the one hand, and the Muslim-Jewish question, so frequently sentimentalized as idyllic before the foundation of Israel, on the other.[17] It is in this context, by the way, that we should note that we are dealing, to that extent, with an implicit tension between a largely Ashkenazi experience, on the one hand, and a Sephardic experience, on the other. As Elie Barnavi, the former Israeli ambassador to France was reminded, when an aged gentleman introduced himself, after a talk, as "the Ashkenazi community of Marseille," the Jews of France are at present overwhelmingly Sephardic.[18]

The metaphor of the Holocaust—*reductio ad Hitlerum*—was so abused during the period leading up to what I have called anti-anti-anti-Semitism that it may prove prudent, in examining the question of the articulation between the Holocaust and colonialism, to proceed cautiously. In which case we would find that one of the most haunting bonds between the two domains is probably that provided by the Grand Mufti of Jerusalem, Haj Amin Mohammad al-Husseini, who spent the years of World War II in Berlin as Hitler's guest, contemplated the construction of a death camp for Jews, modeled after Auschwitz, near Nablus, and helped to organize thousands of Muslims in the Balkans into pro-Nazi military units known as Handselar divisions.[19] During the war period, we are assured by the late Edward Said, the Grand Mufti was "Palestine's national leader." The reference to the pro-Hitlerian Muslim troops in the Balkans lingers in the mind. I remember during that last summer of the anti-anti-anti-Semitism years, shortly before 9/11, picking up a book by Pierre-André Taguieff (*Résister au bougisme*) and being struck by the unflattering evocation of Kosovo, a region whose suffering victims had endowed its name, Kosovo, with an almost sacred aura in the United States. (On the model of *reductio ad Hitlerum*: "If Milosewicz was the new Hitler, the Kosovars were his Jews.") And here was Taguieff, in a long footnote, discussing the Kosovar cause as having degenerated into a mix of "terrorism" and ethnic "counter-cleansing" bespeaking a kind of "mafia."[20] Might that terror, evoked by Taguieff shortly before 9/11, be not the image—but in some small way the continuation—of whatever was cobbled together, under Hitler's auspices, in the Muslim Balkans? And might it not in some measure be a link in a chain issuing in a reality alluded to by Régis Debray, when he reminds us (or claims he is reminding us) that "Al Qaida was born on the side of the Good, in Bosnia-Herzegovina, to the emotional applause of our antitotalitarians"?[21] My claim is not that Hitler is the right metaphor for Islamic extremism, but rather that the best corrective to the abusive metaphor, quite frequent abroad, assimilating Sharon to Hitler might be the patient tracing of the afterlife of the Balkan projects of the Grand Mufti of Jerusalem (who happened, moreover, to be the revered uncle of Yasser Arafat).

Let us turn now to a second instance of contact between the anti-Semitism of World War II and the colonial question. In 1870, following the French defeat in the Franco-Prussian War, a decree, known as the Loi Crémieux, was enacted, granting French citizenship to Algeria's Jews—but not to its Muslims. Why the disparity? It is the subject of an interesting piece written by the young Hannah Arendt in the *Contemporary Jewish Record* in 1943.[22] On the one hand, the progressive elements of the French government, in their struggle with the military, which was running Algeria, saw in the Jews, as Arendt puts it, "the only trustworthy part of the population." On the other, the Arabs were by and large unwilling to renounce polygamy and legally enforced female subservience, two provisions of Koranic law regarded as incompatible with French citizenship. And so the Crémieux law was passed, granting French citizenship in 1870 to Jews but not Arabs, and the result was widespread rioting throughout Algeria.

The law was, to be sure, abrogated during the Vichy regime, but the focus of Arendt's article is a somewhat later development. After the United States effectively liberated Algeria in November 1942, the date on which Pétain famously or infamously refused to leave Vichy for newly liberated French territory, a decision was made by General Henri Giraud, America's man in Algeria, *not* to restore citizenship to the Jews, lest the native Arab population feel slighted or, as he put it, in order "to eliminate all racial discrimination."[23] Here then was an early case of anti-Semitism in the name of antiracism—*au nom de l'Autre*, to use Alain Finkielkraut's phrase. Consider the configuration: In 1870, defeated by the Prussians, France granted citizenship to Algeria's Jews; in 1942, having expelled the Germans from Algeria, a decision was reached to permanently strip the Jews of that citizenship—in the name of eliminating racial "discrimination."

The episode calls for several comments. The policy of not restoring French citizenship to the Jews of Algeria in 1942 was Giraud's, but Giraud was placed in power by Franklin Delano Roosevelt, who thoroughly backed Giraud's policy of "abrogation." That policy was opposed by de Gaulle, and nothing infuriated Roosevelt more than de Gaulle's "vicious propaganda staff," as he put it in a letter to Churchill, "descending on Algiers to stir up strife between" Arabs and Jews.[24] Thus the United States played a role in this classic episode of French anti-Semitism and it was not a benign one.

Consider now an exemplary incident of contemporary French anti-Semitic antiracism, which has its place here because of its congruence with the abrogation of the Crémieux incident just evoked. On November 8, 2001, *Le Nouvel observateur* ran a story on "crimes of honor" in the Muslim world.[25] The central episode in the report concerned a young Jordanian woman sent to assist in the childbirth of her sister in a town north of

Amman. While there, she was raped by her brother-in-law. Calling home in distress, she was summoned back only to discover that her family had commissioned her own brother to murder her in order to protect the family's honor. The reader gasps, but his sense of horror is presumably assuaged when the journalist balances things out, presumably in the name of anti-racism, by implying quite falsely that the Israeli army, realizing that such misogynistic crimes against women were common in Muslim lands, had a policy of raping Palestinian women on the understanding that the women's families would "finish off the job" by murdering the women they, the Israelis, had raped. Gasp and counter-gasp. The only problem is that the second claim (about the Israeli army) was false and the journalist, Sara Daniel, was forced to beat an embarrassed retreat. Can anyone doubt though that she was motivated by the purest desire to establish some balance and thus disarm anti-Arab racism?[26]

Let me turn now to one more point of contact between the wartime tragedy of the Jews and more recent tensions in the Middle East. It concerns one of the more remarkable pieces written about French literature in recent years, Eric Marty's long essay on Jean Genet among the Palestinians.[27] Genet, sometime thief, prostitute and apostle of evil, has been the subject of major works by Sartre, Derrida and, more indirectly, Foucault, so that to write importantly on him, as I believe Marty has, is arguably to write one's way into French intellectual history. The problem Marty assigns himself is how to articulate Genet's endorsement, on aesthetic grounds, of the Nazi massacre at Oradour, on the one hand, and his condemnation, on moral grounds, of the massacre of Palestinians at Chatila, allegedly with the go-ahead of Ariel Sharon, on the other. The works involved are the early *Pompes funèbres* for the aesthetic endorsement and the late *Un Captif amoureux* for the moral condemnation, so that what is at stake in finding a point of articulation between the two is nothing less than establishing the unarticulated premise of the entirety of his *oeuvre*. And it is enough for Genet to wonder out loud whether he would have been so attracted to the Palestinian cause had their struggle not been fought against "the people who seemed to [him] the most tenebrous" for Marty to identify that point of articulation: an antipathy toward the Jews.[28]

But allow me now to fix on the Proustian climax of Genet's book on the Palestinians. The narrator comes to the end of his quest when he discovers the home of a Palestinian mother and son who had befriended him years earlier. It results in what Marty calls an experience of "involuntary reminiscence." An inexplicable Germanic aura seems to emanate from the humble home of mother and son: "The house was not built from materials from the Black Forest, but between it, or rather between the sight of it and the sound of the word *Allemagne* [*Germany*] I intuited the agreement [*accord*] established now when I speak of them: Germany and the Grand Mufti."[29] That is, in the midst of a sentimental visit, apparently to proclaim solidarity with the "wretched of the earth," the aesthetic resurfaces in the form of an "accord," but what that chord mediates is the affirmation—in the person of the Grand Mufti, whom we encountered earlier—of collusion between Palestinians and Nazis.

Marty's essay appears as the centerpiece of a volume in Philippe Sollers' series *L'Infini*. It is called *Bref séjour à Jérusalem*. I confess that when I discovered it, I had my own "involuntary reminiscence" since twenty years earlier I had published a volume in the same series that was centered on the question: what if one were to reread the entirety of Maurice Blanchot's *oeuvre* from the perspective of his early endorsement of acts of terrorism against Jews?[30] Twenty years had passed and here was Marty asking the question: what if one were to read the entirety of Genet's *oeuvre* from the perspective of his late declared hostility to the Jews? The symmetry was striking. As though Marty were attempting to do for (or against) what has been called the new Judeophobia in France what I had attempted to do, successfully or not, for a more classic phase of what has been called the Vichy syndrome.

Here then was the Jewish question pitched at the very heart of French letters. For Marty insisted that for an entire generation it was Genet alone who had kept French literature from degenerating into "the dry-as-dust liturgy of a soon-to-be-abandoned church."[31] Such would be a first justification of the word "Judeocentrism" in my title. But there are other striking cases, two of which I will evoke by way of conclusion. What they have in common is that they are by important members of the "structuralist" generation, sometime Lacanians both, and that they each argue, rather differently, for what they call the existence of a "structural hatred" of the Jews. To speak of the "structural" in these cases frequently tends to mean that one is giving short shrift to the empirical, which in turn means that one is giving voice to what may be regarded as obsessional: whence (again) the Judeocentrism of my title.

The first is Daniel Sibony, mathematician, psychoanalyst and an altogether engaging figure. He argues, in a recent book, that the motivating factor in the Middle Eastern crisis is what he calls a "structural hatred" for the Jews written into the Koran.[32] The sacred book is said to be a plagiarism of the Old Testament whose justification is that the Jews were so eminently unworthy of the divine message they had received that it now had to be confiscated from them. Moreover, for real life Jews, expelled from the text, to have showed up in the flesh in Palestine with a claim on the land is described by the psychoanalyst in terms alternately of a return of the repressed, which would be upsetting enough to Muslims, and of the Lacanian mechanism specific to psychosis—a return in reality of what had been foreclosed from the symbolic—which would be literally maddening.

And then there is the curious case of Jean-Claude Milner, who, we are reminded by Jean Daniel in *Le Nouvel observateur*, is not "n'importe qui."[33] A psychoanalyst, linguist, polemicist and, in the 1960s, a founder at the Ecole Normale Supérieure of *Cahiers pour l'analyse*, one of the most rigorous, or at least intimidating, epistemological projects of structuralism in its headiest years, Milner has recently published a volume titled *Les penchants criminels de l'Europe démocratique*.[34] It is unfailingly intelligent, but more of a para-Lacanian fantasia on the current state of the world than a documented study. Here is the argument: An ever-expanding and war-averse Europe, besotted with whatever it can think of as other than itself, appears to have encountered its own mirror image in an ever-expanding, war-bent Islamic extremism, infuriated by anything it can think of as other than itself. Such is the empirical reality that underlies the argument. The internalization of Europe's specular image or reflection—call it Europe's own *stade du miroir*—occurred, it is argued, at the United Nations congress of Durban and was consolidated around an antipathy to the Jews. It is this "structural" hatred of Europe for the Jews that is Milner's theme, which he encapsulates, rather than argues, in terms of the Jew being what the Lacanians call "the *objet a* of the West."[35] Or the unconscious.

To the extent that Milner does justify what it is the West is repressing in the Jews, the argument is strangely meager. In a postmodern, almost Houellebecquian world intent on limitless technological advance, the Jew keeps alive an almost archaic question: "What shall I tell my children?" To that question, articulating the four poles of parents, children, male and female, Milner gives a Heideggerian name, "quadruplicity," and invites us, since he barely elaborates the matter, to pour whatever Heideggerian profundity we can muster into that rectangular vessel.[36] For it is this profundity that an increasingly superficial and technologized Europe would repress.

My point, however, is not to criticize Milner, some of whose book is indeed impressive. It is to sketch a contemporary configuration. On the one hand, Milner sees a "structural" hatred of the Jews as lying at the heart of European unification. On the other, Sibony, argues a "structural" hatred of the Jews written into the sacred text of even moderate Islam. Each of the books has its undeniable merits, but the marshalling of empirical evidence is not their strong suits. Yet there is a fruitfulness in all this. When the French invoke the "structural," I have suggested, dismissing much of the empirical record but with an impatience that precludes genuine structural analysis, what we are served is less a diagnosis of the current situation than a symptom. And that symptom is what I have called a new Judeocentrism in French thought. For it is the coherence of these two para-Lacanian readings—of Islam by Sibony, of Europe by Milner—that is striking. A coherence, moreover, that is not without its piquancies: Milner's philo-semitic "quadruplicity," designed to pinpoint the specificity of the Jew in modernity, is a borrowing from the anti-Semite Heidegger, even as Sibony's Lacanian model of "foreclosure"—by virtue of which what is excluded in the "symbolic" returns in the realm of the real—was originally a borrowing by Lacan from the writings of the notoriously anti-Semitic psychoanalyst, linguist and militant of Action Française, Edouard Pichon.[37]

Consider as well that for Milner the exemplary contemporary French author is Jean Genet, who figures in the book, on the subject of Jews, as the postwar counterpart to the prewar Giraudoux.[38] (That Milner's most frequently cited Jew is the compulsively anti-Semitic Simone Weil and that the richest paragraph of the book is a surprising parallel between Weil and Genet is a sign of just how pessimistic his take on things is.)[39] The circumstance, moreover, allows for a kind of counter-confirmation of the configuration I have been assembling. "Quadruplicity," the distilled essence of Judaism, we're told, is nothing other than another name for "Freudian sexuality" itself and as such the unmentioned answer to the enigma of the apparent imperishability of the Jewish people that Freud found himself pondering at the end of his life in the last lines of *Moses and Monotheism* (Milner 2003: 121). Milner, that is, pretends to provide a crucial supplement to the last book Freud wrote (even as Sibony claimed to be doing for Islam what Freud had done for Judaism in *Moses and Monotheism*: opening it up to the impurity of its own origins).[40] Moreover, Milner claims, contemporaneous with Freud's *Moses*, the discourse of "quadruplicity" was already present—in 1938—in psychoanalysis, specifically in an early Lacan text written for an encyclopedia, "Les complexes familiaux dans la formation de l'individu" (Milner 2003: 121). The point is worth noting because that rarely cited text just happens to play a role in a recent volume by Didier Eribon devoted—quite differently—to an author who has occupied us in these pages, Jean Genet. (His book is in fact subtitled *Variations sur un thème de Jean Genet*).[41] Eribon's argument is that Genet's way of plunging, through identification, into abjection—be it with that of a coterie of Barcelona transvestites, with the Black Panthers or with the Palestinians—in order to undo that abjection, as it were, from within, is as exemplary an exercise in moral courage as might be imagined. (That Genet, in *Pompes funèbres*, evoking the weakness of the Jews in the camps, feels that abject weakness to be a provocation to hostility more than anything else and that the historical case that best exemplifies Genet's reversal of abjection into pride is Vichy's wartime Milice may point to the limits of the "social isotopy of exclusions" extolled by Eribon in Genet.)[42] Now little could be more coherent with my argument in these remarks than the fact that fully half of Eribon's volume in praise of Genet is an attack on Lacan, deemed to be a homophobe, and specifically on the 1938 text we saw Milner invoking as indispensably linked to the saving "quadruplicity" of the Jews. As though Eribon, who is in no way anti-Semitic (and who even finds room to denounce an overture by Lacan to Charles Maurras in his book), nevertheless felt compelled to affirm the opposition Genet/Lacan and did so, even as he reversed the signs attached to them: The crypto-Judaic Lacan of Milner and perhaps Sibony, in his opposition to the anti-Semite Genet gives way in Eribon to a Genet as moral guide in his opposition to a tendentiously anti-Semitic Lacan. It is a botched coherence, to be sure, but no less coherent for being botched. And it is perhaps the botch no less than the

A New Judeocentrism? 219

coherence that makes it all seem convincingly *symptomatic* of what I have called a new Judeocentrism in French thought.

NOTES

1. Alan Dershowitz, *The Case for Israel* (New York: Wiley, 2003), 208–216.
2. Jean Daniel, *La Prison juive* (Paris: Odile Jacob, 2003), 247–257.
3. Sigmund Freud, *Moses and Monotheism* (New York: Vintage, 1955), 114–117, and George Steiner, *Errata: An Examined Life* (London: Weidenfeld & Nicolson, 1997), 58–61: "Of this pressure, I believe, is loathing bred."
4. For contingent reasons, Finkielkraut was unable to make the trip and these remarks became more lecture than contribution to a dialogue. Since then, in April 2006, Finkielkraut has come to Boston University, where his two lectures—"*Laïcité*: The Secular Ideal in France" and "The Plight of the Jews in France"—have been published in a limited edition, with my introduction, in the context of the First Roger Shattuck Memorial Lecture.
5. Pierre-André Taguieff, *La Nouvelle judéophobie* (Paris: Fayard, 2002).
6. Pierre Vidal Naquet, *Assassins of Memory: Essays on the Denial of the Holocaust* (New York: Columbia University Press, 1992) and Alain Finkielkraut, *L'Avenir d'une négation: Réflexion sur la question du génocide* (Paris: Seuil, 1983).
7. Henry Rousso and Eric Conan, *Vichy: Un passé qui ne passe pas* (Paris: Fayard, 1994), 67.
8. Pierre Nora, "Tout concourt aujourd'hui au souvenir obsédant de Vichy," *Le Monde* (October 1, 1997).
9. Pierre-André Taguieff, *Résister au bougisme: Démocratie forte contre mondialisation techno-marchande* (Paris: Mille et une nuits, 2001), 103.
10. Alain Finkielkraut, *Une voix qui vient de l'autre rive* (Paris: Gallimard, 2000), 67.
11. Finkielkraut, *Voix*, 35–52.
12. Since then, Finkielkraut has taken the Camus matter a step further, suggesting that the articulation of the ethical and the ethnic—*l'éthnique et l'éthique*—in the incriminated passages of Camus' journal bespoke an attitude that was in a profound sense Jewish. See Alain Finkielkraut and Peter Sloterdijk, *Les Battements du monde* (Paris: Pauvert, 2003), 52–56.
13. "Déclaration des hôtes-trop-nombreux-de-la-France-de-souche," Collective statement in *Le Monde* (May 25, 2000).
14. Taguieff, *Judéophobie*, 199.
15. George Steiner, "Sainte Simone—Simone Weil" in *No Passion Spent* (New Haven: Yale University Press, 1996), 172.
16. Jacques Vergès, *Le Salaud lumineux* (Paris: Livre de poche, 1997), 14.
17. That idyll makes short shrift of the second class status—known as *dhimmitude*—of Jews and Christians in Muslim society. This could take a particularly dramatic cast: e.g., the annual public ritual slap in the face administered to the head of the Jewish community. See Emmanuel Brenner, *France, prends garde de perdre ton âme: Fracture sociale et antisémitisme dans la République* (Paris: Mille et une nuits, 2004), 103–104.
18. Elie Barnavi, *Lettre ouverte aux Juifs de France* (Paris: Stock-Bayard, 2002). The figure given by Barnavi is 68 percent Sephardic and 22 percent Ashkenazi.
19. A passage from Husseini's memoirs is chilling in its eloquence in this context: "Our fundamental condition for cooperating with Germany was a free hand to eradicate every last Jew from Palestine and the Arab world. I asked Hitler for an explicit undertaking to allow us to solve the Jewish problem in

a manner befitting our national and racial aspirations and according to the scientific methods innovated by Germany in the handling of its Jews. The answer I got was: 'The Jews are yours.'" Cited in Dershowitz, *Israel*, 55.
20. Taguieff, *Résister*, 61.
21. Régis Debray, *Chroniques de l'idiotie triomphante, 1990–2003* (Paris: Fayard, 2004), 25.
22. Hannah Arendt, "Why the Crémieux Decree Was Abrogated," in *Contemporary Jew Record* 6 (2; April 1943): 115–123.
23. Arendt, "Crémieux," 115.
24. Raoul Aglion, *Roosevelt and de Gaulle: Allies in Conflict* (New York: Free Press, 1988), 149.
25. Sara Daniel, "Le cauchemar des crimes d'honneur," *Le Nouvel observateur*, November 8, 2001.
26. Shmuel Trigano has commented trenchantly on a recent parallel: the effort to twin the plight of Arabs and Jews in France, in the name of human rights, has issued in an implied de facto "de-nationalization" of French citizens of Jewish birth. See S. Trigano, "The Perverse Logic of French Politics," *Jerusalem Center for Public Affairs*, June 2, 2002.
27. Eric Marty, "Jean Genet à Chatila" in *Bref séjour à Jérusalem* (Paris: Gallimard, 2003).
28. Jean Genet, *Un captif amoureux* (Paris: Gallimard, 1986), 239.
29. Genet, *Captif*, 571.
30. Jeffrey Mehlman, *Legs de l'antisémitisme en France* (Paris: Denoël, 1984).
31. Marty, "Chatila," 19.
32. Daniel Sibony, *Proche-Orient: psychanalyse d'un conflit* (Paris: Seuil, 2003), 33.
33. Jean Daniel, "Antisémite, l'Europe?" in *Le Nouvel observateur* (November 12, 2003).
34. Jean-Claude Milner, *Les penchants criminels de l'Europe démocratique* (Paris: Verdier, 2003).
35. Milner, *Penchants*, 105, where the proposition is attributed to François Regnault. Subsequent references to this edition will be indicated parenthetically in the text.
36. The four Heideggerian terms of the *Geviert* are earth and heaven, gods and mortals. See "Bâtir Habiter Penser" in Martin Heidegger, *Essais et conférences* (Paris: Gallimard, 1958), 176.
37. On the "fantastic intinerary of the concept of 'foreclosure,'" see Elisabeth Roudinesco, *La Bataille de cent ans: Histoire de la psychanalyse en France*, vol. I (Paris: Ramsay, 1982), 383–395.
38. On Giraudoux's anti-Semitism as it pervades not only the lament over the Ashkenazi threat to France in the 1930s, but his literary accomplishment, see my *Legacies: Of Anti-Semitism in France* (Minneapolis: University of Minnesota Press, 1983).
39. See Milner, 155. The parallels include the factory for Weil and the prison for Genet, Spain and London for Weil and the Panthers and the Palestinians for Genet, Weil's "maternal indulgence" for Hitler in *L'Enracinment* and Hitler's "sexual fascination" for Genet, not to mention a refusal to perpetuate the world embodied (or disincarnated) by Weil's anorexia and Genet's homosexuality. "The anti-Judaism of the one might well have a connection with the anti-Judaism of the other."
40. Sibony, *Proche-Orient*, 123.
41. Didier Eribon, *Une morale du minoritaire: Variations sur un theme de Jean Genet* (Paris: Fayard, 2001).

42. Eribon, *Variations*, 41. Curiously, the motif of an "unexpected swerve from malediction to exultation," outside of any dialectic and opposed to any theodicy, is defined, against the horizon of Auschwitz, as the essence of Judaism, in what turned out to be Benny Lévy's final book, a latter-day Judaic rewriting of Péguy's *Notre jeunesse*, a reflection on the significance of the author's years as Sartre's guide to Maoism, and a polemical engagement with the universalizing aspirations of the thinker who inspired his own return to Jewish orthodoxy, Emmanuel Lévinas: *Etre juif* (Paris: Verdier, 2003), 17.

14 Dual Narratives on the Middle East Conflict
Analysis of a French Literary Genre, 1967–2006

Denis Charbit

On June 4, 1967, *Les Temps Modernes* published a special issue entitled "The Arab-Israeli Conflict." Aside from the fact that it was huge (over one thousand pages compared to its typical two hundred) and the coincidence that it came off the press twenty-four hours before the start of the Six-Day War, this issue was also special in terms of its mode of presentation. In a departure from the journal's customary stance of unbridled unilateral support in a given conflict (the Algerian and Vietnamese National Liberation Movements, and the partisans of the 1956 Hungarian insurrection), Claude Lanzmann, the editor in chief, deliberately chose to invite both Arabs and Israelis to present their respective views on the conflict. Cognizant of its limited impact, he warned his readers that this contiguous juxtaposition of articles should not be taken as a premise for dialogue that would lead to imminent reconciliation. In fact, the twenty-two articles representing the Arab view were not contrapuntal to the nineteen pro-Israel articles; they were written as though the other half of the journal was simply not there.

This issue of *Les Temps Modernes*, which for years was considered the benchmark in France on the topic, embodies Hayden White's influential concept of "narratives,"[1] even though the word is never explicitly mentioned. The volume in fact was made up of two long narratives, two parallel lines of explanations, causes, conclusions and solutions destined, like railway tracks, never to meet. Their only point in common was publication together, but Lanzmann did not feel the effort had been in vain. Sartre defined it as "inert coexistence" and made a plea to the readers, not the authors. He assigned them the Herculean task of not only reading the part that already had their sympathies—which would only add fodder to their preconceived notions and fundamental beliefs. Instead, he asked them to venture into the opposing articles, not to spot the contradictions or garner arguments in favor of their own beliefs that would simply fuel hatred, but to let themselves be "troubled" (this was Sartre's verb) by the arguments of others.[2]

Dual Narratives on the Middle East Conflict 223

Unfortunately, the abundant output of French language publications on the Arab-Israeli conflict since 1967 has done little to heed Sartre's pedagogical recommendations. Typically, these publications (memoirs, autobiographies, collections of speeches, compilations of interviews) tend to reflect a single viewpoint—whether explicitly or implicitly—that the reader can then accept or reject according to his or her own convictions. This is particularly true for the many tendentious manifestos and fervent apologetics whose sole purpose is to denigrate one cause and/or champion the other.

Do scholarly works display the same traits? Even though academic texts differ from other types of publications in that they are expected to adhere to the strictures of scientific research, they should be subject to the same scrutiny since they can be the vectors of dominant trends if not the *doxa* of the time. Historiography, by pinpointing the myths and preconceived notions of any past conflict, shows that these insinuate into the scientific discourse of any era.

In the remainder of this chapter I examine a different type of narrative, which in my opinion is the only one to have taken Sartre's plea to heart and whose intrinsic value lies in the fact that it presents both narratives on an equal footing. Unlike the special issue of *Temps Modernes*, however—and the difference here is crucial—the two accounts of the Arab-Israeli conflict face off in a formal dialogue with the key protagonists. Despite, or perhaps because they do not share the same views, two key figures meet to debate theroots of the conflict and its future. They put their names to a collective volume designed from the outset to be the expression of two voices (sometimes three, when a third party is deemed necessary).

The implementation of this literary format is not linked to any particularly auspicious time as regards dialogue or the goodwill of their authors. Books of this nature have appeared regularly since 1967 and even though some are better than others, they provide a unique glimpse into the history of the French take on the Arab-Israeli conflict and the course of its history more than any of the other types of publications mentioned previously. Although this format is not exclusively French, France is the only place where the contributors are not only historical figures who shaped the conflict, but who also can be, to use Raymond Aron's term, *"committed spectators."*

In what follows, I do not examine each of these works separately; rather, I discuss how each volume sheds light on the changing nature of the fundamentals of the conflict. The five books, all published between 1967 and 2006,[3] are:

1. Eric Rouleau, Jean-Francis Held, Jean and Simone Lacouture, *Israel et les Arabes: Le Troisième combat* [*Israel and the Arabs, the Third Combat*] (Seuil, coll. L'Histoire immédiate, 1967). Henceforth, Rouleau/Held, 1967.
2. Mahmoud Hussein, Saul Friedlander and Jean Lacouture, *Arabes et Israéliens: Un premier dialogue* [*Arabs and Israelis: A first dialogue*]

224 *Denis Charbit*

   (Seuil, coll. L'Histoire immédiate, 1974). Henceforth, Hussein/Friedlander/Lacouture, 1974.
3. Hamadi Essid and Theo Klein, *Deux vérités en face. Un dialogue* [*Two truths face to face: A dialogue*] Presentation and discussion by Jean Pierre Langellier (Lieu Commun, 1988).[4] Henceforth, Essid/Klein 1988.
4. Pascal Boniface and Elizabeth Schemla, *Halte aux feux* [*Stop the Firing*] (Flammarion, 2006). Henceforth, Boniface/Schemla, 2006.
5. Rony Brauman and Alain Finkielkraut, *La Discorde: Israël-Palestine, les Juifs, La France. Conversations avec Elisabeth Lévy* [*Discord: Israel-Palestine, Jews, France. Conversations with Elisabeth Lévy*] (Mille et Une Nuits, 2006). Henceforth, Brauman/Finkielkraut/Lévy, 2006.

In general, this type of publication appears in the wake of an upsurge in violence—the Six-Day War, the October/Yom Kippur War, the First Intifada or the Second Lebanon War.[5] Although major events of this type most likely prompted the authors' decision to engage publicly in dialogue, the events are not given equal treatment. For instance, Jean-Francis Held and Eric Rouleau dialogue solely and exclusively on the 1967 war and the way it unfolded, thus providing a window on contemporaneous events. History begins, so to speak, in 1967, and the half century of conflict preceding it is relegated to a summary of fewer than twenty pages by Jean Lacouture, the veteran journalist and the editor who moderated the exchange. Because they are journalists and not historians, Held and Rouleau chose not to discuss the roots of the conflict. By contrast, in Mahmud Hussein and Saul Friedlander's book, there is hardly any mention of the key events in the October War that started with the crossing of the Suez Canal by the Egyptian army on the morning of October 6, and ended with the ceasefire signed by the two parties on kilometer 101. These only serve as a catalyst for the authors to focus, on the one hand, on the new consciousness of the Arab nation, which, having swept away its humiliating defeats of the past, can now envisage the existence of the state of Israel in its midst, and to consider, on the other, how the shock of the surprise attack prompted an Israeli society in crisis to view the Arab world in a different light. By contrast to the distancing from the past in the Rouleau/Held book and the orientation toward the future in Hussein/Friedlander, (a future motivated by the Egyptian victory over the previously invincible Israeli Army), Hamadi Essid and Theo Klein return to contemplate the past. Curiously, given its contributors, (the former President of the CRIF, the Representative Council of Jewish Institutions in France, and the Arab League's representative to UNESCO), this book centers more on the Israeli-Palestinian struggle than on the Arab-Israeli conflict.

Most of these dialogues took place shortly after the event that gave rise to the publication. Held and Rouleau wrote in the immediate aftermath of the war (July–August 1967) and the Hussein/Friedlander and Essid/Klein dialogues took place less than a year later (July 25–27, 1974, for the former and October–November 1988 for the latter). The Boniface/Schemla and Brauman/Finkielkraut books disrupt this pattern. The event that prompted both was the Second Intifada that began in September 2000, but more than six years elapsed between the outbreak of violence and publication. In both these cases, the duos—or duelists—acknowledge they had to overcome enormous hesitations before agreeing to dialogue, particularly since they had both been the self-proclaimed spokesmen of their respective camps at this critical juncture. In a sense, their joint appearance in a single volume was newsworthy in itself and may have had as much clout as what they had to say. The prime goal of these books is to reveal the conflicting points of view in the two narratives and attempt to find those points which could lead to agreement and reconciliation. Here again the latter two books differ in that they were less aimed at contributing to future accords as to defusing the atmosphere surrounding debates over Israel in France.

The choice of contributors from 1967 to 2006 clearly illustrates the transformation in the perceptionof the Israeli-Arab conflict in France. The earliest books were written by journalists and chroniclers. As foreign correspondents, they were ideally suited to inform their readers on the unfolding of the crisis which, due to its dramatic flare-ups, spectacular reversals and political and territorial upheavals, deserved an in-depth examination of whether history could have taken a different turn. Held and Rouleau's notoriety derived from their skills and experience: once back from Egypt and Israel which they had covered for their respective news outlets, they were the obvious choices to query political leaders and test the waters of public opinion. In this respect, Jean Lacouture was careful to note when presenting them that they were in no case the spokesmen for either cause but rather career journalists, which did not mean they could not show their true colors. Seven years later, Jean Lacouture was once again the master of ceremonies. Instead of journalists, he invited Mahmud Hussein, the pseudonym of Bahgat Elnadi and Adel Rifaat. These two Egyptian intellectuals were ddeply concered in the conflict but were capable of violating the taboo of dialoging with an Israeli, in this case Saul Friedlander, a historian well known for his works on Nazi anti-Semitism and the Final Solution. The title and the subtitle of the book are soberly eloquent: *Arabs and Israelis: A First Dialogue*. Not *the* first dialogue, which doubtless would have been wrong and in any case pretentious, but *a* first dialogue, suggesting that this dialogue would only have real impact if there were a second. A series with this type of goal had no choice but to start by naming names, "*Arabs and Israelis*" the collective identities in conflict separated for the time being by a coordinating conjunction. Mahmud Hussein echoed the Palestinian voice that was emerging after years of silence, but the conflict with Israel was still primarily cast as one involving the Arab nation as a whole.

Fourteen years later, two public figures—the diplomat Hamadi Essid and the lawyer Theo Klein—accepted the challenge to dialogue. They were not asked to discuss the issues from afar as intellectuals but as de facto representatives of each community, in an attempt to reach a historical compromise. They were both engaged in *a dialogue* on the conflict where *two truths* come *face-to-face* (as reflected in the title). This is because, in the meantime, the conflict had narrowed geographically (since the peace treaty with Egypt) but increased in intensity. From a conflict between many warring states it had become a bitter struggle between two nations fighting for the same land.

Neither Elisabeth Schemla nor Pascal Boniface dismissed this shift, but in the uneasy context of the Second Intifada, Durban, 9/11, the wars in Afghanistan and Iraq, coupled with the unrest in France which broke out in November 2005, the prime concern was elsewhere. By calling their book *"Stop the Firing"* (in the plural, with a play on words [fires/firing] since fires were not only burning in the Middle East but had been kindled in France as well, for instance the Dieudonné affair and the Ilan Halimi murder), they acknowledge their duty and responsibility to modulate the tension they both contributed to in 2000, when she ran a news website (*Proche-orient.com*) and he authored a report commissioned by the Socialist Party that recommended a change in the party's traditionally favorable stance toward Israel. Here again the subtitle selected by the pair is telling: it inevitably begins by mentioning the Middle East, but then links it to *anti-Semitism, the media, Islamophobia, the suburbs*, all suggestive of the subject matter but also of a cause-effect relationship.

The Rony Brauman and Alain Finkielkraut exchange is presented as a "conversation," but no one expects platitudes: "two men who won't even look at each other are not intellectuals who disagree or political adversaries, they are enemies," writes Elisabeth Lévy, the moderator (Brauman/Finkielkraut/Lévy 2006: 14). Compared to the spontaneity with which Elisabeth Schemla and Pascal Boniface agreed to write a book in two voices, it was much more difficult to convince these contributors, in particular Alain Finkielkraut, to take part. The range of topics discussed is more limited: *Israel-Palestine, the Jews, France*. Theirs is, however, the most successful book and the best argued, despite the undercurrent of personal animosity. The title was clearly designed to distinguish it from other works and associated expectations. "Dialogue" is typically meant to imply discussion aimed at finding common ground, but Brauman and Finkielkraut deliberately avoid sham consensus, one of the pitfalls of the genre. The title *"Discord"* still divides them at the end, but has the merit of placing them on a level of verbal exchange of ideas and opinions rather than on a level of impassioned disregard of facts that leads to violence.

One surprising feature that emerges from these books is that no Palestinian has ever taken part. A perhaps even more disturbing facet is that although ethnic background and religious affiliation of the advocates of the Arab or Palestinian cause differ from one book to another—Hamadi Essid is Muslim, Rony Brauman is a Jew, whereas Pascal Boniface does not fit into either of these categories—the Israeli position has always been defended by Jews, either French or Israeli.

The aims of these books are strikingly modest. The authors attempt to make their points, provide information on two societies that mutually disregard and fantasize about each other, not validate claims. "We were not there to make peace, or even to draw up the guidelines or even to make a global appeal, or even write a good book, but to show above all that debate is better than mortal combat" states Jean Lacouture (Hussein/Friedlander 1974: 10). Rather than trying to find a single, overarching truth, the purpose is to accept the idea of *"two lines of truths"* (Rouleau 1967) or *"two truths face-to-face."* Even more minimally, although representing a stance that is eminently praiseworthy, it is hoped that readers' exposure to the two narratives will make them realize that both make sense regardless of personal leanings.

Despite its intrinsic pedagogical qualities, this type of book fails to avoid an aporia. On the one hand, the contributors who revisit the origins of the conflict to seek a compromise are forced to admit that rehashing the past is counterproductive and acknowledge that after having generated their version of the conflict they need to turn the page. This type of book can take the form of an unrelenting, joust as well as a "dialogue designed to bring views closer" (Essid/Klein/Langellier 1988: 221). Even though the authors may not be official representatives of the cause[6] they are known to espouse, they are expected to fulfill this role. *This is what makes the book a dispute.* On the other hand, the two contributors, who can speak independently and are capable of distancing themselves from events, can also be more outspoken or daring politically so as to respond to readers' hopes that the hurdles initially separating them can at least partially be overcome. *This is what makes the book a dialogue.* This continuum from dispute to dialogue corresponds, in general, to a transition from the emotional to the rational. Nevertheless, the participants are torn between these two conflicting demands. In this confrontational situation, each must come to the defense of Israeli or Palestinian policies as a whole and are expected to verbalize the perceptions and interpretations, hopes and fears and visions of the past, present and future emplotted by each dominant narrative. At the same time, they need to show they can trespass borders, and reveal some comprehension of the opposite narrative, since without this, dialogue would be monologue. If each remains riveted to his narrative, the purpose of the book is undermined. Generally speaking, an ideal book of this type should reflect an elementary form of dialectic consisting of a thesis (one stance), an antithesis (the other) and finally, through good will and mediation, a synthesis (some common ground). The books can be seen as ranging from a zero-sum game (one side's wins are the other side's losses) to a win-win situation, or more metaphorically from a showdown to a settling of accounts. Depending on the authors, the tone of the dialogue varies. It can consist of a no-holds-barred sparring contest designed to KO the adversary where the only lesson for the reader is that truth is relative. The drawback is that this holds little hope for future reconciliation. Conversely, the dialogue can be motivated by a genuine wish to resolve differences, end quarrels, overcome obstacles and raw sentiment and place the discussion beyond the realm of the emotional.

The brilliantly argued Schemla/Boniface and Brauman/Finkielkraut books are situated at the confrontational end of this scale that remains. The other end, where dialogue incorporates a search for common ground, is represented by the encounter moderated by Jean Lacouture between Mahmud Hussein and Saul Friedlander. Here, the presentation of both conflicting realities does not undermine these authors' mutual willingness to take the first steps toward the other to achieve, on their level, what the two camps could achieve in the larger arena. By comparison, the chasm separating Hamadi Essid and Theo Klein is much larger. This is mirrored in the layout of the book. The debate, which takes up roughly thirty pages, appears at the end of the volume, and makes it more akin to the format of the special issue of the *Temps Modernes*, since Hamadi Essid's essay is followed in a separate section by Theo Klein's with no option for give and take. This clear division between position paper and debate concretizes the gap between them. Notably, in Essid's paper there is a missing link between his favorable attitude in the dialogue section toward an Israeli-Palestinian peace treaty on the basis of U.N. resolutions, and the indictment in his position paper that constitutes a defense of the Palestinian cause and a demolition of the historical legitimacy of Israel and Zionism. For the Arab side that is favorable to an agreement, the purpose of dialogue is recognition of the state of Israel in exchange for the creation of a future Palestinian state on land occupied by Israel since 1967. But this agreement in no way implies acceptance of any part of the Zionist narrative. Essid continues to see Israel as a *colonial fact*, the title of Maxime Rodinson's article in the *Temps Modernes*. His explanation for the persistence of the conflict remains Israel's refusal to accept the existence of Palestine and he does not even consider the Arab refusal to recognize Israel. Reconciliation thus has limits: it does not imply rewriting of the Palestinian narrative but rather restricts itself to recognizing that Israel is there. All these books reflect an asymmetry: A state exists—Israel—whose legitimacy is challenged. Whereas Palestine, whose legitimacy is never questioned by any of the participants has yet to exist.

The roles are distributed from the outset: Essid and his backers are not on the side of the Palestinians because they are Arabs but because this is the side of justice and victimhood. In his view, Klein only speaks in the name of tribal solidarity: he backs Israel the way Camus chose his *Pied-Noir* mother over justice. Hamadi Essid defines his position in the exchange with Theo Klein by saying he is *"the Arab voice which challenges the Other and at the same time responds to him,"* a somewhat narrow definition of dialogue since it eliminates the feature that makes a dialogue worth it; namely, the willingness to listen to one's counterpart (Essid/ Klein/ Langellier 1988: 16).

While Hamadi Essid's narrative espouses the Arab consensus as a whole, Theo Klein never takes a monolithic stance representing all Jews. While his narrative strives to take the interests of the opposing party into account, Essid rejects the demand to put himself in Jewish shoes.

As compared to the stereotypical Zionist narrative which saw Palestine as a "land without people," Klein revises both the fundamental and the operational ideology because he recognizes the legitimacy of the Palestinian people and supports an Israeli withdrawal from the occupied territories. In other words, the ethical and political demands on dialogue imply, for the Israel side, to change both the narrative and actual practices. The same cannot be said of his counterpart. In operational terms, explains Essid, the existence of Israel can be recognized but not its essence, since on a fundamental level Zionism is still an original sin. *"What is racism if not the exclusion of the other, and what is Zionism if not the exclusion of everything that is not Jewish?"* (Essid/ Klein/ Langellier 1988: 37). Thus, for the Arab advocates, the narrative can and should remain unchanged, and preservation of the original narrative makes it possible to tolerate the existence of Israel. Although he rejects the foundational legitimacy of Israel, he does not exclude a future legitimacy dependent on Israel living in harmony with the state of Palestine.

On a more general level, two types of changes in these publications stand out. The earliest dialogue pairs got straight to the point and expressed their ideological convictions with no personal involvement in the conflict. However, since the late 1990s, each contributor has incorporated something of his own personal narrative. In fact, there is no reason for concealment, because these authors' beliefs were often forged by the impact of the conflict on their personal lives. Thus history on the individual level and history writ large come together even though they are not identical.

The most striking change, however, concerns the role played by France in each of these books. In 1967, Held and Rouleau discuss French policies and the immediate repercussions on local opinion: in Israel the confusion and disbelief, even anger; in Egypt, the gratitude which Rouleau and his colleagues capitalized on to obtain passes others journalists were refused. Both writers confirm that they were surprised by the "inflammatory climate" in France. Nevertheless, the depiction is used to better highlight the fact that the atmosphere was calmer in the Middle East than generally thought. Held takes this paradox even further by commenting that *"Jews or not, the French were involved more intensely than was the case in Israel"* (Rouleau/ Held/Lacouture 1967: 29).

The impact of debate in French grew steadily. Hamadi Essid directed accusations against André Glucksmann and Bernard Henri-Lévy although they had always called for an Israeli withdrawal from the occupied territories and the creation of a Palestinian state; by contrast, he sang the praises of everything that was written in France to negate Israel from Roger Garaudy to Vincent Monteil or Georges Montaron. However, the French dimension, present but in the final analysis secondary in the earlier books, became unavoidable at the time of the Second Intifada. The war did not only take place in the occupied territories and Israel proper; it gave rise to incidents in France directed at places of worship, schools and representatives of the Jewish community. The battle of words and invectives that raged in newspapers and televised debates, on internet sites and radio shows, and involved the same individuals who later dialogued face-to-face, only amplified the idea of a second front. Elisabeth Schemla notes with some anxiety that the Arab-Israeli conflict has indeed been imported to France. Thus the Arab-Israeli conflict no longer impacts solely because of the distress and suffering it continues to cause for the peoples involved. Today, it affects the West and France in particular, for other reasons than oil, because its repercussions are considered to be decisive both in terms of the relationship between the West and the Muslim world, and in terms of the resurgence of anti-Semitism which has been unleashed through hatred and Israel bashing. This is the message conveyed by the most recent set of books which, although they do not achieve a convergence of views, has the merit of replacing one-track thinking on the Arab-Israeli conflict with in-depth considerations of its complexity. By doing so, these volumes align themselves with a more global message: the need to confront contradictory truths and persevere in dialogue even when it is difficult, painful and entwined, even if the wandering in the desert seems interminable before reaching the promised land of reconciliation that will enable people to live together while having differences of opinion.

NOTES

1. Hayden White, "The Question of Narrative in Contemporary Historical Theory" *History and Theory* 23(1; 1984): 1–33.
2. For more on this special issue of *Les Temps Modernes*, see Denis Charbit, "Le conflit israélo-arabe, un numéro des Temps Modernes revisité," *La Règle du jeu*, 34 (mai 2007): 82–145.
3. The topic is far from being exhausted, since two new books came out at the start of the 2008 academic year. The first brings together two of the most famous international figures involved in both the conflict and as artisans of a peaceful solution and whose farsightedness and ability to distance themselves makes them particularly suited for this type of exercise: Boutros Boutros-Ghali, the Egyptian Foreign Minister and Former Secretary General of the United Nations, and Shimon Peres, Former Prime Minister and Foreign Minister and currently the President of the State of Israel: *Soixante ans de conflit israélo-arabe. Témoignages pour l'Histoire. Dialogues croisés avec André Versaille* (*60 years of Arab-Israeli Conflict. Testimonies for History, dual dialogues with André Versaille*; Bruxelles: Editions Complexe, 2008). The second book is more innovative because instead of opposing, as is typical, a representative of each side, it brings together two figures who are both active in the French Jewish community and whose convergences of view override their differences: the political commentator and *Le Figaro* editorialist Alexandre Adler and the lawyer Gilles William Goldnadel, president of Lawyers

Without Borders and the France-Israel Alliance: *Conversations sur des sujets qui fachent avec Clément Weill-Raynal* (*Conversations on Problematic Topics, with Clément Weill-Raynal*; Paris: Jean-Claude Gawsewitch, 2008).
4. Note that Theo Klein used this same dialogue mode with Antoine Sfeir twenty years later in their recent *Israel survivra-t-il?* (*Will Israel Survive?*; Paris: l'Archipel, 2008).
5. In the case of the Hamadi Essid and Theo Klein book, their last exchange took place on the eve of the meeting of the Palestinian National Council in Algiers where they hoped it would ratify U.N. resolutions, and in particular Resolution 181, on the partition of Palestine into two sovereign states.
6. With the exception of Hamadi Essid who, at the time he dialogued with Theo Klein, was the representative of the Arab League to UNESCO.

15 How One Becomes a Traitor

Esther Benbassa
(Translated by Alan Astro)

Within the memory of the Jewish people, the military chief and historian Flavius Josephus stands out as the archetypal traitor.[1] He took part in the Jewish revolt against Rome that began in 66 AD. When his camp was besieged, he betrayed his fellows and surrendered to Vespasian. From the Roman side, he witnessed the fall of Jerusalem and the destruction of the Temple in 70 AD. He abjured neither his faith nor his God, yet remained loyal to Rome. His betrayal led Jews to consign him to forgetfulness, which was most unfortunate, both for him and for the Jewish people, deprived thereby of his brilliant insights into the period. His writings in Greek became part of Christian culture, to be introduced to Jews only nine hundred years later, in a Hebrew adaptation published in Italy in the tenth century.

When does one become a traitor? And in whose eyes is one a traitor? Betrayal resides more in others' perception of one's actions than in the actions themselves. Anything and everything can be subsumed into the category of betrayal, in accordance with the point of view taken. The act of betrayal can be the failure to make good on a promise, the breaking off of a friendship, the postponement of an encounter. Certain moments are more favorable than others to accusations of betrayal. They occur particularly often in difficult or unusual times. Were the Jews who left Spain in order to avoid betraying the religion of their forebearers better than those who converted to Christianity in order not to leave behind their country, their language, their occupations, their positions of status? Who decides what constitutes betrayal? Is it the historians who, supposedly objective, place on the good or bad side those actors who make decisions in accordance with their understanding of the necessities of the moment, the particulars of their own cases and their states of mind? The impossibility of reconstructing an entire period in the past leaves to memory, and then to history, the right to decide who were the good or bad guys.

At all moments of crisis, factions of Jews have fought against other factions of Jews. One cannot forget the Sabbatean heresy of the seventeenth century that almost entirely undermined rabbinical authority throughout the Diaspora. Sabbatai Tsvi, known to subsequent eras as a false messiah, provoked a veritable religious cataclysm, a wave of conversions to Islam and Christianity. Those on the losing side have often been condemned by history as having been on the wrong side. Let us remember as well the battles waged by Hasidim, adherents of a mass mystical movement that caused a scandal within the eighteenth-century rabbinical establishment. Didn't their opponents, the *mitnagdim*, denounce them to the Russian authorities as undesirables and heretics?

With the onset of modernity, Jews who wished to leave the ghetto to partake of Emancipation were fought by followers of tradition. Supporters of the Jewish Enlightenment were especially targeted. Were German-Jewish soldiers in World War I, whose bullets may have hit their coreligionists on the other side, traitors unbeknownst to themselves? Memory of the Second World War is still so vivid that we are hard-pressed to decide whether those who sat on Jewish councils in the ghettos were traitors or unwilling tools of a hostile order.

ISRAEL, THE DIASPORA, GENOCIDE

The founding of Israel constitutes the major turning point in the history of Jews since the destruction of the Second Temple. On the one hand are those who live in the Jewish state, and on the other, those who remain in the Diaspora despite the Zionist aspiration to gather all exiles onto that land. The gap is great between enthusiasm about Israel, the sense of security it affords, and actual emigration there. Supporting Israel does not preclude loving the country one continues to inhabit, its language, its culture, its climate, as one enjoys the comforts it offers.

Zionism, whose birth coincided with the proliferation of nationalist movements in Europe, reinforced in its adherents a Jewish identity that had started to falter in the modern era. It represented the attempt by a minority of Jews to take their fate into their own hands, at a time when modern Europe showed itself incapable of defending them against pogroms in Russia and restrictive measures in societies where they had lived for centuries. Post-World War II mythology posits an unbreakable link between the extermination of the Jews and the founding of the state of Israel, downplaying the role of Zionism from the end of the nineteenth century onwards.

The state of Israel was supposed to undo Jewish history in the Diaspora, as it created a new Jew, the modern-day Hebrew, the Israeli. "Denial of the Exile," which was, in a sense, a betrayal of a centuries-old Jewish identity, was a part of Israeli mentality for several decades before giving way to a more pragmatic view. Israel exists thanks in part to the support of the Diaspora, just as the Jews of the Diaspora gain ever more spiritual sustenance from their links to Israel. An exchange of favors takes place, whereby the Diaspora is gratified emotionally and Israel's basic interests are furthered, since Diaspora Jews are excellent promoters of Israeli policies.

Moreover, Diaspora Jews feel somewhat like traitors to the Zionist cause. Not having settled in Israel, they are afflicted by a sense of guilt that they assuage by moral and especially financial support. For Israelis, this has been a marriage of reason, reinforced by the Six-Day War and the occupation of the Palestinian territories. And Diaspora Jews get to project all kinds of fantasies on a people and a country that seldom correspond to the actual situation of a nation at war ever since its inception, living in rather difficult conditions.

The extermination and suffering of Europe's Jews that preceded the founding of Israel, endowed the country with an almost sacred kind of untouchability. Still, how could one disregard that it was born on land inhabited by another people? It was the biblical, and thus mythical, homeland of the Jews; and an ancestral, actual homeland for the Palestinians. The latter experienced the occupation of the West Bank and Gaza in 1967 as a kind of repetition of what they went through in 1948. The Israelis too replayed the primal scene of the birth of their nation. As Israel was to be perceived as a land for Jews after the genocide, in 1967 the specter of Auschwitz was invoked to justify its new borders. Such reasoning was hammered in further by the right-wing Likud, when it came to power in 1977.

That was when memory of genocide started to emerge more fully not only among Jews but throughout the West. Constant invocation of the Holocaust served to restore Jewish identity in the Diaspora, especially among secularists, before it assumed a major political function both in the Diaspora and in Israel. Such considerations have nothing to do with the real pain and legitimate mourning undergone by survivors. Clearly, no a priori political calculations went into their attempts to convey their experiences and urge all sectors of society to be vigilant lest comparable atrocities occur. Nonetheless, one must carefully distinguish between actual endeavors to recount the traumas lived through and the way those traumas are instrumentalized, even if some strategies overlap.

"THE SHOAH AS RELIGION"

On September 11, 2000, an article of mine entitled "The Shoah as Religion" was published in the newspaper *Libération*. The problem I raised is not taboo in American or Israeli universities, where it is debated openly. The last few decades have seen the Holocaust transformed into a sacred cult with its ceremonies, its monuments, its commemoration days, its temples (the museums dedicated to it) and its high priests. I was so imprudent as to question the uniqueness of the Holocaust, arguing that no genocide is unique: our times have seen enough of them both before and after the Holocaust, and anything that is human is not essentially unique in the sense that it can occur again. This viewpoint enjoys a wide consensus in the scholarly world, with a few exceptions. It certainly does not deny the singularity of each genocide, bound to its historical context and the methods employed. Nonetheless, the aim pursued in each case was the extermination of a group defined in "rational" terms by those programming the operation.

Imagine my surprise when I was attacked by droves of journalists, mouthing the opinions of the high priests of the Holocaust! The criticisms did *not* come from individual survivors or their organizations. By describing the process of sacralization, I had broached a topic that only the guardians of the temple and their spokespeople had the right to discuss. In a country like France, which does not clearly distinguish among intellectuals, amateurs and journalists, the media will provide an outlet to anyone, qualified or not, proclaiming a supposedly eternal truth. However, to question dominant opinion is akin to committing sacrilege.

The first thing held against me was that I had said something politically unacceptable. Indeed, to trace the evolution undergone by the memory of the Holocaust involves saying that the Holocaust does not escape manipulation and that it has been used to reinforce the ever-weakening identity of secularized Jews. Moreover, considering the Holocaust from the same perspective as other genocides places it within long-term history and gives back its fundamentally human—although deeply tragic—dimension. In the opinion of the self-proclaimed guardians of memory, such contextualization brings the Holocaust into competition with other genocides, something unthinkable because of the supposed uniqueness and unspeakability of the event. But if something cannot be spoken, doesn't that mean that memory of it cannot be transmitted? By pushing the argument to its logical consequences, one ends up advocating the opposite of what is sought by all those who expend incalculable efforts to prevent forgetfulness.

Jewish community institutions generally, and in France particularly, are known for their unconditional support of Israel, whatever be its government at the moment. They have consistently gone along with the politicization of the Holocaust that the Likud undertook upon its accession to power. The aura of holiness surrounding the Holocaust and the unassailable victimhood of Jews that follows from it de-legitimize from the start any criticism of the state of Israel, which has been elevated from the real plane to the symbolic. Those who take it upon themselves to criticize Israel have to pay the consequences, except on university campuses that remain on the margins of everyday society—as they do in the United States, but not in France. Such an aura of holiness is quite useful, sheltering the state of Israel no matter what it does to the Palestinians.

Though this arrangement does not always function perfectly, it achieves its aim of parrying the gravest criticisms of Israel. Everyone has to bow before the tyrannical memory of the Holocaust and the requirement to show unswerving support for Israel. Anyone not following this line had better beware; especially if he isn't Jewish, he may be called an anti-Semite at any moment. Such an accusation is anathema in these times when contrition for acts committed against minorities is all the rage. Yielding to the ukases on memory, the West as a whole has sought to purify itself of its crimes, including the one committed against the Jews. It is almost unthinkable to advocate the dose of forgetfulness necessary for life to go on, and to urge transmission of a more positively defined Jewish identity.

In February 2008, at the well-publicized annual dinner sponsored by the CRIF (the Representative Council of French Jewish Institutions)—to which most high-profile French politicians are invited—French President Nicolas Sarkozy made a startling proposal. He urged assigning to every French primary school pupil the responsibility of remembering a particular Jewish child deported from France and killed in a Nazi camp. This suggestion brought about a general wave of opposition among the French population, Jews included. For example, just one day after Sarkozy made his proposal, the well-respected former cabinet minister Simone Veil, herself an Auschwitz survivor, declared her opposition to this initiative, which she called counterproductive. Later, the commission that formed to examine the proposal rejected it. This incident, I hope, will cause people to think more carefully about Holocaust remembrance. It is as though public opinion were warning us that it had grown weary of being tyrannized by official memory.

Instead of accomplishing the difficult task of disseminating Jewish culture, various Jewish organizations and media have for decades preferred propagating the memory of genocide, especially useful for group cohesion. The Jews of North Africa, arriving in France after their native lands had become independent from the end of the fifties on, sought recognition from their Ashkenazic brethren, who regarded them with condescendence. Thus they zealously partook of the memory of a genocide they had escaped, thanks to the fact that North Africa was liberated before France was. In North Africa, Jews had tended to be quite traditionalistic. However, in France, as the immigrant generation died out, religious practice declined among their descendents. They too felt the need for this identity based on suffering.

My article had thus touched several sore points; it was not long before my apprehensions proved justified. Few people had any illusions about these matters, but it was essential that all questioning remain within the community and not be aired in public. That was a problem I had not foreseen. I had written the article precisely to point out how the ubiquitous call for memory downplayed the dynamics of Jewish universalism. The risk was that generations to come would feel alienated from a Judaism defined by what had wrested vitality from it, and not by a future they could build by taking a distance from the past. I urged responsibility toward others rather than the cultivation of a memory that closed rather than opened horizons.

A few years later, in 2005, during the commemorations of the sixtieth anniversary of the liberation of Auschwitz, Simone Veil, president of the Foundation for the Memory of the Shoah, would also speak of the need to strike a balance between the necessity of remembrance and the ethics of responsibility toward others. But we had not yet reached that point.

Whereas in the United States, Norman Finkelstein's *The Holocaust Industry*—though excessive, ideologically biased and far too personal—met only with severe criticism, in France, the author, the publisher of the translation, and Antoine de Gaudemar—the journalist for *Libération* who had reviewed it—were dragged into court by Gilles William Goldnadel. This commercial lawyer, head of an organization called *Attorneys without Borders*, has distinguished himself by the series of lawsuits he brings against those he accuses of anti-Semitism, by which he means criticism of Israeli policies. His favorite target is journalists, whom he attempts to silence by holding this threat over their heads. Of course, he ends up losing all these cases, but that hardly keeps him from embarking on new ones. This is the same man who, linked at one point with far-Right groups and now president of the Association France-Israël, published in November 2001 *Le nouveau bréviaire de la haine* [*The New Harvest of Hatred*].[2] In the midst of a French presidential campaign that fanned fear of street crime and resurgent anti-Semitism, the arrival of this work was hardly coincidental. It came right after 9/11, in the middle of the Intifada, at a point when approval of Israeli policies was at its lowest, as evidenced by public opinion polls and media coverage. The book is of no interest whatsoever except insofar as it plants fear in the minds of Jews. It would be followed by similar works, proudly displayed in the windows of bookshops.

DO JEWS HAVE A FUTURE?

Just a few days following September 11, 2001, appeared the book I wrote with Jean-Christophe Attias, *Les Juifs ont-il un avenir?* [*Do the Jews Have a Future?*].[3] It was our bad luck to have finished it just before the terrorist attacks on the soil of the United States. The central role that the struggle against terrorism and the "axis of evil" would soon assume in the policies of the United States and the West in general quickly blurred the boundaries among the concepts "Muslim," "anti-Semite," "Islamic fundamentalist," "terrorist" and "Palestinian." This lumping together would become permanent in the heated state of public opinion—a heatedness understandable in the fright that took hold of the West, whose fragility had been driven home by the sight of an attack against its greatest power precisely where it seemed larger than life. Again, we must not forget that this was in the middle of the Second Intifada, and a kind of natural confusion formed between Palestinian terrorism and the acts that in a few minutes killed thousands of innocent victims and swept away the self-confidence of the United States.

The week it came out, our book was discussed in the magazine *Le Point*, by some intellectuals who couldn't have read it because they hadn't received it from the publisher. We were reproached for having downplayed anti-Semitism among Muslim Arabs in France. Perhaps, in fact, we had underestimated it. Nonetheless, in light of recent events, the issues of street crime and anti-Semitic acts were rapidly woven into a *leitmotif* of the presidential race. Among our most virulent critics would be Bernard-Henri Lévy, and the future campaigner against the "new Judeophobia" Pierre-André Taguieff,[4] who in a kind of Moscow show trial questioned our status as scholars while paying little attention to the substance of our book. Let it be said in passing that just a few months earlier, the same B.-H. Lévy had, on the part of the Grasset publishing house, expressed great interest in my project for a book to be called *The Religion of the Shoah*. (For reasons not relevant here, I withdrew it from consideration by that publisher.)

Those who attacked my article on the Shoah a year earlier were the first to do the same to our book, which though cautious in its conclusions touched once again upon sensitive issues. A television debate followed, which pitted us against the official guardians of the memory of the Shoah: Serge Klarsfeld and his son Arno, as well as Claude Lanzmann. I had always respected their work, especially that of the two elders, but not what they had come to represent. My first mistake was to be seated next to a Palestinian, though I know neither how nor on what grounds I could have refused. Actually, only a few pages of the book dealt with the Holocaust, but they would be the only ones discussed, so much have Jews been identified with the genocide; what they accomplished before or after is of interest to very few, even among Jews themselves. It took a few minutes for me to figure as a foe of the Jewish people; since I spoke in such terms about the Shoah and happened to be seated next to a Palestinian, the association of ideas was quickly made. Neither Jean-Christophe Attias nor I, researchers working in relative calm, was used to the being in the limelight. We had gotten trapped.

What happened on television was just our first experience of the venom to be spewed upon us. The new political climate made it even easier for Jewish institutions to foster confusion between the struggle against anti-Semitism and the defense of Israel. French Jewry, immersed in the memory of the Shoah for years, would soon become ensnared in constant fear of anti-Semitism. Indeed, some sectors of the Jewish population faced it, especially those living in poor suburbs, victims of a climate of generalized, everyday violence. If anti-Semitism is appalling, so is the day-to-day racism directed at Arabs, Muslims and blacks. The second in no way excuses the first, but it has to be fought just as vigorously. But that was not part of the anti-street crime agenda of the politicians.

After September 11, it was no longer politically expedient to mention racism against Arabs and Muslims. And since politicians entertain various fantasies about Jewish power and the Jewish vote (there are some 530,000 Jews in France), it seemed useful to include the struggle against anti-Semitism as a theme in their campaigns. It was in these same circumstances that the shift rightward of French Jewry began. The left-wing government of Prime Minister Lionel Jospin was reproached for having lacked vigilance. Following our TV appearance, we were attacked verbally on the street by some of our Jewish brothers and sisters. Things having gotten rather painful, we decided to take advantage of an offer to work at a research institute in Budapest, for a few months at least, thereby escaping passions whose depth we were just starting to grasp.

Our detractors felt an urgent necessity to get recalcitrant characters like us back into line, especially since we were Jews and held chairs in Jewish studies (I in Modern Jewish history at the École Pratique des Hautes Études, Sorbonne, and my husband in medieval Jewish thought at the same institution). Group solidarity was what mattered, and universalism was scuttled. The preference went to Jewish intellectuals totally attached to the "tribe." If any resisted, name-calling and other intimidations made them quickly rejoin ranks. The task was completed through connections in the press. Ordinary Jews, plunged in a climate of fear, were only too glad to be offered scapegoats on whom to let out their frustrations.

Luckily, at this moment, we came across courageous journalists and publishers, intellectuals in the true sense of the word. Should anyone claim that real debate has died out in France, let it be known that there are spaces of free speech zealously and painfully guarded by some men and women of the Left and of the Right. Nonetheless, in such a case, one may feel immensely alone. One is seen as a traitor among the Jews, and regarded with suspicion by members of other groups, fearful lest they be seen as not thinking properly. One has been pasted with labels, and not the best ones. One begins to doubt oneself and one's very thoughts. This is a crucial moment, when one might betray even oneself. More or less questionable characters come to offer support, not necessarily for the right reasons. One risks falling victim to their siren song.

Another danger is to assemble an in-group of victims of various kinds, a marginal cocooning strategy tempting to those who go against official doctrines. However, isn't an intellectual supposed to be a vagabond, far from clannish interests, free *not* to belong? That's no doubt a utopic desire, in these morose times. Besides, I have no calling for victimhood and did not feel so much persecuted as pressured. I resisted as well as I could, not without moments of weakness. Coming from a Sephardic family that held its honor and dignity above everything else, I was able to hide my dismay as I searched the better to understand and master the situation. Like a kind of Penelope in reverse, I rewove at night what others had undone during the day. Unsigned letters with obscene drawings arrived at my workplace; I received anonymous phone calls, threatening e-mails. Denigrating letters about me were sent to institutions where I had been invited to speak, in France and abroad.

Happily, our university positions did not depend on the Jewish community, but on the French state. If that had not been the case, we would have long been in deep trouble. Thus we were given the opportunity to measure the importance of something we, like others, often take for granted: the fact that our nation permits us as citizens to escape the pressures of our communities of origin, participation in which is a matter of choice and always revocable. Colleagues where we taught chose to remain outside these community scuffles, and that redounds to their credit. Perhaps they simply did not get what all the fuss was about. Whatever the reasons for it, their silence was a source of comfort.

EVERYWHERE AND NOWHERE AT THE SAME TIME

I had thus been placed outside the community—I, who had never been quite inside it. The ambiguity of being inside and outside had always suited me, because of the distance and freedom that such a position offered. The symbolic expulsion to which I had been subjected had all the weightier a meaning. It reminded me of the excommunication that Jewish authorities could perform before the time of Emancipation, when Jews could not survive outside the community. Such a severe penalty was rarely brought to bear; it functioned more as a threat encouraging obedience to commonly accepted rules and general adhesion to the group, since such norms did not have the force of law. I felt somewhat excommunicated, not without a vague sense of having actually committed a betrayal. I too had refused to follow the consensus adhered to by members of a group as diverse as they are dispersed, and by the media organs that mirror this consensus in a kind of solidarity with the group.

Does a traitor always know why he has become one? In any event, the effects of his betrayal make him realize its extent. Abroad, and especially in the United States, my works translated into English are recommended reading in Jewish studies courses; in Paris, fewer and fewer students of Jewish background were willing to have a renegade like me direct their dissertations. Actually, that was a stroke of luck, because they were soon replaced by others with a more professional attitude toward research, having passed state contests for jobs and already taught some years in lycées. They worked on Jewish subjects as they would have on any other, with a refreshing distance and levelheadedness, and without crises of conscience. They brought to bear the same interest they would have shown if the Mayas or the Cathars had been their object of study. Jewish history suddenly felt more universal, which was hardly to my displeasure. As far as auditors were concerned—and it's a longstanding tradition of the École Pratique des Hautes Études to let in as many as possible—the Jews among them continued to quibble over every word and give their point of view on everything. After all, by being born Jewish, weren't they automatically conversant with the entirety of Jewish history, whether ancient, medieval or modern?

Thus it became more prudent to give up speaking at Jewish centers where my listeners gleefully rewrote history as they liked, to conform to the circumstances of the moment. If I dared present certain proven historical facts, I was met with a barrage of insults and recriminations. For example, no one would listen if I pointed out that the Arabs had not expelled the Jews at the time of the decolonization of North Africa. I tried to explain that Jews had to leave these new states because they had not, for the most part, been involved in the national movements that led to independence (indeed Jews were not always welcome in those movements). I recalled that Jews had been on the side of the colonizers from whom they expected improvement of their status, and that the birth of the state of Israel had poisoned their relations with the other natives. All that could simply not be heard. Before or after my appearances, vituperative articles would appear in the Jewish press, and radio programs would slam me.

A kind of force pushed me into a marginal space where I did not wish to be. I have never had any taste for small, conspiratorial groups. In my youth, I had been a Trotskyite for a brief time—less than a year, if my memory serves me correctly. I could not accept the partisan ideas, the division of the world into them and us. Inchoately I felt that if my comrades succeeded in changing the world, the new order would probably be even worse than the old one. In my native Turkey, I had grown up in a multilingual and multicultural universe, where various groups were not necessarily well-disposed to each other, but where they tried to act as though they were. As a matter of course, I came into contact with other cultures and languages. I was familiar with Islam as well as Christianity, not to mention Judaism, though we practiced it without great punctiliousness. Having circulated in such varied environs, I felt no desire for isolation. To be everywhere and nowhere at the same time has become a way of life for me; whether I've chosen it or not is no longer a question.

My "excommunication" freed me from a Jewish identity that would have suffocated me and cut off my contact with other groups—a hardly avoidable result of recent events and subsequent brainwashing that had affected a number of Jews, including the most open among them. At the age of fifteen I had moved to Israel, where most of my family lived, and studied there a few years. Israel was where I got rid of my inhibitions about being Jewish. In Turkey, after all, we had been a modernized kind of *dhimmis*, "protected" second-class subjects. We did not display our Jewishness openly; our first and last names made it clear enough. We were Jews, but not too Jewish in public, in order to avoid problems. We always feared the worse, even when there was no valid reason to do so. I was raised with the notion that one should learn several languages, in order to build one's life elsewhere. As a result, I don't know any language very well, though I speak quite a few passably.

In Israel, I had nothing to hide. I found the Israelis quite different from me. *I* was Jewish, and *they* Israeli. We did not share the same customs or culture. Slowly, I got over *that* exile as well. Though I did not become Israeli, the weight of being a Jew lightened; I sometimes wonder if that's what being an Israeli means. Some of my intellectual friends in Israel criticize the country's policies, back the Palestinians, make very subversive statements in the media, and they are not ostracized. That is no more true after Gaza war Freedom of expression there was more developed than within the French Jewish community, which tracks every word you say and demonizes you as soon as you step out of line. I often go to Israel, where I have numerous familial and professional ties. There, no one has ever kept me from supporting the Palestinian cause, even if arguments can become quite intense. I have no problem with being Jewish and feeling profoundly close to Israel; nonetheless, I don't see Israel as the ultimate safety net.

In France I learned that as a Jew you may not criticize Israel, and that it is your duty to back it in all circumstances, even when its policies are wrongheaded and inhumane. Apparently, centuries of suffering, and genocide itself, have not made us more sensitive to others' afflictions. Israel is a country like any other, though it was founded by people who had suffered. Suffering doesn't make you any better. Worse: the stance of absolute victim, the supposed superiority of Jewish suffering, has immunized us against compassion. The suffering of the Palestinians is part and parcel of the existence of Israel. It's a country that belongs to two suffering peoples, who can't manage to share it equitably. They have their backs to each other right now; maybe in the future they'll work side by side. At least I hope so.

INSIDERS AND OUTSIDERS

As the issue of anti-Semitism was becoming central in France, the defense of anything Israel did went without saying. While there were those who exploited fear of anti-Semitism in order to protect Israel's image, the majority of Jews were simply frightened. Instead of trying reasonably to deal with such a negative climate by working out strategies for groups to live together, those who had something to gain from fear fueled it with alarmist statements on TV and radio, while squelching any calls for calm and reconciliation. In the meantime, the community withdrew into itself. Anti-Semitism united a group whose members had long spread their efforts among universalist causes. At the same time, there reemerged an apprehension rooted in the past, which some sought to use for their own purposes, and anyone who tried to swim against the current was tyrannized. Journalists and politicians went along with this, lest they be branded anti-Semites. More and more Jews became radicalized, boxing the leadership into corners they had created for themselves.

Emotions reached a fever pitch, though they were occasionally dampened by reality, as when a young woman who claimed to have been the victim of an act of anti-Semitic aggression later revealed having made it all up, or when arson against the Sephardic social center on the rue Popincourt, attributed to Muslim Arabs, turned out to have been the work of a Jew. But there was a kind of confusion among Bush's campaign against the "axis of evil" (the finest moment of which has been the occupation of Iraq), anti-Arab sentiment among the native French (with its source in decolonization), ordinary racism and the party line of the Jewish community leadership, who used emerging anti-Semitism to meet pressure put on it by Israel to increase emigration from France.

Even if one may argue that such phenomena have been exaggerated and the resultant fears exploited, it would be foolish to ignore the widespread identification of French Muslim Arabs with Palestinians, their strong resentment against Jews who have been more successful as a minority, and the resultant anti-Semitic attitudes and behaviors. Muslim Arabs, as well as sub-Saharan Africans, are outsiders insofar as they are targets of social and economic discrimination. That feeling is reinforced by the nearly complete absence of members of their groups among higher-ranking civil servants and political figures. They look at Jews as insiders, close to sources of power—as Jewish community leaders often claim to be, when they declare themselves to be "guardians of the values of the Republic." The hostility of outsiders toward power is directed in the first instance against those at the center, but also against those who are weak because they, too, are a minority: the Jews.

In this tense context I came to understand how the Holocaust and the creation of the state of Israel had slowly eroded the universalist outlook of Jewish intellectuals. Anyone who did not bow to community dictates and showed disagreement was a traitor. All means were employed to stifle dissent, even when they involved going outside the community. Well-formed relationships obviated the need to ask explicitly that articles by a certain scholar occasionally not be published, that his or her books not be reviewed, that he or she not be interviewed on radio or TV. Indeed, such petty rebuffs are not intolerable, but they foster malaise in those of us who exist professionally only when our work is noticed and our viewpoints elicit reactions.

Far-Right Jewish websites, whose content would cause shudders if it were not put up by Jews, have come to play an essential role in sullying reputations, branding certain individuals with the odious label "anti-Semite." It is easy to imagine breaking into a cold sweat as one ponders the possibility of such a fate. But do those who fear Jews like them? No one seems to be asking that basic question. Those who today pour vitriol on Islam, Islamic fundamentalism and terrorism—which they roll into one thing—may tomorrow vent their wrath on the Jews, as happened at times of crisis in the unpredictably changing France of the nineteenth and twentieth centuries.

In addition to the Jewish activists I have described, there arose, in 2003 and 2004, die-hard secularists, whose rhetoric is somewhat different. They claimed that the French Republic was endangered by some 1,500 Muslim schoolgirls wearing veils. The effects the girls' attire caused on the educational climate could have been dealt with serenely, without enacting a law, but we must not forget that secularism is the sole remaining issue capable of serving as a rallying point in France. The points of convergence between the Jewish activists and the die-hard secularists are many. We are witnessing a "betrayal of the intellectuals" of the kind Julien Benda described so eloquently in the 1920s; in our times, it is the response to an identity crisis France is going through as it confronts various challenges: The expansion of European Union, globalization, obsolescence of its social programs, structural unemployment, uncontrollable ghettos on the fringes of its cities and the exhaustion of a culture that is no longer seen as a beacon of civilization. Our intellectuals are betraying their mission by promoting a vague nationalism that rejects Muslim Arabs and blacks.

KEEP UP THE FIGHT?

Though the Palestinian cause has been transformed by some into an all-encompassing ideology, there are those who support it simply out of a desire for justice, thereby fulfilling their proper role as intellectuals and journalists. They do so, despite the strong temptation to adopt a reactionary position that would safeguard their tranquility and, occasionally, even their livelihood. Provocative stances have never been less appreciated than in these gloomy times. However, not all abdicate their responsibilities. History has shown many times that France has a conservative, reactionary streak. Nonetheless, it is also a birthplace of human rights and of many a struggle for freedom; that legacy has not been totally effaced.

Intellectuals covet the honors, great and small, that authorities bestow upon them. The fragility of their status makes them cross easily from one side—or from one extreme—to the other. That is a risk no one, and certainly not I, can be sure of escaping. Thus it is a cause both for gladness and regret that the power of intellectuals has been greatly eroded in this era of globalization, free markets and cyberspace. Nonetheless, in France, and especially within the limited parameters of its capital, their voices are occasionally heard; something remains of their erstwhile prestige, but their impact is no longer the same. The importance of in-groups among Parisian intellectuals cannot be discounted, whether the networks formed are the result of elective affinities or sheer cliquishness. In the provinces, concerns are light years away from the internecine struggles of the capital.

I am fortunate to be Jewish in that it spares me from being labeled an anti-Semite. I can be accused only of self-hatred. That term was used in the 1930s to describe Jews who had internalized anti-Semitism to the point of detesting their Jewish selves and occasionally even committing suicide. Naturally, I am far from any such attitude. But I am no less Jewish for asserting that Israel and the genocide do not constitute the bases of my Jewish identity. I urge filtering our sense of affliction so that it may be experienced in a positive way. For that reason, I believe that it is time to move from the cultivation of memory to the study of history. It seems to me that the essential lessons of the genocide can only be transmitted, once the survivors are gone, by historians who will take a distance from the searing memory of those who went through it. It is historians who will secure a permanent place for that tragic event.

What remains of the expulsion of the Jews from Spain—one of the greatest traumas of medieval times, the witnesses to which have long disappeared—if not historical accounts of the period during which that catastrophic occurrence took place? By neutralizing the intense affect elicited by that tragedy, history has freed successive generations from its unbearable weight. This is hardly the same as forgetting the event; instead, history provides the continuity and fosters the creativity necessary for a constant renewal of Jewish existence.

If French Jewry shows less vitality than its American counterpart, one reason is that France demands conformity and centralization, while it mutes diversity. It is an urgent necessity to compose a new form of diasporic Jewish identity in this country, faithful to Israel but autonomous. That would be the only kind of Judaism capable of producing values relevant to today's world and responsibly engaged in it. Where are the heirs to the nineteenth-century Jews committed to Marxism, socialism and anarchism, who sought to change the world and, so doing, the Jewish condition? Where are Jewish musicians like the Gershwin brothers, so universalistic as to base their *Porgy and Bess* on the lives of African Americans? Where are those eager to follow in the footsteps of the American Jews who in the 1960s lent essential support to the black struggle for civil rights? Not only did the catastrophe of World War II make European Jews lose confidence in their countries; the current self-isolation of Jews here is symptomatic of a crisis caused by a focus on Israel and a refusal to stop mourning the genocide.

These patterns were all too evident following the torture and murder of a young Jew named Ilan Halimi in January 2006. It is most likely that his kidnapers assumed he was rich because he was Jewish, even though he had a modest job as a clerk. The trial of the persons accused of this murder began more than three years later, after a long inquiry, on April 29, 2009. And when the murder first became known, community officials, chastened by earlier false alarms, proceeded cautiously. But at the annual CRIF dinner shortly afterwards, government figures mentioned anti-Semitism as a motive for the murder, thereby prejudging results of an investigation then still in its early stages. The president of the CRIF took it from there. Emotions soon reached a climax among the rank and file of the Jewish community.

In an article published in *Le Monde* of February 25, 2006, I called for calm, urging that this crime not be interpreted primarily as an assault against the Jewish community. I was assailed by dozens of e-mails. Unfortunately, I focused more on negative reactions than on expressions of support from those like me, fearful of mass hysteria. Shaken by the frenzy, I censored my remarks to the media; no one was ready to listen to reason. The greatest alarmists were predicting an end to Jewish life in France.

There followed a mass demonstration against this crime, where Jews found themselves isolated, so far had they pushed an ethnocentric interpretation. This was a further sign of a turn inward that risks making the Jews of France foreigners in their own country, cutting them off from the nation as a whole. Far-Right activists under the tutelage of Philippe de Villiers joined the march—another symptom of the new political orientation of a community that had always tended to vote for the Left. Nowadays, Islamophobia has made the far Right an acceptable force. A few days later, someone of "French" origin (i.e., not Jewish, Muslim or black), met a fate similar to Ilan Halimi's; no sooner had that happened than a Muslim Arab was killed at Oullins in what was probably a racist attack. None of these murders can be condoned, and it is certainly worthwhile to consider closely the causes of such recurrent violence emerging within French society. But neither of the latter two cases called forth mass demonstrations.

THE LONG, DIFFICULT COMBAT FOR COEXISTENCE

In 2004, right in the middle of the Intifada, Jean-Christophe Attias and I organized a day of encounters at the Sorbonne, entitled "Jews and Muslims: Sharing History and Constructing Dialogue." We wished to bring to the same podium scholars, media commentators and community activists who generally did no more than hurl invectives at each other. Our aims were to foster dialogue by delving into the factors that enabled members of our groups in the not-so-distant past to live together despite grave conflicts, and to see what elements could be reproduced of those earlier modes of coexistence. In the climate of anti-Jewish and anti-Arab sentiment, the event was somewhat defiant. We took up the gauntlet before some one thousand young and not so young people, assembled in the great lecture hall of the Sorbonne. Their reaction was positive, as was that of the media, a great number of whose representatives attended. Without falling into excessive optimism, it can be claimed that this gathering of concerned citizens began a process whereby tensions were reduced. Similar colloquia were organized by others, elsewhere. The proceedings of ours appeared in 2006.[5]

Encouraged by such an achievement, we spent the next two years organizing a week-long series of events to be called "Paris: The Wager of Coexistence."[6] We scheduled panels, lectures, debates, concerts of world music and films. The municipality of Paris, other levels of government, private institutions, the media, various organizations, cooperative politicians from various parties—all worked together to produce a great success that lasted from March 19 to 26, 2006.

However, throughout our preparations, we came up against arrogance and indifference on the part of Jewish institutions, the Jewish press and radio, and dogmatic Jewish intellectuals. Fortunately, there were a few positive exceptions. However, the Foundation for the Memory of the Shoah denied us a grant because, no doubt, its officials would have preferred that they, rather than we, decide the speakers to be invited.[7]

Attempt at coexistence does not seem to be a priority. Everyone is in favor of living together, but it depends upon with whom. Certainly not with Muslim Arabs and blacks. And what's the good of life together, since it just leads to assimilation. In fact, the implicit demand is that it's for them to live with us, and not vice versa. This denotes the absence of any realistic strategy as well as the amateurism throughout all echelons of Jewish community leadership. This state of mind is only reinforced by the fact that they have the ear of many politicians, of whose support they consider themselves forever assured.

"Paris: The Wager of Coexistence" opened on March 19, 2006, a few days after publication of my article on Ilan Halimi. As a reprisal, many representatives of Jewish institutions who had finally agreed to take part, canceled on Friday, March 17, well aware that the series of events was beginning that Sunday. Though it was no doubt the result of a decision taken at a group level, this attempt at sabotage was not followed universally; a few Jews, more courageous and independent than others, stayed on the panels. The meeting rooms were packed for several days with hundreds of people of all religions, political tendencies, walks of life, and not just from Paris. Taboos on what could be said had fallen, a veritable place for free speech had been opened. Representatives of a great majority of media organs were there as well. So all was not lost; hope still existed that we were not condemned to hate one another forever.

On June 5, 2006, I published an article with François Burgat, calling for an end to the financial boycott by Israel and Europe that risked starving the Palestinian people. In this case, the first thing held against me was having coauthored a piece with a scholar at the Centre National de la Recherche Scientifique (CNRS) who had been accused of sympathy for Islamic fundamentalism. In fact, I did not meet him until after the appearance of the article. When he suggested we collaborate, we agreed on a number of common points, which certainly did not mean I approved of everything he had ever written. My second offense was to advocate suspension of the boycott after Hamas had been elected. I do not see why anyone would imagine I support terrorism because I urged that a people stop being punished for voting a certain way, when no consideration had been given to why they had done so. The war against the Hezbollah in July–August 2006 and the brutal attack against Gaza in December 2008–January 2009 will probably not change the situation. These offensives no doubt lead to a quagmire. One day, negotiations will become necessary among all those involved, including Hamas and Hezbollah, who will be forced to normalize, renounce terrorism and recognize Israel.

The article I wrote with Burgat earned me the labels "community-biased, antisecular, supportive of fundamentalism." This was in a piece in the weekly *Marianne*, authored by Martine Gozlan, known for her irrational positions on Islam. So now I was "community-biased," without knowing for sure to what community I belong. I hope it is to the community of men and women who, despite the risk of occasional errors of judgment, hold dignity and freedom to be nonnegotiable and resist as much as possible caprices of the moment.

At the present time, some months after the Gaza War, and even if 95 percent of French Jews supposedly supported Israel in this war, I cannot but ask myself this question: How to be a Jew after Gaza? The general climate of confusion in France has given a new impulse, among some groups, to a combination of anti-Israeli sentiment and anti-Semitism. It is impossible not to be aware of this worrisome evolution. On April 6 and 7, 2009, during a conference I organized in Paris on the Israeli-Palestinian conflict, I realized how much more difficult it had become to discuss these issues. Yet, how can a Jew accept what happened in Gaza? And how can a Jew accept this transformation of anti-Israel hostility into hostility toward Jews as such? Perhaps a new path has to be opened toward a new way of being Jewish.

ACKNOWLEDGMENT

This article was originally published in French under the title "Comment devient-on un traître?" in the journal *De l'autre côté* 2, August 2006, 26–44, with subsequent changes made by the author in 2009.

NOTES

1. Pierre Vidal-Naquet, "Flavius Josèphe ou du bon usage de la trahison" ("Flavius Josephus, or On the Proper Use of Treason"), introduction to the French translation by Pierre Savinel of Josephus' *The Jewish War* as *La Guerre des Juifs* (Paris: Minuit, 1977). [Author's note.]
2. Gilles William Goldnadel's *Le nouveau bréviaire de la haine* (Paris: Ramsay 2001) references the title of Léon Poliakov's *Le bréviaire de la haine* (Paris: Calmann-Lévy, 1951), one of the first historical overviews of the Holocaust, translated into English as *The Harvest of Hate* (Philadelphia: Jewish Publication Society of America, 1954). [Translator's note.]
3. Esther Benbassa and Jean-Christophe Attias, *Les Juifs ont-ils un avenir?* (Paris: Lattès, 2001), soft cover ed. (Paris: Hachette, 2002). English translation: *The Jews and their Future: A Conversation on Jewish Identities* (London: Zed Books, 2004). [Author's note.]
4. Pierre-André Taguieff's *La nouvelle judéophobie* (*The New Judeophobia*; Paris: Mille et une nuits, 2002) was translated by Patrick Camiller as *Rising from the Muck: The New Anti-Semitism in Europe* (Chicago, IL: Ivan R. Dee, 2004). [Translator's note.]
5. Esther Benbassa and Jean-Christophe Attias, ed., *Juifs et musulmans: une histoire partagée, un dialogue à construire* (Paris: La Découverte, 2006). [Author's note.]

6. In French, "Le Pari(s) du vivre-ensemble," is a complicated play on words. *Paris* is, of course. the capital of France, but *pari* means "wager." [Translator's note.] In 2008, Esther Benbassa and Jean-Christophe Attias organized a second edition of this event, focused on cultural diversity at school (see www.parisduvivreensemble.org). [Author's note.]
7. In her e-mail of March 7, 2006, Anne-Marie Revcolevschi, director of the Foundation for the Memory of the Shoah, put it this way: "Despite the objective of fostering coexistence, which we support wholeheartedly, the general composition of the panels seems to us to emphasize what separates the groups involved rather than what brings us together." [Author's note.]

Contributors

Cyril Aslanov is an Associate Professor at the Hebrew University of Jerusalem and currently the head of the Institute for General Humanities. His main fields of interest are diachronical linguistics, contact linguistics, as well as linguistic and literary pragmatics. His main publications are: *Pour comprendre la Bible: la leçon d'André Chouraqui* (Éditions du Rocher, 1999); *Le provençal des Juifs et l'hébreu en Provence: le dictionnaire Sharshot ha-Kesef de Joseph Caspi* (Peeters, 2001); *Evidence of Francophony in Medieval Levant: Decipherment and Interpretation* (MS. BnF. Copte 43, The Hebrew University of Jerusalem Magnes Press, 2006); *Le français levantin jadis et naguère: à la recherche d'une langue perdue* (Honoré Champion, 2006).

Alan Astro is a Professor of Modern Languages and Literatures at Trinity University in San Antonio. He has published twenty-five articles on writers as diverse as Bashevis, Beckett and Borges. He also was the editor of *Yiddish South of the Border: An Anthology of Latin American Yiddish Writing* (University of New Mexico Press, 2003), and of *Discourses of Jewish Identity in Twentieth-Century France* (*Yale French Studies* 85, 1994).

Esther Benbassa is a Professor of Modern Jewish history at the Ecole Pratique des Hautes Etudes (Paris). Among her publications in English: *Haim Nahum. A Sephardic Rabbi in Politics, 1892–1923* (University of Alabama Press, 1995); *A Sephardi Life in Southeastern Europe. The Autobiography and Journal of Gabriel Arié, 1863–1939* (with Aron Rodrigue, University of Washington Press, 1998); *The Jews of France. A History from Antiquity to the Present*, (Princeton University Press, 1999); *History of Sephardic Jewry, XIVth–XXth Centuries* (with A. Rodrigue, University of California Press, 2000); *Israel, the Impossible Land* (with Jean-Christophe Attias, Stanford University Press, 2003); *The Jews and their Future. A Conversation on Jewish Identities*, Zed Books, (with J.-C. Attias, 2004); *The Jew and the Other* (with J.-C. Attias, Cornell University Press, 2004). Her last book, *Suffering as Identity*, (published in French in 2007, Guizot Prize of the Académie Française in 2008) will be published in English in 2009.

Contributors

Fethi Benslama is a psychoanalyst, a Professor of Psychopathology and the Dean of the Department of "Sciences Humaines Cliniques" at the University of Paris-Diderot (Paris VII). He is the founder of the journal *Intersignes* 1990–2003. He participated in several edited volumes and he has published numerous studies on psychoanalysis, Islam and Europe in the contemporary era. Among his main publications: *La nuit brisée*, (Ramsay, 1988. Translated to Arabic); *Une fiction troublante* (éd. de l'Aube, 1994. Translated to Arabic); *L'islam à l'épreuve de la psychanalyse* (Aubier, 2002. Poche Flammarion, 2004. Translated to Arabic); *La virilité en Islam* (collective work with N. Tazi, Ed. de l'Aube, 2004); *Déclaration d'insoumission, à l'usage des musulmans et de ceux qui ne le sont pas* (Flammarion, 2005).

Lamia Ben Youssef Zayzafoon is an Assistant Professor in the School of Arts and Humanities at the University of Alabama at Birmingham. Her areas of specialization are postcolonialism, feminist literature and theory, Francophone film and literature, and the literatures of Africa with a specific emphasis on Islamic and Maghrebian studies. She is the author of *The Production of the Muslim Woman: Negotiating Text History and Ideology* (Lexington Books, 2005). Her current book project investigates the interrelations between memory, narrative and power in Western and Maghrebian accounts of WWII.

Bruno Chaouat is an Associate Professor of French at the University of Minnesota where he teaches contemporary French literature and thought. He is the author of *Je meurs par morceaux. Chateaubriand* (Presses Universitaires du Septentrion, 1999). He has also written on testimony, Jewish figures in literary theory, debates about the representation of the Holocaust. His main interest is in contemporary polemics in France, especially on French Jewish questions. He has published in journals such as *Modern Language Notes, Diacritics, Critique, French Forum, Romantisme*. He is currently working on a book on the return of melancholy in French thought, literary theory and art history. An excerpt of this manuscript will appear in 2009 in *Yale French Studies*.

Denis Charbit is a Senior Lecturer of Political Science at the Open University of Israel, Raanana, since 2002. He also teaches French culture at Tel-Aviv University and Bar-Ilan University. He has published in the fields of French Contemporary intellectual history, Israeli politics and Zionist thought. Recent publications include a Zionist anthology entitled *Sionismes. Textes fondamentaux* (1998), a new edition of *Theodor Herzl's Altneuland* (2004) and *Qu'est-ce que le sionisme?* (2007). He is currently editing the December 2008 issue of French review *Les Temps Modernes* devoted to Israel as a Jewish and democratic state. He also published an essay on French Jewish culture and literature in David Biale (ed.), *The Culture of Jews*.

Contributors 253

Anny Dayan-Rosenman is an Associate Professor of French Literature at the University of Paris-Diderot (Paris VII) in the Department of "Literature. Arts. Cinéma." Her work focuses on the relation between writing and history and also on the role of traumatic memories in the construction of collective identities. She has published numerous articles on Vercors, Georges Perec, Romain Gary, Albert Cohen, Albert Memmi, Patrick Modiano in *Les Temps Modernes*. She has also published two books: *La guerre d'Algérie dans la mémoire et l'imaginaire* (with Lucette Valensi, (ed.), Bouchenne, 2002). Et *Les alphabets de la Shoah. Survivre. Témoigner. Ecrire* (CNRS Editions, 2007).

Nathalie Debrauwere-Miller is an Associate Professor of French and Francophone Literature at Vanderbilt University. Her research focuses on Jewish studies and feminist theory. She is the author of *Envisager Dieu avec Edmond Jabès* (Editions du Cerf, 2007). She has also published numerous articles and book chapters on Edmond Jabès, Emmanuel Levinas, Hélène Cixous, Marcel Proust, Maryse Condé and Simone de Beauvoir in Europe, Canada and in the United States. They appear in journals such as *Modern Language Notes, Literature & Theology, French Forum, Romanic Review, Sites, Dalhousie French Studies,* and in *les éditions Minard* and *Presses Universitaires de Vincennes*. She is currently completing a manuscript entitled *La Crypte du père: Hélène Cixous, Sarah Kofman, Eliette Abécassis et Anne Goscinny*.

Nacira Guénif-Souilamas is an Associate Professor of Sociology at the University of Paris Nord and a research fellow at Experice (Paris XIII–Paris VIII). She has published *Des beurettes aux descendantes d'immigrants nord-africains* (Grasset, 2000, translated to Arabic in 2004). She has co-authored with Éric Macé *Les féministes et le garçon arabe* (L'Aube, 2004). She has edited *La république mise à nu par son immigration*, (La Fabrique, 2006) and contributed to a number of book chapters and articles in journals such as *La Revue Européenne des Migrations Internationales, French Politics, Culture and Society, Mouvements, VEI Diversité*. She is currently completing a series of chapters for a forthcoming edited volume *La fracture postcoloniale, Frenchness and African Diaspora,* and a book project on *The Otherness from Within*.

Ethan Katz is a research fellow at the Center for Advanced Judaic Studies at the University of Pennsylvania (2009–2010) and will be an Assistant Professor of History at the University of Cincinnati starting in the fall of 2010. His book project deals with the history of Jewish–Muslim relations in France from World War I to the 1980s. Previous publications include his articles "Displaced Historians, Dialectical Histories: George L. Mosse, Peter Gay, and Germany's Multiple Paths in the Twentieth Century," *Journal of Modern Jewish Studies* (July 2008), and "Memory at the Front: The Struggle over Revolutionary Commemoration in Occupied France, 1940–1944," *Journal of European Studies* (June 2005). He is also a contributor to the forthcoming *Encyclopedia of Jews in Islamic Lands* from Brill Publishing House.

Maud Mandel is an Associate Professor of Judaic Studies and History at Brown University. She is the author of *In the Aftermath of Genocide: Armenians and Jews in Twentieth-Century France* (Duke University Press, 2003). Her current book project, *Beyond Anti-Semitism: Muslims and Jews in Contemporary France*, will be published by Princeton University Press in 2009 (with fellowship support from the American Council of Learned Societies, the American Philosophical Society, and the Memorial Foundation for Jewish Culture). Her recent articles include: "Assimilation and Cultural Exchange in Modern Jewish History," in Jeremy Cohen and Moshe Rosman, (eds), *Rethinking European Jewish History* (Littman Library, 2008) and "Transnationalism and its Discontents during the 1948 Arab/Israeli War," *Diaspora: A Journal of Transnational Studies*, 12(3) (Winter 2003): 329–360.

Jeffrey Mehlman is a University Professor and a Professor of French Literature at Boston University. His books include: *A Structural Study of Autobiography:Proust, Leiris, Sartre, Lévi-Strauss*; *Revolution and Repetition: Marx/Hugo/Balzac*; *Cataract: A Study in Diderot*; *Legacies: Of Anti-Semitism in France*; *Walter Benjamin for Children: An Essay on His Radio Years*; *Genealogies of the Text: Literature, Psychoanalysis, and Politics in Modern France*; *Emigré New York: French Intellectuals in Wartime Manhattan, 1940–1944*; and (with Denis Hollier) *Literary Debate: Texts and Contexts*. His translations of Lacan, Derrida, Laplanche, Blanchot and others have played an important role in the naturalization of contemporary French thought in English. He is currently completing a memoir, *Adventures in the French Trade: Fragments toward a Life*.

Johann Sadock teaches in Foreign Languages and Literatures at MIT. He was guest co-editor of a recent issue of *Contemporary French and Francophone Studies/Sites: Séfarade-Francophone/Sephardic-Francophone* (Spring 2007). He has published in journals such as *Sites*, *Paragraphes*, *French Contemporary Civilization* and *Infini*; and in edited volumes such as *Transnational Spaces and Identities in the Francophone World* (University of Nebraska Press, 2009), in *Encyclopedia of Jews in the Islamic World* (forthcoming, 2009) and in *France in the Twenty-First Century/La France au XXIe siècle* (Summa Publications, forthcoming, 2009). His Web project, *Au-delà du regard: rencontres multiethniques*, and his documentary, *Black, Blanc, Beur: parlons-en!*, are based on interviews with young people and deal with ethnic diversity in France.

Contributors 255

Lawrence R. Schehr is a Professor of French, Comparative Literature, Gender and Women's Studies, and Theory at the University of Illinois. He has published numerous studies of nineteenth- and twentieth-century French narrative, as well as works on queer theory and contemporary cultural issues. His books include *Flaubert and Sons*; *The Shock of Men*; *Alcibiades at the Door*; *Rendering French Realism; Parts of an Andrology*; *Figures of Alterity*; and *French Gay Modernism*. Most recently, he has published a translation of Willy's *The Third Sex*. Forthcoming works include a monograph on subversions of verisimilitude in French Realism and a study of the representations of masculinity in contemporary French culture. He is also the editor of the journal *Contemporary French Civilization*.

Lincoln Z. Shlensky is an Assistant professor of English at the University of Victoria, where he specializes in postcolonial literature and film, cultural studies, Caribbean literature, and Jewish studies. He is currently preparing a manuscript entitled *Islands of Memory: Postcolonialism, the Holocaust, and Literary Politics*. His recent publications include: "Lost and Found: Aharon Appelfeld's Hebrew Literary Affiliations and the Quest for a Home in Israeli Letters," *Prooftexts* 26: 3 (Winter 2006); and "'To Rivet and Record:' Conversion and Collective Memory in Equiano's Interesting Narrative," in *Slavery and the Cultures of Abolition*, Peter J. Kitson and Brycchan Carey, (eds), (Woodbridge: Boydell and Brewer, 2007).

Philippe Zard is an Associate Professor of Comparative Literature at the University of Paris X-Nanterre and a member of the "Centre de recherche en littérature et poétique comparés." His research focuses on the political and religious imagination in modern fiction: the myth of the West, the crisis of culture, the representations of the French Revolution in the European narrative or dramatic fiction. He has published *La Fiction de l'Occident: Thomas Mann, Franz Kafka, Albert Cohen* (PUF, 1999) and edited with Anne Tomiche, *Littérature et philosophie* (Artois Presses Université, 2002) ; and with Alain Schaffner, *Albert Cohen dans son siècle* ("Colloque de Cerisy", (ed.) Le Manuscrit, 2005), and *Sillage de Kafka* ("L'Esprit des lettres", (ed.), Le Manuscrit, 2007).

Index

A

Algeria, 2, 4, 11, 15, 19n6, 19n13, 26, 27, 30, 31, 32, 33, 67, 72, 74, 77, 96, 107, 122, 124, 170, 181, 194, 197, 200, 214

Algerian Forces for National Independence (FLN), 96, 98, 124, 200

Algerian War, 3, 107, 194, 198, 199, 200, 202

Allouche, Jean-Luc, 86, 89, 90

Amara, Fadela, 9, 10, 21n22

Anidjar, Gil, 1, 19n5, 93, 103n3, 104n28, 158n13, 198, 205n2

Anti-Israeli, 5, 143, 165, 166, 248

Anti-Semitism, 2, 3, 6, 11, 12, 13, 16, 17, 18, 20n26, 29, 30, 32–37, 45, 50, 56, 58, 59, 61, 62, 93–99, 101, 102, 143, 151, 152, 154, 165, 166, 167, 181, 188, 189, 193, 195, 201, 202, 203, 209, 211, 213, 214, 225, 226, 230, 237, 238, 242, 243, 244, 248

Anti-Zionism, 12, 13, 17, 33, 67, 152

Anticolonialism, 213

Antiracism, 151, 214, 215

Arab league, 85, 113, 224, 231n6

Arab Muslim (Arabness), 1, 3, 8, 9–18, 21, 171, 69, 76, 80n16, 93, 100, 136, 192n23, 203

Arab nationalism, 26, 27, 72, 94, 10, 11, 13, 26, 72, 94

Arafat, Yasser, 6, 7, 143, 159n30, 168, 184, 191n14, 214

Arendt, Hannah, 213, 214, 220n22

Aron, Raymond, 6, 20n21, 223

Aryan (Indo-European), 20n26, 58, 59

Ashkenazi Jews, 10, 19n13, 88, 186, 191n4, 199, 202, 213, 220n18, 221n38, 236

Assimilation, 9, 13, 50, 59, 60, 61, 62, 64n13, 72, 201, 213, 247

Attias, Jean-Christophe, 237, 238, 246

Auschwitz, 14, 50, 56, 213, 234, 236

B

Balfour declaration, 27

Banlieue (cité), 10, 12, 13, 17, 19n4, 108, 180, 186–190, 193n23, 193n27

Barbie, Klaus, 14, 22n44, 212

Barnavi, Elie, 6, 19n8, 20n13, 213, 220n18

Barrès, Maurice, 42, 43, 53

Bedouin, 48, 69

Begin, Menahem, 6, 89

Benaïssa, Slimane, 16, 67–80

Benbassa, Esther, 3, 10, 11, 12, 14, 18, 19n9, 20n14, 21n29, 21n37, 22n41.

Benjamin, Walter, 115, 119n17, 158n10

Benslama, Fethi, 16, 94, 99–103, 103n22

Bensoussan, Georges, 106

Bensoussan, Philippe, 106

Berbers, 88, 95

Beur (Beurette or Rebeu), 9, 11, 21n29, 61, 168, 175–177, 190n1, 199

Bible, 19n13, 53, 73, 79n13, 186

Bitto, Simone, 116, 117

Black Panther, 112, 141, 143, 145–148, 152, 156, 218

Black September, 106, 112, 118, 141, 147

Black, 3, 9, 12, 14, 21, 22, 147, 152, 180, 189, 190n2, 192n23, 193, 195, 196, 199, 204, 205n1n4, 215, 238, 244, 245, 246, 247

Blanchot, Maurice, 112, 119n13, 149, 154, 216

Index

Blum, Léon, 31, 203
Bouganim, Ami, 86–89
Boukobza, Shoshana, 86, 90
Bouraoui, Hédi, 94, 98–102, 102n1
Bourguiba, Habib, 97, 98
Brauman, Rony, 11, 12, 13, 15, 20n25, 22n41, 187, 192n21, 224, 225, 226, 228

C

Camus, Renaud, 18, 211
Chahid, 129, 130
Chirac, Jacques, 7
Chouraqui, André, 16, 37n5, 68, 73, 76, 77, 78, 79n6, 91,
Cinema, 16, 105, 107, 113–117, 117n2
Citizenship, 3, 4, 9, 27, 31, 55, 56, 74, 97, 98, 102, 164, 174, 201, 214
Cohen, Albert, 15, 41–54, 88, 89
Colonialism, 3, 11, 27, 30, 37, 56, 73, 95, 96, 97, 152, 205, 212, 213
Colonization, 2, 3, 4, 8, 9, 11, 14, 19, 107, 194, 202
Commemoration, 15, 22n43, 132, 234, 236
Communitarism (communautarism), 8, 9, 10, 11, 21n28, 21n33, 189
Conan, Eric, 210
Conseil Représentatif des Israélites de France (CRIF), 35, 165, 170, 172, 224, 236, 245
Consistoire, 165, 172
Crémieux Decree, 3, 220n22

D

Darwish, Mahmoud, 115, 182, 191n8
De Gaulle, Charles, 4, 5, 6, 7, 41, 198, 214
Debray, Régis, 210, 213, 220
Decolonization, 2, 3, 8, 9, 11, 19n13, 86, 194, 200, 202, 203, 241, 242
Democracy, 14, 67, 185, 210
Derrida, Jacques, 158n26, 212, 215,
Dhimmis, 3, 74, 194, 241
Diaspora, 10, 11, 42, 43, 47, 82, 87, 102, 205, 232, 233, 234
Dieudonné, 22n44, 226
Discrimination, 10, 11, 30, 96, 99, 100, 107, 180, 188, 191n1, 201, 214, 243
Drumont, Edouard, 13, 42, 59, 60
Durban, 13, 217, 226
Duty of memory (competition of memory), 14, 22, 22n42, 73, 189, 235

E

Emancipation, 10, 21n34, 50, 233, 240
Enlightenment, 139, 194, 233
Exile, 4, 11, 42, 44, 45, 46, 53, 68, 74, 75, 76, 82, 83, 86–91, 96, 99, 100, 127, 148, 194, 233, 241

F

Fascism, 34, 37, 43, 51, 53, 145, 151, 210
Fatherland, 123–128, 135
Finkielkraut, Alain, 7, 9, 11–14, 21n24, 21n36, 21n37, 22n41, 22n44, 63n2, 158n29, 185–189, 191n15, 192n21, 192n23, 192n27, 209–214, 219n4, 219n6, 220n12, 224–228
Fisher, Joseph, 25, 38n1, 39n27, 39n41
Fontaine, Pierre, 31, 39
France, 1, 2–12, 14, 16, 18, 19n7, 19n9, 19n13, 25, 27, 28, 29, 31, 33–37, 38n8, 55–62, 80, 82, 85, 88, 96, 97, 105–111, 114, 125, 141, 142, 163–171, 174, 180, 181, 184, 187, 189, 192n27, 193–205, 209, 211–216, 219n26, 222–226, 229, 230, 235–238, 242–248
Franco-Judaism, 10
Francophone, 1, 2, 16, 18, 18n1, 26, 67, 68, 73, 76, 98, 102, 105–108, 111, 114, 116, 117, 118n2
French Jewry, 20n13, 27, 35, 38, 165, 238, 245
French revolution, 8, 35
Freud, Sigmund, 94, 127, 128, 133, 138, 138n18, 152, 209, 218, 218n3
Front National (FN), 174, 184
Fundamentalism, 9, 10, 243, 247, 248

G

Gaza War, 18, 205, 242, 248
Genet, Jean, 17, 136, 141–159, 215, 216, 218, 220n27, 221n39, 221n41
Genocide, 22n43, 50, 53, 95, 101, 151, 210, 211, 219n6, 234, 235, 236, 238, 242, 244, 245
Gentile, 58, 59, 62, 63n8, 71, 151
Gitaï, Amos, 90, 116
Globalization, 244
Glucksmann, André, 229
Godard, Jean-Luc, 105–108, 112–116
Gulf War of 1991, 11, 17, 163, 173, 174, 185

H

Hadj, Messali, 33, 97
Halimi, Gisèle, 93, 96–98, 102
Halimi, Ilan, 226, 245–247
Hamas, 247
Hebrew, 20n34, 37n1, 42, 43, 73, 87, 95, 112, 117, 149–154, 232
Hegel, 93, 154
Heidegger, Martin, 217, 220n36
Hezbollah, 7, 16, 131, 134, 135, 247
Hitler, Adolf, 26, 28, 30, 33, 50, 97, 114, 143, 148, 210, 213, 214, 219n19, 220n39
Holiness, 83, 125, 126, 235
Holocaust, 56, 60, 64n11, 95, 101, 111, 112, 119n4, 147, 151, 194, 199, 210, 211, 213, 234, 235, 236, 237, 238, 243
Human rights, 100, 205, 220, 244
Humanism, 60, 127
Hussein, Saddam, 163, 166, 168, 192n14, 212
Imam Hussein (Ali's son), 129, 131–138
Husseini, Hadj Amin Mohammad al-, 25, 213

I

Immigration, 3, 10, 19n13, 27, 36, 61, 64n13
Imperialism, 28, 30, 32, 33, 36, 163
Importation, 1, 8, 13, 17
Indigènes, 156, 194, 197, 199, 200
Integration, 9, 10, 60, 62, 172, 173, 174
Intelligentsia, 3, 7, 42, 67, 98, 212
Intifada, 1, 2, 3, 5, 8–15, 17, 19n3, 105, 106, 141, 158n22, 181, 184–189, 200, 201, 202, 224, 225, 226, 230, 237, 246
Invasion, 34, 36, 131, 167, 168, 180, 184
Iranian Revolution, 132, 133
Iraq War, 2, 8, 110
Ishmael, 31, 76, 101, 182, 194
Islam, 133, 135, 142, 166, 170, 172, 200, 217, 233, 241, 243, 248
Islamism, 69, 93, 99, 100, 129, 213, 217, 237, 243, 247
Islamophobia, 8, 13, 20n27, 195, 202, 226, 246
Israel, 1, 2, 3, 4, 6–16, 19n10, 26, 37, 41–46, 49, 51–54, 58, 67, 68, 69, 71, 73, 75, 77, 81, 83, 84, 85, 87–95, 98, 101, 104n30, 106, 109, 111–116, 147, 148, 151, 152, 158n22, 163, 165, 169, 171, 173, 175, 180–189, 191, 193, 194, 201, 204, 212, 222–230, 233, 235, 238, 241, 243, 244, 247
Israélite, 1, 10, 21n34, 27, 28, 30, 31, 35, 94

J

Jabès, Edmond, 75, 79n7
Jacques, Paula, 86–88
Jarblum, Marc, 25, 35
Jewish immigration, 28, 33, 36
Jewish Labor Oganization, 32
Jewish nationalism, 10, 11, 13, 28, 51, 72, 244
Jewish question, 1, 15, 34, 61, 70, 211, 213, 216
Jihad (djihad), 14, 128, 129, 134, 141
Jospin, Lionel, 7, 238
Judeocentrism, 17, 209, 210, 215, 217, 219
Judeophobia, 8, 11, 12, 13, 15, 17, 20n26, 21n36, 193, 209, 216, 238

K

Kabyl, 180, 190, 197
Kamikaze, 130, 131, 142, 144, 145
Kattan, Naïm, 87
Kessel, Joseph, 81–85, 90
Kibbutz, 87, 88, 112
Koran (Qu'ran), 10, 71, 73, 79n8, 125, 128, 129, 214, 216

L

Lacan, Jacques, 134, 138, 140n19, 216–218, 254
Lanzmann, Claude, 107, 111, 112, 113, 211, 212, 222, 238
Lebanon War, 18, 224
Lévinas, Emmanuel, 185, 186, 188, 191n16, 191n18, 192n23, 221n42
Lévy, Bernard-Henry, 21n36, 22n41, 188, 189, 192n24, 192n25, 192n27, 229, 238
Lévy, Elisabeth, 12, 20n25, 224, 226, 238
Likud, 19, 234, 235
Literature, 75, 93, 94, 98, 100, 102, 154, 156, 197, 211, 215
Lyotard, Jean-François, 62, 64n15, 146.

M

Maghreb (Maghrebian), 2, 4, 8, 9, 10, 11, 18n1, 21n29, 33, 56, 67, 73, 74, 75, 76, 77, 99, 163, 166, 172
Mardam-Bey, Farouk, 3, 10, 11, 12, 13, 19n11, 21n27, 193n27
Marie L., 195, 196, 202
Marker, Chris, 106, 111, 116, 117
Marrus, Michaël, 20
Marshall Pétain, 7, 20n16, 210, 214
Marty, Eric, 143, 156, 157n2, 215, 220n27
Martyrdom (martyr), 16, 50, 54, 101–141
Maurras, Charles, 211, 218
Memmi, Albert, 4, 20n18, 56, 93–103n10, 104n30, 104n31
Mendès-France, Pierre, 203
Middle East, 1, 2, 6, 11–13, 17, 18, 27, 37, 67, 86, 93, 95, 102–112, 119, 131, 156, 157, 166, 167, 168, 170, 175, 185, 191, 194, 196, 201, 215, 216, 222, 225, 229
Mitterrand, François, 5, 6, 7, 164, 182, 189, 203, 210
Modernity, 43, 100, 194, 217, 233
Morocco, 3, 4, 19n6, 19n13, 67, 73, 77, 86, 88, 101, 197
Mujahid, 128, 130, 133
Multiculturalism, 8, 9, 189

N

Nakba (Naqba), 3, 90, 194
Nasser, Gamel Abdul, 76, 96
Nation (nationhood), 3, 4, 10, 11, 13, 15, 42, 43, 49, 50, 51, 55, 56, 57, 62, 63, 69, 72, 75, 94, 98, 100, 106, 107, 111, 114, 116, 148, 163, 166, 174, 198, 200, 202, 213, 226, 239, 240, 244
Nazism, 3, 20n26, 30, 36, 43, 51
North Africa (North African), 1, 2, 10, 16, 18n1, 18n9, 19n13, 20n17, 21n29, 26, 27, 28, 36, 38n10, 74, 77, 86, 95, 96, 97, 102, 108, 164, 170, 173, 193, 194, 197, 198, 201, 203, 212, 236, 241
Nuremberg law, 3

O

Obscurantism, 10, 67
Occupation, 27, 35, 56, 60, 89, 97, 117, 124, 131, 185, 188, 232, 234, 242
Oppression, 4, 5, 34, 67, 95, 96, 98, 99, 100, 111, 124, 136, 147, 152, 168
Oslo accords, 101
Ottoman Empire, 27, 197

P

Palestine, 1, 2, 7, 11, 15, 16, 17, 19n13, 25–36, 37n9, 39n32, 40n53, 40n61, 41–47, 52, 58, 69, 72, 78, 82–85, 92n15, 95, 101, 111, 118n1, 143–148, 157n3, 168, 182, 186, 187, 190, 191n14, 212, 213, 216, 219n19, 224, 226, 228, 229, 231n5
Palestinian Liberation Organization (PLO), 6, 7, 118, 143, 191n14
Palestinian nationalism, 101
Palestinian occupied territories, 69, 101, 184, 187, 194, 202, 229, 230
Palestinian revolution, 17, 141, 143, 144, 146, 152, 155
Paxton, Robert, 20
Pieds-Noirs, 68, 178n54, 199, 200
Pioneers, 32, 46, 48, 49, 51, 82, 84, 87, 88
Pogroms, 4, 82, 85, 233
Popular Front (PF), 31, 203
Promised Land, 47, 86, 88, 99, 116, 119n18, 200, 230, 240
Propaganda, 10, 33, 36, 52, 59, 91, 99, 101, 115, 214
Protectorate, 2, 19, 19n6, 20n14
Protocols of the Elders of Zion, 6, 21n35

R

Race (racialism), 8, 20n26, 27, 42, 43, 51, 53, 59, 60, 94, 103n, 148, 150, 151, 193, 196, 201, 204, 238
Racism, 11, 12, 13, 19n7, 20n26, 34, 43, 51, 94, 97, 151, 163, 168, 171, 174, 181, 188, 189, 195, 201, 214, 229, 238, 243
Repression, 5, 110, 124, 155, 202
Republic (republicanism), 6, 7, 8, 9, 10, 12, 16, 28, 30, 46, 55–58, 80n16, 106, 107, 108, 188, 198, 199, 201, 204, 243
Riots, 13, 17, 28, 30, 31, 34, 38n23, 39n31, 189, 199
Rousso, Henry, 20n20, 210, 219n7

S

Sabra and Shatila, 3, 141, 150, 184, 200

Said, Edward, 156, 213
Sanbar, Elias, 3, 10, 11, 13, 19n11
Sarkozy, Nicolas, 7, 189, 190, 192n28, 203, 204, 236
Sartre, Jean-Paul, 15, 55–64, 143, 146, 148, 158n16, 215, 221n42, 222, 223
Secularism, 8, 72, 73, 98, 100, 189, 243
Secularization, 72, 123, 125, 126
Segregation, 4, 86, 87, 96, 203
Semitic, 4, 20n26, 93, 101, 194, 196, 203, 205, 214, 217
Sephardic Jews, 3, 9, 16, 20n13, 31, 74, 76, 81, 86, 108, 112, 191n4, 194, 198, 199, 201, 202, 203, 213, 220n18, 239, 242
September 11 (or 9/11), 19, 141–143, 158, 200, 202, 212, 213, 226, 234, 237
Sharon, Ariel, 6, 19n3, 157n2, 191n11, 213, 215
Shiism, 132, 133, 135
Shiite Islam, 131, 132
Shoah, 2, 11, 14, 15, 17, 22n44, 25, 35, 37, 112, 211, 234, 236, 238
Sibony, Daniel, 216, 217, 218, 220n40, 254
Six-Day War, 5, 18, 222, 224
Slavery, 14, 22n42, 22n44, 194, 200, 205
Soury, Jules, 42
Spain, 19n13, 13, 76, 232, 245
Stereotypes, 11, 203
Stora, Benjamin, 38n7, 38n10, 40n55
Suburbs (suburban development), 1, 9, 10, 13, 17, 19n4, 86, 108, 109, 196, 200, 226, 238
Suez Canal, 2, 224
Suicide bombers (attacks), 16, 141, 124, 125, 129, 131, 133, 136, 183
Sunni Muslim, 131, 136

T
Taguieff, Pierre-André, 9, 12, 14, 20n26, 21n35, 21n36, 22n37, 22n41, 210, 213, 219n5, 219n9, 220n14, 220n20, 238, 248n4
Tarnero, Jacques, 106
Taubira law, 22n42
Terrorism, 5, 8, 10, 12, 16, 31, 33, 130, 142, 144, 145, 147, 148, 150, 164, 165, 200, 213, 216, 237, 243, 247
Thora, 151

Tribalism, 9, 21n33
Trigano, Shmuel, 21n33, 159n, 180, 181, 182, 187, 190n3, 191n5, 220n26
Tsahal, 112, 149, 150, 185, 187
Tunisia (Tunisian), 3, 4, 16, 19n6, 19n13, 20n14, 27, 67, 73, 93–102, 168, 197, 203

U
United States, 1, 2, 61, 64, 148, 158, 163, 166, 185, 205, 210, 213, 214, 235, 237, 240
Universalism, 8, 9, 10, 53, 56, 61, 72, 76, 198, 199, 201, 236, 239, 242, 245

V
Veil, Simone, 236
Vergès, Jacques, 212, 219
Vichy Regime, 3, 4, 7, 26, 35, 37, 62, 107, 199, 107, 194, 199, 200, 203, 210, 214, 216, 218
Victims (victimization, victimology), 12, 14, 22n44, 31, 59, 67, 89, 96, 109, 114, 147, 165, 170, 188, 191n6, 195, 197, 210, 213, 237, 239
Vidal-Naquet, Pierre, 158n29, 210n6, 248n1
Violence, 8, 12–16, 21n27, 30, 35, 49, 51, 53, 81, 86, 91, 100, 101, 109, 115, 117, 135, 142, 149, 163, 165, 167, 173, 195, 212, 224, 226, 238, 246

W
Weizmann, Chaim, 41, 46
West Bank, 187, 234
Wieviorka, Michel, 21n36, 21n38, 188, 191n13
World War I, 26, 27, 182, 233
World War II, 15, 26, 37, 97, 182, 210, 213, 233, 245

X
Xenophobia, 29, 112, 165, 166

Y
Yom Kippur War, 101, 184, 199, 224

Z
Zionism, 2, 4, 6, 11–17, 26–36, 41–48, 51, 53, 54, 67, 72, 94, 152, 213, 228, 229, 233

For Product Safety Concerns and Information please contact our EU
representative GPSR@taylorandfrancis.com
Taylor & Francis Verlag GmbH, Kaufingerstraße 24, 80331 München, Germany

www.ingramcontent.com/pod-product-compliance
Lightning Source LLC
Chambersburg PA
CBHW062125300426
44115CB00012BA/1820